A Theory of Assembly

A Theory of Assembly

From Museums to Memes

Kyle Parry

University of Minnesota Press
Minneapolis
London

This project was supported in part by a grant from the Arts Research Institute at the University of California, Santa Cruz.

Portions of the Introduction and chapter 4 were published in "Generative Assembly after Katrina," *Critical Inquiry* 44, no. 3 (2018): 554–81; copyright 2018 by University of Chicago Press; all rights reserved. Portions of the Introduction were published in "Kyle Parry reviews *Assembly*," *Critical Inquiry* 46, no. 1 (2019): 252–56; copyright 2019 by University of Chicago Press; all rights reserved.

Published by the University of Minnesota Press
111 Third Avenue South, Suite 290
Minneapolis, MN 55401-2520
http://www.upress.umn.edu

ISBN 978-1-5179-1315-1 (hc)
ISBN 978-1-5179-1316-8 (pb)

A Cataloging-in-Publication record for this book is available from the Library of Congress.

Printed in the United States of America on acid-free paper

30 29 28 27 26 25 24 23 22 10 9 8 7 6 5 4 3 2 1

For Natalie

Why do we call something a "number"? Well, perhaps because it has a—direct—relationship with several things that have hitherto been called number; and this can be said to give it an indirect relationship to other things we call the same name. And we extend our concept of number as in spinning a thread we twist fiber on fiber. And the strength of the thread does not reside in the fact that some one fiber runs through its whole length, but in the overlapping of many fibers.

—Ludwig Wittgenstein, *Philosophical Investigations*

We speak, we write, we do language. That is how civilizations heal. I know the world is bruised and bleeding, and though it is important not to ignore its pain, it is also critical to refuse to succumb to its malevolence. Like failure, chaos contains information that can lead to knowledge—even wisdom. Like art.

—Toni Morrison, "No Place for Self-Pity, No Room for Fear"

Contents

Introduction *Assembly as Cultural Form* 1

1 *What Is Assembly?* 45

2 *Art, Assembly, and the Museum* 91

3 *Memes, Assembly, and the Internet* 135

4 *Generative Assembly after Disaster* 179

5 *The Powers and Perils of Media Assembly* 213

Conclusion *From Paranoid to Reparative Assembly* 257

Acknowledgments 273

Notes 277

Index 315

Introduction

Assembly as Cultural Form

There are numerous terms for the expressive strategies people put to use on a daily basis across this warming planet. When a young child strings together the words "cat," "hop," and "tree," she exercises the human capacity for *narrative.*[1] When magazine editors publish photographs of farmworkers picketing for better protections and compensation in the midst of a pandemic, they seize on the evidentiary power of *representation.*[2] When artists code scripts that generate inscrutable images on demand for a fee, they test the aesthetic (and economic) possibilities in *abstraction.*[3] The range of such cultural forms is broad and diverse, from those that cut across fine art and the digital everyday, like *performance* and *parody,* to those that once tended to require (at least in their more official guises, before computers became widespread) special training and equipment, such as *mapping* and *visualization.* Ever the subject of experimentation, the many varieties of expressive strategies continue to inspire critical and philosophical debates. Each also serves as an umbrella term for a still more plural array of ways in which citizens, activists, artists, designers, and content creators use the media available to them—from sidewalks and exhibition spaces to social networks and algorithms—to think, speak, act, and interact, and thus to have a say in their own and others' lives.

Given not just the number but the quite ingrained status of these different cultural forms, it might seem foolhardy to argue for the introduction and elaboration of one more. And yet this is not only possible, but necessary. This is because the form in question, which I call "assembly," is not some exotic add-on known only in obscure internet forums, nor is it an esoteric aesthetic subspecies confined to academic journals. Rather, assembly has both seen a long history of use and enjoyed a recent, dramatic expansion. In this book's assessment, assembly has become increasingly powerful and pervasive, first and foremost as a type of expressive artifact and communicative practice in its own right, but also as one among many strategies practitioners can creatively combine. Gathering projects from the humorous and brief to the serious and hard-won, *A Theory of Assembly* argues that, with the rise of digital and social media, assembly has come to equal narrative, representation, and other dominant cultural forms in its capacity to move audiences and mobilize publics, and just as crucially, to do harm. What we need, I contend, are new terms and taxonomies for artistic, activist, and everyday media practices whose lifeblood is expressive gathering, whether as small as a provocative visual comparison undertaken by one person or as large as the whole history of internet memes undertaken by millions.

Part of why these terms and taxonomies are needed is a longstanding imbalance.[4] Despite the incessant hum of cultural formal invention (and despite digital technologies greatly amplifying that hum), European and North American writers have tended to prioritize certain cultural forms over others, with storytelling and mimesis (another term for representation) as the most commonly studied and celebrated among them.[5] No doubt there have been efforts to introduce otherwise unnamed cultural forms, and this includes Lev Manovich's influential contention that a form deserving of the name "database" has begun to supplant narrative in its importance and reach.[6] (I'll say more about this below.) Moreover, for the many writers working to undo the persistent Eurocentrism of art history, the interpretation of so-called "non-Western" cultural practices involves a refusal to adhere to prevailing Western assumptions around expressive strategies. (I think, for instance, of Carolyn Dean's distinction between "representational" and "presentational" objects in Inkan contexts.[7]) At the same time, as narrative and representation continue to enjoy pride of place, attempts to address the spectrum as a whole remain relatively rare. This book contributes to that much needed effort by showing that any rigorous accounting of available and valuable artistic and cultural practices in the internet era will be incomplete without assembly and its many subfamilies. From where I sit, to research and teach art and digital and visual culture *without* acknowledging assembly-based and assembly-infused projects is to leave unremarked a widely practiced form of cultural production that, simply put, matters.

But there is further reason why assembly deserves such extensive treatment. From acting as an engine of disinformation to opening unanticipated potentials for remembering, from reinforcing reductive accounts of gender to helping link social and environmental justice movements, assembly is of *particular* consequence in contexts of political and ecological struggle. It can offer an especially powerful means of intervening in prevailing accounts of certain disasters (chapter 4); it can also act as a method for justifying forms of slow and structural violence that unequally fall upon communities of color (chapter 5). It can support remarkably connective modes of aesthetic expression (chapter 2); it can also corrode the norms that sustain democratic life (chapter 3 and Conclusion). In other words, assembly is not only a forceful tool in the hands of the progressive and the emancipatory; it is also an insidious weapon in the hands of the reactionary and the antidemocratic. The power of assembly to support renewal and repair is also a power to undermine those things, quickly, widely, and repeatedly. Seeing, reading, and remaking assemblies—these are essential tasks. *A Theory of Assembly* shows just how much of this work remains to be done.

An Initial Definition and an Initial Set of Examples

So, what is assembly, such that it should be understood as equaling storytelling and representation, not only in the richness of its expressive capacities and the breadth of its distribution but also to the extent to which it can both mitigate and instigate violence and injustice?[8] In chapter 1, I offer a full-fledged framework for the term, showing how uses of assembly cut across all manner of platforms, times, and places while also exhibiting significant expansions in accessibility, frequency, and influence in the digital era.[9] For now, a more concise approach will have to suffice.

Here's the quick version. Assembly places expressive relationships front and center. To assemble is to convene, collate, and compile. It is to organize, arrange, and configure. An assembly is *any combination of expressive elements that maintains and seizes on the appearance of selection and arrangement.* To undertake or participate in assembly is *to contribute to the constitution, configuration, or use of an assembly at any scale.*

The longer version begins by clarifying the term "cultural form."

For the purposes of this book, cultural forms are the "medium-nonspecific" or "transmedia" structures and strategies that animate acts of communication and interaction.[10] The book also welcomes N. Katherine Hayles's more sweeping take: different cultural forms embody "different cognitive, technical, psychological, and artistic modalities," and they offer "different ways to instantiate concepts, structure experience, and embody values."[11]

Like other cultural forms, assembly is both a type of thing and something people do. (One can, for instance, encounter an assembly in a museum or a social media feed, but one can also participate in collaborative or "crowd-sourced" assemblies, like participatory archives.) Whereas narratives conjure up events and characters and representations convey scenes and subjects, assemblies convene what I call "constituents." These constituents are often things like words and images, but other kinds of entities can also act as the constituents of media assemblies, such as objects, numbers, and sounds, or even humans and nonhumans.

What ultimately distinguishes the cultural form of assembly is the way people engaged in the form make use of those constituents.[12] With most cultural forms, the point is, more often than not, to provide the reader/viewer/user something effectively transcendent, such that some separate and coherent thing, such as a picture, story, visualization, or performance, supersedes the component parts. Kurt Vonnegut rightly emphasizes the role of the imagination in these processes: "The imagination circuit is taught to respond to the most minimal of cues. A book is an arrangement of twenty-six phonetic symbols, ten numerals, and about eight punctuation marks, and people can cast their eyes over these and envision the eruption of Mount Vesuvius or the Battle of Waterloo."[13] In the case of assembly, by contrast, the relations between constituents, collections of constituents, and the overall arrangement are much more porous and, as it were, democratic. The different constituents function like citizens: they remain apart from each other as separate, discernible elements (such as one among many pictures or one among many instances of a meme); they persist in distinct and meaningful positions; and they also are in conversation, collaboration, and sometimes conflict with the constituents that precede, exceed, or surround them. From obvious differentiation to an unruly flurry of impressions, these intersecting, overlapping, and often nonlinear relationships among constituents generate multiple expressive, experiential, and semantic effects, provided the reader of (or participant in) the assembly is ready to engage and coproduce them.

Among the more common variations on assembly are the *viral comparisons* that circulate through social media platforms. These comparisons characteristically involve the readily shareable unification of disparately sourced media, in many cases as means of revealing unacceptable contradictions, but perhaps most often as a comforting amusement. (Comparative assemblies frequently, but not exclusively, look like what W. J. T. Mitchell calls "imagetexts," which is to say "composite, synthetic works . . . that combine image and text."[14]) Among the most poignant examples of the contradiction-oriented work of viral comparison is a juxtaposition of news photographs of people wading through floodwaters in New Orleans after the levees broke in 2005 (Figure I.1). In this assembly, which I analyze at the outset of chapter 4, the photo of the pair of white people is captioned as "finding" goods while the photo of the Black person is captioned as "looting." The comparison was widely shared, helping to set off a national reckoning with racialized media-framing and with the structural (and often fatal) undervaluing of Black lives.

Whereas the Katrina comparison is a participatory one-off, the prolific and widely shared work of Uğur Gallenkuş (to pick just one among many possible further examples) indicates the potential for comparative assembly to become an activist-artistic mode in its own right. In this case, it is by way of one image of peace, safety, and belonging, typically a stock image or a canonical Western painting, fused with a second, typically photojournalistic image of conditions of war, suffering, and injustice (Figure I.2). While producing a momentary delight at unexpected fusion is a risk for certain comparisons made by Gallenkuş, it's the driving purpose of others, among the more successful of which is the "Woman Yelling at a Cat" meme. In the germinal instance of this meme, a Twitter user was delighted to no end by the pairing of two already viral images: on the left Taylor Armstrong, at that time a cast member on the television show *The Real Housewives of Beverly Hills,* pointing and yelling, and on the right a seemingly angry (or maybe just smug) cat sat at a dinner table. Users across Reddit and other platforms

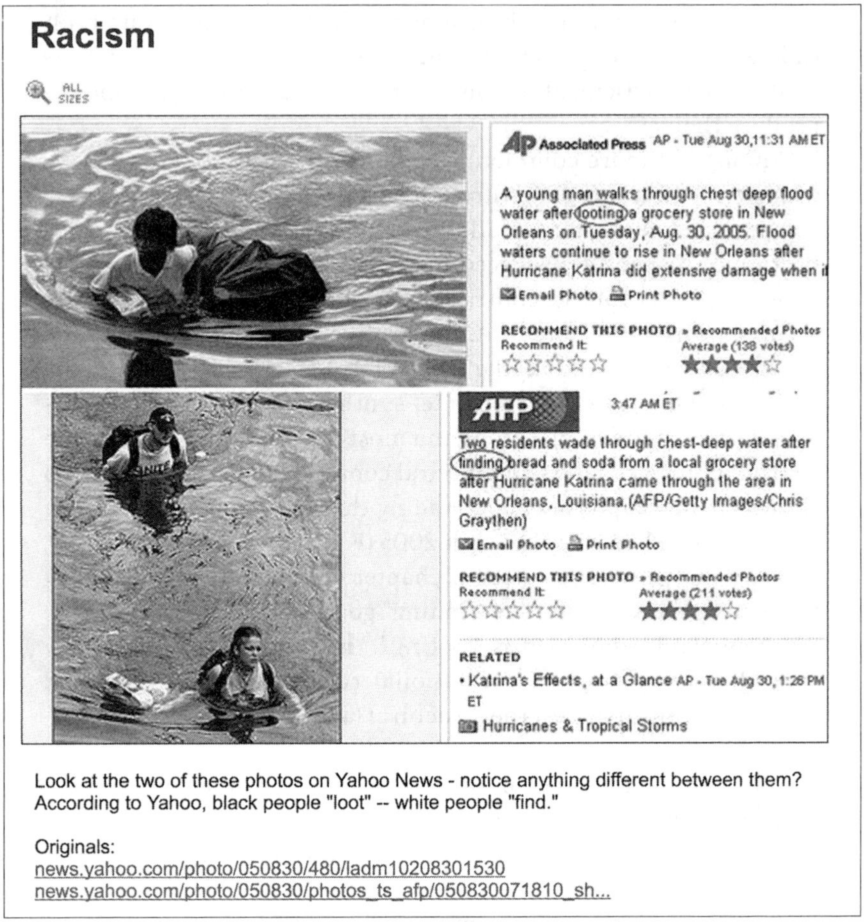

Figure I.1. A "viral comparison," this is among the earliest instances of media or "generative" assembly undertaken in response to Katrina. "Racism" as posted to Flickr by dustin3000 (2005).

took this playful pairing as the opportunity for variously trivial, funny, relatable, and repugnant acts of digital visual contribution (Figure I.3). Although these three and countless other examples could be interpreted through frames like storytelling, representation, and performance, to apply these more dominant terms would mean overlooking the work they do in placing selected constituents into compelling arrangements. Doing so would also distract from the degree to which the force or the appeal of this expressive work

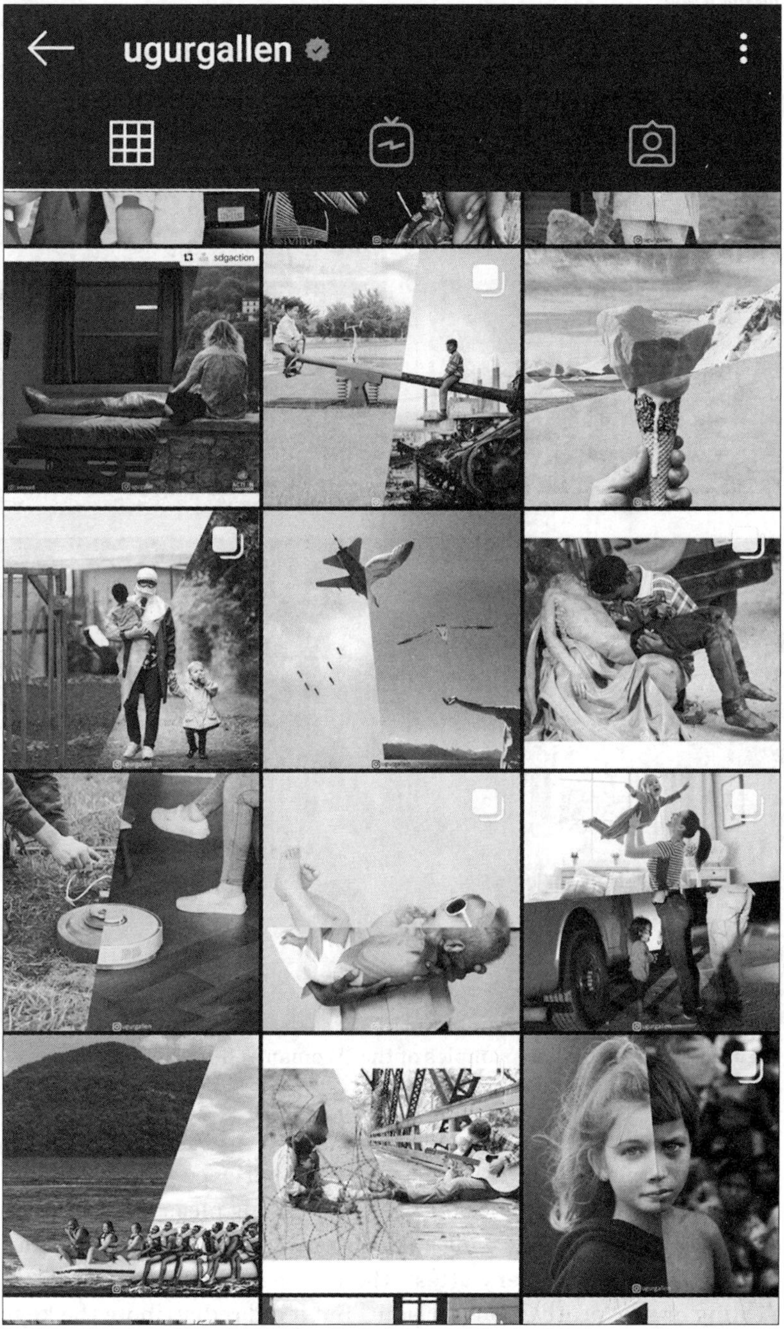

Figure I.2. A view of Instagram posts by Uğur Gallenkuş, all of which engage in comparative assembly. Screenshot, September 2020.

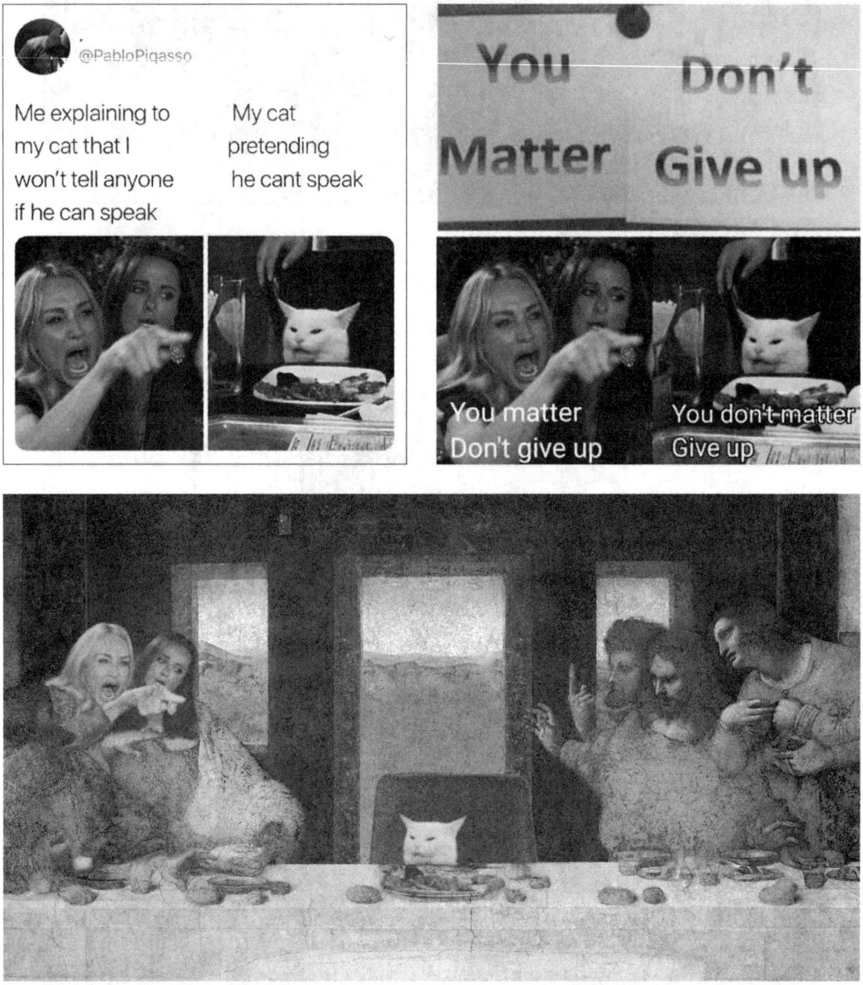

Figure I.3. A selection of examples of the "Woman Yelling at a Cat" meme. All collected in 2019.

is the provision of an assembly-based experience of dwelling in analogies and disanalogies (or of simply taking pleasure in certain visual pairings). As the long histories of political cartooning and before-and-after imagery attest, the internet didn't invent the revealing or provocative comparison.[15] But it did redistribute the keys to anyone with access to Photoshop (or even just a free "meme generator" tool), so much so that comparative assemblies are, for now anyway, a quotidian and political rhetorical staple of millions of people's daily or even hourly media diets.

Less common but no less important types of assembly appear in contexts quite different from rapid-fire social media, such as the art gallery or the art museum. In places like these, designations and taxonomies do not tend to be unofficial and protean, but established and orderly. That means there are dominant categories, things like general type (e.g., art or not-art), medium (e.g., sculpture), movement (e.g., Mexican muralism), and origin (e.g., outsider art). There are also authorities, from scholars, curators, and tour guides to metadata standards and usage guidelines, working to ensure the normative repetition of those categories. Of course, all efforts to retain established orders notwithstanding, many aesthetic practices continue to elude such organizational schemes.[16] To borrow Hanneke Grootenboer's language, many artworks and art practices might indeed inhabit well-worn (and often quite accurate) categories, even self-consciously, but they are also "embedded in an ever expanding network of shapes and forms," and they exist "as a result of a shaping and reshaping of these forms."[17] One of this book's arguments is that the actual, lived palette of possible artistic forms and strategies well exceeds current habits of seeing, and one of the most important missing pieces (particularly in the digital era) is art that specifically and strategically commits to aesthetics of compilation and configuration, relation and arrangement—to assembly.

In chapter 2, I elaborate this argument through a critical typology of art in the mode of assembly. That means addressing everything from a sequence of internet-sourced photomosaics, to basalt columns on an island off Reykjavík, to a recuperative gathering of animated GIFs. Indicative of the considerable scope of assembly, my examples cut across mediums, genres, and subject matters, reaching as far back as Hieronymus Bosch's *Garden of Earthly Delights*. What binds this large and heterogeneous set of instances of "aesthetic assembly" is not, as E. H. Gombrich would have it, the projects' appeal to "the habits and mental sets we acquired in learning to read representations."[18] Instead, it is their appeal to the habits and mental sets we acquired in learning to read relationships. Take a deceptively simple piece like *Nocturnes II* by Milagros de la Torre (Figure I.4). From one vantage, the work is indeed a sequence of photographic representations of a digital clockface at an angle, and

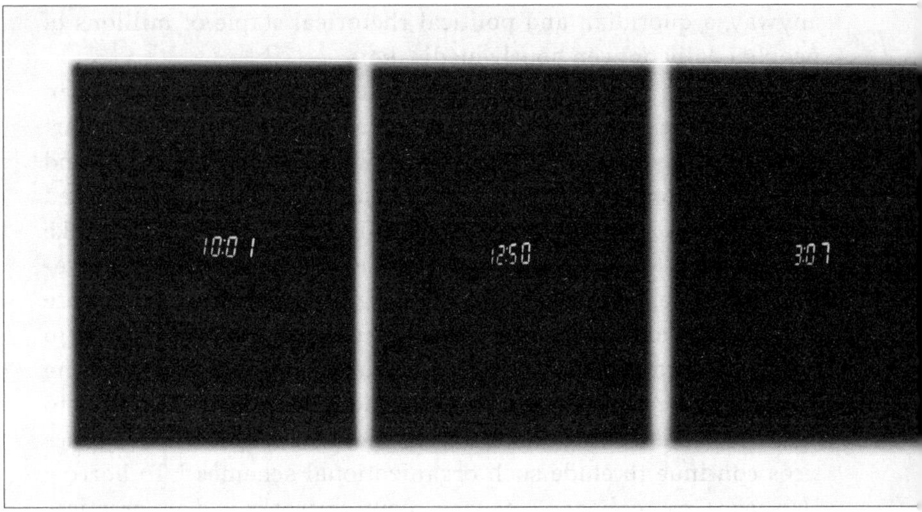

it is in that sense a poetic image of night that also implies a story (or many stories) of insomnia.[19] From another vantage, however, the work is a confluence of constituents, not just the five individual images, but the elements consistent across those images: the numbers, the colon, the light they cast, the dark that surrounds them. To read this work well, in other words, is to linger in the fact and the potentials of those constituents' expressive interplay. That can mean a kind of experiential immersion in the mode of "firstness," as with watching subtle variations in the light (such as the seeming differences in intensity among the lines that make up the numbers, or the variation across the blurring of the frames). It can also mean interpretation in the mode of "secondness," or what Mitchell calls the "onset" or "event of recognition" of an image (in this case, an assembly of images).[20] One can work with the dense meanings and potentials in the artist's configuration, such as its gathering of a darkness that doesn't fade, or the way it "alludes to a varied and complex network of personal responses and references such as our sensations of the notion of time, of the activities induced by the night, of insomnia, and of the border between sleep and wakefulness."[21] One can also glimpse would-be emulations on social media, such as repeat images of an alarm clock fused with text overlays for a modest mapping of the unruly thoughts of a sleepless night, an ephemeral assembly scanned by a few, soon replaced.

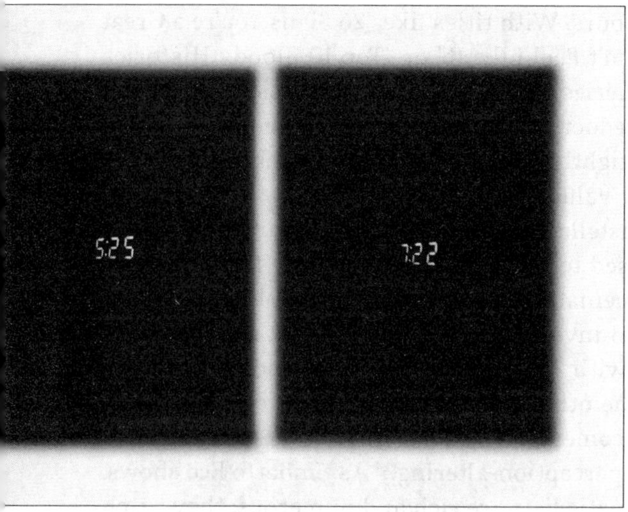

Figure I.4. Repeated views of a digital clock afford an expressive interplay. Milagros de la Torre, *Nocturnes II,* 2002. Archival pigment print, 16 × 52 inches.

Artists (and curators and still others) working in the mode of aesthetic assembly can produce countless further variations on such experiential and interpretive generativity. They can do so through many media and platforms, not just through assemblies of images, but through installations, "warm" databases, transhistorical exhibitions, or even activist actions. Crucially, those who engage in aesthetic assembly do so in a manner that does not seek to overcome the fact of combination. Instead, they make that fact into the primary source of emotional, semantic, political, or still other effects. In so doing, they speak to the promise of reassembly: that, as Jacques Rancière puts it, "every situation can be cracked open from the inside" (or so one might sometimes hope), and that, at their best, artistic works and practices (and the people who engage and question and make use of them) can help "reconfigure the landscape of what can be seen and thought."[22]

As yet another kind of assembly, the *thematic list* hovers between viral comparison and aesthetic assembly: while it can be read quickly, it also tends to take nontrivial quantities of time and resources to produce. On the generally less remarkable but still quite successful side of this family within a family are the many varieties of shareable lists and "listicles" that "infotain" (and some might say prey on) those in the midst of commutes or other contemporary downtimes. Perhaps you have seen one, maybe even in the last twenty-four hours. With titles like "26 Signs You're a Great Boss—Even If It Doesn't Feel Like It" or "Top 10 Bloody Histories Behind Common Surgeries," these lists perform basic functions of rapid education and reductive representation, but they are also, in the vein of assembly, tightly packaged symbolic combinations that consolidate particular values and concerns, and that readers scan and pass along as constellations worthy of temporary diversion.[23] Not necessarily opposed to but still quite divergent from this end of the subfamily of thematic lists are the various abstract, activist, and quasi-archival inventories produced by artists and other media practitioners with all manner of social and experimental intentions. Here the otherwise orderly exercise of placing one thing after another becomes the means to produce kaleidoscopes of meaning-making and perception-altering.[24] As Umberto Eco shows, examples of such thematic lists are rich and numerous: they reach back to antiquity and extend into the very fabric of the World Wide Web, which Eco characterizes as a massive exercise in inventory.[25] Although not his intention, Alan Liu likewise speaks to a long history of such media forms, particularly in his suggestive reframing of the premodern time tables of Eusebius of Caesarea as "patchy" assemblages capable of historical and semantic linking.[26] Among the most cited instances in the realm of art is a list of both familiar and untested artistic potentials I analyze in the second chapter: Richard Serra's late 1960s *Verb List,* a typology of verbs ("to differ," "to disarrange") and subject matters ("of simultaneity, of tides").

Another poignant example from the mid-1970s was a response to a question posed to multiple artists by Lucy Lippard, Ruth Iskin, and Arlene Raven: "What is feminist art?" Rather than answer in the mode of argument, allegory, or abstraction, Joan Snyder opted for what Eco might call a "chaotic enumeration,"[27] only not in the sense that the two-page handwritten list fails to make any sense (Figure I.5), but in that it dwells in a multiplicity of perceived features of the "feminine sensibility," embodying the simultaneously resistant and collectivist character of feminist art.[28] Albeit to much different effect, that dual character is again on display in a collaborative variant on the thematic list undertaken several decades later called *Art + Feminism.*[29] Here it is not an explicit enumeration put on paper; it is an ever-expanding, theme-driven inventory to which volunteers add by way of action. They add to this inventory by attending gatherings dedicated to creating and improving one

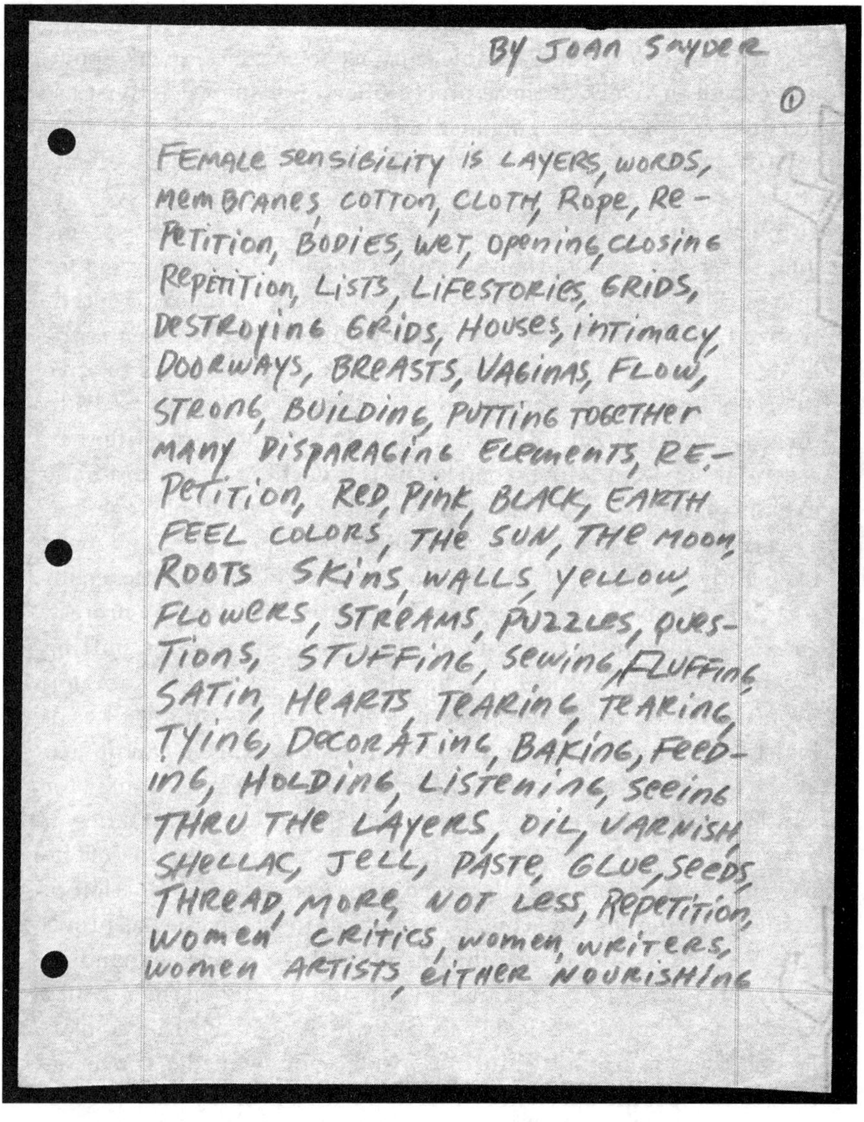

Figure I.5. Joan Snyder's enumerative response to "What is feminist art?" (1976/77). Woman's Building Records, 1970–92. Archives of American Art, Smithsonian Institution. Courtesy of the artist.

Wikipedia article after another on otherwise underrepresented communities across the arts: cis and trans women, nonbinary people, and Black people, Indigenous people, and people of color. As in-person and virtual "edit-a-thons" grow in number, and as the people involved become more informed and connected in the process, so also grows the available capacity to see, cite, speak about, and curate the work of these practitioners. Ephemeral activist assemblies can beget enduring media ones.

Still other types of assembly take shape and produce effects at scales even larger than *Art + Feminism*. These can involve vast numbers of participants, even tens of millions, and often extreme quantities of visual, verbal, and other constituents. My name for this family—*distributed assembly*—embraces the paradox of decentralized gathering.[30] One of the most important examples is the hashtag, typically (and correctly) framed for its functions relative to access and dissemination. Adding a hashtag to a post tends to increase the likelihood of it being #discovered. But there is another, essential sense in which the rise of the hashtag was a dramatic expansion in the capacities of broad publics to assemble together. This is not to say that people could literally gather better and more frequently because of the hashtag (although, as Zeynep Tufekci observes in a book on the power and fragility of networked protest, activists can come to see "no need to spend six months putting together a single rally when a hashtag could be used to summon protesters into the streets; no need to deal with the complexities of logistics when crowdfunding and online spreadsheets can do just as well").[31] It is to say that many people using the same hashtag for similar reasons are engaging in a mutually informing practice of assembling media constituents from virtual removes. One of the key implications of such dispersed practices is the production of malleable, heterogeneous media assemblies to which one has provisional access by way of search, assemblies that, as ever-expanding aggregates, can "say" something no individual could on their own, a kind of distributed political speech of which no body, user, or platform is the sole origin.[32] Think, for instance, of the media, conversation, and affect produced in connection with a hashtag like #MeToo, based on the phrase used since 2006 by Me Too founder Tarana Burke, or the perspectives and commitments circulated through campaigns like #CiteBlackWomen, initiated by Christen A. Smith in 2017.

Of course, another, quite different implication of hashtags, digital archives, memes, and other avenues of distributed assembly is of a different order: the enhancement of hidden datasets that feed into everything from market research and "behavioral surplus"[33] to crime-prediction algorithms (or, in Ruha Benjamin's terms, "crime production"[34]). Hidden troves of data constituents also play a role in the production of new and unseen images by machines for machines (and for the states and businesses that make use of those machines), what Trevor Paglen calls an "invisible visual culture," and what Joanna Zylinska calls "nonhuman photography."[35] One form of assembly occasions another, and the way one contributes to media assemblies has many varying effects, not always visible, on what kinds of assembling and disassembling are possible for oneself and others going forward.

Viral comparison, aesthetic assembly, thematic list, and distributed assembly are just four among multiple versions of a cultural form that is both extremely widespread and insufficiently theorized. I present these initial examples because they support the argument that assembly has both long existed and recently become newly ascendant thanks to digital and networked technologies, along with the structures and incentives that spread and embed those technologies. I also present these examples because they begin to answer a line of skepticism certain readers will inevitably (and understandably) bring to *A Theory of Assembly.* Maybe (this line of skepticism goes) the book is simply taking existing cultural forms, like montage, assemblage, bricolage, collage, or the aforementioned "database," and pretending they are all cut from the same cloth. Maybe it ought to be framed as montage and assemblage meeting the internet. Or maybe the book ought to be framed as an update of Manovich's claim that many new media artifacts are, like databases, "collections of individual items, with every item possessing the same significance as any other."[36] This initial cluster of examples answers these doubts by pointing to a distinct and powerful way of using and making media that takes shape at widely varying scales. Each version of assembly I have cited centrally involves seizing on combinations of constituents that remain both separate and highly interactive, combinations that can sometimes have the "same significance as any other" but that more often exhibit complex gradations of importance and intensity. And each centrally involves engendering meaningful or moving (or at least momentarily diverting) effects out of those combinations that could not (or not quite) be engendered otherwise. In short, assembly is all about relationships, from the simple to the complex, from the small to the sprawling, from the clear to the enigmatic. We are overdue in recognizing just how many cultural practices thrive on relational rather than representational, narrative, database, or other modes of expression.[37]

This isn't to say that other expressive forms can't exhibit similar characteristics, such as an instance of "database narrative" in which the layout speaks as much as the "data" and the storytelling, or a project of sound collage that opens itself up to the contributions of outsiders. (The latter is on display in certain stretches of the radio show *Over the Edge* in which the host invites audience members to phone in improvised contributions to the show's emergent soundscape.[38]) Nor is it to deny the conceptual overlaps between assembly and database, both a shared call to shift our premises around cultural forms and a mutual (but, in the case of assembly, not exclusive) emphasis on the significance of media practices that, as Hayles puts it, "construct relational juxtapositions," or that can readily welcome new elements without "disrupting their order."[39] However, the presence of overlaps is not reason to suspend inquiry—not even close. We must think outward from what is out there, and we must follow the connections as they exist and emerge. Time and again, this book will present projects and practices for which "montage," "database," and other proximate terms are insufficient, or for which an emphasis on the fusion or "dance" or "complex ecology" of cultural forms, including between assembly and narrative, proves essential.[40] This will be true of expressive actions at the smaller end of the scale, like the juxtaposition in response to Katrina. It will also be true of much more diffuse undertakings, including the vast, anarchic world of memes.

Forming language and critical frameworks for these practices serves to expand the palette of artistic possibility, a shift with implications for practices of description, production, purchase, display, and critique across art, art history, and museums. It grants overdue attention to (and provides new analytical armature for) the remarkable inventiveness (and insidiousness) of assembly-based and assembly-infused cultural production in the internet era. And it helps to counter the understandable but overbearing influence of storytelling and image-making in strategic conversations around aesthetic and activist responses to large-scale disasters and to slow and structural violence.

Plural Reading, or Family Resemblance as Method

If one set of doubts facing *A Theory of Assembly* turns on the suspicion that instances of assembly are really just instances of other, already-known cultural forms, another set of doubts turns on the seemingly impossible heterogeneity contained within the concept. A Redditor's "exploitable" recasts the Bing search engine as more obscure than the dark web (chapter 1). An artist collective lofts a two-mile line of balloons with Indigenous iconography over the Mexico–U.S. border (chapter 2). A "meme warfare consultant" helps launch a repugnant meme that makes its way to the president's Twitter account (chapter 3). A digital archive includes a visualization of keywords that places both marginalized and dominant perspectives on a disaster side by side (chapter 4). Social media accounts attempt to undermine the science of climate change through deceptive comparisons (chapter 5). How can such manifestly different projects be analyzed together in any meaningful way? Shouldn't their medium specificity, thematic disparity, and dissonances of tone and purpose make such inquiry impossible?[41]

One answer to these important questions is the framework for assembly presented in the first chapter, in which I define assembly as a mixture of constituents and positions, selection and configuration. Another is a matter of distinct approach. This book assumes that conversations around what cultural forms exist and matter will remain unnecessarily limited if they shy from the possibility of actively comparing uses of "old" and "new" media that otherwise seem too different to compare. Along these lines, *A Theory of Assembly* pursues a method that anyone in art history, visual studies, digital studies, or other fields could take up, what I call—in conversation with practices like "close," "distant," and "surface" reading—*plural reading.*[42]

The conceptual foundations of plural reading rest in a well-trodden terrain: the philosophical notion of family resemblances.[43] Albeit not in so many words, the notion has been in circulation in Europe since at least as early as the thirteenth century.[44] It finds

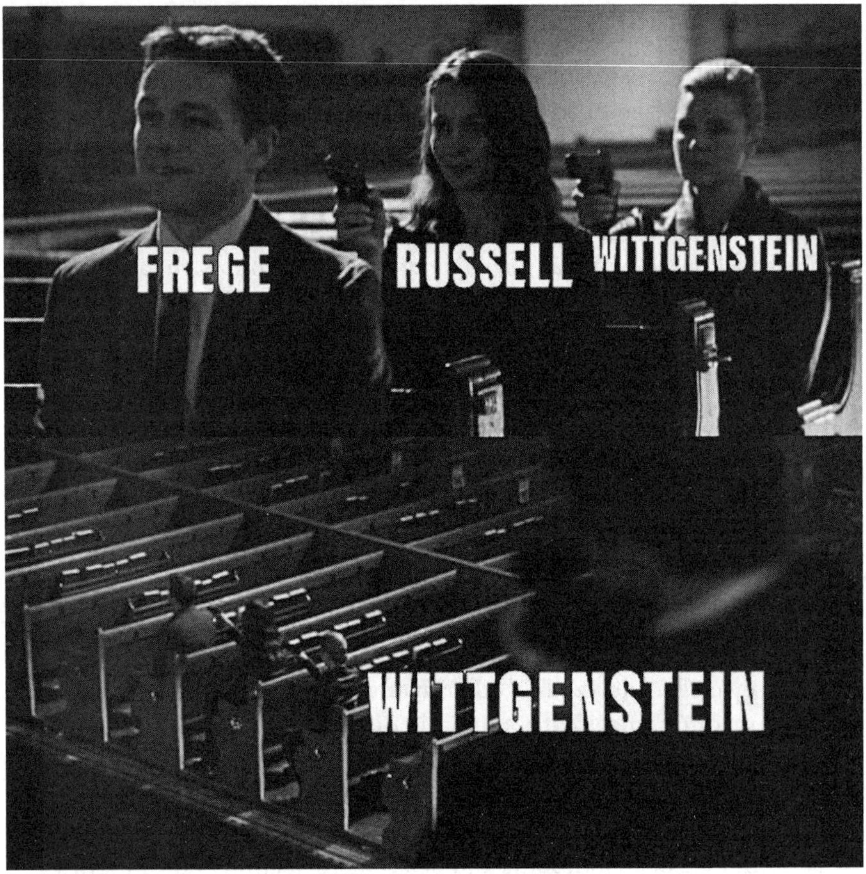

Figure I.6. An "object labeling" meme in which Bertrand Russell targets his predecessor Gottlob Frege, while (early) Wittgenstein targets his mentor Russell and (later) Wittgenstein targets his earlier self. Anonymous, circa 2019.

its most potent articulation in *Philosophical Investigations,* a book in which, as several image memes recall, Ludwig Wittgenstein disavowed not just his mentor's but also his own work (Figure I.6).[45]

What are family resemblances? Say we are trying to determine what binds a particular set of things together, what makes them of a piece with each other. We could attempt to distill an essence across many uses: the thing that is common to all of them, the universal shared trait. But countless phenomena, including Wittgenstein's oft-cited example of a game, end up defying such an approach. Multiple things can deserve the name "game," and yet no single feature will necessarily unite all of them, nor safely delimit their boundaries. Maybe *most* involve some amount of play, for instance, but not *all* of them will, or not all of them will require that feature in order to be understood as games. (I think of a war game, in which play is not an integral component.) Reading for family resemblances neither dispenses with the work of analysis nor acts as though the world were hopelessly undefinable. Instead, it shifts the interpretive practice. One examines the many overlapping and diverging features across multiple cases, such as ball games, board games, and card games. (I should note here that it's well worth considering the roles of media assembly in video, role-playing, and what Ian Bogost calls "persuasive" games.[46]) What results is a markedly plural exercise of interpretive watching and listening. We observe a carousel of analogy and disanalogy; in Wittgenstein's words, we "see how similarities crop up and disappear," both dominant similarities and less common ones.[47] As daunting as this method might initially seem, it is merely a matter of revising one's assumptions around how diverse things can interrelate. Whether studying concepts, media, cultural practices, or still other matters, what one encounters is a network of linking similarities that are not necessarily shared across all cases, or at least not to the same degree. In other words, there can be commonalities that link nearly all cases while nevertheless not being essential or universal.[48] Just as importantly, there can be binding commonalities that might be shared by only a handful of family members (a small subfamily within the overall family) but are nevertheless highly significant and worthy of critical and interpretive attention.[49]

This book turns Wittgenstein's philosophical response to problems of categorization into a flexible method for analyzing culture and media.[50] This has been done in partial ways before me, such as when philosophers have countered monolithic definitions of art with more porous schemes based in family resemblances. But this book's use of family resemblances is not quite the same as these others. Rather than compare types for the sake of a more inclusive taxonomy, we inductively compare and speculatively categorize instances of cultural production for the sake of thinking and practice, sometimes emphasizing very large commonalities, like assembly, other times more particular ones, like the practices of "expressive folksonomy" in meme cultures (chapter 3) or "emergent archiving" after disaster (chapter 4).[51]

As many readers will recognize, plural reading's precedents aren't limited to family resemblances. One important precursor is Heinrich Wölfflin's influential use of a double slide projector in art history classrooms. Another is André Malraux's recombinatory museum of the imagination or "museum without walls."[52] There is also the comparative work of Charles Robert Cockerell and other nineteenth-century figures influenced by his rich assembly-based "drop-scenes."[53] Finally, more recently, Tina Campt infuses her striking practice of "listening" to archival, state, and identificatory images with methods of reassembling and comparing, including what she calls at one point "stereoscopic and stereophonic juxtaposition."[54]

What plural reading adds to such precedents is both the emphasis on generating flexible and sometimes speculative categories *and* the considerably higher levels of heterogeneity, quantity, and scale invited into the mix.[55] One way to summarize the stakes of plural reading is to say that it offers a way of remaining assured and attentive amid the forbiddingly complex analogical networks that characterize digital and visual culture. One opts to persist with analysis while comparing collections of things that exhibit variously general, frequent, and rare similarities. Meanwhile, differences need not fall out the window. They remain there, too; in fact, differences become even more evident and important because we have adopted a flexible and intersectional way of seeing that does not accept rigid binaries or settled systems, but emphasizes overlapping frames, soft borders, gray areas, and outliers. As Mieke Bal puts it in defense of anachronism and "interhistorical" exhibition in art, "approximation does not come at the cost of historical difference; on the contrary, it enhances it, deploys it as a tool to sharpen how and what we can see."[56] In Campt's terms, an assembly of images that forgoes a single, "unifying attribute" can produce "patterns of similarity that yield multiplicity and difference."[57]

As if elaborating the interpretive combinatorics of Aby Warburg's unfinished *Mnemosyne Atlas*,[58] and building on Griselda Pollock's Warburg-inspired "virtual feminist museum" that "break[s] all the museal and art historical rules of what can be put together with what,"[59] we come to see that there are families of media and culture that constitute families for reasons other than their technical basis (like photography) or their broadly common domain (like social media) or their historical affinities of style or geography (like Dutch still life). Instead, there are families based on other kinds of similarities and "exploratory relations" that are often quite unfamiliar, understudied, and "unnatural."[60] Form, function, effect, mode, material—there can be many kinds of linking similarities that point to the existence of a particular family, even if the "members" of that family derive from quite different cultural, geographical, and historical contexts. Along these lines, as I emphasize again in the conclusion, the plural reading of assembly shares affinities with well-established queer and feminist approaches, including what Eve Kosofosky Sedgwick calls "reparative reading." This is a fundamentally relational mode that seeks to "organize the fragments and part-objects she encounters or creates,"[61] a mode that, as Olivia Laing puts it, works to "find or invent something new and sustaining out of inimical environments."[62] To read for family resemblances is, at its most vital, to read for renewal.

Of course, at the end of the day, it is not the conceptual basis but the actual, achievable fruitfulness of plural reading that matters most, and in that sense a new slate of examples is in order. Let's start with a nondigital one: Louise Bourgeois's 2006 work *10 AM IS WHEN YOU COME TO ME* (Plate 1). The title of this piece (of which Bourgeois made ten unique versions) refers to the point in the morning when Bourgeois's longtime assistant, Jerry Gorovoy, would arrive at the studio. In interview, Gorovoy recalls the artist's "whiplashes": something "deep inside her" would be triggered or unlocked, and this something would "re-emerge as aggressive and self-destructive impulses."[63] His role would be to "calm her down," and this is, in his recollection, what Bourgeois "wanted to convey in the suite of hand poses," that Gorovoy's arrival meant the return of safety and the readiness to work again. The assembly itself gathers one configuration after another of their hands (Bourgeois's has a wedding ring), sometimes in isolation, sometimes overlapping. With those hands and arms reaching both outward and to each other, the work is a rendering of friendship and warmth; it is also something of a "map of their working relationship" and of the "varied successes" artist and assistant can realize.[64] Meanwhile, by way of the consistent grids of the musical score paper, it embeds associations with the nourishments of music ("its rhythm, structure, beat") and with personal memories along these lines.[65]

Though quite divergent in tone, medium, and subject matter from the other projects I've already presented (and it isn't digital), from the perspective of plural reading, *10 AM* is highly germane. Reading the Gallenkuş assemblies and the "woman yelling at cat" meme in conjunction with Bourgeois's work, it is apparent that, for all their blatant dissimilarities, they nevertheless carry important family resemblances. One of these resemblances already in play is the expressive strategy of media assembly. Another is more elusive and particular: the use of the hand as a consequential constituent. In the Gallenkuş juxtapositions, there are hands that grasp for love (adults and children), hands that are absent (the child in tears beneath the child laughing), and hands associated with peril (the hand beneath the glacier or near the mine). In the meme, there are both the very present and forceful pointing hand and the barely recognized hand behind the cat. In addition, in at least one iteration, the parody of *The Last Supper,* there are the multiple gesturing hands as rendered by both Leonardo da Vinci and *The Real Housewives.* Finally, in the Bourgeois piece, there is an equally playful and intensive engagement with the idea of hands as bodily constituents that take on certain positions and that can come into intimate relation (and conflict) with those of others. A more conservative perspective would dismiss these as merely coincidental or unimportant overlaps. Taking the time to dwell in the possibility of a subfamily, however, one can recognize that these are all instances in which constituent hands draw the eye, indicate human presence, intensify the qualities of expressivity, and serve as sources of tension and power. This much could (and should, for my part) be interesting to practitioners who ponder aesthetic possibilities. But the question from the perspective of plural reading is whether and how it might be valuable to pursue this subfamily further for the sake of understanding and critique, perhaps finding a vein of aesthetic or activist ore, or running into conceptual questions that deserve further study.

One way to do this is to look outward to other projects that bear these same family resemblances: the cultural form of assembly and the expressive use of gathered hands. Not surprisingly, what Ryan M. Milner and Whitney Phillips dub the "ambivalent internet"[66]

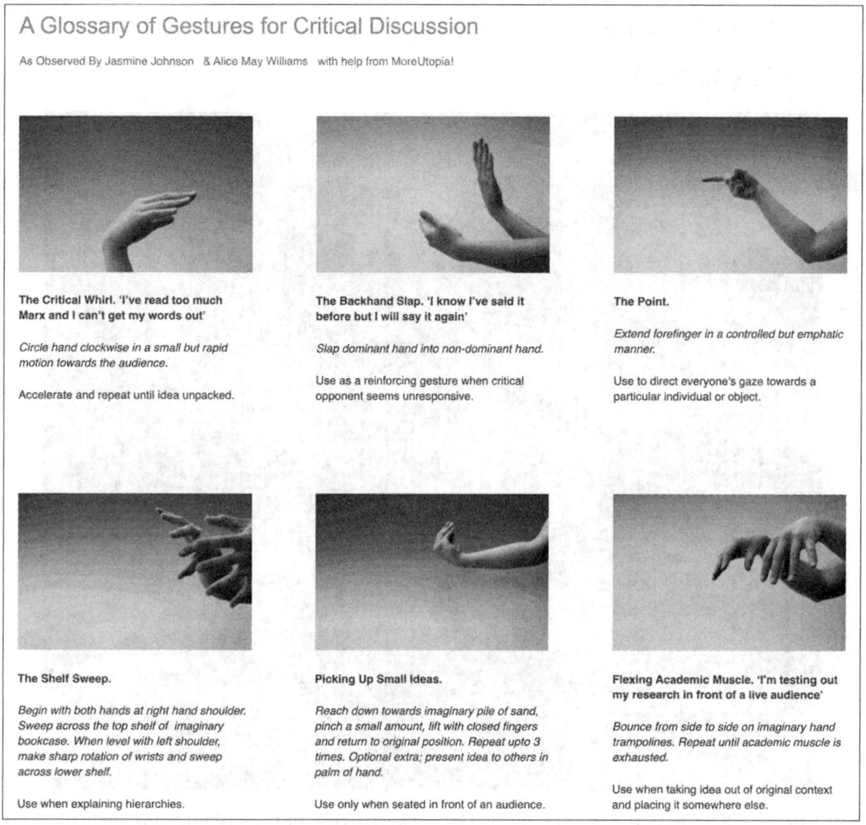

Figure I.7. Jasmine Johnson and Alice May Williams with MoreUtopia!, *A Glossary of Gestures for Critical Discussion,* 2013. Screenshot, September 2020 (criticalhandgestures.tumblr.com).

is rife with the latter. One example is a delightful use of Tumblr. A pair of artists present "A Glossary of Gestures for Critical Discussion"; the looping GIFs of emphatic hand gestures (in conjunction with their clever captions) make for a satirical ferment while nevertheless speaking to an attentiveness to academic habits in all their specificity and eccentricity (Figure I.7).[67] Several years later, meme producers adapted a longtime schoolyard gimmick in which you trick someone into looking at the "O.K." circle you make with your thumb and the index finger. Somehow this game ended up being coopted by white supremacists, so that in 2019, a memetic rendition of the first-ever imaging of a black hole as the universe tricking us

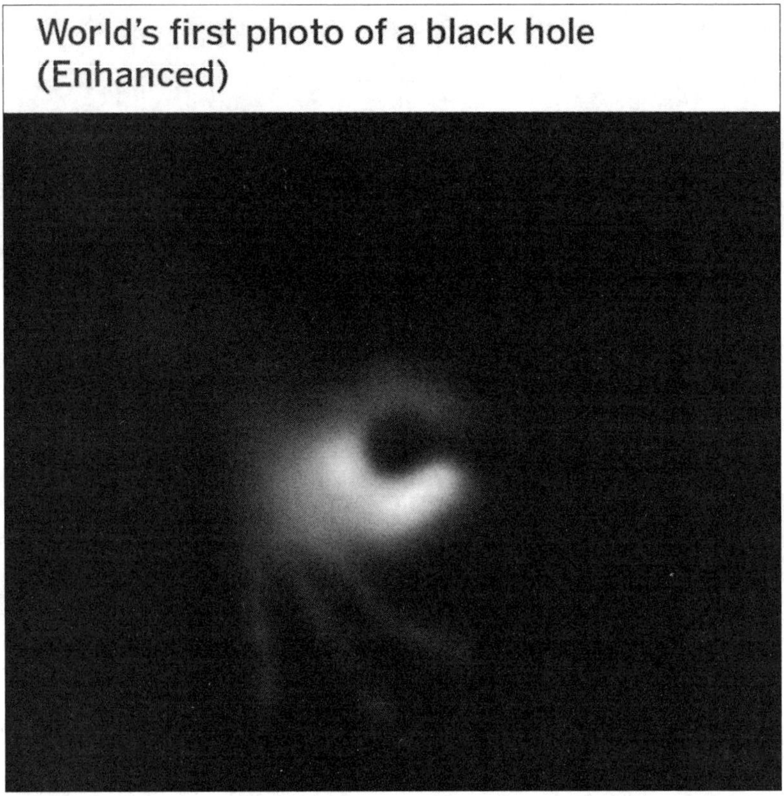

Figure I.8. A playful meme about the imaging of a black hole (apparently unintentionally) cites a violent one. Anonymous. Collected in 2019.

all into seeing the circle becomes tainted by an apparently unwelcome citation of networks of racist ideology (Figure I.8).[68] As a final example, on the now-ascendant (as of 2022) platform TikTok, several among the never-ending stream of memetic "challenges" invite people to do things with their hands for the camera. In one case, users flash one or two hands in imitation of a sequence of hand emojis, either trying to match what's already been done or creatively adding new variations on the theme. In another, very different challenge, users hold up fingers as they listen to TikToker Kenya Bundy read twelve negative scenarios regularly dealt with by Black Americans on the basis of race. If you have any fingers remaining by the end, then you have privilege (Figure I.9).

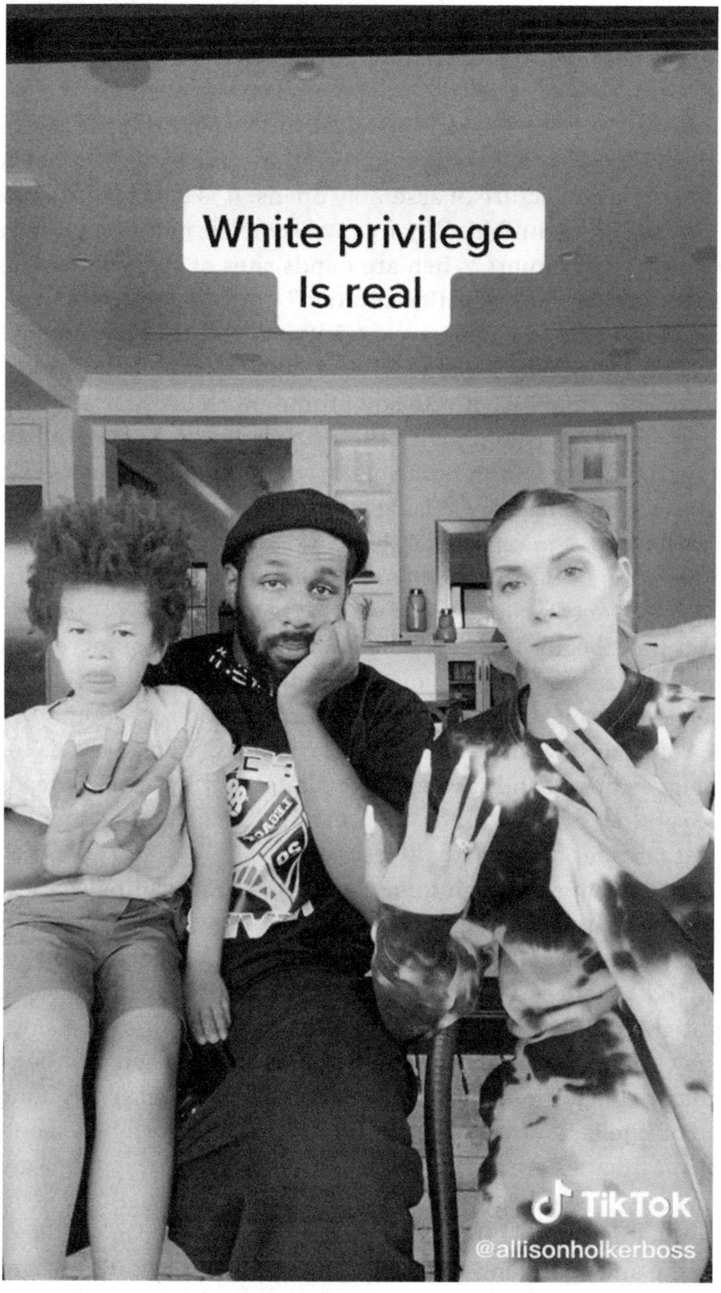

Figure I.9. Fingers configure privilege on the TikTok account @allisonholkerboss in 2020.

A pluralist approach welcomes the considerable discomfort that emerges here. On the one hand, you get that sinking feeling that you've merely glommed on to some arbitrary feature. On the other hand, you find that there is good reason to persist: that the very feeling of trouble is (one hopes) a sign of potential. It is not just because the big picture of assembly opens. It is also because interesting questions unfold. What can assembled hands say that assembled faces cannot? When are hands sites of interconnection?[69] When are they sites of differentiation? To what degree do smartphones and emojis kill the eccentricity of gesture? To what degree do visual assemblies save them? And, finally, how might these different uses of hands point to something much broader about how humans index and count with their fingers, or as Benjamin Peters put it, "have digital tools built right into their hands"? Peters elaborates: "By pointing or orienting ourselves to different objects, our digits have long manipulated the world around us. This is nothing new: what is new is the commanding degree and scale to which, in the past seventy years or so, trivially large reservoirs of computing power have begun to be consolidated in the hands of increasingly powerful data-rich institutions—corporation and state alike—and much less so self-organizing groups of people. Socioeconomic privilege continues to scale with digital privileges."[70] From hands in an analog studio to hands as vectors of digital privilege, plural reading relies on exactly these kinds of uncertain, speculative, and multiplicative cascades of inquiry.

Lest it seem as though I am claiming plural reading carries no risks or limits, let me emphasize that it does. Among the major risks is that one ends up leaving out significant aspects of the projects and practices analyzed. As certain family resemblances are highlighted, other distinguishing features can fall to the side. In some cases, such as a humorous dance craze, this will not be particularly concerning, but in other circumstances one risks doing a kind of intellectual violence, acting as though cultural and contextual specificities are not important, or effectively stripping a given project of its felt meanings or political force. Another risk is more general. It is possible that hyperinductive analysis can end up performing and endorsing what Ariella Aïsha Azoulay calls an "imperial right." One assumes an entitlement to freely select, decontextualize, and reclassify—a forced removal of existing categories in favor of newly imposed ones.[71]

There is no easy answer to these problems. Perhaps they can be partly mitigated by means of the habits and orientations of the inquiry, including a consistent reticence around selecting examples about which one cannot pretend to know much or, more importantly, that do not "want" such study, or through the selection of examples that themselves embody anti-imperial, antireductionist commitments. For my part, I have sought to point to the limitations of my analyses (including the limits of my knowledge) while nevertheless insisting on the relevance of my selections.

Among the most important of my guiding criteria in these selections is a commitment to touch upon as many digital and nondigital mediums as possible (thus showing the reach and flexibility of assembly). Another is a desire to mix quite canonical and well-known examples (like the Bosch painting or memes that went "mainstream") with projects and practices that have not yet received the attention they deserve. Still another has been the overarching argument about the ambivalent powers of assembly in relation to violence and injustice. And yet one more criterion is a desire to suggest a potential history of assembly. It is a *supposition* of this book (i.e., not an argument it pursues in depth) that assembly well precedes the twentieth and twenty-first centuries. (As is evident, my historical and theoretical scope is largely limited to European, North American, and English-language contexts.) I have been further convinced of the merit of this idea by the handful of scholars who point to projects from the eighteenth century in which the expressive power of configuration proves integral. For instance, John O. Havard proposes that the remarkable satirical cartoon *Political Electricity; or An Historical & Prophetical Print in the Year 1770* could be seen as an instance of expressive assembly.[72] Even more suggestively, a book that will be published during production of this one, Kelly Wisecup's *Assembled for Use,* gathers understudied examples of early Indigenous American "compilations." For Wisecup, these compilations, which took forms as varied as medical recipes, poetry scrapbooks, and vocabulary lists, all involved "juxtaposing and recontextualizing textual excerpts into new relations and meanings" and served to "remake the very forms that defined" their writers' "bodies, belongings, and words as ethnographic evidence."[73]

Plural reading is the most effective means I have found to evade the dominance of oversubscribed (but obviously important) cultural forms while also providing critically flexible typologies of the potentials and pitfalls of assembly in response to social and ecological oppression and harm. It is my strong sense that, as digital and networked technologies increasingly blur what were only provisional lines between media (and between life, culture, and technology), and as more and more voices and perspectives enter planetary-scale experiments in cultural forms, the need for plural reading will become all the more pronounced. Plural reading might fail at times, but without it we won't adequately meet the remarkable heterogeneity and citational ferment of the internet era. We will also overlook much needed tactics and countertactics in the daily maelstrom of mediated democratic struggle.

Through the Lens of Assembly

A Theory of Assembly joins books like *The Age of Sharing* and *The Ecology of Attention* in placing front and center a single, essential concept: *assembly*.[74] So far, I have emphasized how assembly names a distinct cultural phenomenon. That phenomenon is an increasingly prevalent expressive strategy set apart by the visible and intensive use of compilation and configuration; it is especially open to analysis through the method of plural reading; and it is of particular (though not always positive) consequence in response to events and conditions of destruction and injustice.

The last thing I must discuss before launching into the chapters is something else assembly names, which is *a way of looking at the world*. In many respects, this way of looking matches up with the concept of assembly as I have so far presented it. That is to say, if you look through this book's "lens" of assembly, then your attention will be drawn to expressive projects that do not characteristically narrate or represent the world, but instead rearrange it. In another important sense, however, this book's lens of media assembly tends to at least partly (and sometimes thoroughly) scramble that more stable perspective on cultural and communicative life. It does so by consistently bringing other things into view: other features, other scales, and most notably, *other forms of assembly and assemblage.*

I can best clarify this more complicated dimension of the book's theoretical project through a reworked version of this now commonplace metaphor of the conceptual lens. The usual idea with this metaphor is relatively straightforward. Something of intellectual interest is seen in finer detail by way of a certain governing concept. Researchers might, with a meaning closer to the literal, characterize given research projects as efforts to reinterpret something (such as environmentalism) through a particular lens, or they might employ a similar language for certain turns of mind, speaking to shifts in perception, a "lens switch." At the same time, the metaphor of the lens also suggests something akin to a "point of view."[75] Researchers are adopting certain perspectives, vocabularies, and commitments over others.

Although the technology of the lens is rarely discussed (the term comes from the Latin for "lentil"), the implicit notion in these cases tends toward that of a magnifying glass, as in a single piece of "glass or other transparent substance with curved sides for concentrating or dispersing light rays."[76] But it turns out that actual lenses are almost always plural in nature. Telescopic lenses, smartphone lenses, single-lens reflex (SLR) camera lenses—quite a few things we imagine as discrete lenses are, in fact, made up of structured arrays of several simpler lenses or "lens elements" (Figure I.10).[77] In other words, lenses are collections or arrangements of lenses. Typically, the lens elements that make up these arrangements align in groups, filtering and focusing light waves in particular ways for the receptive surface, whether an emulsion or a charged couple device. As different blends and different positionings of lenses yield different visual and informational results, what is at stake is often an improvement in image quality, but there can be other reasons to favor one arrangement over another, such as a preferred type of image for consumer cameras or a certain kind of visual data necessary for research purposes.

It is also possible to refuse these more normative approaches to lens assembly. Among the more suggestive demonstrations of this possibility is a lens that is not unidirectional but multidirectional, as in the north-south-east-west camera built by the artist Aïm Düelle Lüski. Instead of a clearer, more beautiful, more comprehensive, or more useful image, the multidirectional lens yields a melding of four distinct views in a single, enigmatic exposure. As Azoulay emphasizes, these exposures "address the groundless effort to violently split, and later allegedly seam together, one geographical and urban unit according to national and ethnic lines."[78]

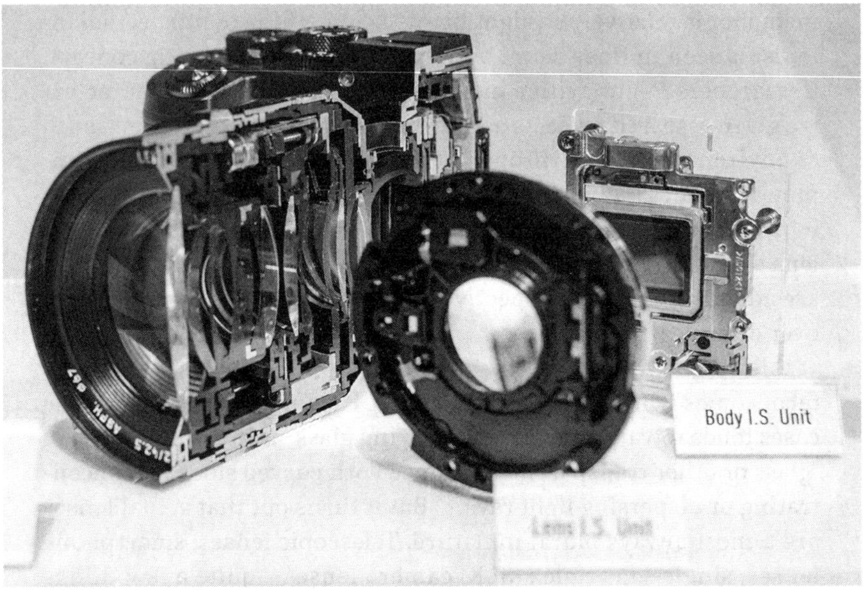

Figure I.10. As revealed by a split-open SLR camera, a lens can be (and often is) an assembly of lens elements. Kārlis Dambrāns, "Panasonic camera, IFA 2015." Cropped. CC BY 2.0.

In employing the lens of media assembly, this book tends toward this more open-ended and indeed plural idea of a lens that comes from the technology itself. This takes shape in two key ways. For one, my approach to given contexts and problems will consistently undergo switches, as though media assembly's internal lens arrangements have been adjusted on the fly. Quite often these switches will be from artifact to practice, moving from what something *is* (like an ark built after disaster or a sequence of climate change memes) to what those things involve or yield (like an arts nonprofit in the same area as the ark), or to how their effects stretch out over time and place (like the effect of the persistent "drip" of these climate change memes). Another kind of switch involves scale, moving from a vision of assemblies made by individuals (like a GIF), to things made by distributed participants (like a digital environmental justice atlas), to endeavors undertaken in widely dispersed and not always intentional fashion (like the distributed mediation of the Mexico–U.S. border). Whether an appreciation for the effects of a process or an attention to multiple scales rather than just one, the virtue of this malleability is a considerably expanded account of how assembly-based efforts are effective and consequential. Assembly matters not only for what it expresses but also for what it enables and enacts across time and place. One other advantage of these switches is a responsiveness to the circumstances of networked life. The smallest actions can have the biggest effects (and the largest actions can have the least effect). Practices of digital assembly matter and mutate across multiple orders and registers. The point is not that it is wrong to focus on assembly in the sense of media assemblies, like viral comparisons or thematic lists. It is that, given the complexity and richness of art and media, there are always other lens configurations one ought to consider using. One of these is a shift from static artifact to in-process practice. Another is the switching of scales.

A second, more "plural" habit of this book's lens of media assembly might be phrased thus: I open the lens of media assembly to creative recombination with other conceptual lenses; I do so to see and think something better, differently, or anew. The lenses with which I combine media assembly are quite varied, from analogy and folksonomy to structural violence and intersectionality. At the same time, there are certain cognate lenses that prove especially enabling throughout the book. They fall into two broad categories: on the one side, theories of assemblage and, on the other, theories of political and popular assembly.

Lenses under the umbrella of assemblage reach back at least as far as the wonderfully roving (if also sometimes frustratingly opaque) 1980 book *A Thousand Plateaus*. There Gilles Deleuze and Félix Guattari defy more dominant Cartesian and Newtonian precepts by suggesting that the world is replete with something called "agencement," a term that is most often (and somewhat deceptively) translated into English as "assemblage."[79] Assemblages are not a type of art in this case.[80] Rather, they are certain kinds of entities in the world. They are porous aggregates; these aggregates are made up of evolving, heterogeneous elements and relationships among those elements; and the aggregates exist, operate, and transform across multiple scales.[81]

Manuel DeLanda provided the first full-fledged explication of this novel concept. According to DeLanda, the most accessible example of an "assemblage of heterogeneous elements" is a particular kind of martial "whole," one which is "composed of a human being, a fast riding horse, and a missile-throwing weapon."[82] This is the most accessible example because it clearly cuts across "entirely different realms of reality: the personal, the biological, and the technological." Other assemblages, much larger in scale and much more varied in character, from a prison to a city to an entire nation, likewise cut across different realms of acting and becoming, but with dramatically more elements, dynamics, and relationships in play.

Over the past several decades, numerous scholars have built on these complex (and often elusive) theoretical foundations. Among the many, many examples one could cite are: Jane Bennett arguing that a power grid is an assemblage exhibiting a kind of agency[83]; Hayles on the power of "cognitive assemblages" (from automated personal assistants to the entire internet) that act as "arrangement[s] of systems, subsystems, and individual actors through which information flows, effecting transformations through the interpretive activities of cognizers operating upon the flows"[84]; or finally Jasbir Puar reconceiving a host of interrelated phenomena—terrorists and terrorism, the "homonationalism" of states, the turbaned body, the theoretical apparatus that pursues these concepts, sexuality—as evolving, mutating, dynamic aggregates of elements.[85] Still other examples likewise assert a conceptual reworking of supposedly stable things as unruly, in-process, malleable arrangements, finding assemblage a useful term for phenomena as varied as melancholy, climate-change policy, Bollywood, tourism, and the brain.[86] Are these thinkers all using the *same* lens of assemblage? My analogy suggests a more nuanced approach. We assess how different elements are used and fused, making sense of the concepts' internal "arrangements" while also pointing to a consistent way of seeing: the view to heterogeneous aggregates.

Along a different and more recently established track, several theories of assembly share this emphasis on heterogeneous aggregates (or what Hayles calls "a provisional collection of parts in constant flux"[87]), but they tend to find their primary departure point in the concrete fact of people gathering and organizing toward political ends.[88] In some sense, this has meant paralleling theories of assemblage by emphasizing plurality, relationality, and connection over individuality and discreteness. But it has also meant retaining a focus on the things that cultural and especially political actors do (or struggle to do) under limiting and sometimes hostile conditions. One influential strand of such assembly-based thought is found in the work of Bruno Latour, who, in collaboration with an array of artists and writers, asks what kinds of political assemblies are possible and effective, how techniques for representation support (and sometimes undo) these assemblies, and whether gatherings of people (and objects) can ever manage to successfully negotiate the spaces between their mutual concerns and "contradictory attachments."[89] In both Elise Danielle Thorburn's 2012 account and Michael Hardt and Antonio Negri's subsequent book, to assemble is to risk an often unsuccessful political organizational mode that mortal creatures already do and might yet do better.[90] For these thinkers, assembly feeds into more horizontal and emergent forms of organizing; it even has the potential to provide "the organisational terrain for the common politics to come." In Judith Butler's 2015 "performative theory of assembly," likewise inspired by the spate of political gatherings in the early 2010s (and a key influence on the present book), to assemble is to engage in a relational, expressive, and manifestly plural "performative enactment" that requires the alignment of vulnerable bodies in time and space.[91] To assemble is thus also to actualize the potential for affinity and cooperation across sometimes seemingly insurmountable degrees of difference, quite often in shared opposition to conditions of what Butler calls the "differential distribution of precarity."[92] Such assembly can also be, as Jonas Staal puts it, the occasion for "the creation of spaces in which we perform the popular to compose our understanding of being a people differently" in the mode of "assemblism."[93]

As a final example, in the work of Jason Frank, these more concept-driven visions of assembly give way to a historically situated investigation of the enduring importance of popular assembly in Europe and the United States. For Frank, there has long been a political aesthetic problem: unlike the sovereign monarch, the "people" are not consolidated or visualizable in a single figure; instead, "the people must see themselves assembled in order to feel their power."[94] By pursuing both spontaneous and planned acts of "collective staging," whether in protests, rallies, barricades, or insurgencies, aggregates of people make themselves "visible and tangible as a collective entity possessing a creative and sovereign will."[95] The often energetic and even "sublime" act of gathering toward political ends is an engine of democratic imagination; it remains "one of the principle, dynamic, and most historically persistent sites of this form of political enactment."[96] Meanwhile, whether through lithographs, photographs, paintings, or other media, "images of peoplehood" serve to "mediate the people's relationship to their own political empowerment—how they understand themselves to be a part of and act *as* a people."[97]

When I survey these heuristic summaries through this book's lens of media assembly, I *partly* see things with which I have quite a bit of agreement (such as the causal force of multi-scalar assemblages like cities in the DeLanda sense, or Hayles's emphasis on interpretation and decision-making, or the expressive and performative functions of popular assemblies). I *partly* see things about which I have questions (such as the potential overinvestment in popular assemblies as positive and effective political forms, or the paradoxical emphasis on the expressive strategy of representation in certain cases, or what appears to be an unnecessary tendency to see assemblages as everywhere and fundamental rather than particular). But what I *primarily* see are terms, ideas, convictions, and ultimately ways of looking and listening with which to come into conversation and combination.[98] And, thus, with respect to the world of theories based in assemblage, for instance, *A Theory of Assembly* takes ample inspiration from the basic commitment to recognize arrangements of heterogeneous elements on their terms, *as* arrangements, and to think through the interactions of multiple scales. The book also makes tactical use of a distinct lens element from the work of Deleuze and Guattari: "deterritorialization." Without this notion, the museum exhibition I address in chapter 2, for example, would be too much given over to assessment in terms of story and history. With this notion, I can better analyze its drive to disaggregate histories of extractive colonization and creative destruction in California through acts of aesthetic and interpretive recombination. I can also turn to other, more radical projects in this vein.

To put this all a different way, like theorists of assemblage, I am interested in how the figuration of assembly/assemblage proves enabling, whether for untested kinds of analytical comparisons, for thinking in terms of process and arrangement, or for the blurring of material and subjective acts and dynamics. At the same time, although I find "assemblage" compelling, I do not use it to name the cultural form in question because the concept misses the sense of purposeful organization, because it risks obscuring the roles of individual and group agency so important to projects of activism and repair, and because it does not as readily bridge the analog and the digital. By contrast, "assembly" has the virtue of evoking both the fleshly gathering of people and the orderly construction of machines.[99] The term thus primes us to observe the algorithmic and the archival as much as the authorial and the artistic, and the ability to think across these spheres proves especially valuable in the contexts that animate this book, from art, visual culture, and memes to disaster and slow and structural violence.

With respect to the world of popular and political assembly, the relationships between this book's lens and the ones found there are more numerous. For one thing, *A Theory of Assembly* makes evident the degree to which media assembly has several significant roles to play in both the exercise and afterlife of political gathering. (This is a lens of media assembly before, at, of, and after political assembly.) Media assemblies can act as spurs toward such physical assemblies. People assembling together can make visual and other kinds of media assemblies, such as memory quilts, free libraries, and digital archives, that reflect and remember the ongoing work of social and political convening (or that work to communicate the demands of an assembly of people without singling out a leader, as in the signatures arranged in circles known in English as "round robins" or in Japanese as "umbrella-style joint covenants"[100]). Finally, during actual in-person gatherings, there is expressive power in stances and actions that involve gathering and configuring bodies, combining and aligning voices, relating and arranging gestures.

One of the most poignant (but basically entirely forgotten) examples I have encountered along these latter lines had fishing boats rather than people as its primary media constituents. In July 1989, several months after the grounding of the *Exxon Valdez,* at the time one of the worst petroleum disasters in history, a group called F.I.S.H. (Frustrated Independent Fish Harvesters) attempted to stop an oil tanker from docking at a terminal near the Kenai River in southern Alaska. With the salmon harvest devastated after not just one but multiple oil spills, the members of F.I.S.H. sought to bring attention to their ongoing plight and the risk of further pollution events from the lack of accountability. The power of this action was, of course, the sheer physical vulnerability involved, not just the boats against the tanker, but also the local fishing industry (or one could say the local fishing "assemblage" in the Deleuze/DeLanda sense) against the global petroleum one. The power was also the expressive and disseminatable impact of the flotilla as a kind of media artifact. Together these boats made a provisional, moving assembly that embodied a refusal to accept the status quo. Individual photographs, including an especially striking one that shows wakes parallel to each other and to the long tanker itself, offered some virtual afterlife to this ephemeral configuration (Figure I.11).[101] Then, some twenty years later, a different kind of media assembly emerged that would both extend and rework the activist labors of F.I.S.H. A library and archive entity called ARLIS (Alaska Resources Library and Information Services) digitized a set of slides that included these photographs (which were taken by photographers contracted by the Governor of Alaska to document the spill, the cleanup effort, and related events). That batch of digitized photographs was then uploaded to the photo sharing platform Flickr (Plate 2). Ever since, should one somehow chance upon these images (and it is not likely that one would), one will find the marine demonstration as one assembly among many, situated between a batch of photos of a man fixing a fishing net and another that documents a second resistant flotilla, this time in Prince William Sound in September 1989. (Another blockade, in April of 1993, succeeded in suspending oil transportation over several days.[102]) One act of assembly begets another.

A second version of a hybrid media-political lens of assembly shows how media assemblies can be construed as instances of popular and political assembly in themselves. (This is a lens of media assembly as political assembly.) This notion finds a departure point in Butler's crucial insight that "forms of assembly already signify prior to, and apart from, any particular demands they make."[103] "Showing up, standing, breathing, moving, standing still, speech, and silence are all aspects of a sudden assembly," Butler writes. How do we get from assembly-based enactment in streets and at oil terminals to assembly-based enactment on canvas and in silico? We see that assemblies perform meaningful signifying work prior to

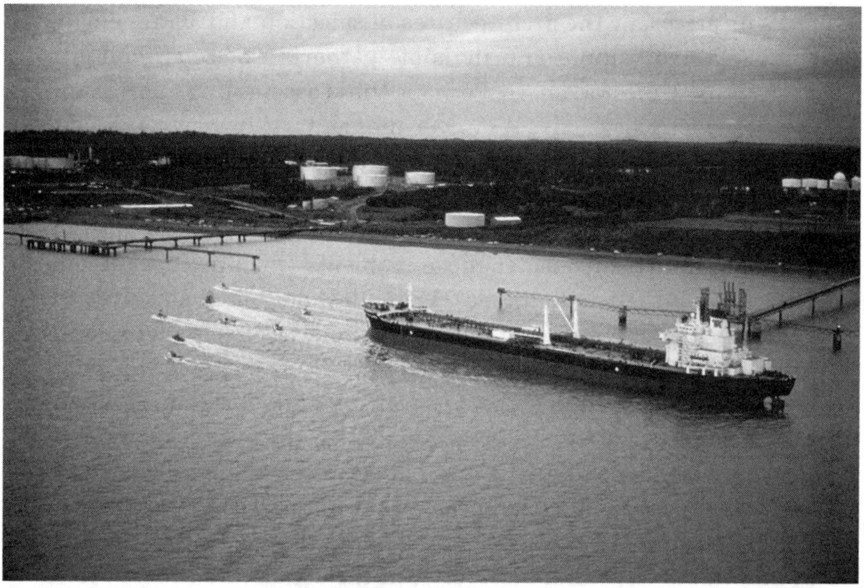

Figure I.11. "Aerial of commercial fishing boats of the Frustrated Independent Fish Harvesters (F.I.S.H.) attempting to blockade an oil tanker from docking, protesting oil spills that were preventable" at the Kenai River (Cook Inlet) on July 20, 1989. From a digitized slide collection of Alaska Resources Library and Information Services (ARLIS) as posted to Flickr.

and alongside what their words and images explicitly say, show, or enable. Put a different way, the very fact of the assembly's appearance and circulation is itself an "expressive action" or "politically significant event."[104] Thus, when audiences encounter artifacts and practices of media assembly, they encounter not only ideas, impressions, and information but also performative assertions, including the power (and the call) to intervene in public conversation, mediation, and memory, however thoughtfully, powerfully, or routinely.

Carrying forth in this speculative manner, it seems possible that, in certain cases, such as media assemblies produced or undertaken in response to violence (and here I am echoing Azoulay's concept of the civil contract of photography), assemblies do more than perform expressive actions; they also act like democratic intersections, proposing implicit and provisional polities or citizenries.[105] In these cases, nominally aesthetic uses of assembly, such as the juxtaposition of multiple characters or perspectives, the alignment of faces or places, or the architectures of selection and arrangement, conjure a provisional and invisible gathering of relational citizens across time and space. Perhaps these assembling expressions can act as provocations—however momentary, however flawed—toward future convening, whether mediated or live, around the ecological and social violence in question or around still other events and histories.

Finally, one can consider those moments when political assemblies don't just include media assemblies, but are themselves involved in and expressive of much larger ones. (This is a lens of political assembly as media assembly.) In the Conclusion of this book, I will point to one such case: the meme-spiked storming of the United States Capitol on January 6, 2021. Suffice it to say for now that the fused lens of media and popular assembly anticipates exactly these kinds of occurrences, when the persistent assembling and disassembling that occur through social media explode into events where the difference between the actual and the mediated no longer applies, but where, nevertheless, blood is spilled and democracy is further eroded. Crucially, this book also anticipates the reverse, in which the blurring of popular and media assembly is the means of profound reflection, reinvention, and repair.

A Summary of What Follows

A Theory of Assembly begins by establishing a framework for assembly, which is the focus of chapter 1, "What Is Assembly?" This framework takes shape in two phases. In the first, the goal is a workable definition of assembly. It is one thing to gather, as I have done here, a sequence of related examples; it is another to systemically map the features that set this cultural form apart from others. I do so with the help of Rick Altman's theorization of narrative through its characteristic materials, activities, and drive. I argue that this triad applies to assembly: its materials are constituents and positions; its activities are selection and configuration; and there is a drive to perceive and interpret (and, especially in the digital era, to pursue and participate in) assembly. The second phase of theorizing assembly involves several elaborations. Assembly is more than a type of media artifact; it is also something people do. Assembly is not confined to individual media artifacts; it can take place at widely varying scales. Finally, assembly need not center on a single artifact; it can involve vast networks of objects and interactions. The chapter closes by addressing an idea one might assume is implicit to a theory of assembly: that "everything is a remix." I suggest that this notion (however well-intentioned) is inaccurate and even harmful, emphasizing histories of cultural appropriation.

Like all the remaining chapters, chapter 2, "Art, Assembly, and the Museum," brings the lens of assembly to bear on a particular sphere of cultural production, in this case the uneasily distinguished domain of art. First drawing on Serra's *Verb List* for orientation and then addressing likely major objections against including assembly in art history and theory, the bulk of the chapter's contribution turns on a critical typology of art as assembly. My contention is that at least two key dynamics distinguish what assembly can do in art. Assembly-based art can analogize; it can also reconstitute. Of key interest here is the capacity for art and curatorial and art-centered activist practices to link what would otherwise remain separate. Equally important is their capacity to shape new (or newly recovered) configurations of perceptual, social, and political life. The chapter closes with a discussion of art and museums in relation to carbonization and decarbonization in the era of climate emergency.

Chapter 3, "Memes, Assembly, and the Internet," shifts the conversation from the fine, slow, and enduring to the popular, quick, and ephemeral. Following a discussion of the difficulty of defining "meme," this chapter parallels the opening one in adopting a two-phase approach. In the first phase, I argue that among the most significant and novel practices yielded by memes is the assembly-based practice of rapid reclassification I call "expressive folksonomy." In the second phase, I zoom out to consider not just one subpractice, but the entire history of this sprawling cultural domain. As things stand, there are numerous broad scholarly frames for memes, including folklore, street art, and conversation. While recognizing the value of these other frames, I argue for one that is both more particular and more encompassing: hyperdistributed media assembly. Among the key affordances of this reframing is attention to the remarkable capacity of memes for performing and encouraging antidemocratic communication and action. The chapter closes by proposing an even broader and more speculative application of the lens of assembly. The expressive strategy, far from being confined to a select set of artifacts and practices, is a distinguishing property of the internet era.

Although the fourth and fifth chapters continue to apply assembly to particular domains, they shift the focus from broad cultural genres to enduring social problems. In chapter 4, "Generative Assembly after Disaster," the enduring problem is the dissonance between what is necessary and valuable from media and culture after disaster and what ends up actually being produced. As was tragically plain during Katrina, which is the focus of the chapter, prevailing conditions of mediation and remembrance tend to favor variously reductive, racialized, and biased framings over and against nuance and attention to differential violence. Taking stock of the remarkable range of cultural projects that emerged in the wake of this unnatural disaster, from the viral juxtaposition cited above to a Kara Walker exhibition to an online memory bank, I argue that among the most powerful means of intervening in these prevailing conditions is the practice of "generative assembly." This practice characteristically involves seizing on the transformative power in recombining the data and media of disaster and recovery. The chapter closes with two very different reflections, first on the broad field of distributed assembly after Katrina, and second on the "configural" nature of Walter Benjamin's famous catastrophe-centered reading of the "angel of history" and Jesse McCarthy's subsequent reidentification of the angel with a monumental installation by Walker.

Chapter 5, "The Powers and Perils of Media Assembly," turns from the visible extremes of sudden, major disasters to the oft-ignored realities of slow and structural violence. In line with the broader tendency discussed throughout the book, dominant assumptions around cultural responses to such violence tend to dwell on the forms of narrative and representation (and this is true of Rob Nixon's influential account of slow violence). However, some of the most influential projects undertaken in response to nonsudden, routine, and distributed violence tend to rely, either predominantly or to a significant degree, on the form of assembly. From "conceptual reassembly" to "thematic counter-mapping" to "memetic drip," citizens, activists, artists, scholars, and designers use assembly to help forestall (or sometimes help occlude or justify) the persistent facts and effects of poisoning, debilitation, and other forms of environmental, social, and technological harm. The chapter closes with a discussion of the strengths and limits of the concept of slow violence in an era when both slow and "fast" violence continue to disproportionately impact Black people, Indigenous people, and people of color—and thus the need for "inventive vigilance."

The book concludes by reframing the power and pervasiveness of assembly in the digital era. Not only is assembly ever more widely practiced, it is also increasingly ambivalent. This doesn't mean that the practice is somehow undecided or wishy-washy. Rather, assembly's increasing capacity to support progressive and emancipatory causes coincides with an increasing capacity to work against those very efforts. The events of January 6, 2021, were an especially harrowing example of the pernicious potentials in the form. Not only did uses of assembly help make the event thinkable, but the event also itself constituted a kind of "critical opalescence" of assembly; neither strictly physical nor entirely virtual, the event chaotically fluctuated between popular assembly and media assembly. The conclusion closes by invoking the words of thinkers whose work opposes the premises assembled that day: Toni Morrison, Eve Kosofsky Sedgwick, and Judith Butler. Together these writers point to how forms of reparative assembly can and must work both in spite of and against violent exercises of assembly in the paranoid mode.

At the outset of her 1982 film on the lives of rural women in Senegal, *Reassemblage: From the Firelight to the Screen,* Trinh T. Minh-ha offers a brief and intriguing assertion of intention: "I do not intend to speak about," Trinh says, "just speak nearby." As Trinh would later clarify, "speaking nearby" is a form of speaking that "does not objectify, does not point to an object as if it is distant from the speaking subject or absent from the speaking place," a form that "reflects on itself and can come very close to a subject without, however, seizing or claiming it."[106] It is a speaking that is "brief" and "whose closures are only moments of transition opening up to other possible moments of transition."

Having had the fortune of taking a class with Trinh, I have long appreciated the notion of speaking nearby, not only for its eloquent evasion of distanced knowing, but also for its recasting of the idea of "about," this ordinary word now sounding strangely spatial. It was only in writing this introduction, however, that I felt the weight and the challenge of this intervention's dual emphasis: on the one hand, the supposedly placeless speech about others that can be understood as what *is* happening, and on the other, what *ought* to happen—humble, situated, avowedly interdependent speech near and alongside others. For a long time, the research and writing for this book took place within the confines of my notebooks and electronic devices. Working at this virtual remove, I could maintain the illusion that what was going on when I addressed questions of public violence and environmental and social justice was an exercise of demonstrating how much assembly matters. In other words, I could assume that, although I was acting as though the objects of my inquiry were absent from my speaking place, I was doing so with good intentions and as informed a perspective as I could adopt. In moving to make this work public, however, and in doing so amid the protests and conversations that have followed from the police murder of George Floyd, I confronted the actual, positioned, and necessarily limited aggregate of ideas, references, and choices that sat before me. One shortcoming I noted was the frequency with which I use theoretical concepts from white, male, cisgender artists and theorists as departure points. Another shortcoming was the relation of nonaffiliation I tended to enact in researching and writing about disaster and slow and structural violence. I proceeded as though these things were out there in the world, open to examination, there for me to respond to by way of concept and example, and not phenomena with which my own life, and the structures that make and inform that life, were interlocked.

In seeking to address these aspects of the book, I have worked to revise not just the people and projects cited, but the concerns and critical positions foregrounded.[107] I have also sought the perspectives of writers who occupy a similar set of subject positions and who, to put it bluntly, take the time to address the locations and limitations of their work. Along these lines, one passage, written by Catherine D'Ignazio and Lauren F. Klein for the introduction to their book *Data Feminism*, stood out as especially forceful:

> We write as two straight, white women based in the United States, with four advanced degrees and five kids between us. We identify as middle-class and *cisgender*—meaning that our

> gender identity matches the sex that we were assigned at birth. We have experienced sexism in various ways at different points of our lives—being women in tech and academia, birthing and breastfeeding babies, and trying to advocate for ourselves and our bodies in a male-dominated health care system. But we haven't experienced sexism in ways that other women certainly have or that nonbinary people have, for there are many dimensions of our shared identity, as the authors of this book, that align with dominant group positions. This fact makes it impossible for us to speak *from experience* about some oppressive forces—racism, for example. But it doesn't make it impossible for us to educate ourselves and then speak about racism and the role that white people play in upholding it. Or to challenge ableism and the role that abled people play in upholding it. Or to speak about class and wealth inequalities and the role that well-educated, well-off people play in maintaining those. Or to believe in the logic of *co-liberation*. Or to advocate for justice through equity.[108]

Having sat with this passage and others like it, I find that one partial (but I hope still worthwhile) thing I can do is speak nearby these writers. I write this book as a white, straight, cisgender, stably employed man, father, and husband who arrived in the United States as the son of two white, straight, cisgender, and graduate-educated immigrants from Wales and (apartheid) South Africa. I have not been on the receiving end of sexism, ableism, and racism. Slow and structural violence have not directly impacted my life. I have never lived through a disaster. I do not start my car knowing I could become the next victim of police brutality, nor have I walked the streets of the cities I have called home under the persistent threat of sexual assault. (This list is, of course, incomplete.) Nevertheless, I join D'Ignazio and Klein in the belief that the privileges of my positions, the gaps in my experience, and the inevitable structural complicities of my lifeway prescribe rather than preclude participation in the project of resisting the forces and structures of violence and inequity I have had the nonnatural, nonneutral, and fully constructed fortune to avoid. That I have ended up relying on ideas and artworks presented by white scholars and artists with relative frequency while participating in this project, even after efforts at revision, seems to me to only further reveal the unlearning I (and others in similar positions) need to undergo. In short, I present this book, which is aligned with social and environmental justice causes, and which often attempts to speak near and with projects addressed to those causes, with as full an acknowledgment as I can muster of its situated, privileged, and imperfect nature.

Far from being *the* theory of assembly, this is one among many possible theories, and it is written in hopes of catalyzing further efforts to contest and rework both established hierarchies of cultural form and, to borrow Karen Barad's phrase, "what matters and what is excluded from mattering."[109]

1

What Is Assembly?

In the digital era, a cultural form deserving of the name "assembly" has come to equal narrative, representation, and other dominant cultural forms in its reach and influence, particularly in European and North American contexts, and particularly in response to circumstances of harm and injustice. In future chapters, I elaborate this argument across multiple spheres, from art and memes to disaster and slow and structural violence. In this chapter, the task is more concentrated. If assembly is to be added to the roster of known and valued expressive strategies, and if it is to be valuable to see both digital and predigital uses of media through this lens, then it will be necessary to have a firm grasp on what sets this strategy apart from others. In other words, I now answer in depth a question only briefly addressed in the introduction. What is assembly?

Assembly Defined

Whereas forms like collage, montage, database, and assemblage have had the benefit of essays and exhibitions, media assembly has not, and that means both the delight and the peril of establishing a reliable definitional framework more or less from scratch. I find help from an unexpected source: Rick Altman's 2008 book *A Theory of Narrative.* Albeit not in so many words, part of what Altman provides there is a method for specifying the nature and distinction of what I am calling "expressive strategies" and "cultural forms," these medium nonspecific structures that shape how people read, communicate, and interact.

Altman's method begins with the establishment of certain precepts that must, in his assessment, be respected, and that I will also respect. First, Altman says, any definition of enduring value "must be based on a willfully diverse corpus": the theorist must "guard against a corpus that is artificially limited by a combination of personal taste, ease of access, historical trends, or hidden cultural preferences."[1] Second, the definition must "maintain a balance between restriction and inclusion," which is to say that it cannot entertain all possible examples, but it also must not unreasonably forgo "potentially useful examples." Third, the definition must specify multiple criteria rather than one single criterion; it cannot overemphasize one seemingly essential characteristic at the expense of others. Finally, relevant subcategories "must not be confused with the category itself," such as when one would use "men" for "humans," or when one would take a familiar notion like a beginning–middle–end structure and allow this to stand in for narrative as a whole.

With these four precepts established, the Altman-esque method proceeds to the work of constructing a framework. Crucial to its power, the framework does not take the form of a few, reductive sentences. Rather, in the vein of what this book calls plural reading, it traces three interlocking characteristics that jointly set the phenomenon apart. Although I do not necessarily agree with Altman on all counts with respect to narrative, I find this three-pronged approach quite effective for the purposes of distinguishing assembly from other cultural forms. I thus join Altman in structuring my definition of assembly around three characteristics: the materials for assembly, the activities of assembly, and the drive to assemble.

The Materials for Assembly

All forms of expression need stuff with which to speak, say, perform, or show. With narrative, the necessary materials include actions (as one might expect), but they also include characters, as Altman emphasizes. For assembly, it is certainly possible for the materials to include events and characters, but because assemblies need not produce the effect of a story, their defining materials are of a different order. The question is how to distinguish those materials.

Constituents

The initial but incomplete answer is to say one can use basically anything. After all, if the name for the cultural form is "assembly," and if the basic notion is that assemblies centrally involve placing expressive and symbolic elements into meaningful relationships across a variety of scales, then effectively any images, words, objects, or other media should be able to serve as the materials for assemblies. And indeed, in this chapter and elsewhere, I show how the form of assembly takes place by way of all manner of entities, from plywood and keywords to epoxy, pixels, and people.

A more thought-through answer maintains this stance on assembly's radical openness to materials while also insisting on the specific character of those materials. Image memes provide an accessible bridge into this terrain (Figure 1.1).[2] The joke in this one is simple and silly: everyone knows the surface web, few people know the deep web, and even fewer know the dark web, but yet fewer know the farthest reaches of the internet: the second page of hits in a Google search, or the even more rarely visited *first* page of a search on Microsoft's far less popular Bing search engine.

Now, according to the good but only partial view on assemblies' materials, this digital assembly is made up of a set of elements: a drawing of an iceberg; a photograph of a deep-sea creature in alien-seeming waters; and a second photograph of a rarely sighted, "living fossil" of an animal, the goblin shark. What is missed is the sense in which those elements are discrete *constituents* of something. To say those elements are "discrete" is to say they are separable in both the making and the receiving: the image of the goblin shark is an image in its own right, and that image could easily be found and shared on its own or reused in a different context. To say they are "constituents" is not to say they are "voters" in an "asymmetric relationship" with more powerful "representatives," as in the more stratified political sense.[3] It is to say that these different elements have expressive and mnemonic power in the more deeply democratic sense, adapting Raúl Sánchez Cedillo's account of the political term "constituency." Constituents don't just impact what assemblies communicate or activate. They give the assemblies life, sometimes through quite coequal and horizontal relationships but other times through more uneven and hierarchical ones. If any of this meme's constituents were removed, then it would risk a radical and even fatal alteration. The assembly could come undone.

Part of what gets lost in saying that assemblies can use any kind of signifying stuff, then, are the constitutive roles played by the discrete elements of assemblies (and, often, the elements of which they're made) in the diverse things the assembly affords. What *also*

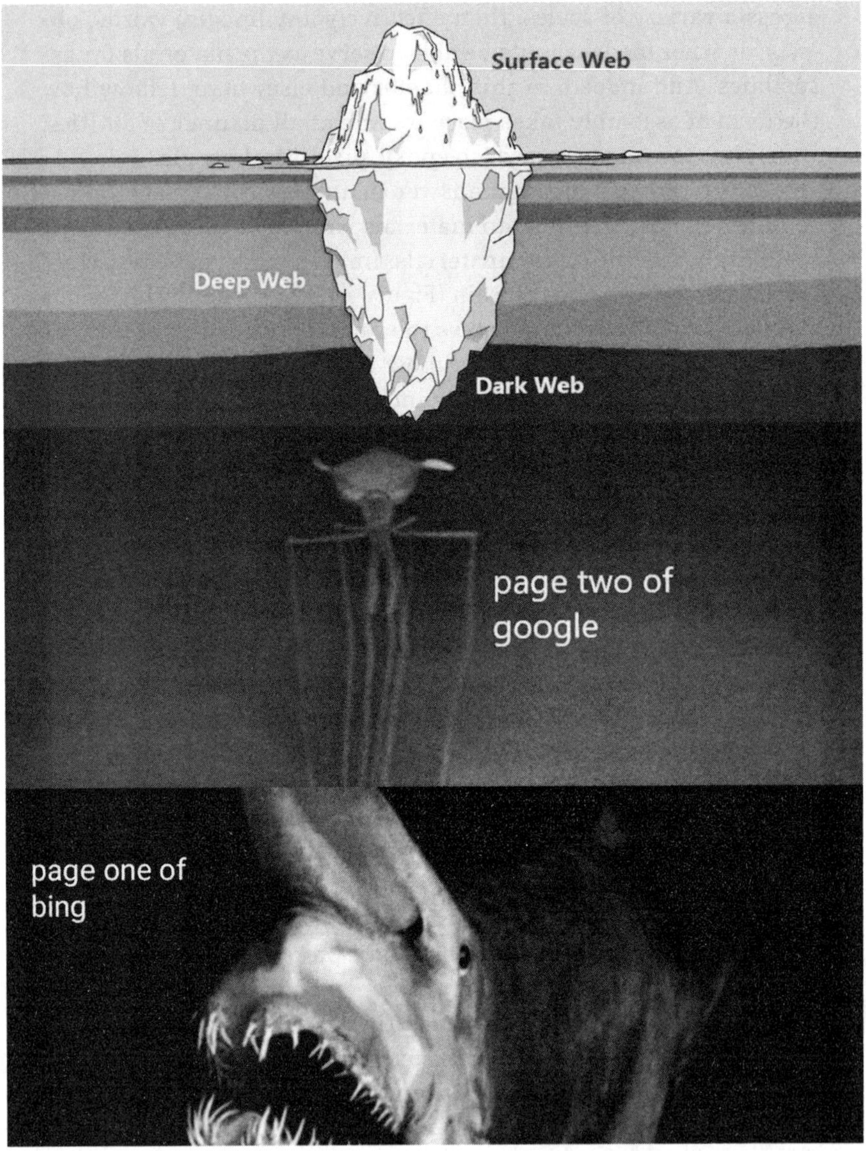

Figure 1.1. Words and images as the constituents of a digital assembly—making light of the less-trafficked corners of the web. One among many iceberg-tiers parody memes. Posted to Reddit by firetti in 2019.

gets lost, importantly, is the crucial dimension of interplay between those constituents. In the case of this dark-web meme, that interplay between constituents is relatively limited and predictable, as a humorous intervention presides over most (though not necessarily all) of the available meaning. In the case of other more internally rich and complex assemblies, however, there is considerably more potential.

Among the many, many examples one might pick are the covert assemblies of the artist Guanyu Xu. (I should emphasize that my turning to an artistic example is not meant to indicate that art is inherently more complex or sophisticated in its use of constituents, although artists can, of course, do remarkable things with assembly.) The raw materials for these assemblies, which he brought together under the title *Temporarily Censored Home,* were hundreds of images he had stashed in his suitcase on a return trip to China to see his parents, with whom he had never shared his sexuality. (In writings and interviews about his work, Xu, who was born in China and emigrated to the United States, identifies as gay.) The stashed images consisted mostly of his own photographs, printed at varying sizes, but also an array of magazine cutouts, postcards, and other pictures. Whenever his parents left for work, Xu would proceed to transform the apartment's rooms into resplendent, queer installations of many expressive constituents—into assemblies. Elegantly lit, oddly blending harmony and chaos, these intersectional assemblies mix many different styles, contexts, and references. In the dining room, for instance, a large photograph of Xu at a table holding hands with a man with a large, electrified cross behind him dominates the view, while in the foreground a photograph of a chandelier sits below the dining room's own chandelier. In a different assembly, now in his parents' bedroom, Xu has draped large, poster-sized nude photographs of himself and others over the bed. Meanwhile, staid images of tourism and daily life look on from the dresser in the corner (Figure 1.2).

In reading these assemblies (technically, the photographs of and as these assemblies), one finds ample and not fully predictable affect, meaning, and experience, and this is because of the numbers and types of objects-become-constituents already in the rooms and the inherent richness of the provocative gesture of installation and deinstallation in secret. Indeed, complex assemblies like these act

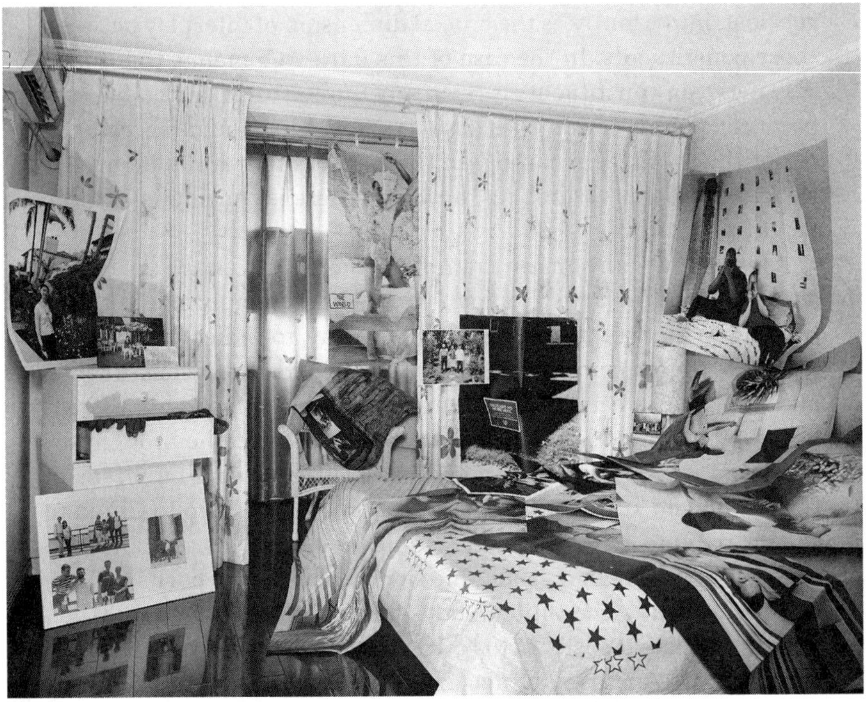

Figure 1.2. Guanyu Xu stages a dissident, ephemeral assembly in his parents' bedroom. *Parents' Bedroom,* 2018. Archival pigment print, 40 × 50 inches. Copyright Guanyu Xu. Courtesy of the artist and Yancey Richardson, New York.

as variegated expressions; they present multiple, overlapping "sub-assemblies" of interacting constituents. *My Desktop* is especially instructive along these lines (Plate 3). Right away, the double sense of the title becomes apparent. On the one hand, the top of his desk in his parents' home hosts an enigmatic configuration of postcards, souvenirs, and magazines. On the other hand, the screen of the laptop hosts a dense agglomeration of porn. As these two sub-assemblies present measures of contrast such as the lively and the sedate, the erotic and the organized, and the public and the secret, the array of constituents tacked to the windows start to speak, too. Some of these constituents are colors asking to be seen together, or pages that curve and converge. Between a graffito of "freedom" and the multiple instances of American flags and American colors, part of what is assembled here also seems to be what Xu calls a "space of mutation": the fantasies of what one will find in America, fueled by popular culture and dreams, and the actualities of what one does find there. What also gathers here is a more reflexive proposition about the way that images come into shifting and provisional relations in an era of visual abundance, from those images that become the stuff of love and lust to those that buttress ideas and memories of family, nation, and travel. The convening of these constituents is not meant to convey a single, decided meaning, but to furnish an encounter with a space of crisscrossing media constituents capable of coproducing multiple levels of feeling, connotation, and enigma.

Xu's markedly pluralist take on the project redoubles the point. The work was partly "a way of disrupting the heterosexual structure that's embedded in the home and familial relations." It was also "an exploration of intersectionality" and the fact that, as both "a gay person and a foreigner," he was "not completely free" in either China or the United States. With this project, he sought to "bridge dialogues about both countries, which in certain ways are quite similar."[4] The project also presents another layer of expression that defies easy summary. In Xu's words, his exercises in assembly build "parallel but converging spaces and times." They visualize both the "co-existing presence of differences" and the dissolution of "borders of opposition."[5]

Such a spirit of openness and analogy is crucial to maintain as one seeks out the most vital and impactful family resemblances across the wide range of projects and practices based in assembly. As different as the dark-web meme and Xu's installations are, they point to the same basic principle: while the materials of assemblies are theoretically unlimited, the way that they come packaged is distinct, as is the way they work in harmony and in dissonance. Often derived from a much larger pool, or even glut, of potential elements, these materials must function as interdependent constituents, ready to participate in the production of meanings and affects through relational interaction with each other and with the viewer/reader/user in turn. As other examples in this book will show, and as the internet-like surfeit and nonlinearity of Xu's installations attest, the rise of speedy networks and interconnected devices has dramatically expanded the potential for tremendously varied kinds of media elements to become the constituents of expressive assemblies. Meanwhile, highly complex assemblies, involving many (even millions) of media artifacts can take shape, often with multiple contributors working to expand and modify them at anonymous removes, from digital archives to viral dances.

Positions

Having specified assembly-based materials as constituents, one could easily overlook the second genus of materials that distinguishes assembly. A second, far less labor-intensive project by Xu puts it on display. On June 11, 2020, amid the massive wave of protests following the police murder of George Floyd, Xu added to his hundreds of existing Instagram posts. Using the gallery format, Xu's post comprises two photos, first of the letters *B*, *L*, and *M* (Black Lives Matter) pasted across a trio of windows, the second of a pair of signs affixed to lampposts reading "Back the Blue," as in back the police (Figure 1.3). Xu's caption explains the pairing: "my neighborhood, the same block #blacklivesmatter."[6]

The constituents of this assembly include the two photographs, the caption, and the hashtag, but also the attendant metadata, like his username, the date, and the number of likes. Crucially, the *positions* of those constituents are essential materials of concern in themselves, both for the person or persons assembling and for the person or persons interacting with the assembly in turn. In this case, the positions of text and metadata are set by the design of the platform, but what is not set is the order of the images in the gallery. Whether or not he thought about it, Xu ended up placing the Black Lives Matter photograph before the Back the Blue photograph. The effect is to emphasize the priority of the first over the second, or to locate the author's sense of a justified starting point over a wrong departure. In theoretical terms, this means that engaging this assembly is not just a matter of engaging its constituent materials. It is also engaging its component positions. Users do so within the more diffuse assemblage of ideas and impressions that is Xu's account or within their own algorithmically arranged feeds.

The same is true of all assemblies: reading assemblies is reading constituents *and* their relative positions. And once again there is a spectrum of complexity. A second example of the use of positions as material in assembly—this one likewise produced in defense of Black lives—points to the more intensive end of the spectrum: the closing sequence of the 2006 film *When the Levees Broke: A Requiem*

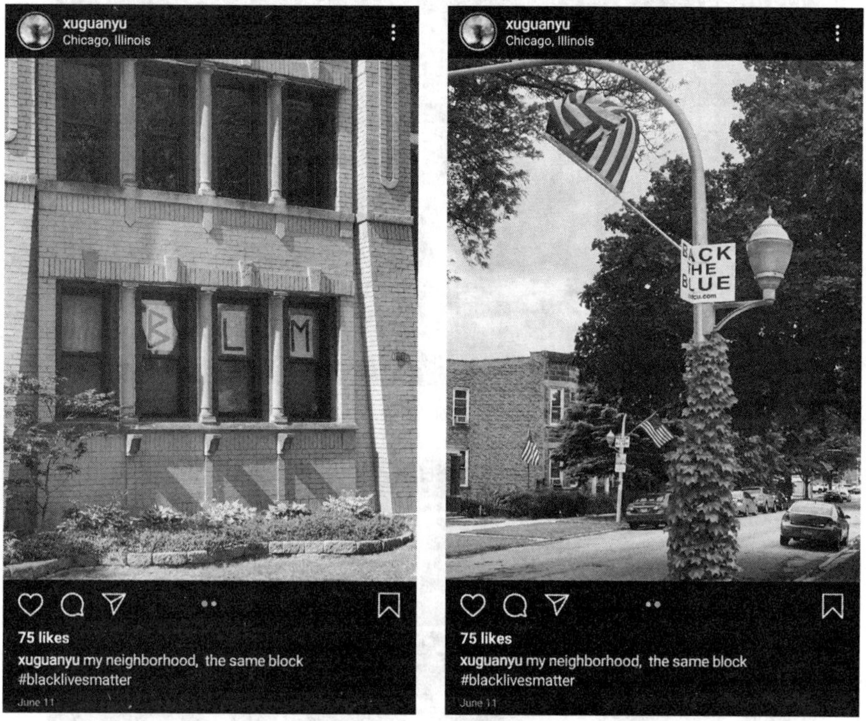

Figure 1.3. A digital assembly of two photographs and attendant metadata that seeks, among other things, to mark the unexpected proximity of opposing political stances. Instagram post in carousel format. Guanyu Xu, "my neighborhood, the same block #blacklivesmatter," 2020.

in Four Acts (Figure 1.4). Directed by Spike Lee, the film recounts Katrina, the massive hurricane and preventable flood of over eighty percent of New Orleans that took at least eighteen hundred lives and displaced hundreds of thousands more. (I discuss uses of assembly after Katrina in chapter 4.) In the closing sequence, each of the film's interviewees, from whom viewers have heard often harrowing and sometimes uplifting testimony for several hours, announce their names and their hometowns. Each speaker either holds or sits behind a picture frame. While some of these frames are unadorned wood, others are quite ornate. Upbeat jazz plays throughout the sequence.

As with Xu's juxtaposition, the presence and interplay of constituents is plain to see, not just the frames and backgrounds, but

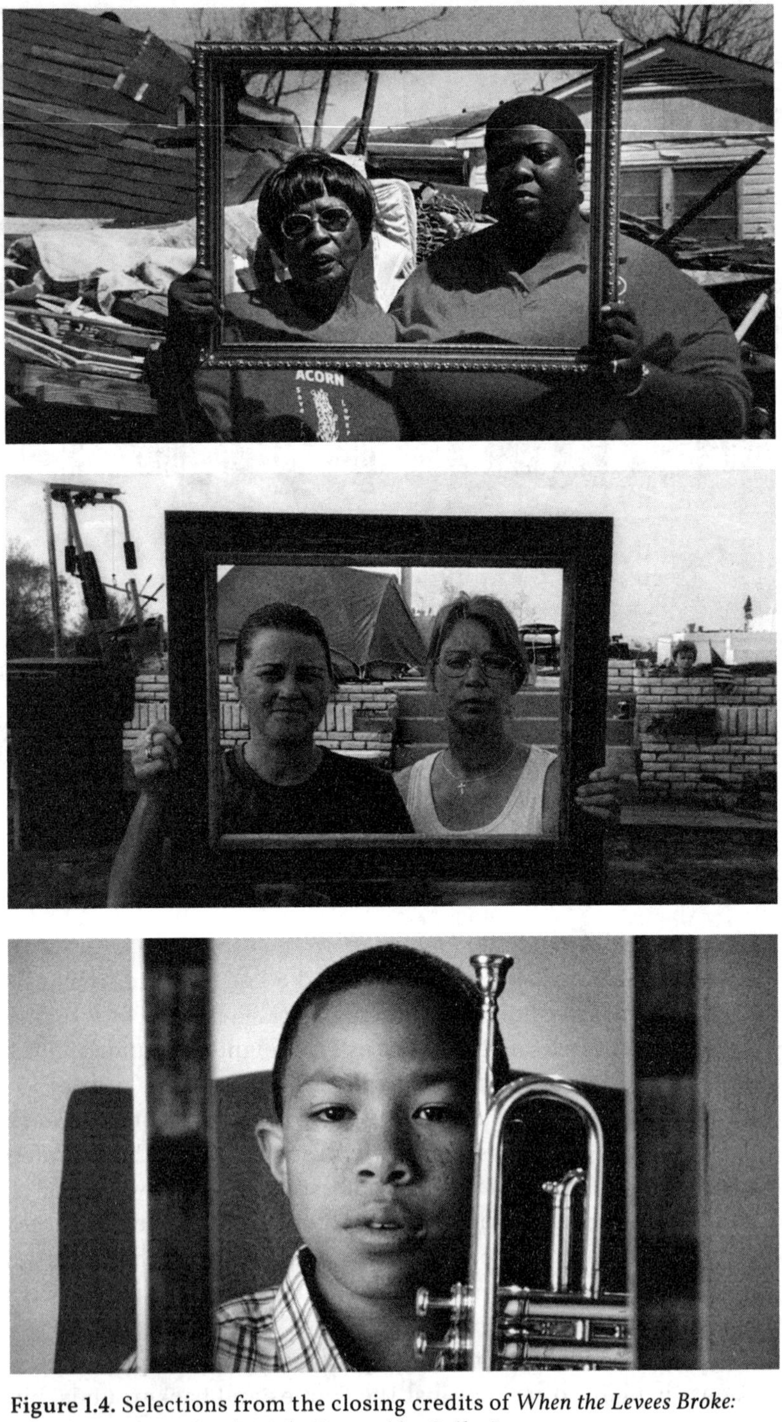

Figure 1.4. Selections from the closing credits of *When the Levees Broke: A Requiem in Four Acts* (2006), directed by Spike Lee.

(wonderfully and movingly so) the words, faces, voices, locations, and clothes of the people themselves. Equally important is the layered and expressive nature of those constituents' positions. For one thing, the frames sit between the viewer and the speaker; they also sit within the frame of the camera. The effect of these placements is rich and paradoxical: both an emphasis on the importance of this person and a reminder of their occupying particular sets of social and economic positions. The variable of position is also at work in the organizing of the subsequences. One might expect clear parameters for how one speaker is positioned after another, such as their role in the film, or their perspective on the disaster (e.g., survivor, observer, researcher). But there is a jazz-like freedom in the mixture, with the force and pleasure of the overall sequence as the apparent dominant ordering principle. This is an instance when the interplay of constituents and positions is also an interplay of two forms of assembly. Like a protest or a march, this is a convening that "speaks" apart from, before, and alongside anything it particularly says.[7] And like the "people" seeing themselves acting in emergent concert in the event of a demonstration, this use of media assembly asserts a collective power to intervene in prevailing conditions of mediation and memory, a power that was widely asserted across a range of digital and nondigital contexts after Katrina.

Choices about where to locate materials make a difference for many cultural forms, from the timing of the appearance of characters in stories to the stances of people in visual compositions. But the variable of position is such a fundamental aspect of how assemblies ask to be interpreted that it must be understood as an essential building block in its own right. And just like the material of constituents, the material of positions is the site of tremendous creativity (and exploitation) in the internet era. Juxtaposition is just the beginning.

The Activities of Assembly

It is not enough to delineate what a cultural form includes. One must also speak to what takes place in and through the form: its characteristic *activities*. According to Altman, a narrative will look, feel, and act like a narrative only when the story follows the movements of a character "from action to action and scene to scene."[8] Meanwhile, there also must be what Altman calls "framing." This is the effort on the part of the narrator to delimit scenes and actions.

With assembly, the activities of assemblers are similar to those of narrators in some respects. But because the materials for assembly are constituents and positions rather than characters and events, the activities of assembly are once again of a different order.

Selection

Selection is the process by which the person, persons, institutions, or software—or even a distributed "cognitive assemblage," to use N. Katherine Hayles's term—responsible for the assembly makes choices around what to include and what to exclude. Within art contexts, it is often a source of frustration or fascination (or critique) why certain things have been included in exhibitions and artworks and not others. Within the digital context, there are many other dimensions and tensions that can emerge. With memes, for instance, part of the humor of a given example can derive from the insider sense of the meme maker having opted to include a reference that is both familiar and unexpected. That is, there is an evolving (but known at least to insiders) set of possible references, and the selection of certain constituents and positions over others is distinct and expressive. Beyond memes, there is the possibility that a critical element of the viewing experience involves selection, whether because the viewer has opted to view certain parts of an artwork over others, or because the work itself depends on the addition that the viewer/user makes, such as the movements of a mouse in a web browser for an interactive visualization. It is also important to consider the lack of diversity and flexibility in the constituents and positions around certain things due to algorithmic biases, a phenomenon I will refer to again in other parts of the book, in dialogue with Safiya Umoja Noble and Mimi Ọnụọha, among others.

Made up of expressive constituents, assemblies rely on processes of selection, whether careful and considered or automated and algorithmic. Moreoever, typically by virtue of their mode of appearance, assemblies tend to foreground rather than obscure their basis in this activity. In other words, assemblies thematize and intensify aspects of expression and communication long known and employed, from the configuration of bodies in paintings to the difficult choices of a curator presenting a mixture of material under the physical limits of a gallery space or the programming limits of a web browser. Assemblies also embody the shifts in potentials for cultural production brought on by the rise of smartphones and the internet. Their devices interconnected, people (and algorithms) select and arrange. Their choices of contribution become the stuff of speaking and convening, however inventive, potent, or habituated.

Configuration

Whereas selection is the activity that follows from the need for constituents, *configuration* is the activity that follows from the fact of positions. The constituents of assemblies must go certain places and not others, and they must exist within a medium or platform that will host and disseminate them.

One helpful way to grasp the activity of configuration is to imagine its work at multiple scales. The most fine-grained scale is configuration at the level of individual constituents. Such and such a constituent has been positioned here rather than somewhere else. Choices around how to configure positions might be actively made by assemblers, but it is also possible that they are indirectly decided, such as by a genre, format, or algorithm (or there might be no discernible ordering factor).

At the far broader scale is the configuration of the overall assembly into a particular media artifact or set of artifacts. The aggregate of constituents and positions must have a medium in which it is enduringly located and by means of which it can travel (or undergo modification).[9] The venue might be a film, an empty portion of a museum, or the boxes and pages of a graphic novel. It might be a particular template in visualization software, an online archive, or even a collectively remembered concept for a meme.

In between the configuration of individual constituents and the incorporation of the assembly into one or more media artifacts are the processes of configuration of multiple constituents and multiple positions together. The assembler attends to the positions and interactions of subassemblies within the overall assembly. Importantly, other things can be added to the configuration at this level, such as headings, page numbers, links, or hashtags.

From the comedic effect achieved through graphic means in the dark-web meme to the protest-like credit sequence, each of the examples I have presented so far is an exercise in configuration at one or more of these levels. Like any media project, each also necessarily involves one further type of configuration, which is the positioning of the audience or user, or in more abstract terms, "interpellation" or "hailing." These examples all share in configuring the audience/user as a reader or viewer of expressive relationships. In other examples, configuration also involves participation, with the audience/user positioned as a would-be contributor or "interactant."

Among the more poignant examples of the latter is an influential project within the realm of net art called *How Do You See the Disappeared? A Warm Database,* hosted by the nonprofit arts organization called Rhizome. In developing this project, Chitra Ganesh, and Mariam Ghani responded to the "data-driven surveillance techniques that particularly targeted immigrant groups" in the wake of 9/11 by soliciting a form of what they evocatively labeled "warm data." Unlike the "cold data" of state authorities, these data would document experiences of the disappeared without revealing their identities or making them even more vulnerable. To gather these data, Ghani generated a web-based questionnaire she hoped "no two people would ever answer in the same way." (The prompts included things like "describe a place you see when you close your eyes at night" and "which muscle do you use the most in your normal daily activities?") What eventuated was "a hypertext essay, watercolor portraits of the Disappeared" and "visualizations of the answers, as well as accounts of activist efforts and links to political resources."[10]

In both the questionnaire and these final products is a stirring effort to seize on the activity of configuring another, nonhomogeneous group of assembled constituents: the audience. For the user who has been subject to forms of targeting, this is an opportunity to assert, albeit anonymously, an alternative "data body," and it is an experience of being perceived and positioned as an actual, mattering political constituent. Meanwhile, for other visitors, the project presents one assembled provocation and facilitation after another. The richly curated version on Rhizome, notably invoking the more dominant frameworks of representation and storytelling, describes it thus: "As visitors traversed the website, they would encounter calls to action, resources, and stories of efforts underway to aid the disappeared. The project was not merely a representation of a political and social problem—it aimed to spark direct action and bring about change." In other words, Ganesh and Ghani seized on a crucial digital affordance: making action and response an integral element of their expressive arrangement.

The Drive to Assemble

Drive is the third and likely the most easily forgotten component of any thorough definition of assembly. Because of narrative drive, Altman argues, humans can perceive narratives in all kinds of texts that are purpose-built as narratives, but also in an array of other circumstances.[11] Hayles also speaks to this drive: "We take narrative in with mother's milk and practice it many times every day of our lives—and not only in high culture forms such as print novels. Newspapers, gossip, math story problems, television dramas, radio talk shows, and a host of other communications are permeated by narrative. Wherever one looks, narratives surface, as ubiquitous in everyday culture as dust mites."[12] Following on this principle, Altman specifies that narrative motivations form a necessary element for any narrative text to come to life. Altman further argues that "a strong narrative drive can generate the very factors necessary for recognition of narrative."[13] (For example, Altman says, even something as simple as a line can be seen as a character that thins and thickens.) The reader or viewer can also withhold or suspend their narrative drive by dwelling on catalogs of details within a narrative scene, for instance, thus temporarily undoing the otherwise normal procession of the story.

The drive to assemble shares some of these characteristics but not all of them. The key shared aspect is the capacity and willingness to perceive the cultural form at work (or as possible to pursue) when confronted with the prompts to do so. This drive (which could also be called "configural" or "relational") is active when those prompts are purposefully constructed, but it also seems fair to say that, as with narrative, many situations, texts, and objects can be invested with the characteristics of constituents, positions, selection, and/or configuration. (And indeed, the perceptual drive to see faces and other "gestalts," or "meaningful patterns and whole-relations in the stimulus array,"[14] is relevant here.) At the same time, if the notion of the drive to assemble follows Altman's formulation too closely, it risks reinforcing a frame of isolated agency and responsibility. Of equal importance to an appreciation for the more local, readerly, and individually inventive drive to assemble is an appreciation for what Hayles calls "systemic and relational perspectives."[15] As Hayles might emphasize (and as theories of assemblage help suggest), in the networked era, both the fact and the workings of the drive to assemble—to perceive, pursue, and remake mediated relationships—are highly distributed. The "transformative potentials" of this drive aren't just widely visible, as in the varieties of assembly-infused online curating or the daily churn of memetic production; they are also "enabled, extended, and supported by flows of information." It might even be ventured that technical and nonhuman agents, from phones to algorithms to whole platforms, likewise carry, embed, activate, exploit, and "live" this drive.[16]

Some projects make the drive to assemble especially evident. On the more intimate end of the spectrum is a project called *SIXSIXSIX* by the Cameroon-born Nigerian and Igbo artist Samuel Fosso. Fosso is a savant of the self-portrait who, as Okwui Enwezor observes, "took the photographic discourse of African identity to a space that exceeded the borders of individualised memorial and commemoration, and into a significant socio-cultural, as well as political temporality."[17] The project's title refers to the number of photographs of which it consists and (by way of the numerical reference to the Antichrist) to the numerous disasters that have followed Fosso throughout his life, including illness, civil war, and forced migration.[18] Over several weeks, returning time and again to a specialized chair that maintains the same body position (usually for the purpose of mug shots), Fosso sat for one Polaroid after another, all close-ups in a studio, all under the conceit of producing a different expression in each case. For Fosso, the larger meaning of this arduous undertaking lies in survival and determination in spite of accumulating disaster: "I carry on, I persist, I stay alive, and I produce. . . . You have to know how see the decent, the good, and also not to despair."[19] The recurrence of faces is also a kind of reparative allegory: "Things don't disappear; they change. They do not get lost, even a fragment of something remains something."[20]

Viewed through the lens of assembly, the project is also an occasion for viewing and interpreting constituents in consequential positions. Placed in a book, the photographs generate constant internal juxtaposing and sequencing while also literally adding to the project's weight. Some hundred years before Fosso's project, film theorist and filmmaker Lev Kuleshov showed how different impressions could be produced by following shots of the same facial expression with shots of different objects.[21] Here it is accumulating fusions of the same face in different guises. Provided the viewer doesn't page through too quickly, certain pairings can become mutually and multiply expressive: analogous gazes across divergent expressions, sharp and seemingly sudden contrasts in feelings, one state as seemingly the step to the next, persistent emotional ambiguity, the self in one moment seeming to look over to the self in another (Plates 4 and 5). Part and parcel of such analogical display, clusters of photographs over multiple pages can seem to trace the silent phenomena of internal worlds, like the persistence of a painful memory or the hidden progress of a new thought. As Fosso puts it: "When you look at my work, it's my body that is looking at me. It's my way of seeing."[22] All this makes for a generative convergence of the drive to perceive the expressive strategy of assembly, the drive to encounter the expressive strategy of performance, and the further drive to discern some kind of underlying story or allegory. Among this work's many actions and affordances, then, is the way it excites and seizes on viewers' readiness to engage assemblies as assemblies, doing this through a method of generative constraint, placing mutually evocative constituents in orderly positions within a supporting medium.

A second "project" that stands out relative to drive is not a one-off, but rather countless related instances, from chalk drawings to png files. Since the late-nineteenth century, based in a much longer history of configuring logical intersections, everyone from mathematicians to school children have produced diagrams that array the similarities and differences between two or more phenomena.[23] The most famous of these logic diagrams is the one conceptualized by John Venn in 1880. Most often a deceptively simple cluster of two or three overlapping circles, a Venn diagram gathers what Venn characterized as "the imperfect knowledge of . . . relations" among sets that "we may possess, or may wish to convey."[24] This variation on assembly has had applications ranging from "counting to actuarial science, and from biology to English drama," as well as "industrial design and automated industrial manufacturing."[25] More recently, Venn diagrams became a meme, as various users, with interests ranging from emotions and television shows to cheerleaders and robbers, make light (or wry observation) of the overlaps and

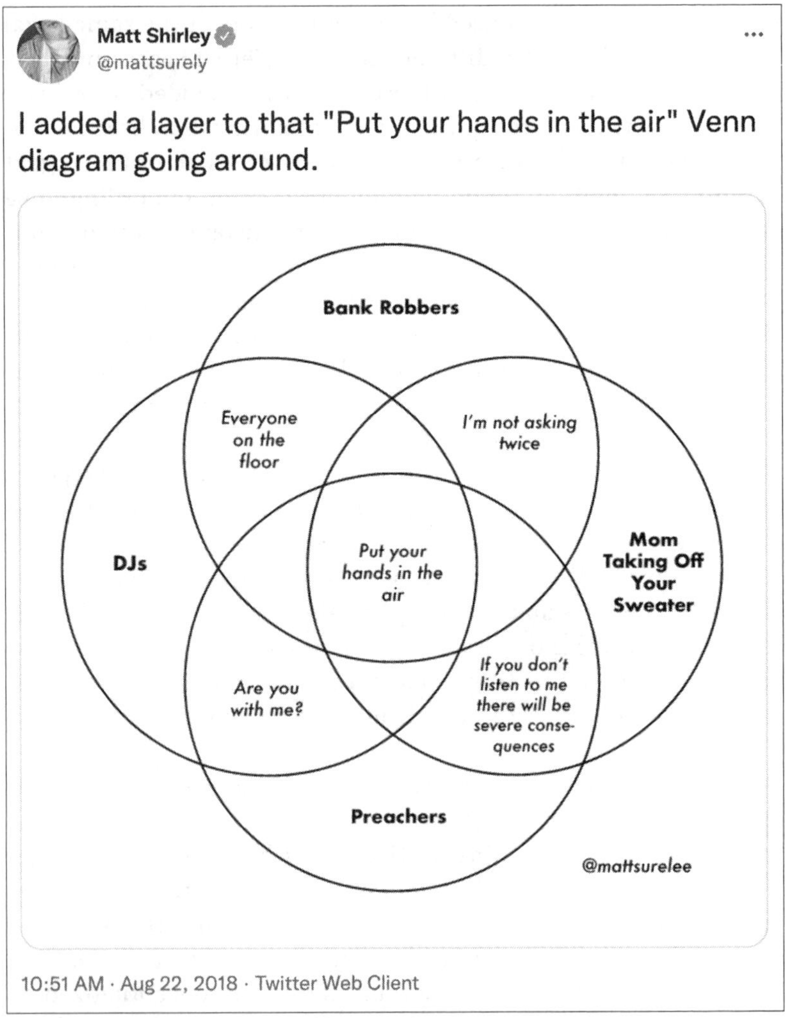

Figure 1.5. From tool of logic to viral meme, the Venn diagram embodies the drive to assemble. Matt Shirley adds a layer to the "put your hands in the air" Venn diagram meme, August 22, 2018.

distinctions between various entities, not just in pairs but also in trios and quartets (Figure 1.5).

Logic diagrams are relevant to the drive to assemble in multiple respects. At one level, the wide array of applications reveals the fundamental importance of not only narrating and picturing the world, but rearranging it. This drive to assemble has long existed, and it has long been actively encouraged. (To take 1960s England as an example, many children were given the task of "sorting and classifying objects by size, colour and shape"; they did so by "placing them in spaces marked out on the floor by chalk outlines or wooden hoops."[26]) At another level, the more recent parodic use of these diagrams reveals the recursive quality of the drive to assemble, inasmuch as pushing the limits of comparative assembly became a momentary visual and social obsession. Although there are many reasons one might find these memes compelling, at least one dimension is an apparent delight in seeing unexpected overlaps and linkage points between otherwise disparate phenomena. What's more, the success of one of these diagrams is, in part, an indication of the apparent (and partly comedic) interconnection of everything everywhere. Further still, the exercise of asserting similarities and dissimilarities is so constant across social media and AI that a pocket of humorous diagramming constitutes both a mirror and a departure, with the exercise seizing on that collective drive and making light of it at the same time. Finally, there is the uncomfortable and violent side of all this, which is that the neat and tidy division of classes of people has been party to so many crimes that the exercise of neat and tidy division toward a humorous recognition is a delight in spite of the horrors of settled classification. Indeed, it is an essential observation about assembly that the strategy is not exclusively empowering or progressive. Assembly can be put to numerous ends, including those that are oppressive and dehumanizing.

In his closing reflections on narrative drive, Altman writes: "The one thing we can claim with great assurance is that whenever narrative drive causes a text to be read as narrative, the reading will foreground narrative material and narrational activity."[27] An analogous assertion holds for the drive to assemble. When the drive to assemble causes a text, a set of images, a performance, or another use of media to be read as an assembly, the reading will emphasize the dimensions of constituents and positions, and it will involve attention, however intensive or limited, to the activities and legacies of configuring and selecting. Faced with audiences willing to respond to the cues and scaffoldings of assemblies, the makers and disseminators of assemblies enjoy seemingly limitless options in how they might populate and organize these generative structures, whether through juxtapositions, arrays, sequences, constellations, or still other forms.

Digital devices are not just the bridges to these assemblies. They are also the engines, as the reservoir of possible constituents constantly expands, and as the distribution of the drive to assemble across people and machines becomes increasingly widespread and even seemingly immanent. At the same time, in a manner true to the paradoxes and contradictions of the internet, these expansions can coincide with dramatic reductions, as the formats and venues through which much actual assembly occurs remain largely restricted to those designed for the sake of profit by corporate entities. Among the more exciting democratic potentials of the internet was the way in which a relatively dormant drive to assemble could manifest at a much wider scale, in many more formats, at much higher speeds, in the wonderfully labile space of the web browser, from GeoCities to net art to whatever newly invented URL. The subsequent canalization of the drives to represent, narrate, perform, and assemble into the drive toward for-profit social media is a threat, no matter however richly one can configure its galleries and threads, nor how richly one can cultivate networks of novel affiliation. Part of what drives this book's theory of assembly is the need to discern countermovements against these attempts to domesticate and monetize the form. In other words, defining assembly is not just an intellectual correction of an imbalance. It is also an assertion of enduring collective powers. The internet, in its most democratic forms, embodies an ongoing commitment to the activities by which assemblies come to matter: these agents of assembly, configuring these constituents, in these arrangements, working to amuse, move, or even transform others and maybe themselves be amused, moved, or transformed in turn.

Assembly Elaborated

The above framework provides the terms and orientations necessary to interpret instances of assembly across a wide spectrum of media, and without the encumbrances of typical divides, such as the fine and the popular, or the digital and the nondigital.[28] The framework also contains the building blocks for a necessary expansion, moving from the drive to perceive and interpret assemblies to the drive to *pursue and participate in assembly.* In the digital era, this double quality of assembly, as both artifact and action, has become especially evident and significant, as effectively anyone with adequate access to the internet can pursue and participate in the form. They can do so quickly and without much thought; they can also do so in intricate and intensive ways. They can do so in isolation, in direct collaboration, or at an anonymous remove. And they can do so with not just one but many—even a vast multitude of—expressive artifacts in play.

Assembly Is Also Something People Do

Counterintuitive and multipart, this expansion of the definitional framework of assembly is best conveyed through a sequence of aphorisms. The first (already broached) is deceptively simple: assembly doesn't name just a type of cultural object or expressive artifact; it also names something people do with, across, and beyond objects and artifacts. I say this is deceptively simple because it sounds like I am stating the obvious: assemblies don't just make themselves; flesh and blood people make them. But the key idea here is more particular. One way to get at it is to convene multiple further examples in the vein of plural reading.

It helps to lay them side by side. Some readers might prefer to treat these blocks of description like they would paragraphs of linear prose, reading each from start to finish. Others might prefer to treat them like a cluster of images, quickly scanning each one, then returning for details as necessary:

(a) In 1900, W. E. B. Du Bois contributed an unprecedented exhibit to the Exposition Universelle in Paris, for which he won the gold medal as "collaborator" and "compiler."[29] As Whitney Battle-Baptiste and Britt Rusert put it, Du Bois compiled in a manner out of step with the broader imperial order of the exposition, which "imagined the white race as lifting up the rest of the world out of barbarism and backwardness."[30] In collaboration with a team of students at Atlanta University, Du Bois convened a set of mutually allusive media artifacts that sought to "demonstrate the progress made by African Americans since the Civil War," as well as to establish "the

Black South's place within and claim to global modernity."[31] Anchoring the exhibit were two sets of highly innovative visualizations of statistics and information cutting across the history of slavery, emancipation, Reconstruction, and Jim Crow (Figure 1.6). The visualizations were innovative in their bold and colorful visual style, anticipating the graphic languages of the Bauhaus, which would not come for decades; they included "renderings of national employment and education statistics, the distribution of black populations across the nation, a comparison of literacy rates in the United States relative to other countries," as well as a "map depicting routes of the African slave trade."[32] Set alongside these renderings was a collection of photographs that depicted "the physical and social heterogeneity" of Black Americans across Georgia, a collection that made it "difficult," as Aldon Morris puts it, "to reach any conclusion other than that the people reflected in these images embodied a beauty and grace of their own not describable by white standards of beauty."[33] Accompanying the visualizations, photographs, and other materials was a remarkable "three-volume, handwritten compilation of the Black Codes of Georgia, stretching from the slave codes of the colonial and antebellum periods to the segregationist policies and laws of the present."[34]

(b) Over one hundred years after the Exposition Universelle, several people undertook creative emulations of Du Bois's visualization work. In 2017, for a project called *But to Be a Poor Race,* Theaster Gates produced "response paintings in which the statistical data gathered and made visual by Du Bois has been reduced to abstract color fields and geometric motifs"; to these Gates added a bound series of *Jet* magazines, with the spines of these volumes bearing poems written by the artist. In 2019, for her exhibition *In Absentia,* Ọnụọha produced a series of images that rework the Du Bois graphic language: some are poetic (including one that appends "What / are we / trying to prove" to a spiral visualization); others are more documentary and interventionist, including maps of the Indian Removal Act, ICE (U.S. Immigration and Customs Enforcement) detention centers, and regions of the United States with the highest incarceration rates. Finally, starting in 2019, a group of scholars and designers for the network

Dignity + Debt visualized racial disparities around student debt in the Du Bois style.[35] They also helped produce "design specifications and coding tools to help designers, artists, developers, writers, and scholars who want to visualize their data" in that same manner.

(c) In April 2012, two months after the murder of Trayvon Martin, Martine Syms began to accumulate links to news stories, opinion pieces, primary documents, and other materials related to the events and their aftermath on a website called *Reading Trayvon Martin* (Figure 1.7). Scrolling through these links, viewers/users could not click away three overlaid objects, the things Martin, a Black teenager, wore and carried just before George Zimmerman shot and killed him: a hooded sweatshirt, an Arizona Iced Tea, and Skittles. The project continued until 2020.

(d) The fourth example is many together. Starting in the early 2000s, across 4chan, 8chan, and 8kun[36] bulletin boards, on Instagram "meme pages," in private and public Facebook groups, on subreddits and Parler profiles, in Discord, Telegram, YikYak, and other apps' forums and group chats, people posted, reposted, and commented on easily reshared verbal and visual-verbal aggregates like listicles, image memes, image macros, and quickly rendered charts that attacked ideas and efforts aimed at repair and justice around matters of racial violence, inequality, and oppression and, in their stead, asserted and elaborated white-supremacist, white-nationalist, and other cognate frameworks.

(e) Finally, in 2020, Alayo Akinkugbe (at the time an undergraduate) established @ablackhistoryofart, an Instagram page dedicated to "highlighting the overlooked Black artists, sitters, curators and thinkers from art history and the present day" (Figure 1.8). Many of the posts are concise assemblies of individual artists' work along with information and commentary. Others offer windows into current exhibitions, or they tell stories of Black figures in historical portraits, or they use individual paintings to explore Blackness across art history. Akinkugbe regularly responds to followers' comments, building on their observations, answering questions, and often laying down no small share of effusive emojis.

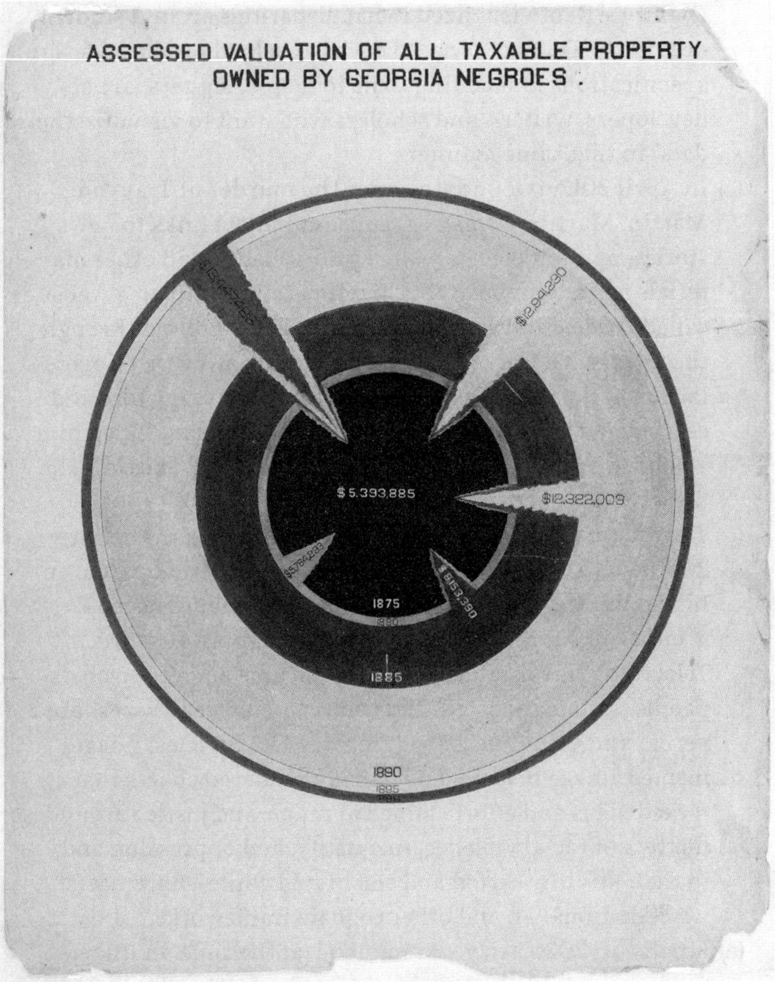

Figure 1.6. "Assessed Valuation of All Taxable Property Owned by Georgia Negroes." Chart prepared by W. E. B. Du Bois and collaborators for the "American Negro" Exhibit of the American Section at the Paris Exposition Universelle in 1900. Ink and watercolor, 710 × 560 mm. Library of Congress Prints and Photographs Division.

As I hope is obvious, I am not suggesting these examples are somehow fundamentally similar in theme or orientation. Rather, they are distinct engagements with racist structures and ideologies, one in defense and the rest in different modes of defiance. Together these

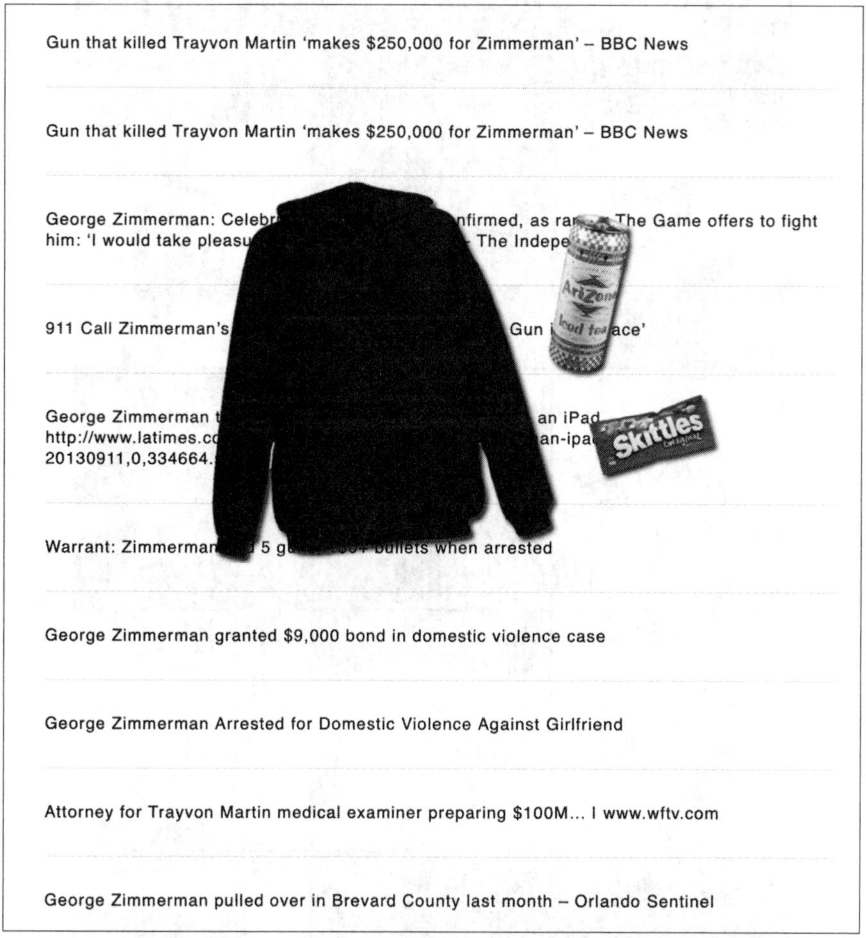

Figure 1.7. A multiyear accumulation of links and an arduous response to the murder of Trayvon Martin. Martine Syms, *Reading Trayvon Martin* (readingtrayvonmartin.com), 2012–20.

engagements point to the presence and consequence of assembly in the mode of pursuing, participating, and performing.

Seeing how this is so depends on a lens switch. So far, I have focused on how image memes, artworks, and other media artifacts can manifest assembly in the materials they gather. Now we see that there are practices, processes, and performances distinguished by those very same things. *Reading Trayvon Martin* is perhaps the

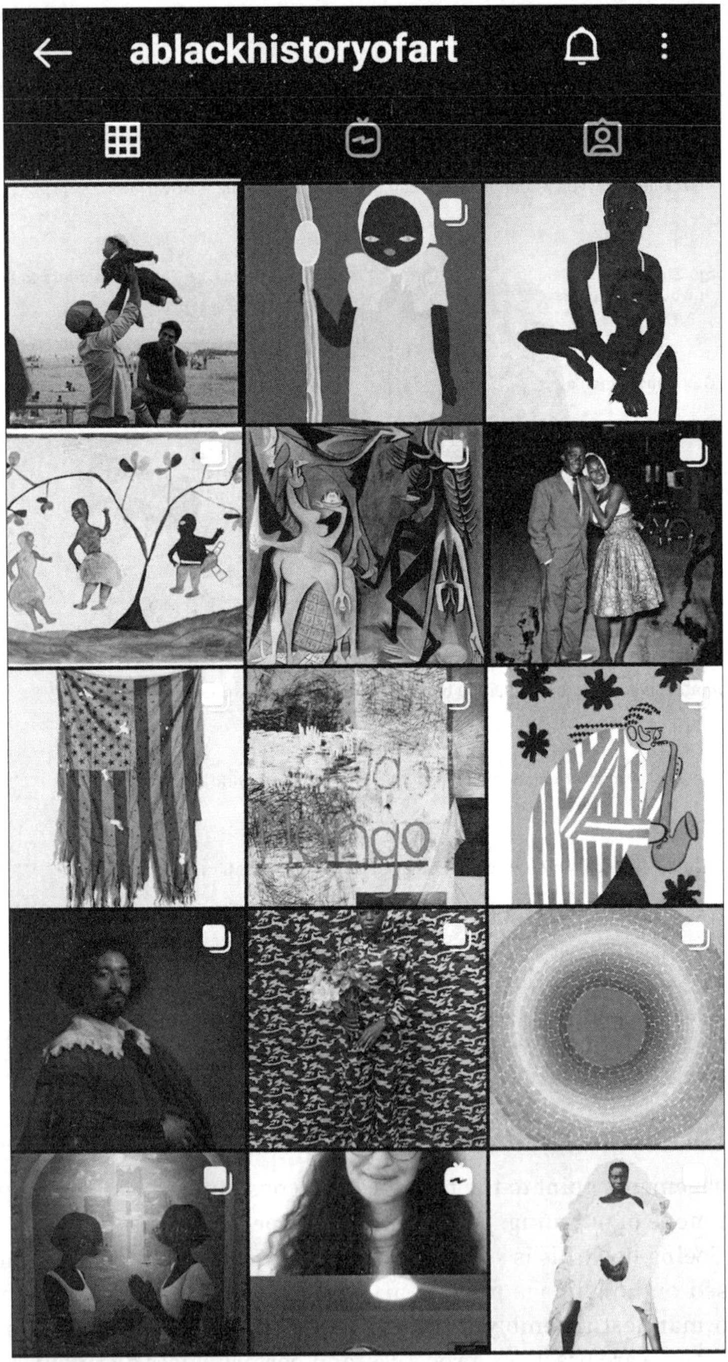

Figure 1.8. A persistent and vibrant aesthetic assembly: @ablackhistoryofart. The project was started in 2020 by Alayo Akinkugbe. Screenshot, July 2021.

most immediately accessible in this respect. What audiences encountered wasn't a static artifact, nor could it be understood without reference to its developer. Rather, Syms's project, as a web page, was an act of collection and accumulation in process; it was an active and public pursuit. Not only that, this pursuit was imbued with meaning: it was a public performance of attention to the shifting conversation around this widely discussed event by a young Black woman artist/citizen/maker/reader. In other words, to read this project well was to read it as an instance of pursuing meaningful media assembly, not just in the immediate aftermath of an event, but in an ongoing, public, and arduous manner.

Reading the other examples well likewise requires combining the lens of performance with the lens of media assembly. In the case of the Du Bois project, for example, it is crucial to the richness of the project that not just one or two, but dozens of visualizations were produced. This work of assembling did not simply elicit the drive to compare and contrast views and ideas among viewers (i.e., the drive to see and read assembly). It also made for a whole graphic language and intellectual precedent pursuable in art and data a century later. Equally important, the dozens of visualizations depended on a drive to assemble and permute information gathered by, for, and from dozens of Black citizen collaborators. Still further, there is a crucial performative dimension to the writing out and inclusion of the codes in the overall imperialist and white-supremacist macroassembly that was the Exposition Universelle. The editors of the visualization volume put it this way: the inclusion of the Black Codes "ultimately conveyed not a utopian and happy narrative about black progress in a forward-looking, modern nation, but a sense of the gains that had been made by African Americans *in spite of* the machinery of white supremacist culture, policy, and law that surrounded them."[37]

What becomes evident through the lens switch, then, is that there are not just a few, but multiple senses in which media assembly can manifest as acts, undertakings, and performances. For one thing, the sense of coded performance in *Reading Trayvon Martin* is in effect again in the responses to Du Bois by Gates and Ọnụọha; in both these cases, the subject positions of these artists as Black artists working in the United States matters to the significance of their engagement with Du Bois as an influential figure and with the particular histories of struggle, thriving-in-spite, and creative response with which they interact by way of convening and juxtaposing. In a different vein, the dimension of assembly as repetition and accumulation, again a part of Syms's unfolding compendium of links, is crucial to the social and visual cultural intervention made in @ablackhistoryofart. The latter makes of that repetition and accumulation a lively social dimension, drawing together an increasingly large selection of followers (which includes artists and art institutions) who can speak to each other and to Akinkugbe, or just listen and learn.

Albeit to much different and violent effect, the aggregate of examples in (d) likewise use the persistent posting of media, of quick and shareable visual, verbal, and sonic recycling of racist premises, to facilitate an active social dimension by reasserting certain rhetorics, defending particular sensibilities, and emitting and endorsing aggressive emotions and actions. Indeed, these instances of assembly have a social linking function, what Hito Steyerl, via Dziga Vertov, calls a "visual bond," even serving as avenues of recruitment for younger, unformed political citizens.[38] Among the many possible countertactics here are those on display in the student-debt visualization by Dignity + Debt. In assembling a tool kit for citizens to produce clusters of visualizations suffused with the graphic and social imagination of Du Bois, the network has made this visionary project into something anyone with the know-how, inspiration, and access can take up, thereby expanding the reach of its meanings and the spectrum of its participants. In facilitating a student contest and a #DuBoisChallenge inviting "Du Boisian replications," the network has also helped to make that work of assembly visible and interconnected, and it has therefore richly emulated the collaborative and pedagogical dimensions of the original undertaking.

To say assembly is something people do is to speak to the material fact of any work with assembly. But it is also to speak to an expanding spectrum of expressive and communicative possibilities, possibilities that are often generative and progressive (but by no means always).

Assembly Takes Place at Widely Varying Scales

The second elaboration of this book's definitional framework picks up where the second leaves off. Assembly isn't just something people do; it is also something that takes place across widely varying scales, from the small and individual to the massive and anonymous.

In its rich mixture of intimacy and provocation, one assembly that stands out on the former side of the spectrum is a serial sculpture produced in 1969 by Danish feminist artist Kirsten Justesen (Figure 1.9). Titled *Circumstances,* it is four partly transparent epoxy casts of the artist's then-pregnant body. One torso holds snapshots of family members that imply an album the child will join. Another holds pamphlets from a social organization focused on maternity. A third holds plastic flowers that together seem to speak to living and loving emergence. And a fourth holds fur that is comfort, protection, violence, and otherness both buried and expressive. Together these configured constituents make up a partial and memorable materialization of a pregnant mother's contradictory "circumstances." This is existing life and new life as unfolding arrangements subject to biology, history, patriarchy, and chance.[39]

From the perspective of this book, *Circumstances* isn't just a sculptural work. It isn't just an aesthetic assembly either. It's a practice of "discrete" assembly at a "micro" scale. The artist has performed a work of dissident compiling and configuring that continues to act through relatively small and transportable means. Against the general invisibility of the pregnant body, there is an *insistence* on placing this body in the gallery four times over. Against the picture of pregnancy from the dominant outside, there is a *pressing* of a single body against moldable material that holds physical images. And against an image of motherhood as either pure selflessness or blissful wholeness, there is a *filling* of the womb with variations on that larger outside world that both are and are not linked to the growing child. The localized fact of the work—the physical assembly of torsos—is one legacy of these actions. It is also the site of their small-scale repetition and elaboration through belly-to-belly configurations with audiences. Day after day, passing viewers form temporary (and maybe typically quick and distracted but perhaps at times deeply felt) unions with Justesen's past acts. They might well wonder what the story behind the project is, or what argument it seeks to make. But these are questions that follow the body-sized aesthetic assembling in which they have already become the latest participant, a present, passing union (visitor and assembly) with a past, intimate union (mother and child).

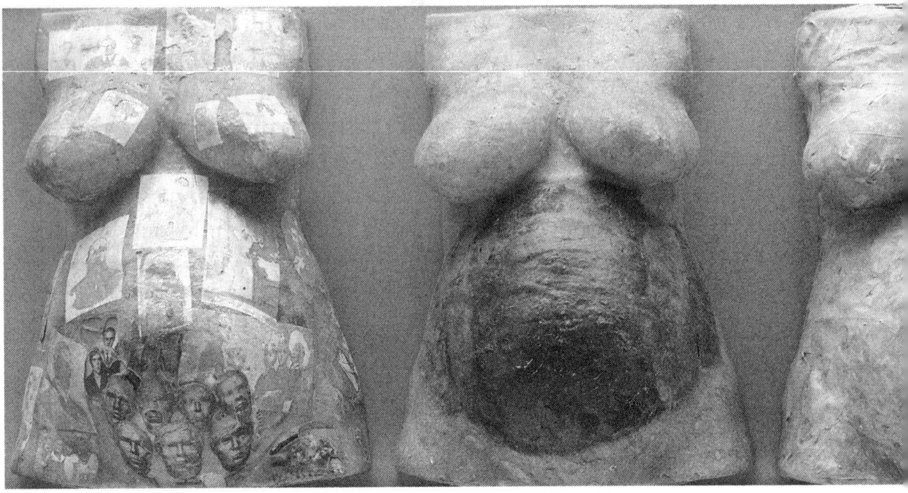

If *Circumstances* is discrete assembly at a micro scale, then the Du Bois's project is collaborative assembly at a meso scale, and that implies a third mode of distributed assembly at a macro scale. Especially instructive on this front is a project on which I once collaborated called the Japan Disasters Digital Archive (JDA) (Figure 1.10).[40] Led by the Reischauer Institute of Japan Studies at Harvard University and started in 2011, the JDA's focus was a sequence of disasters part natural and part social: a massive, 9.0 earthquake; a tsunami that reached as far as six miles inland; and the nuclear meltdown at Fukushima Daiichi that released harmful radiation while also displacing tens of thousands of people. Couched as a networked and participatory archive, this was more like an "archive that is not one," as adding items was not typically a matter of preserving the actual materials, but of adding links to tweets, videos, photos, articles, and still other media. The consequence of this para-archival approach was partly an expansion of research potentials with the unusual distinction of being led from outside Japan, which has seemed to some a dubious distinction (understandably). But it was also the furnishing of assembly-based potentials. The JDA made possible in rapid, digital, and not always elegant form what Arlette Farge observes in the quiet and the slowness of analog archives: the way archives can serve as a "vantage point from which the symbolic and intellectual constructions of the past can be re-

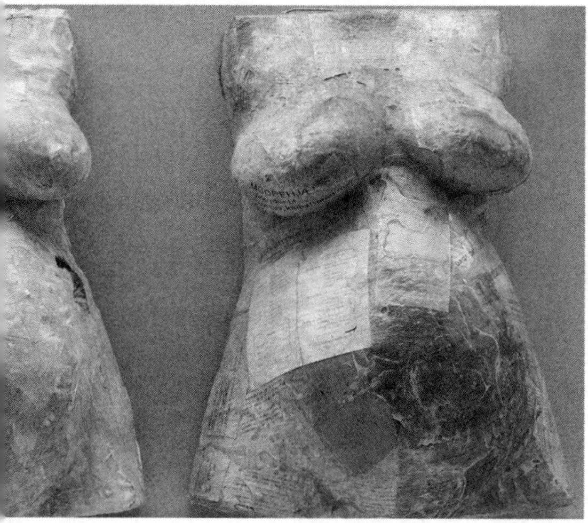

Figure 1.9. Kirsten Justesen, *Omstændigheder* [Circumstances], 1969. Four fiberglass-reinforced epoxy sculptures, approximately 58.5 × 44.5 × 25.5 cm. The work arrays four epoxy casts of the artist's then-pregnant body. Artwork owned by SMK, the National Gallery of Denmark, Copenhagen. SMK Photo / Jacob Schou-Hansen. Copyright 2021 Artists Rights Society (ARS), New York / VISDA.

arranged."[41] Engage the search function, and one moves through a massive assemblage of images, data, and words, akin to what Farge calls the "the whirlwind of the kaleidoscope." Engage the map function, drill down to materials filtered by time and place, and one sees the actual and media lives of the disaster in neither "settled story" nor accurate picture, but in a heterogeneous constellation full of "ruptures and dispersion." View or make a user-generated "collection" of items within the archive's database, and one interacts with a subassembly of media within a superassembly of items (and relations between items). Like the overall archive, these subassemblies were not necessarily narratively coherent, nor did they offer a single visual representation. They were mixed aggregates open to varying engagement and ongoing reassembly, and the usual logics of the iconic image or the overarching story receded from this "forest without clearings." Rather, it became possible to emphasize "continual combination and recombination of action and reaction, change and conflict."[42]

In terms of the question of assembly across scales, a chart conveys what prose struggles to organize: how this locus of distributed assembly was (and, at the time of writing, remains) multiple forms of assembly overlapping and crisscrossing (Figure 1.11). In the first column, I note different practices of media assembly: some take place at micro scales, some at meso or macro, and some move

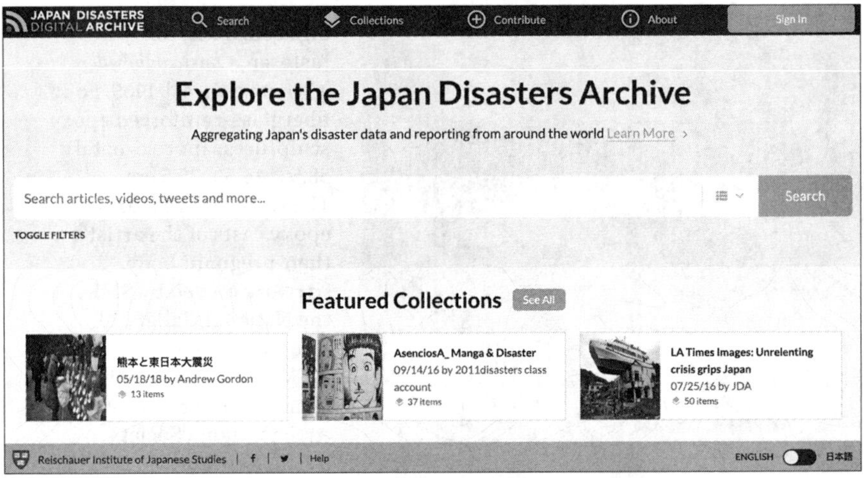

Figure 1.10. Homepage of Japan Disasters Digital Archive, 2019. From the home page onward, the user is positioned to both explore and reshape the digital archival assembly.

between all three. I then specify the materials of the given practice of assembly, as well as my sense of the typical participants, activities, and effects. Finally, I indicate how a given mode of assembly works within the JDA before then offering a mix of assessments and open questions in the form of brief comments.

The chart may make the juxtaposition with *Circumstances* seem all the stranger. And yet all I am doing is insisting on an addition to the kinds of broad, multiscale statements people make all the time. (For instance, we can stay small to say that a single Facebook post misrepresents young trans people's motivations for gender-affirming surgery, and we can also zoom out to say, without hesitation, that thousands of trans TikTokers and YouTubers are collectively transforming available representations of trans lives and trans struggles.) As the JDA example makes evident, the significance of this multiscale approach is both intellectual and practical. As one might expect for an experimental project faced with technical challenges and subject to shifts in public attention, this para-archive struggled to attract the hoped-for levels of engagement. In laying out the overwhelming variety of assembly-based practices for which the site serves as a locus, I am perhaps indicating part of why this has been the case. It is an open question whether shifts in the design of the project could make these different scales of activity more tractable, and therefore more conducive to widespread use.

One last thing to emphasize about assembly's multiscale quality is the matter of transmission and translation. Discrete acts of assembly can translate into distributed ones and, in so doing, take on additional significance.[43] The digital makes this especially possible. A striking example emerged amid research for this book. The young climate-justice activist Greta Thunberg refuses to attend school on Fridays until adults adequately address the climate emergency. She does so with a sign that labels the act "skolstrejk för klimatet," or "school strike for climate." The small-scale act of verbal-performative assembly disperses into a larger one. Other students do the same, and they do so in groups, and they do so in configuration with other signs, messages, images, and ideas. Large-scale affiliations, as groups bound in assembly to the assertion of climate justice, are part and parcel of the physical and political assembly of walkouts, strikes, demonstrations, and assertions of practicable paths forward. Meanwhile, other more distinctly contemporary portals of assembly join the collective media generativity. There are, for instance, half-absurd memetic images circulating through social media channels that permute cultural fragments (GIFs, slogans, dances) with enduring political determination and small-scale practical interventions. There are also swipeable galleries that transmit information on ways to undo the engines of climate change in a fast and fashionable format. The impulse to call all this storytelling, representation, or conversation is understandable. But what we are speaking to with those terms is multilevel, mutually configuring interaction, the emergence of one mode of constituent-driven relation after another. This is assembly at many intersecting scales at once. Scale variance is also scale proliferation.

Assembly Need Not Center on a Single Artifact

Sprawling instances of assembly like the JDA might seem to stretch this book's conception of assembly to its limit. But we can't stop there. This is because there are instances of distributed assembly that take a qualitatively different form. The key difference is that they do not center on a single, managed location to which an audience would travel to engage the legacies of assembly-based practice, such as an exhibition space, a book, or a website. Instead, as

Practice	Materials	Participants	Activities
collating and arranging disparate data assemblies	collections of images, videos, websites, tweets; typically links, sometimes files	curators of data assemblies, project leaders and hired staff on networked archive side	cross-institutional formation of contracts around uses of shared materials, incorporation of materials into networked archive
horizontal data curation	aggregated digital materials, metadata, authored collections	project leaders and staff, students, researchers, interested publics	annotation of existing items, addition of new items, arrangement of items from within the networked archive into private or public subcollections, addition of titles and descriptions to these subcollections
archival authoring	aggregated digital materials, outside additions from authors, resulting authored presentations	project affiliates, students, researchers	constructing linear or multilinear presentations that make use of and link back to materials in the archive
teaching and learning supported by media assembly	readings, discussions, collections, archival essays	students, teachers, programmers, guests	reading and discussion in the style of a seminar coincide with project development and critique, as in a design studio course
conversation and dispersal through networks	short-form writing, linked materials, comments, likes	project leaders and staff, students, followers	adding material to associated social media accounts relevant to archival themes and responding to comments as necessary and interesting

Figure 1.11. The varieties of media assembly in the Japan Disasters Digital Archive. Chart by Kyle Parry.

At Work in the JDA	Comment
From archival collecting to collecting archives: the original collection of archived websites became one among multiple data sets.	Many archival projects assemble what is otherwise dispersed. How might networked assemblies also enhance the assemblies from which they draw?
Whereas we expect archivists and curators to do acquiring and arranging, this project invited participant to pursue those same activities. The materials and perspectives widened.	Open-ended models do not necessarily yield interest, perhaps because of lack of reward structures and time. Finding ways to invite indirect contributions, such as through social media, could be useful.
Could an idea of "archival authoring" be anything other than a contradiction? A significant dimension of the JDA sought to answer in the affirmative. Archives can become sites of expressive assembly.	This is a novel communicative mode: expression takes place within rather than beyond an archive. This proves challenging. Making this form extremely simple to produce and read could be helpful.
The project came to include a grant-funded seminar. Alongside more traditional means of learning, such as discussion, the collections served as a creative and conversational waypoint and reservoir.	These are among the most promising uses. Students are motivated by the context, and the archive is generative of conversation and contribution. This could be done for multiple classes at once, working in dispersed fashion.
The archive project maintained social media accounts dominated by news and resources related to the disasters.	The project of assembly is occasion for ongoing distribution. There is symbolic and attentional value in the act. Discussion is rapid and interactive. Archives as conversational catalysts.

the school strike begins to suggest, both the activities and the legacies of assembly, the artifacts generated or transformed, are widely dispersed. Not only that, those activities of distribution and consolidation can take place over long periods, sometimes with no end in sight, and sometimes almost entirely out of sight. In short, there can be forms of communicative combination that have neither center nor author but, nevertheless, do not lack specificity or force.

One way to demonstrate this further twist on the idea of assembly as practice is to look to the work of artists who operate in precisely this mode. As a version of what Ceci Moss calls "expanded internet art," Kari Altmann's work (or really a strand of that work) is an illustrative case. At one level, Altmann is what Moss calls "the custodian of a growing database," with that database composed of many subsidiary and offshoot databases.[44] Altmann uses what she calls a "mutated search algorithm" to consistently gather and arrange images found online. This process is on display with the flexible "eco-conscious lexicon"[45] for *Garden Club,* which Altmann calls "an evolving look at the overlapping meanings and tactics of 'virality' and eco-philosophy across cultures, ecologies and social information networks" (Figure 1.12).[46] At another level, Altmann is a kind of self-respondent: out of these assemblies of constituents—she calls *Garden Club* a "wild" feed and an "encrypted vocabulary"—different artworks, editorials, and the like are "born" as installations, presentations, video compilations, and sculptures. "By inserting herself into the stream" of her own found materials and those in surfeit around her "and codifying it according to her own logic," writes Moss, "she develops a vision that twists the rapid systematization of information."[47] This is an approach to art not unique to Altmann but widely practiced by means of algorithms, collaborative maps, and mutating software. In Mark Leckey's words (as quoted by Moss), artists working in this mode conceive of their practices as dispersed in such a way that audiences and interactants find "no object to look at as such," only a "nodal network that you're in the midst of."[48]

Although assembly in the distributed mode does frequently center on the way that "data collection and management are integral to the structure of our world," it is not restricted to that concern, nor is it restricted to the digital sphere. Take Jenny Holzer's *Truisms*

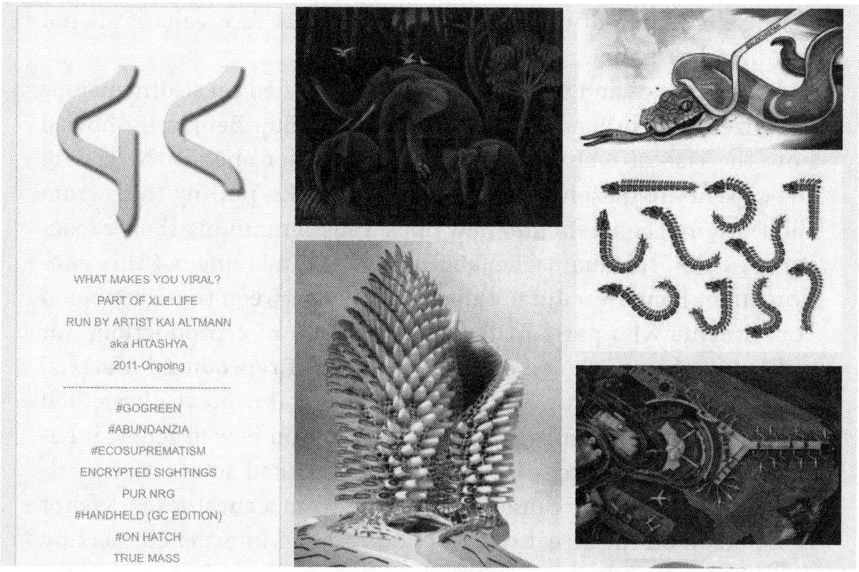

Figure 1.12. Kari Altmann, *Garden Club,* since 2011. Series, social feed, editorials, videos, installations, etc.

(1978–87). The project began with a single artifact: a typewritten, thematic list populated by laconic statements conceived by Holzer, from "abuse of power comes as no surprise" and "relativity is no boon to mankind" to "sloppy thinking gets worse over time."[49] Crucially, Holzer saw to it that this original verbal assembly was more catalyst than core. Its constituent statements appeared on posters and granite benches, in the middle of baseball games and on T-shirts at the Venice Biennale. In this sense, the artwork was "dematerialized," to use the term in conceptual art, but it was also delocalized and distributed, as Holzer's verbal assemblies formed temporary unions with the things that surrounded them (people, advertisements, scenes).[50] In Robert Storr's terms, "Holzer's work . . . pursues its viewers into their privacy" while also "confronting them in public."[51] For Holzer, the release from a single location for the work was a way of evading the limitations of normative display. "With the outdoor work you might startle people so much that you have a prayer of changing their thinking a little bit, or even prompting them to take some kind of action. . . . And because the content of the writing is taken at face value, it is not dismissed as art."[52]

Smartphones and social media have amplified these dimensions of Holzer's and others' work. In the 1930s, Walter Benjamin showed how the rise of technologies for reproduction meant the rise of the capacity to disseminate copies of artworks, pulling them from their original contexts into new ones, thus scrambling their capacity to exhibit the quality he labeled "aura."[53] In laying out this phenomenon, Benjamin did not discuss links between the distributed constituents who participated in this action of reproduction, nor did he emphasize the emerging aggregate of reproduced material around a given artist or subject. In the digital context, these tacit dimensions of Benjamin's intervention take on new urgency; it becomes possible to recognize multiple, distributed actors participating in a para-aesthetic practice. Anyone from a curator to a visitor to a person on the street with a phone and an internet connection performs distributed assembly by way of the reproduction and redistribution of individual works and fragments of works. As much is evident when one searches #jennyholzer on Instagram. What one encounters is a provisional and partial assembly reliant upon the dispersed actions of many different constituents (Figure 1.13). Individual works, pieces of works, exhibitions, reproductions on t-shirts, reproductions in the form of tattoos—users redirect the constituents of Holzer's practice into their own discrete assemblies (their photorolls and their social media accounts). Holzer once had to paste aphorisms to surfaces throughout New York City. Now armies of documentarians and disseminators, including a Holzer aphorism-sharing Twitter bot called @holzertron, allow her constituents to travel and endure as part of a widely distributed assembly of traces and copies.[54] Tellingly, Holzer's more recent projects on gun violence, AIDS, voting, police violence, and climate justice use methods of visual projection and display on trucks and other media, such that the constituent names, phrases, and sentences are easily read, photographed, and shared. In other words, Holzer now seizes on the strategy of distributed assembly at a wider scale than ever before. Like (but not exactly like) expanded internet art, this work "reproduces, travels, and accelerates across different spaces and forms, always reconstituting itself, always circulating, assembling, and dispersing."[55]

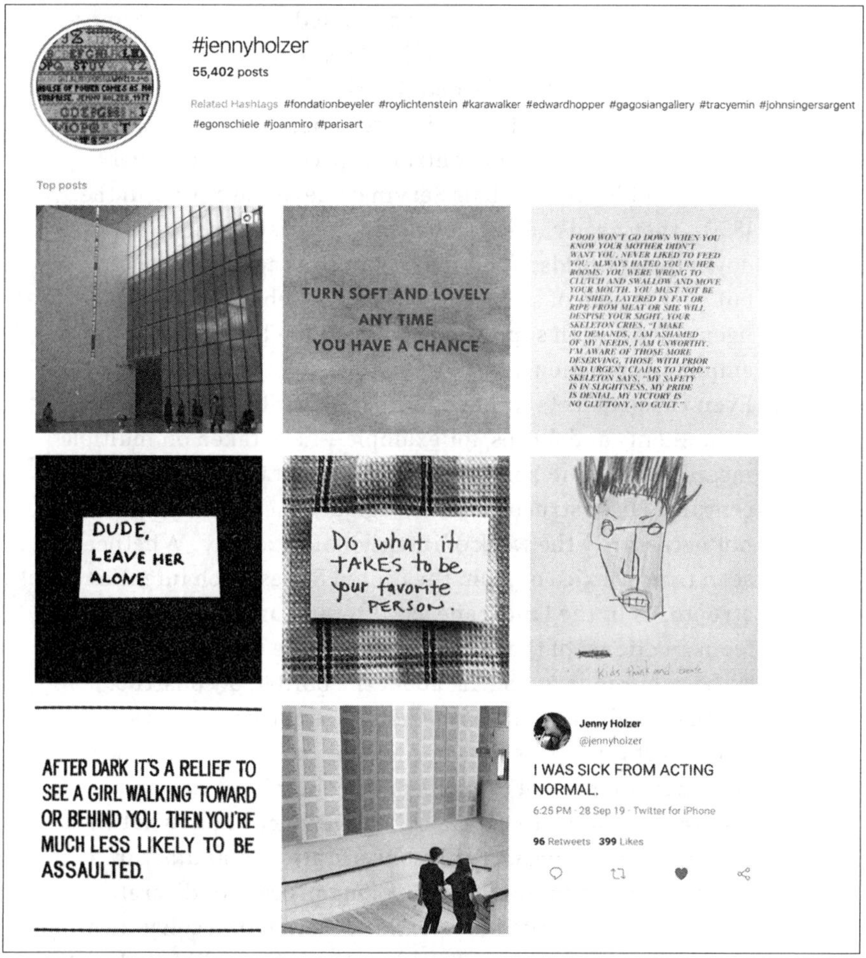

Figure 1.13. Top posts tagged #jennyholzer in early 2020. Instagram, January 2020.

Of course, as wide-reaching as Holzer's and expanded internet art's assembly-based work is, it is not the final word on what decentered assembly can involve. Yet another version of assembly exceeds any single person or group, as well as any fully mappable list of artifacts. Among the many ways into this proposition is a 2018 scholarly collection called *Border Spaces: Visualizing the U.S.–Mexico Frontera.*[56] The phenomenon in question is evident across passages like these:

(a) Before maps delineated worlds and fixed them in place, most people experienced the borderlands as a land in motion. It was land marked by ebbs and flows—as people set in motion by inclination, dislocation, commerce, violence, and empire met and vied for control of space. When surveyors like Daniel Payne and Luis Servín came to the border in the 1890s, they used cameras, obelisks, and mathematics to pin down these worlds in motion, not only as agents of states, but also as men of science—sustaining webs of "global intelligence" that both supported and circulated widely beyond empires and nations.[57]

(b) Even those objects intended as permanent markers—monuments and fences, for example—have taken on multiple meanings and interpretations throughout the twentieth century. These structures, although at times aesthetic, are not necessarily the work of intentional artists. . . . Whether seen from Mexico or from the United States, such intentional structures in the landscape are, literally and figuratively, "constructions" of the borderlands and the border itself.[58]

(c) At best, border art, and art about the border, deconstruct, rupture, and intervene in the notion of borders. At its worst, border art reinscribes the borderline, or la linea, and the assumed supremacy of the state and economics.[59]

(d) [These essays] say to us in a collective voice: look, what we call today our "border reality" was crafted, manufactured, and willed into being through a long process of discrete actions that attempted to wrestle into order and coherence the landscape of cross-cultural relations that collided along these natural and man-made terrains.[60]

Most obviously, these passages point to the enormous, radically complex, highly contested, and violent phenomenon that first emerged as idea, reality, and abstract legal entity in the nineteenth century: *la frontera,* the Mexico–U.S. "border." Also at stake is what a theory of assembly would characterize as the distributed and constantly evolving work of media assembling of, in, around, across, for, and from that phenomenon. That is to say, as part and parcel of what the third passage above calls a "long process of discrete actions" that wrestle with (and take advantage of) the border, there has been a crisscrossing network of media practices around this phenomenon taking place over a long period and over vast stretches of space: effectively a collective exercise in materially consequential distributed assembly not yoked to a single artifact. This is the massive, multiperson, multicollective, now partly automated practice of all signifying and mediating related to the bifurcating border.

All of this could sound like an unnecessarily jargony way of naming what one author helpfully calls "a borderlands panorama of knowledge" developing over time.[61] Along the lines this chapter has sought to make persuasive and tractable, however, there is virtue in approaching the broad process of mediation and visualization as a contested and contradictory practice of assembly (and indeed also disassembly). It isn't just that we see how specific artifacts involve assembly-based forms of expressing and conveying, such as in photo albums that survey border sites, in some cases leading to unintended expressive effects.[62] It is that we become aware of a basic and consequential tension in the collective work of social and environmental visualization and mediation. On the one hand, there is the enduring possibility of individuals and collectives participating in contesting and reworking the vast assembly of ideas, stories, frames, impressions, images, binaries, and divisions that is the mediation of the border between Mexico and the United States, as with a comparative assembly produced by Jordan Engel, whose Decolonial Atlas I discuss in chapter 5 (Figure 1.14).

On the other hand, there is only ever partial and provisional access. Indeed, if you explored the Wikimedia commons category "Mexico–United States border" in 2021, you would see both an individual image of stark difference (a photograph of the border taken by a member of the U.S. military, given pride of place) and an overwhelming mix of perspectives in the varieties of media gathered below. There was a video of a political speech by Bernie Sanders; there were historical maps and political comics; there were photographs of signs and injuries. Part of what we can say is materialized here is the long and still-unfolding material and virtual legacy of distributed assembly, a legacy with which millions of people interact, but one that they never see in total or frozen form. The results of the search, like the gathering of essays in an edited collection, are a glimpse of ongoing acts of reassembly beyond measure. And

The Decolonial Atlas
@decolonialatlas

If a line can be drawn, it can be erased. If a wall can be built, it can be toppled.

📷: The US-Mexico border bisecting Nogales Arizona (right) and Nogales Sonora (left).

#NoBorder #NoWall

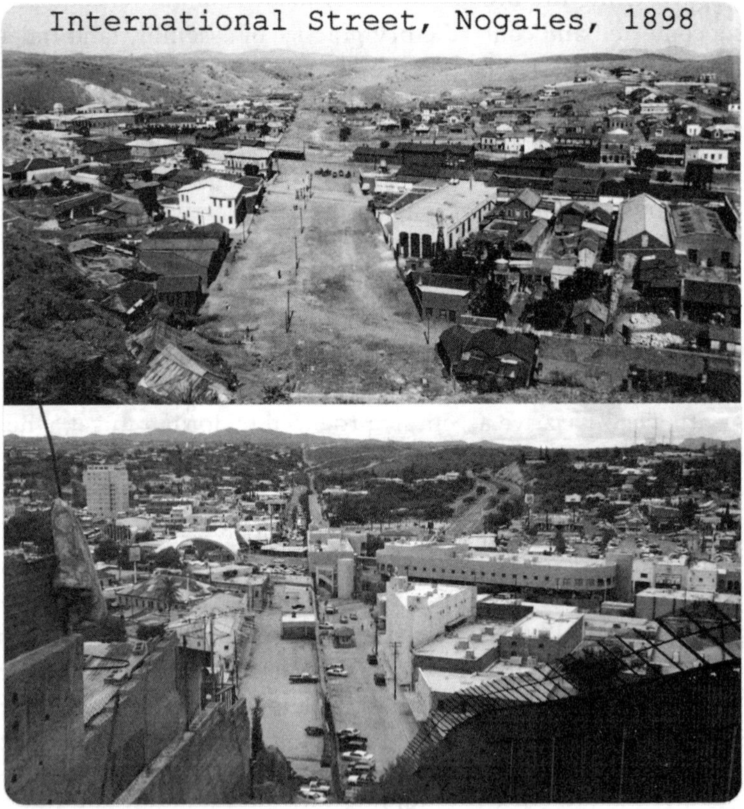

9:12 AM · Sep 12, 2021 · Buffer

Figure 1.14. Twitter post by @decolonialatlas with a visual juxtaposition of historical and contemporary photographs of International Street in Nogales, Arizona, and Nogales, Sonora, September 12, 2021.

perhaps this condition of knowing and unknowing is part of what one contributor has in mind when speaking to the virtue of physical gatherings that confront the media assembly of the border head-on. "Even our meeting today is another way of thinking about borders," says Amelia Malagamba-Ansótegui. "We represent different territories, or mapped places, cartographically and ideologically speaking, with distinct visions, histories, and perspectives. Gathering together, seeing border art and spaces from each other's point of view is critical."[63] In a time when the border is all the more contested and deadly, and in which it is a means to drum up political support for xenophobic causes, it matters that we come to recognize the ongoing process of assembling and disassembling something as consequential as this by means of a massively distributed process of cultural and communicative selection and configuration. Future research along these lines would take this from a more speculative to a specifying notion, working to delineate particular dynamics. There would be newly identified avenues of resistance, reinvention, and reform through newly identified avenues of configuring and reconfiguring the many constituents and subassemblies that make up the overall superassembly.

Is Everything a Remix?

First assembly's materials, activities, and drive, then the pursuit of and participation in assembly across widely varying scales—is all this just an elaborate way of recycling the quintessentially digital mantra that "everything is a remix"? That mantra forms the title of a TED talk and a documentary.[64] It is also an idea asserted by several scholars in the field of remix studies.[65] The notion is compelling: acts of borrowing and appropriating are creative fundamentals, from the earliest instances of human culture to the teeming, networked present.

Is a theory of assembly a way of effectively reinforcing this conception of media and culture? As understandable as this move might be, it misses the mark. For one thing, it is an overcorrection. In some sense, it is appealing to oppose dominant hierarchies of cultural form by saying, "look, it isn't only important that we acknowledge assembly; it's also important to acknowledge that those things we think stand apart from processes of recombination really do not." The problem with such a move is that it undermines the work of insisting on assembly as powerful and widespread. What is more useful is an evasion of the underlying premise. When someone takes the perspective that "everything is a . . ." (and one can readily find claims that "everything is a story"), the response is to read that perspective for the value statement that it is: "Everything *that I presently claim as important* is an x." We then proceed to develop more flexible and reflexive accounts of cultural worlds. This book's account emphasizes the sheer abundance of artifacts and practices that seize on the transformative promise of media constituents placed into generative relationships. This is not to say that such a promise is absolutely everywhere. It is saying the workings of assembly are increasingly widespread. It is saying assembly can prove especially enabling when it becomes a guiding communicative or collaborative strategy (though it can also fall short, fail, and deceive). And it is saying we will not adequately meet the richness and complexity of networked cultures when we remain wedded to the current roster of cultural forms and expressive strategies.

The other reason not to equate a theory of assembly with a notion of pervasive remix is this: the universalizing version of remix is not seen the same way by all parties. If you are in a position of relative cultural power, and if you do not find you or your forebears have been subject to systematic and violent taking, you might not find it particularly alarming to look out at histories of cultural expression and see remix in every direction. But if you are not in such a position, and if you are all too aware of what Beretta E. Smith-Shomade calls the actual "material consequences" of appropriation, then an unqualified vision of pervasive remix might well strike you as nonneutral and even dangerous.[66] In other words, the perspective that everything is a remix risks reasserting a position of cultural and imperial privilege and precedent, even when it is meant as a useful provocation. It can *seem* like everything is a remix, and many remarkable acts of creative expression are shot through with influences and emulations. But the actual circumstances of cultural production are far more uneven.

Does this mean that a theory of assembly advocates only originality? Does it call for the perpetual policing of cultural exchange?

No: it calls for attention, action, and care within the shifting limits of the possible. Questions concerning how we assemble, why we assemble, with whom and for whom we assemble, and when and where we assemble are just as important as the elemental question of what we assemble.

2

Art, Assembly, and the Museum

At some point between 1967 and 1968, Richard Serra drew up a tidy list of heterogeneous terms (Figure 2.1). Four columns across two sheets of paper, the list consists of a variety of actions, some of them quite tangible (to chip, to sever), others more abstract (to complement, to continue), and still others caught in between (to support, to expand). Although you wouldn't know it from the title, *Verb List* also includes a variety of themes and subject matters. These likewise cut across the material (of felting, of ionization), the conceptual (of grouping, of context), and the ambiguous (of reflection, of friction). "When I first started," the artist later explained, "what was very, very important to me was dealing with the nature of process, . . . and I really just worked out pieces in relation to the verb list, physically, in a space."[1] Given over to conceptual as much as sculptural experimentation, Serra also came to treat *Verb List* as an art object in its own right, including it in a group show in Milan in 1969 and eventually gifting a second version to the Museum of Modern Art in New York in 2012.[2]

If *Verb List* is invoked in art-historical contexts, it is usually in accordance with Serra's summary. As a compilation of what Serra calls "actions to relate to oneself, material, place and process," the work is, in Samantha Friedman's terms, a "linguistic laying out of possible artistic options."[3] For Rosalind E. Krauss, it is a text in which the verbs become "themselves the generators of art forms."[4] And for Lynne Cooke, it amounts to an "an artist's statement" or even a "credo."[5] Although I do not deny the accuracy or importance of these readings (Serra's uses of steel, rubber, and rock really do test one ambitious material act after another), it is a pair of others that take priority here. For one thing, *Verb List* places this book's key premise—that assembly ought to join the roster of available and valuable expressive strategies—right in the center of modern and

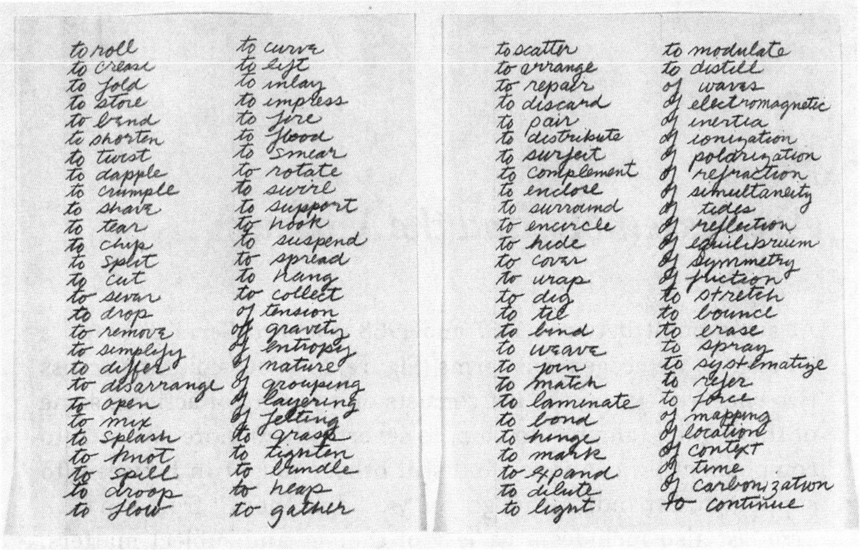

Figure 2.1. A "linguistic laying out of possible artistic options," an assembly-based thematic list, and a model for a critical typology of art as assembly. Richard Serra, *Verb List*, 1967–68. Pencil on two sheets of paper, each 10 × 8 ½ inches. Museum of Modern Art. Copyright 2021 Richard Serra / Licensed by Artists Rights Society (ARS), New York.

contemporary art. It does so because the work both embodies and encourages the strategy. When confronted with this rich agglomeration of lexical constituents, viewers can find their drives to read and perceive assemblies set in motion: Are there implicit messages in Serra's selections and placements? Why does "of mapping" follow "to force"? Why are certain perennial artistic themes here (nature, time) and not others (God, beauty, power)? How would this action alter the way an artist addresses this or that subject? Meanwhile, the work volunteers a vision of art as a drive to recombine: this possibility following this possibility following this possibility, ad infinitum.

Quite by accident, *Verb List* also points to what a theory of art as assembly ought to do.[6] Like *Verb List*, such a theory should take as given not just the sheer variety but also the legibility of "possible artistic options"; it should name both the well-known and the marginal among those options; and it should avoid reinforcing dominant schemes of which actions and themes matter most. At the same time, a theory of art as assembly must also remain true to its lens. That means "filtering" the view of artistic potentials such that those based in assembly, including those that seize on the recombinatory and accumulative potentials in digital technologies, come into focus. It also means emphasizing the potentials of aesthetic assembly for projects of social and ecological justice and repair.

In other words, what is presently lacking, and what I now offer here, is a critical typology of art in the mode of assembly. There are certain prevailing terms and taxonomies that confront anyone who enters an art museum or an art history classroom (e.g., Fauvism, modernism, allegory). And yet there are, as Serra demonstrates, other possible indexes of actions and subject matters to which artists and curators (and the audiences or "constituents" of artworlds) can relate themselves. These alternative indexes tend to remain implicit; they hide in the interstices of artists' notes and statements; they dwell in the asides of critics and in the searching conversations of gallery visitors and account followers. In offering a critical typology centered on aesthetic assembly, I can help to variously correct, augment, or redirect the habits of mind that impact which works and practices find their way into circulation and collection, how those projects are seen and interpreted, and thus what they ultimately manage to do. Neither natural nor neutral, aesthetic terms and taxonomies act on us. A theory of assembly argues we ought to act on them in turn.

Immediate Objections

There are at least three angles from which more traditional art history will immediately object to this whole operation. Because these objections demonstrate the sometimes stultifying entrenchment of dominant art-historical schemes, and because addressing them will help underscore what a typology of assembly aims to offer by contrast, I will respond right away, rather than let them linger.

The first objection is legible in the oft-quoted provocation from an 1890 essay by artist and critic Maurice Denis. "It should be remembered," Denis writes, "that a picture—before being a warhorse, a nude, or an anecdote of some sort—is essentially a flat surface covered with colors assembled in a certain order."[7] The basic notion here is relatively simple: any given picture is, before anything else, a collection of ordered visual material. The implications of this notion are far-reaching. What Denis is suggesting (and it is important to remember there was a range of people thinking in similar terms at this time) is that artistic production can and must be freed from the habituated notion that an artwork really exists and matters only when it functions to mimic or to allegorize or to recount.[8] In this recognition and in the confidence to follow it there is much of the impetus for the torrent of abstract and conceptual art that would follow in the ensuing decades. Indeed, the work of an artist like Serra finds sustenance in exactly such a proposition. Not only do whole indexes of artistic possibility precede and exceed the well-trodden expressive strategies of representation, allegory, and storytelling, but there is also no escaping the fact of materials and actions to which artists must somehow relate themselves.

The objection that derives from all this is that trying to select out assembly as a distinct strand of artistic production is an effectively redundant measure that misses the actual pervasiveness of the phenomenon. According to the Denis line of thinking, not just some, but all works of art are instances of assembly. This is because anything and everything artistic, from decolonial net art to narrative painting, can be reconceived as a combination of ordered elements. To try to select out certain examples as assembly (such a line of thinking goes) does not just miss this essential truth. It also misses the critical insights (and the historically crucial freeing of artistic drives) that follow from seeing all instances of making pictures or building sculptures, or whatever the work might be, as exercises in collation and arrangement of one kind or another.

The response to this objection is to grant the primary point that most anything aesthetic is conceivable as a gathering and ordering of elements but also refuse the effect of covering and occluding that overemphasizing this point can have. In making the fact of combination the characteristic that links all instances of art (and presumably all instances of visual and material culture), one also paradoxically restricts the available roster of artistic possibilities. This is because one forestalls attention to those forms of artistic practice in which assembly is actively thematized as such, those in which it is the driving form and the distinguishing characteristic. The distinction of those practices is precisely what a critical typology of assembly in art aims to assert. These practices join all fellow aesthetic practices in the primal act of combining expressive elements, but their legiblility and power fundamentally depend on the work they do as assemblies, combinations, and configurations. In other words, instances that fall under the rubric of assembly characteristically intensify and elaborate their basic status as "colors" (or nails or marks or words or pixels or still other constituents) "assembled in a certain order." And the rise of digital and social media only amplifies the speed, frequency, and inventiveness with which assembly-based works and practices can come into existence, circulate, and matter.

A second objection is effectively the inverse of the first. This is the idea that any artist that would intensify and elaborate their work's engagement with assembly would be veering in the wrong direction. They would be failing to do what any and all works of artistic quality ought to do, which is to rise above the fact of combination to become something else. Such a perspective has a long (if also largely unconscious) history within European and Anglo-American thought.[9] In effect, it is a vision of art as that exercise in which the work of combining aesthetic elements is transcended in favor of something variously skillful, powerful, awe-inspiring, enlightening, unprecedented, or transformative. This much is evident in brief moments throughout centuries of critical literature, in phrases of derision like "mere arrangement" or "mere catalog." The precept is also evident within the sphere of philosophy of art, and perhaps no philosopher is as forthright in this respect as Susanne K. Langer. "An artifact as such is merely a combination of material parts," Langer writes. "A work of art, on the other hand, is more than an 'arrangement' of given things—even qualitative things. Something emerges from the arrangement of tones or colors, which was not there before, and this, rather than the arranged material, is the symbol of sentience."[10] From this perspective, works and practices based in assembly do not enjoy full citizenship within the domain of art.[11] They cannot shake the pedestrianism of strict combination.

If the notion is that certain would-be artworks are "nothing more than" arrangements, the best response is to hijack the notion and say that numerous artworks and art practices are nothing *less* than arrangements. Whether in sculptures, lists, installations, GIFs, or still other media, instances of assembly are consciously and thoroughly driven by the transformative potential of expressive relationships. This is not to say that *nothing* emerges from the arrangement, but that the thing or things that emerge are not somehow on an entirely different and higher plane of importance than the "arranged material." Rather than participate in traditions that would have the value of an artwork depend on the degree to which it exceeds the actual combinatory makeup of the works' colors, elements, positions, and so on, assembly-based works speak in and through the arrangements of (or in or made by) the work itself. An especially poignant example of this commitment is a photograph within Milagros de la Torre's *Untitled (Poland)* (Figure 2.2). For this project, two key verbs are "to remove," since the walls of a house were stripped of their family photos, and "to document," as the walls were then photographed. In the image in question, what was once a convergence of eight of a family's photos has transformed into something else. Gone are the scenes and details those photos held; what remains are the positions marked by the outlines of their frames, the nails that held those frames up, and the patches of wall they covered. A kind of found expressive arrangement, the shadowy assembly makes for an "interplay of present absences and omitted presences," one that is both evocative (of family, of proximity) and provocative (of death, of erasure).[12] Other projects of aesthetic assembly likewise seize on the generativity of lingering there in the sometimes chaos and sometimes precision of arrays of positions and open-ended relations among constituents. When artists make such work, they engage in a widely pursued but still undertheorized dimension of how humans interact in and through media. To collect, to juxtapose, to arrange, to sequence, to reconfigure—these forms of artistic possibility matter not only as supplements or stages. They matter in their own right.

The last major objection sits between the first two. Let's say one grants the rebuttals to these objections (that assembly is distinct, that assemblies are nothing less than arrangements). One might still object that people have been doing and talking about combinatorial art for a long time. Artists and filmmakers such as Georges Braque, Pablo Picasso, Filippo Tommaso Marinetti, Hannah Höch, Alexander Rodchenko, Sergei Eisenstein, Linder Sterling, Peter Greenaway, and Betye Saar (to name just a few) have long experimented with different methods for combining media in which the work and appearance of combination is essential. The products of

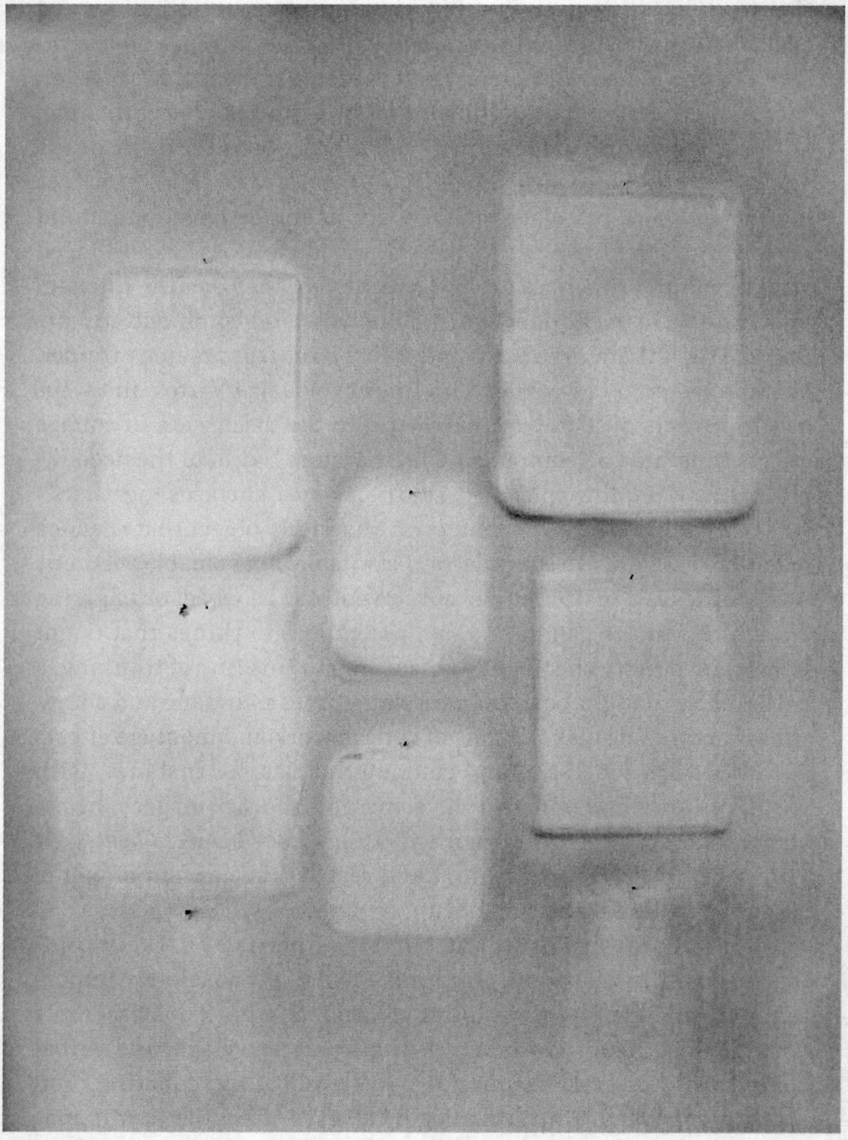

Figure 2.2. A found assembly. Milagros de la Torre, *Untitled (Poland),* 2005. Archival pigment print, variable dimensions. Copyright Milagros de la Torre. Courtesy of the artist.

this work have not been ignored (the all-too-usual prejudices and exclusions notwithstanding); rather, arts of recombination are integral to the history of modern and contemporary art. Moreoever, these practitioners have not operated in a kind of conceptual fog, without terms and taxonomies. Quite the opposite: from books and articles to landmark shows and university courses, practices like assemblage, bricolage, collage, and montage have long found harbor in the texts of critics, scholars, and curators.[13] And indeed such terms and practices are not relegated to the past: the intellectual transits between modernist composite and combinatorial art and the digital era are many and important, from memes framed as Dada redux to Lev Manovich's linking of Dziga Vertov and web-based projects of "database narrative" to the discussion of collage effects generated on computers, and therefore "without the need literally to cut photographs or paste their paper surfaces together."[14]

Taking all this into account, one can readily object that the idea of adding assembly to the palette of available and valuable aesthetic possibilities is a matter either of reinventing the wheel or of giving a seemingly quite general name ("assembly") to things that ought to be named more specifically. According to this line of thinking, a better project might be to map the sometimes mundane and sometimes remarkable elaborations of collage work and montage effects across net art, video art, and computer art (as, for instance, with Joe Hamilton's hallucinatory layering of airborne imagery, brush stroke, and architectural fragments in his 2014 *Indirect Flights*). Or it might be best to avoid all that and restrict the concept of media assembly to digital and nonartistic spheres.

A critical typology of art as assembly responds by both welcoming and refusing the point. On the one hand, it is absolutely important to recognize the continuities of art (and nonart) qua assembly with the long history of practices that center on visual and verbal compilation, as well as quasi-archival collecting, collating, and rearranging. What Christina Poggi calls the "freedom to mix materials and media" is a hallmark (and even taken for granted, says Poggi) feature of a great deal of important modern and contemporary art.[15] The rich uses of that freedom have had enduring influences in multiple domains of visual culture, not just the digital. At the same time, numerous critics have developed crucial insights not only into what exercises of compilation, configuration, and arrangement can achieve but also into how these exercises parallel social and technological developments and disruptions throughout modernity.

And yet to refuse to entertain the idea that yet more combinatorial genres, forms, and strategies exist and matter would do a disservice both to these histories of practice and inquiry and to those that fall under this umbrella I label "assembly." After all, if I understand historians in these areas correctly, terms like "assemblage," "montage," "collage," and "database" point to specificities of form and to specific discourses about and from those forms.[16] According to Patrizia McBride, for instance, the "genius" of montage "lies in rendering, at a basic structural level, the semblance of a world in shambles while avoiding depicting it in an illusionistic or naturalistic fashion."[17] As a different example, Poggi writes that the cubists contested the "homogeneous, unified field of representation," and therefore asserted a "different process of cultural exchange, one in which the signs of the fine arts and those of popular culture proved to be of equal value." Finally, in speaking to the notion of "database aesthetics," Christiane Paul writes that the term is "frequently used to describe the aesthetic principles applied in imposing the logic of the database to any type of information, filtering data collections, and visualizing data."[18] Sharon Daniel writes that a "'conception' of the 'beauty' of a database is not located in the viewer's interpretation of a static form but in the dynamics of how a user inflects the database through interaction with its field or frame."[19]

From where I sit, observations like these and the many more that could be cited, including with respect to archives and "archival art," do not point to the need to protect and further entrench existing terms, but to the value of flexible engagement with the terrifically complex network of family resemblances across artistic worlds, or what Griselda Pollock calls, via Aby Warburg, art and visual culture's "patterns and persistences across time, location and media."[20] These patterns and persistences will inevitably look different depending on your positions and purposes. And this means that what we ultimately face at the confluence of assembly, montage, collage, assemblage, database, and other forms is a situation of resonance rather than redundance.

While this book recognizes and indeed celebrates the richness and wide applicability of combinatorial approaches across modern, contemporary, digital, and net art, it also maintains a defense of the actuality and importance of its focal form. As *Verb List* and *Untitled (Poland)* begin to suggest, and as the other examples in this chapter will elaborate, assembly is that expressive strategy in which the component elements are mutually distinct constituents and positions, and in which the appearance and logic of selection and arrangement—the fact and the ferment of expressive relationships—are integral rather than incidental. Furthermore, and crucially, aesthetic assembly is not restricted to the level of the single artwork. It can be undertaken across artworks, in the modalities of organizing and curating. It can also be something in which audiences and activists (and even machines) participate by means of the gathering and distributing afforded by digital and networked technologies.

To Assemble, To Array, To Infuse, To Incorporate, To Participate, To Distribute

All art is assembly; no good art is assembly; plenty of combinatory art is already known and interpreted through better lenses. However understandable these objections are at first blush, they end up pointing to the need for a critical typology that will trace key potentials in aesthetic assembly across analog and digital spheres.[21]

Step one is to establish the major types of assembly in this imperfectly delineated context of "art."[22] The first of these is "assembly-based." Here "based" indicates that from which something derives; it also indicates the power or resources from which a structure or activity draws, as in a database. Assembly-based art is art that is structured around or fundamentally dependent on a version of expressive or interactive gathering. The way things are put together is not just a partial concern, such that the work yields something greater than the sum of its parts. Rather, it is essential to how the artists, curators, or collaborators undertake the enterprise itself. Part and parcel, the assembly is read and understood, or reused and reshared, through rhetorics and logics of compilation and configuration. The viewer or user or contributor dwells within and makes use of the sums, subtractions, divisions, and multiplications of the component parts, clusters, and overall whole.

As has been evident, assembly-based art is not confined to one or the other medium, format, or era. Take, for instance, the deceptively simple assembly-based action "to array." In the format of sculpture, an artist such as Lungiswa Gqunta, in her *Lawn 1,* can organize one after the other broken Coca-Cola bottles in a definitive grid that welcomes no visitor and that rearranges both a specific method of making walls threatening and the enduring effects of apartheid in South Africa. In the format of photography, an artist such as Trevor Paglen, in his *They Took the Faces from the Accused and the Dead . . . (SD18)* (2020), can arrange hundreds of (only partly censored) mugshots that had been provided without consent by the American National Standards Institute to developers seeking to train facial recognition software. In the format of the browser, the opportunities to array are legion, from constellations of keywords in a net-art discussion list (Alex Galloway, Mark Tribe, and Martin Wattenberg, *Starrynight*) to a ladder of differing image results for the same search term based on geography (Taryn Simon with Aaron Swartz, *Image Atlas,* 2012–present), to a vast stream of links to Latinx net-art projects that themselves frequently involve bringing media into structured visual and interactive arrays (Brian Mackern, *netart_latino database,* 1994–2004). Finally, the work of arraying can combine the visual and the computational, as when an artist takes thirteen years of digital drawings, quite a few of which, it turns out, are derogatory in nature,[23] and arrays all five thousand of them in an image file that is 21,069 by 21,069 pixels, and sells the work via Christie's as a string of data in a blockchain (a nonfungible token, or NFT) for $69 million, the third-highest price fetched by a living artist (Beeple [Michael Joseph Winkelmann], *Everydays: The First 5,000 Days,* 2021). Across all these cases, there is a basic, shared gesture of not only systematically organizing constituents in a given format but also making the appearance and activity of arraying into an integral dimension of the work.

Alongside art that makes assembly integral is art that partly includes, or *infuses,* as I prefer to think of it, assembly. This type finds ample expression in an artwork that is seemingly impossibly divergent from the other examples in this book but that, in its canonical status and in its theological and quasi-erotic bent, helps to emphasize assembly's wide net: Hieronymus Bosch's altar piece (that actually wasn't one), produced between 1490 and 1510 and commonly called *Garden of Earthly Delights* (Plate 7). The enigmatic artist has been associated with "madness," "heresy," and "membership [in] some licentious sect," but also with "adherence to the 'Modern Devotion' movement."[24] Meanwhile, this "phantasmagorical" triptych has yielded quite disparate attempts to determine what Hans Belting calls "the argument that is the message of this work."[25] While, for instance, an early interpreter claims that *Garden* is all about "the vanity and emptiness of the world" (the monk José de Sigüenza, writing in the sixteenth century, as recalled by Belting), another interpreter, several centuries later, imagines it presents an "ideal realm of love" (art historian Wilhelm Fraenger).[26]

Although not its intention, Belting's account provides a crucial waypoint toward understanding the relational and configural dimensions of this work, and in particular the way it infuses assembly into its cultural formal field. For Belting, while *Garden* lacks a "coherent linear narrative," it nevertheless does present a kind of "narrative structure," one that manages to be both "stringent" and "thoroughly subversive."[27] What makes that narrative structure subversive is the simultaneous adherence to and departure from contemporaneous norms around religious painting. There is, for instance, a relatively familiar scene in the left panel, with Adam and Eve shown together before the Fall, but the middle panel that follows is not, as convention would have it, either the world after the Fall or even quite the Paradise from which they were expelled. Instead, it is some other, magnificently wrought paradise entirely. Though the details of this other paradise adhere in many respects to the descriptions in the Bible, they do so in an unprecedented and risky "paraphrase." The third panel only intensifies this striking eccentricity. While it is full of iconography one might expect from a rendering of the Last Judgment in this time and place, it is also a radical break from the middle panel's distinctly utopian vision, instead rendering both familiar and surreal scenes of disaster, or what Belting thinks of as hell on earth, a kind of "contradictory form of realism."[28]

To say this work is assembly-infused is to more or less accept Belting's account of the tripartite juxtaposition along the lines of narrative while *also* respecting his call to linger in the "artist's chosen form of expression." For Belting, this is a work released from "the mimesis of the world" and instead bound to the "creative imagination." It is the result of the "poetic freedom [Bosch] claimed for himself." Bosch is "appealing to the viewer's imagination, calling for everyone to undertake his or her own personal interpretation of this panorama of repeated motifs."[29]

Heeding both Bosch's and Belting's appeal, I venture an interpretation through the lens of assembly. Bosch didn't just address his poetic freedom to paradise and disaster. He also addressed it to the more-than-one, the many, and the assembled, and not just once or twice, but widely and repeatedly, as though he were obsessed by the fact and the ferment (and the folly) of human and nonhuman relationships. In the left panel, this is evident by way of absence, with only the human characters presented in any kind of company or union (albeit an instance of union, between Adam and Eve, that is understood to precede all others). By contrast, the middle panel, which Belting calls a "counter-image of civilization,"[30] is assembly many times over. Whether crowding beneath a strawberry or joining oversized birds in a pool, human bodies, most but not all with light-toned skin, are variously making, finding, and forcing connections. There are couplings; there are gatherings; there are stampedes. Bosch is presenting us with an effervescent catalog of fleshly recombination. (One pair of writers puts it this way: "There are so many naked limbs asunder, intertwined in so many bodily configurations, that any sense of proportion, scale, or order is overwhelmed by the sheer amount of visual activity."[31]) The third panel breaks all this. A vision of hell on earth, it is also a vision of disassembly. Any convergences are convergences of people in extremis, such as the mad dispersal into an unlit pool near the upper edge of the image or dismemberment and no escape inside a lantern and on a knife's edge. Meanwhile there is also the horror of isolation: the surreal digestion through a bird, being impaled by the strings of a harp. In short, however much Bosch engages in subversive acts of narrative sequencing (or striking representations of objects and creatures), he also seizes on the expressive strategy of assembly in both the content and the poetic form of the work. From the use of the contrasting panels to the sheer variety of bodily configurations, this is a wickedly generative patterning of living relations as rare, then overflowing, then radically imperiled and distorted.

For some, it might be unacceptable to read this work for the phenomenon of assembly, particularly because those encountering the panorama in its original spheres would not have employed such a framework, but perhaps also because it seems much tidier to confine assembly to the digital era. And yet, in its "formative power" and "transhistorical surplus," *Garden* embodies an approach to the production of aesthetic media that has been and will continue to be repeated in the worlds of offline art, contemporary art, outsider art, and whatever other art.[32] This is an approach in which assembly is a quality among other qualities, or in which only particular "subregions" of the work or the practice have assembly as their animating principle.

In their affordances of manipulation, remix, and interactivity, digital technologies multiply these potentials for infusion. I think, for instance, of a work of browser art that couldn't be further removed from *Garden,* Olia Lialina's oft-cited *My Boyfriend Came Back from the War* (Figure 2.3). There the infusion of assembly occurs within a few clicks. What begins as a simple line of text ("My boyfriend came back from the war. After dinner they left us alone.") soon becomes, by way of further clicks, a triad, then a quartet, then a quintet of delineated still images, looping GIFs, and phrases. (As Manovich observes, unlike a work of cinematic montage, in which images replace each other, in this instance that he would call database narrative and "macrocinema" and that I think of as the fusion of storytelling, looping montage, and digital assembly, they persist, as "each new image is juxtaposed not just with one image which preceded it, but with all the other images present on the screen."[33]) While users piece together a narrative, they also actively participate in constructing different kinds of assemblies, with constituent phrases sometimes seeming to connect with each other (like "forgive" and "Who asks you?") and images taking on subtle layers of resonance by way of proximity (the 20th Century Fox logo and the window). Not surprisingly, Lialina's project inspired not just one or two works by other artists, but a whole array. Together these works form a constellation of media artifacts (even a kind of small-scale aesthetic meme) sometimes directly and sometimes loosely yoked to the original. An inflow of spatial assembly in the germinal work becomes an outflow of imitative reassembly across the subsequent ones.

Such responsive work points to yet other modes of aesthetic assembly. These modes are not legible in the works themselves, but in what is done with those works, in the ways they are placed, per-

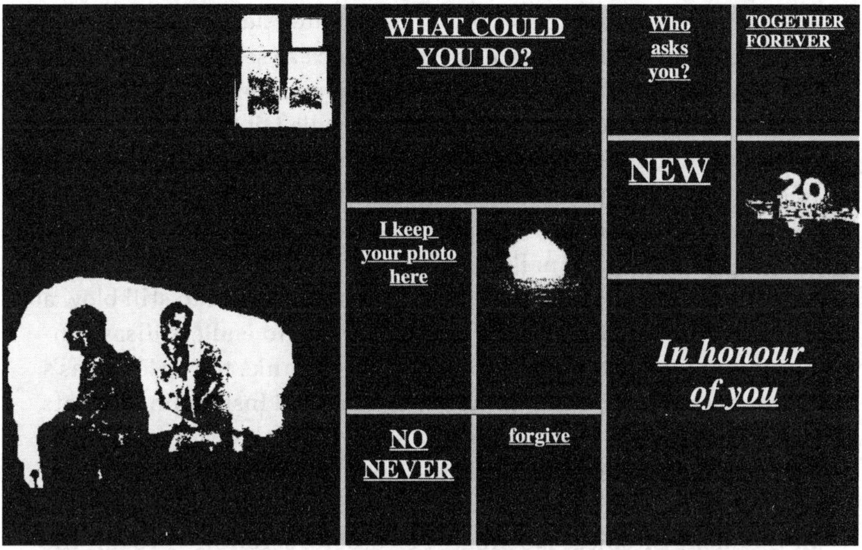

Figure 2.3. An example of assembly-infused art in the digital sphere. Olia Lialina, *My Boyfriend Came Back from the War,* 1996. Screenshot, 2021.

formed, and distributed. Take *Garden.* In 1939, the work was moved from El Escorial to the Museo del Prado, where it has figured in the ready-at-hand gathering of works by "an immensely popular artist" still "capable of mobilizing hundreds of thousands of visitors."[34] In 2019, a replica greeted visitors to an exhibition at Gropius Bau in Berlin. In the latter case, by virtue of its incorporation into this assembly of some two dozen works exploring and metaphorizing gardens (including the grid of broken bottles by Gqunta), the enigmatic work became a newly positioned constituent. Its renderings of flesh, flora, and fauna acted as an analogical reservoir for an era of endless disasters and enduring potentials. At work here is the power of institutions to incorporate artworks into assemblies of their choosing, often toward the consolidation of existing categories, but sometimes also in more generative modes that might, to borrow Joseph Keckler's terms, "totally rearrange the molecules of [one's] existence" while also ensuring there is "an open space there too."[35]

In the digital era, images and artworks can find that, as David Joselit puts it, "their insertion in networks" has them set in motion, where they become "capable of changing format—of experiencing cascading chains of relocation and remediation."[36] *Garden* is a paradigm case of this kind of distributed aesthetic assembly. On Pinterest, different boards gather *Garden* as seen in fashion and tattoo, adding to a long history of copying and remediating Bosch's work.[37] In a more involved vein, a "transmedia triptych"—a film, interactive, and virtual-reality documentary—provides new means of exploring the work's many corners while also adding audio reflections, thus altering the importance of constituent figures, faces, and brushstrokes.[38] Finally, in that frantic sphere of remediation that is social media, "the 500-year-old painter who can still blow a 16-year-old's mind" finds his work subjected to endless disassembly and reassembly.[39] Every few minutes, thanks to Nig Thomas's @boschbot, a fragment is posted to Twitter and Instagram accounts that now overflow with "shareable slithers" of the triptych (Figure 2.4).[40] Some people take this as the opportunity for memetic reassembly, transforming the loosened constituents into *Garden* memes in the mode of object labeling.[41] For others, scrolling through the advertising-laden assemblage that is their feed, the posts are brief and maybe momentarily inspiring flashes of "thought in visual terms."[42] Some of these flashes allow one's "attention to fix on the fantastic or absurd details"; some fix that attention on cracks and other material traces; some make Bosch's work "feel new again"; and others (especially more recent posts for which Thomas adds custom captions) make light of its most eccentric details.[43] A painting of utopia and dystopia has become the means for variously humorous, predictable, and insightful reuse.

To Analogize, or Analogy in Spite of All

Having expanded the discussion from one to three major types of aesthetic assembly, I arrive at a position that is both daunting and compelling. If the terms of this critical typology are fruitful, then not just a handful, but potentially tens of thousands of projects and practices stand open for consideration in connection with assembly. Meanwhile, there are no obvious methodological guardrails that would safely limit where an inquiry concerned with that massive swath can go. What remains compelling is what successful navigation of these challenges can afford. Neither fixed in a particular movement nor yoked to a single medium, a critical typology of art as assembly can focus on the open-ended question of how to

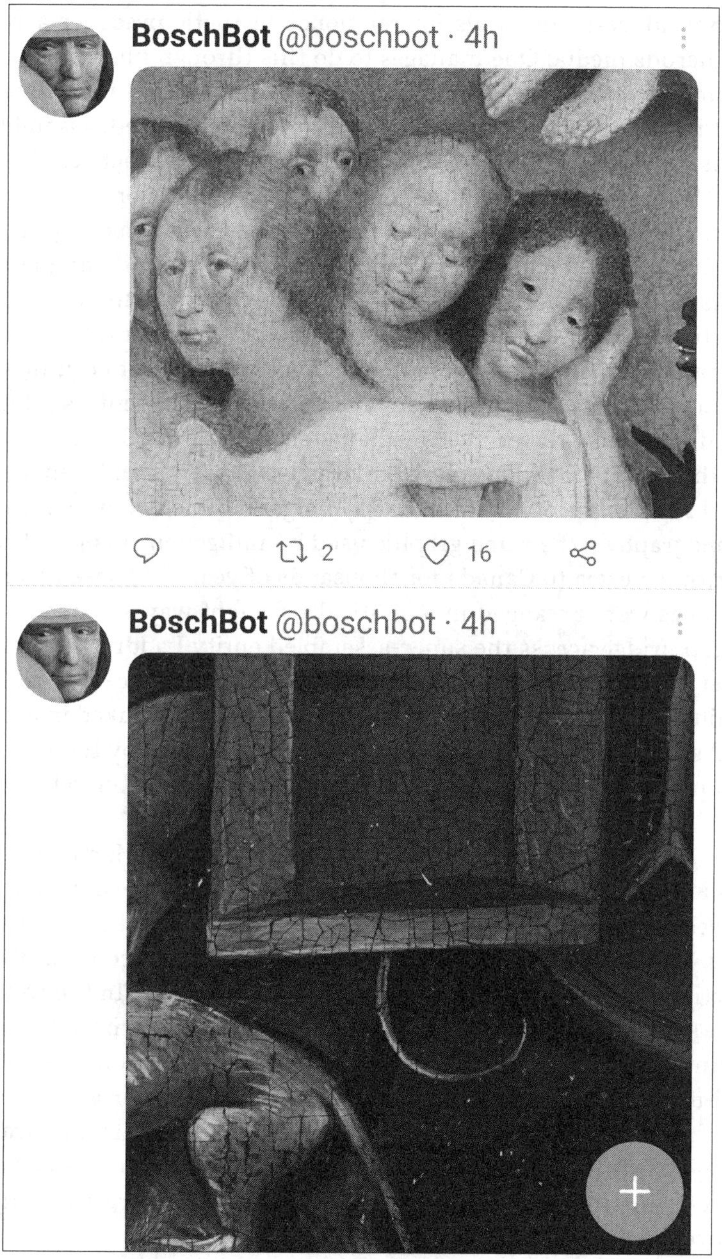

Figure 2.4. @boschbot regularly disassembles the enigmatic triptych, incorporating the painting into feeds and inviting new memetic assemblies in turn. By Nig Thomas, started in 2016.

better address potentials for relational aesthetic practices across numerous media. One manages to do this through plural reading. That means drawing out certain distinct and important family resemblances among assembly-based, assembly-infused, assembly-subsumed, and still other configural projects and practices. These will be resemblances of function, effect, or implication that do not necessarily appear in all cases, or at least not to the same degree.

One of the most powerful of these dynamics finds ample expression in a 2015 work by the interdisciplinary artist collective Postcommodity called *Repellent Fence* or *Valla Repelente* (Plate 8).[44] A testament to sheer aesthetic persistence, the project culminated in an assembly two miles long and composed of twenty-six tethered balloons, all ten feet in diameter, floated one hundred feet in the air. The balloons were "enlarged replicas" of an "ineffective bird repellent product" that "use[s] indigenous medicine colors and iconography—the same graphic used by indigenous peoples from South America to Canada for thousands of years."[45] These floating replicas were arranged in a politically fraught way, serving as an aerial bridge across the super-assembled entity I addressed in the first chapter: the militarized border that separates Mexico and the United States. Postcommodity's sequenced balloons linked in material symbolism what had long been lived and known by Indigenous peoples: the desert that links Douglas, Arizona, in the United States, and Agua Prieta, Sonora, in Mexico.

At the time made up of Raven Chacon, Cristóbal Martinez, and Kade L. Twist, three artists of Indigenous Southwestern American descent, Postcommodity describes *Repellent Fence* on their website as a "social collaborative project among individuals, communities, institutional organizations, publics, and sovereigns." In the collective's eyes, one of the work's key functions is to memorialize existing links and create yet more. The bridge of balloons serves to "bi-directionally reach across the U.S./Mexico border as a suture that stitches the peoples of the Americas together—symbolically demonstrating the interconnectedness of the Western Hemisphere by recognizing the land, indigenous peoples, history, relationships, movement and communication." That all of this also constitutes an instance of art richly infused with assembly is by no means obvious from such descriptions. And yet this is a project that draws much of its power from human and nonhuman constituents placed in surprising, enriching, and memorable combination, and that both exhibits and invites a drive to social and imaginative reassembly. This is evident in both the windswept memorial itself and the dialogues that made the performance possible. "The intentions for these generative dialogues are," Postcommodity writes, "to form local and external capacities for the recovery of transborder knowledges that have been arrested through binary discourses." And the broader goal is to "identify and support indigenous and border community interests, desires, concerns, and goals for creating a more safe, healthy, and culturally appropriate borderlands environment for its citizens."

Apparent in this accounting of the project is something that takes place through and alongside the effort to loft the balloons into consequential arrangement; it is the placement of people and institutions into unexpected positions and productive conversations. These are gatherings of constituents—momentary chats with border agents, searching conversations with young people, lugging materials around with volunteers—catalyzed by the artistic drive to build an assembly over a binary. To some degree, Postcommodity aims to represent and emplot borderlands stakeholders, particularly those whose claims to the land have been sidelined by the constant consolidation of imperial borders. But it also aims to reconfigure the relationships of those stakeholders by threading multiple narratives and encounters into an unprecedented sociotechnical assemblage of contracts, conversations, barriers, ropes, cinder blocks, gas, and photographs. Here, as one member of Postcommodity emphasizes, the work of "land art" is not a cutting into the land; it is an occasion for a metaphor, a suture that dissolves while the work's constituent acts and interactions endure in memory and document, including the associated film.

A social performance and an ephemeral installation, to be sure, *Repellent Fence* is also a powerful demonstration of the particular dynamic of aesthetic assembly I label "to analogize," or analogy in spite of all.[46] The collective indicates this when they write that the project, by way of its "generative conversations," serves as "a means of broadcasting *complex approximations about the complexity* of movement (peoples, cultures, ideologies and capital) of U.S./Mexico transborder systems."[47] If I read these words correctly, then there is a twofold insistence in *Repellent Fence* to which acts of aesthetic assembly are especially poised to respond. For one, although oversimplification and dualism are pervasive temptations, not just within art but across all manner of modern and indeed imperial worlds, it is necessary and empowering to find ways to think, speak, and interact across seemingly unbridgeable divides. Second, although one might hope for clear and distinct truths about situations of mutual concern like the foundation, structuring, policing, and abolition of the borders that have devastated and interrupted Indigenous lifeways, it is quite often only "complex approximations about the complexity" that are concretely possible, and therefore meaningful and interesting, at least until there is a substantive and enduring breakthrough.

Postcommodity is not alone in this dual emphasis. Kaja Silverman, for instance, offers a call to reconceive a myriad of things through the lens of analogy: photography, art, the human psyche, being, the whole world. This lens, Silverman emphasizes, is not built to direct us toward "sameness, symbolic equivalence, logical adequation, or even a rhetorical relationship."[48] Rather, it is built for the simultaneous recognition of similarity and difference. "Every analogy," Silverman writes, "contains both similarity and difference. Similarity is the connector, what holds two things together, and difference is what prevents them from being collapsed into one."[49] Neither strict sameness nor total difference, analogy persists in spite of the forces that might threaten to overdifferentiate or to conflate. Analogy also finds materialization in art.

As experiments in the "analogical basis of the photographic image," the artworks Silverman addresses are quite different from *Repellent Fence.*[50] Nevertheless, there are widely applicable similarities across Silverman's and Postcommidty's projects. Insisting on conversations and aesthetic practices that function in spite of dualism and simplification "across diversity and interests," and pursuing such an insistence in order to generatively yield neither exact copies nor exact theories, but instead "complex approximations about the complexity," these projects of analogy are premised on an equally productive, generous, and fierce kind of nonbinaristic, analogical thinking in which "similarity is the connector" and "difference is what prevents them from being collapsed into one." Indeed, both in spite of and because of the violence of the border, Postcommodity analogizes its shapes, its symbolisms, its absurdity, its negotiation, and its would-be overcoming.

That the projects' mutual affinity is larger in meaning and application than this pair alone becomes evident through others that pursue analogy by way of assembly, even when faced with circumstances that would sever and separate. Potential examples are legion, from the more affective and intimate (I think of Anne Carson's negotiation of links and gaps between herself and her estranged brother in the eulogy *Nox*) to the more social and performative (I think of the grid of singing mouths in Lorna Simpson's *Easy to Remember* or the sequences of habit-revealing video and screen captures from users' mobile devices in Kate Hollenbach's *USER_IS_PRESENT*) to the more political and conceptual. At the latter end of this spectrum is a project by Joan Fontcuberta called Googlegrams. Silverman explains: "Fontcuberta begins a Googlegram by locating an image that is 'an icon of our time,' and that is linked to one or more words. He then conducts a Google image search with this word or set of words, and reconstitutes the iconic image with the jpegs to which this search leads through a freeware photomosaic program."[51] The images that Fontcuberta reconstitutes in this manner are many and various, including photographs of the Twin Towers on fire or a picture of torture and abuse at Abu Ghraib, as well as others less yoked to recent history, such as the first permanently fixed photographic image, *View from the Window at Le Gras* by Nicéphore Niépce.

In the vocabulary of this chapter's critical typology, what has happened here is that a single method of assembly-based analogy (combining disparate images from the internet) supports the production of a variety of complex approximations of images (the photomosaics), as well as the opening of various possible experiences and interpretations of those images (the drive to read and interpret analogical assembly). Silverman's engagement with the work centers on the ten thousand distinct but linked images that make up the artist's reconstitution of *View from the Window.* (The images are derived from the search terms "photo" and "foto.") Quoting Fontcuberta, she observes how each of the constituent photographs "still [has] a meaning by [itself]." That meaning isn't the sort "we mobilize by identifying what is 'in' a photograph," Silverman writes: "It is, rather, the inexhaustible significance that every being should always have for us, and that the photographic image helps us to experience."[52] Silverman also points to how the appearance of these images to Fontcuberta's search depended on the links "forged by other Internet users," links that "reflect their predilections, antipathies, rivalries, and desires, instead of our own." Proceeding in this way, Fontcuberta "opened the door of his work to images that were tagged and uploaded by thousands of other users, and in which their affects were still lodged."[53]

If Silverman helps us see arts of digital analogy as the means toward seemingly impossible intensities of connection across difference, Fontcuberta helps us see them as spurs toward thinking and questioning under fraught circumstances. With Googlegrams, those labors of aesthetic reflection find a focal point in something he calls "archive noise."[54] To read this noise is to adopt a dual approach to the assembly of images. On the one hand—and here Fontcuberta provides helpful terms for the experience of many media assemblies—"a hyperopic vision privileges the composite whole," such that one engages what the many analogies make together, the full photograph. On the other hand, there is a "myopic view" that "privileges the little component units that make up the coarse graphic texture." For Fontcuberta, the exercise of shuttling between hyperopic (whole) and myopic (component) views is the stuff of an analogical process: one produces otherwise inaccessible associations and interpretations across the "causal, spatial, temporal, metaphorical." Such a "dense relational constellation" is not unique to Googlegrams; it "obtains inside every archive." And the artistic act of creating an analogical field through assembly can facilitate and support the drive to engage that constellation. It can also "light up the space between memory and the absence of memory, between useful data and the undifferentiated magma of raw information." This is analogy both in spite of and because of digital abundance.

The point of placing Silverman's reading alongside Fontcuberta's is not to say that one person is wrong and the other is right. Instead, it is to do exactly what the work poses, which is zoom in and out from one practical and interpretive possibility to another, precisely the kind of potential that can open in the "analogizing in spite of all" of a massive digital visual assembly. Adopting the closer myopic view, for instance, there is the power of assembly-based analogy in a plural reading of a photomosaic's constituents, such as the images Fontcuberta derived from the search terms associated with knowledge and conversation (Figure 2.5). Encountering such an as-

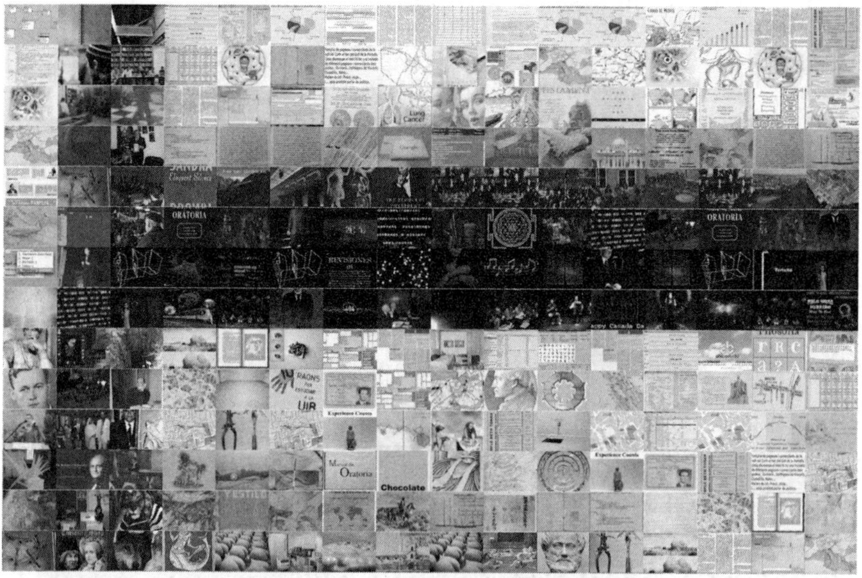

Figure 2.5. A detail of a subset of the constituent photographs, algorithmically compiled from across the internet, making up Joan Fontcuberta's *Googlegram: Guantánamo,* 2006. Courtesy of the artist.

sembly in person (or in zoomable form online), the viewer comes into relation with individual faces, texts, images, and words, as well as provisional and almost entirely purely imagined, but no less interesting, connections between those images. These imagined connections are important, because they assert the value of plural interpretation in an age both beset by echo chambers and brimming with analogical potential.

Adopting the wider hyperopic perspective, however, there is what is embodied in the photomosaic these constituents produce, which is an interrogation cell at a site of indefinite imprisonment and lack of due process: the U.S. military prison at Guantánamo Bay (Figure 2.6). Far from a field for generative recombination, the full image is (from a perspective possible within the United States, anyway) a vision of powerless participation in an economy of images that often works in the service of violence, oppression, and injustice. It is as though the self, in shifting perspective from the chaotic subassemblies to the whole image, had transformed from agential constituent and interpreter into confused and complicit pixel. The

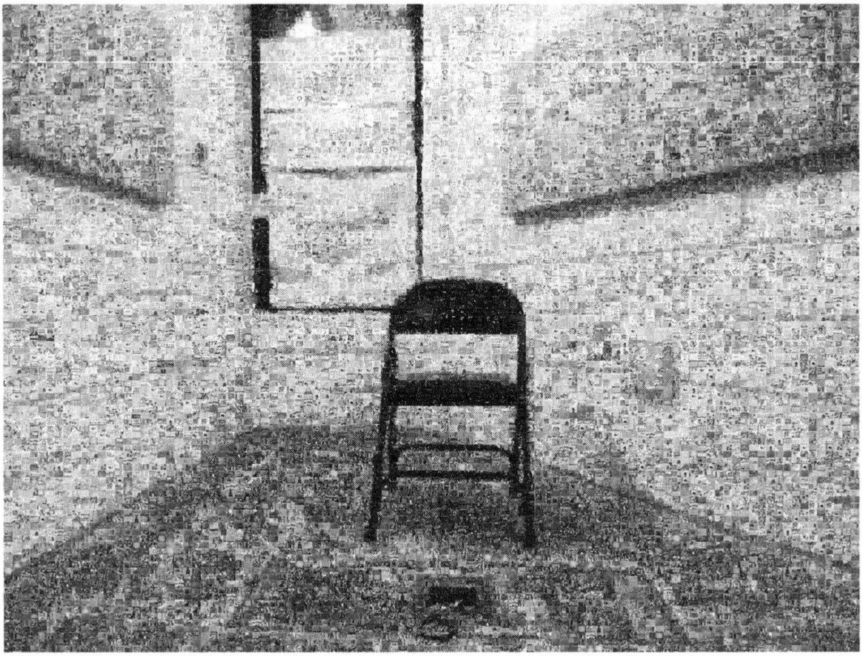

Figure 2.6. Full view of Joan Fontcuberta's *Googlegram: Guantánamo,* 2006. Interrogation cell at Guantánamo secret U.S. detention center. The photograph has been refashioned using photomosaic freeware linked to Google's image-searching function. The final result is a composite of ten thousand images available on the internet that corresponded to the following words as search criteria: "curiosity," "knowledge," "wisdom," "philosophy," "research," "erudition," "culture," "oratory," "eloquence," "chat," and "gossip." Courtesy of the artist.

assembly-based analogizing in Googlegrams thus speaks to the contradictions of media abundance, both the dramatic potential for unexpected kinship and the constant problems of conflation, division, amnesia, and denial. One can readily imagine analogous images built with the image results for other key terms: border, wall, *la linea,* migrant, United States, Mexico.

In their facilitation of unexpected links, projects of analogy could be accused of overriding difference or creating false equivalences. But these are risks rather than premises of this kind of aesthetic work. Done well, done thoughtfully and generatively, analogical assembly can gather shared problems; it can materialize kernels of correspondence; it can take what is otherwise overlooked and make it into the stuff of new (or newly recovered) life and thought. Whether confronting the violence and the complexity of borders, navigating the archival noise of contemporary image economies, or addressing still other concerns, to do analogical assembly well is to maintain serious attention to actual (or, in the case of borders, enforced) differences while also risking the assertion of unseen overlaps and enduring correspondences. Avoid collapsing the two—or the two hundred or the two million—into one. But also avoid making actual kinship into none.

To Reconstitute, or Deterritorialization and Reterritorialization

Assembly doesn't just name a type of artifact; it also names something people do across widely varying scales. This means that any sufficiently inclusive typology of art as assembly must expand to include practices and projects that rely on the form, partly or fully, but that do so beyond the level of the single artwork. The typology must even extend to practices that don't require the production of artworks as such, as with uses of media assembly in and as museum-directed activism.

For different reasons, such as chance, proximity, and resonance, I find three projects converging along these lines. The first of these appeared at the de Young Museum in San Francisco in 2019. Called *Specters of Disruption,* it began as an inquiry into the museum's copious holdings, many of them artworks but many not, including a wide array of objects taken from colonized peoples. Involving tens of thousands of objects, and thus not feasible without digital tools, newly arrived curator Claudia Schmuckli performed this inquiry "with an eye toward identifying patterns that would suggest a storyline within an institutional subconscious." Finding many such patterns, the challenge became editing them "into a presentation that wasn't topical or reductive, but discursive and expansive."[55] Schmuckli answered by selecting and arranging ninety-eight objects, many of them never previously shown at the museum, including a newly acquired video installation by Carrie Mae Weems called *Lincoln, Lonnie, and Me–A Story in 5 Parts.* Huey Copeland describes the installation as "framing American history as a racialized theater of deadly repetition," serving to explore "both the tragedies of the past and the ways in which their farcical returns might be negotiated."[56] In arranging the assembly into five rooms, Schmuckli engaged in what Copeland refers to as a constant spiraling and "looping back." Here those loops and spirals turned around the theme of disruption, which Schmuckli cast as "a foggy business signifier that has become synonymous with Silicon Valley, deep within the natural, topographical, cultural, and mythological fabric of the Bay Area."[57]

The second example is also an exhibition, but it is one that emerged on the internet in 2020: *Well Now WTF?* Faced with the shutdown of physical art worlds due to the Covid-19 pandemic, curators Faith Holland, Lorna Mills, and Wade Wallerstein commissioned "multiple generations of net artists" to produce work in a format that "has the capacity to hold vast complexity and persist despite varying network protocols," the animated GIF (Graphics Interchange Format). The GIFs were media constituents in frantic permutation: virus, blast, virus again, phone, moon; a computer chip exploding into a cloud of hot dogs; surveilled subjects become computer-drawn lines then dollar signs. The "rooms" housing these GIFs carried titles that spoke to discord, disarray, discomfort, and distraction in a world beset by suffering, ineptitude, and disinformation: "The Clean Room," "Bed of Nails," "Stay Home and Masturbate," "Clusterfuck Closet," "Pants Optional," "So Sad Because the Art Fairs Were Cancelled," "Washing Your Fucking Hands," "In These Indoor Times," "Burn It Down," "Deep Dark Gem Corner," "Kiss Me I'm Asymptomatic," and "Zoom Link Plz." As is evident, the point was not to offer a solution to the troubles of the pandemic. Rather, the curators saw their work as "a net art reclamation" aimed at, among other things, "re-connecting the communities that got separated by time, distance, and filter bubbles."

The last example likewise emerged during the pandemic, but it was neither an artwork nor an exhibition. It was a movement trained on the museum that holds *Verb List,* the Museum of Modern Art (MoMA). Called Strike MoMA (or Strike ~~MoMA~~), the project had, at the time of writing, two iterations, first as a series of protests and other actions against the museum in its current form, then as a period of conversation and planning around further actions and the future of the institution. The project's core aim was "disassembling" and abolishing MoMA, doing so "in light of its harmful history."[58]

At one level, these projects share in the relational power of assembly. Although it did include works like El Anatsui's fabric made of bottle caps and copper wire *(Hovor II)*, the dimension of assembly in *Specters* was not a matter of gathering works that themselves embody this cultural form. Rather, the use of assembly in *Specters* was a "transhistorical" (or even nonhistorical or critically anachronistic[59]) mode that reaches back to the early-modern *Kunstkammer* ("art chamber") or "cabinet of curiosities," as well as to certain "modernist display trends," in which avant-garde works were displayed "together with objects coming from non-Western cultures belonging to different historic periods, a procedure that was soon naturalized and served various agendas."[60] And yet it was also, like a spate of recent exhibitions, more reflexive and intentional than the modernist precedent, a distinct deemphasizing of "historiographical concerns in favour of thematic or formal ones," and it relied on arts of selection and arrangement in the process.[61] *Well Now WTF?* joined *Specters* in working in the mode of adventurous consolidation and display, but it specifically took an assembly-laden format (the GIF) and made it into the means for permutations of configural incorporation, with no work quite standing on its own. The online exhibition also made the distributed gathering of people—the artists in question physically set apart by the pandemic and the larger community of net artists—into a driving theme. Finally, Strike MoMA might not have produced or curated art as such, but it repeatedly worked at the union of media and political assembly. It did so through its actions (media assembly supporting political assembly). It also did so through a consistent release of content through social media, presenting an unfolding assembly of messages, many of them assembly-infused and meme-like in their appearance and tone. Among other things, these posts emphasized strategies and aphorisms (e.g., "your network is your net worth"), pointed to the harmful investments of board members, recalled intersecting histories of oppression and liberation, and satirized certain political practices deemed ineffective.

But these projects also bear meaningful family resemblances beyond their basis in assembly. This becomes apparent in moving through what is a network of "patterns and persistences" rather than the repetition of a single, shared essence. Consider, for a start, one of many subassemblies within *Specters* (Figure 2.7). In some

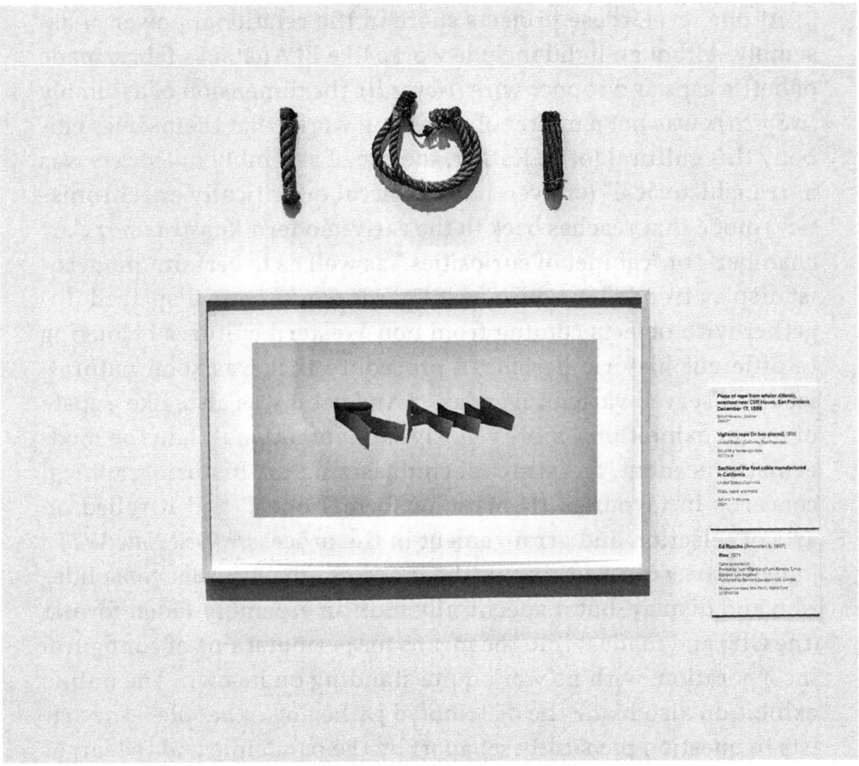

Figure 2.7. Installation view of *Specters of Disruption,* de Young Museum, San Francisco, August 15, 2018, through November 10, 2019. Constituent 1: Edward Ruscha, *Raw,* 1971. Color screenprint: sheet = 407 × 661 mm (16 × 26 inches); image = 276 × 546 mm (10 7⁄8 × 21 1⁄2 inches). Printed by Jean Milant and Fumi Kaneko, Cirrus Editions, Los Angeles. Published by Bernard Jacobson Ltd., London / Fine Arts Museums of San Francisco, museum purchase, Mrs. Paul L. Wattis Fund, 2000.131.50. Constituent 2: Vigilante rope (in two pieces), 1856, San Francisco, California, United States. Fine Arts Museums of San Francisco, gift of Mrs. Vanderlynn Stow. 50731a–b. Constituent 3: Piece of rope from the *Atlantic* (whaling vessel), wrecked near Cliff House, San Francisco, December 17, 1886. Rope, 15 × 2 cm (5 7⁄8 × 13⁄16 inches). Fine Arts Museums of San Francisco, gift of Horace L. Crocker. 38353.1. Constituent 4: Section of first cable manufactured in California, United States. Rope, wood, and metal, 12 × 2.5 cm (4 3⁄4 × 1 inch). Fine Arts Museums of San Francisco, gift of C P. Wilcomb. 26011. Photography: Randy Dodson. Copyright Fine Arts Museums of San Francisco.

ways arranged like one might expect (on a white wall, with labels nearby), this is still a surprising configuration: a trio of pieces of rope with one from a whaling boat wrecked off the coast of San Francisco in 1886, one labeled a "Vigilante rope (in two pieces)," and one labeled a "section of the first cable manufactured in California." Into this assembly of de Young holdings, Schmuckli has incorporated another artifact, not an anonymous one but a named artwork by a famous artist, Ed Ruscha. This piece is likewise made up of three elements: a trio of reposed and uneven letters composing the titular word RAW.

Faced with this unusual aggregation, configured by it into a mode of "encounter that opens up new critical relations," those scanning its constituents and positions can find themselves presented with a range of visual-tactile impressions: *to coil, to turn, to tighten, to twist.*[62] They can also ponder material analogies with other objects within the show, from the bulbous hanging wire of Ruth Asawa to the aforementioned work by El Anatsui. But the most important interpretive vector here takes a cue from the curator's framing. The room is titled "From Gold Mining to Data Mining," and its wall text speaks to histories of extraction and the forced (and often deadly) removal of Indigenous and Mexican peoples in the region now known as California. With these histories in mind, one can read the subassembly for the dynamic in question, what I call "to reconstitute." In this version of the dynamic, there is an effort to use the familiar, sanctioned practice of curating to make these histories at least partly present again, but in a different way, relying on the assembly of material parts, fusing histories often kept apart, and introducing the provocative addition of the Ruscha piece. María Íñigo Clavo and Olga Fernández López call this "the association of artworks, artefacts, and material culture belonging to different contexts, times or social spheres in a new epistemological, contemporary framework," an association that helps question dominant narratives while also creating a "deepened" and "more complex sense of transhistoricity."[63]

The expressive consequences are several. For one thing, while the trio of ropes echo exhibits in a courtroom, they also speak to the intersections and overlaps of the worlds that brought them into being. Commerce (the whaling boat) worked in conjunction with state-sanctioned citizen policing and genocide (the vigilante rope, the extrajudicial use of which would have been supported by the deceptively named Act for the Government and Protection of Indians) and the infrastructures of colonial modernity (the cable) to enable white settlers, as the wall texts emphasize, to "mercilessly" force Indigenous and Mexican people off their lands. Meanwhile, the ironically fabricated and oddly reposed "raw" seems to verbally reconstitute—not intrinsically but in this assembled context—a premise of a right to extract the materials (or indeed the people perceived as) "below," awaiting use. The artwork also implicitly incorporates the images of Western expansion eventually proffered out of Ruscha's adopted home of Los Angeles, the way these images have long worked to sanitize, justify, and erase the very events in which the three objects played a part (and that cleared the way for the historically white-dominated culture industries of southern California). It is not that Schmuckli and her collaborators have narrated something that hasn't been narrated by anyone else, nor have they represented something that hasn't been represented before (silences, gaps, and erasures notwithstanding). Rather, they have fused undertold stories and undercirculated representations with a novel assembly: they have offered a memorable materialization of "entrenched historical presumptions" in suggestive configuration within a museum directly connected to these histories.[64] This stood to help generate (one hopes) necessary thoughts, more emphatic associations, enduring reassessment, and yet further possible connections.

Looking outward into other subassemblies in the exhibition, the work of reconstitution in response to the contradictory valences of disruption took numerous other forms, including a moment in which a woven microchip sits alongside a religious vision of life force, seeming to gesture toward rich discussions around what Michelle Raheja calls "imagining indigenous digital futures."[65] Another instructive instance was an oblique pairing. On the one side was Thornton Dial's 2004 *New Light*, an assemblage of fence and wire recalling the arrival of electric power in his hometown of Emelle, Alabama, in the late 1930s. On the other side was Thomas Cole's 1847 *Prometheus Bound*: a rendering of Prometheus bound by Zeus for gifting fire and knowledge to humans, a work apparently encoded with a hidden abolitionist message (Figure 2.8).

Knowing the divergent backgrounds of these artists, one could

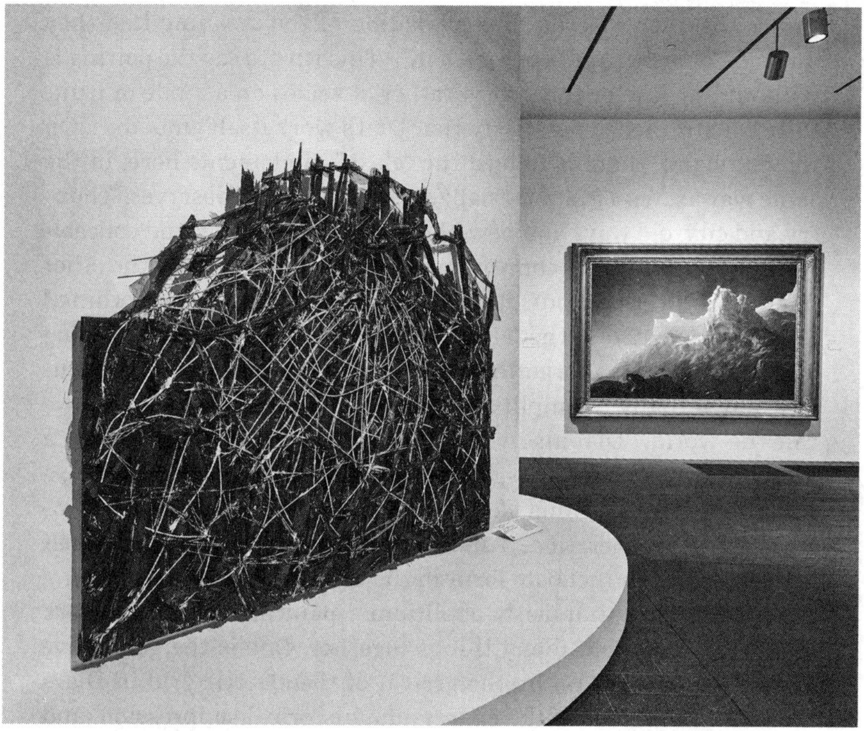

Figure 2.8. Installation view of *Specters of Disruption,* de Young Museum, San Francisco, August 15, 2018, through November 10, 2019. Constituent 1: Thornton Dial, *New Light,* 2004. Wood, wire, twine, caning, cloth, wire screen, cow bone, enamel, and Splash Zone compound on wood, 81 ½ × 94 × 8 inches (207 × 238.8 × 20.3 cm). Fine Arts Museums of San Francisco, museum purchase, American Art Trust Fund, and gift of the Souls Grown Deep Foundation from the William S. Arnett Collection. 2017.1.15. Constituent 2: Thomas Cole, *Prometheus Bound,* 1847. Oil on canvas, 64 × 96 inches (162.6 × 243.8 cm). Fine Arts Museums of San Francisco, museum purchase, gift of Mr. and Mrs. Steven MacGregor Read and Joyce I. Swader Bequest Fund. 1997.28. Photography: Randy Dodson. Copyright Fine Arts Museums of San Francisco.

easily see strict binaries here: outsider–insider, Black–white, folk–fine. But such a response would embody a blunter mode of assembling, what Jacques Rancière characterizes as the "junction of elements that is supposed to create a clash" and thus spur recognition. As with the assembly of ropes and "RAW," the mode of reconstitution here is more fractal and open-ended; it is "a way of putting things together with no presupposition of the meaning that they must make by being made together."[66] This isn't to say the pairing is without purpose or trajectory; rather, it seizes on a mode of fruitfully constrained generativity that Dial's work itself embodies. On the one hand, there is indeed the "clash" of elements here, in the same way as *New Light* materializes, as Paul Arnett observes, "country and city, old ways and new, the fence of separation and concealment and the wires of connection and illumination."[67] On the other hand, as Fred Moten puts it in an essay on "coming from nothing," Dial is committed to the "eloquence of things," and in assembling many things, often forgotten or neglected things, he is able "visually and verbally to amplify the macrophonic assemblage that we call the world." Dial also works, according to Moten, to make "a kind of uncut imaginative generativity that studies generativity; a generativity of the thing, *de re,* that is inseparable from its degeneration and regeneration." And in this way, part of what can be felt and generated in inchoate form in the encounter with this pairing of an allegorical, implicitly abolitionist painting and Dial's work is not one thing but many things together. One is the generative disruption brought on by the arrival of the electric grid in Dial's hometown. Another is the expression, historical suppression, and ongoing risk of what Moten calls, in a phrase as seemingly relevant to Dial as to Black Twitter, "the anarchic principle of creativity in exhaustion."[68] In short, to reconstitute isn't only to recover, but to unmake and remake, toward hard-won realignment and rebirth.

Particularly as one considers the insistently material and museal qualities in the Dial–Cole pairing, the idea that reconstitution takes place across not just the subassemblies of *Specters* but all three projects I have cited can seem all the stranger. But *Specters* isn't assembly-based and assembly-infused reconstitution in its final form; it is but one version in a web of possibility. What *is* binding for this dynamic is the work of breaking down and remaking the constituent elements of something, whether by means of aesthetic (and aestheticized) objects, looping GIFs, or performative action. And an integral means of doing so is the hazarding of novel and often provocative configurations of constituents, configurations that seize on the "interconnectivity between what once was and what is yet to come."[69]

Part of what makes the example of Strike MoMA so relevant here is the way it expands the sense of what that interconnectivity can entail and achieve. Art-centered, assembly-based reconstitution can be about the past; it can be about the past in the present; it can also be about the future in the present and the future beyond the present. Strike MoMA exercised assembly (and other tactics) as a means of taking things further, of asking how things might yet be arranged. In other words, the disruptive and coconstructive gatherings that made (and make) up the movement do not settle on just one set of alternative arrangements (such as forcing a reconstitution of the board of the museum, which is insufficient for this project), but on multiple contexts in which different or overlooked or new constituents (and relations between constituents) take on new life, rebalancing power, redistributing resources, changing the shape of this museum and of art more broadly. As a fusion of media and popular assembly, a thematic list on the Strike MoMA website provides a rich example of these intersections. After a sequence of negative statements—the things the movement refuses—the list shifts to a sequence of affirmatives: "Yes to partisans of art. Yes to art embedded in the culture of movements. Yes to aesthetics rooted in struggle. Yes to art for its own sake, if that means we are down with creating and conspiring to get free, whatever our style, school, or medium." The list then moves to a heterogeneous list of constituent players. There are those who make up art: "Meme-makers and abstract painters, monument topplers and postmodern sculptors, designers of banners and drawers of lines, unpopular musicians and obscure sound artists, live-streamers and cinephiles, war-dancers and pole-dancers, dream-diviners and archive-searchers." There also those who refuse to take part: "critique-ers of institutions and those who never recognized the institution in the first place. Artists of all kinds that do not recognize such distinctions in their life and work." As is evident here, Strike MoMA is absolutely about the mode of disruptive protest, but it is also about using differing modes of media assembly to reconstitute aesthetic and social worlds.

The GIFs of *Well Now WTF?* echo the disruptive orientations in Strike MoMA's acts of reconstitution, but they also point to the intensification of other modes, allowing the irreverent and the serious to coexist in looping visuals (Plate 9). Humorous but heartfelt, the name of the exhibition says that something is going on where the whole world is in question. And the intractable and yet engaging GIFs suggest something runs ahead of us and behind us, out of reach and yet right there, a shock: "What the fuck?" Part of the notion is that art might be rethought and that now dormant net art practices and networks could be reconstituted in the wake of the pandemic. A further notion is that effectively everything can be rethought and remade. Indeed, for a theorization of assembly as reconstitution, the project looks like a generative provocation toward reconsidering the terms and premises through which one undertakes just about anything, not because it is fundamentally good (or profitable) to disrupt, as might be imagined in Silicon Valley, but because, as Wendy Hui Kyong Chun observes, the homogenizing and atomizing technologies of that place have made "true disruption" both increasingly elusive and increasingly necessary.[70]

Incorporating new lens elements into the lens of media assembly will allow me to take up the implicit call of *Well Now WTF?* with respect to reconstitution. In this case, what proves most useful is a set of elements from the world of theories of assemblage, what Gilles Deleuze and Félix Guattari call "deterritorialization" and "reterritorialization."[71] As Manuel DeLanda explains, if the broad notion of "agencement" or assemblage is the idea that one can construe all manner of individual entities as interactions among heterogeneous components (from books to whole societies), and if given assemblages are almost always themselves components of larger ones, then the notion of territorialization names the relative homogeneity or heterogeneity of those components. In other words, to quote DeLanda, "territorialization" refers "not only to the determination of the spatial boundaries of a whole—as in the territory of a community, city, or nation-state—but also to the degree to which an assemblage's component parts are drawn from a homogeneous repertoire, or the degree to which an assemblage homogenises its own components."[72] Assemblages that draw from quite homogeneous sets of components are highly territorialized. So too are assemblages that enforce uniform relations or positions among their otherwise heterogeneous components. Deterritorialization is a process through which the homogeneity of components (and of their interactions) is variously contested or even destroyed. And reterritorialization is a process of reclaiming or reworking existing territorializations.

Seen through this hybrid lens of media assembly and de/re/territorialization, the work of reconstitution across these projects appears in a new light. Take *Specters.* In its efforts to reconstitute histories of disruption by way of assembly, the exhibition puts into practice contradictory processes. The process of *territorialization* is the routine maintenance of the homogeneous relations of the institution by way of an exhibit that adheres to the norms of the museum. (The objects carry standardized descriptions. Museum staff conceive and execute the exhibition. In mounting this exhibition, as any other, the museum affirms its nonnatural right to maintain authority over the land on which it sits.) The process of *deterritorialization* is the upheaval of the institution's typical arrangements of its histories and self-identifications by way of the aesthetic reconstitution of its artifacts. (Although much of the "museum methodology and classification system" is maintained, there is still a shift in its focal subject matters, and there is still a commitment to reassembly that "cuts right through the constraints of time, space, culture, and geography"[73] while also addressing disruptive and destructive histories.) Finally, the process of *reterritorialization* is projective and potential. The show that situates the museum and its region in a complex history of foggy disruption is potentially the show that points the way toward meaningful structural change. There could be alterations of the constitution and functioning of the overall institution, as well as of that institution's relation to local communities. There could even be, in Hito Steyerl's words, a seed of resistance to the well-worn fact of museums as "instruments for prolonging stasis by preserving the tyranny of a partial, partisan history" and a glimmer of how museums can instead help reassemble "the future of public space, the future of art, and the future as such."[74]

While I haven't seen evidence that such reterritorialization occurred in the wake of *Specters,* the exhibition's emphasis on reimagination moves me to consider something akin to what Ariella Aïsha Azoulay (an active participant in Strike MoMA) calls "potential history," which is to say potentials for reconstitution and reterritorialization that were dormant or proximate. No doubt, one of these (which Azoulay might well support, and which I, too, see as ultimately necessary) is to find ways to relinquish and redirect the colonial wealth to which *Specters* directly refers. Another is a partial analogue for those actions that was, at the time of writing, made available by local organizations, including the Sogorea Te' Land Trust. A women-led urban collective that "facilitates the return of Indigenous land to Indigenous people," the group made one of its central projects a land tax across the water from the de Young in the East Bay.[75] Similar to land taxes in other settler colonial contexts, the Shuumi Land Tax is "a voluntary annual contribution that non-Indigenous people living on traditional Lisjan Ohlone territory make." These funds support Sogorea Te's work of "rematriation, returning Indigenous land to Indigenous people, establishing a cemetery to reinter stolen Ohlone ancestral remains and building urban gardens, community centers, and ceremonial spaces so current and future generations of Indigenous people can thrive in the Bay Area." For the de Young, the land tax would not be Shuumi (a Chochenyo word that translates as "gift") but Yunakin (meaning "village") for the Ramaytush Ohlone, whose ancestral lands are the San Francisco Peninsula. Such a payment by the museum, or by the museum in conjunction with its non-Indigenous visitors, is one concrete possibility for reterritorialization in response to the histories of extraction it assembles. A far cry from ceding land, capital, and property, the land tax would nevertheless serve to acknowledge and contest, at least in part, longstanding colonial relationships and habits. In the language of art as assembly, this is a matter of welcoming a disruptive constituent into the mix, an addition to the overall configuration that not only forces a new view on the arrangement but also materially alters what that arrangement yields.

Although it might echo a gesture of institutional revision in this vein, the deterritorialization and reterritorialization enacted by Strike MoMA is more difficult, forceful, and intersectional. The dissident assembly involves a multiweek mapping of the many-faceted process of dismantling MoMA, including divestment, asset transfer, the redistribution of properties, "reparations, rematriations, and Indigenous land restoration," and a way to provide for the "just transition of workers to cooperative self-management and solidarity economies." At the heart of these acts of visionary convening is a demand first (in terms the movement does not, as far as I am aware, use) to deterritorialize—"we extract our imagination from its orbit, our energies, resources and labor power"—then critically reterritorialize in turn. And this is done with the ultimate goal of a MoMA whose component parts and interrelations are not monocultural and hierarchical, but heterogeneous and horizontal, "controlled by workers and communities, not billionaires and their enablers." Viewed through the lens of assembly, Strike MoMA exemplifies a radical and repeatable method for assembly-based and assembly-infused efforts at reconstitution and reterritorialization. The lifeblood of this method is uncompromising demands for dramatic reterritorialization of both one museum and the ideology of the museum in general, with these demands pursued through disruptive assembly in multiple hybrid forms. And yet this does not mean that art or houses for aesthetic display and debate must fall away. In this approach, as in the recuperative irony of *Well Now WTF?,* reconstitution and reterritorialization remain vital, plural, disruptive, and playful. Couched in a critically affirmative mode, movements to radically reconstitute like Strike MoMA are visions of "actions to relate," not to oneself, but to many others (and many other institutions and communities and publics) engaged in analogous and interlocking projects across the planet, from Puerto Rico to Palestine and beyond.

It is well worth asking where else efforts at assembly-based and assembly-infused reconstitution might go. One compelling avenue is under discussion in the book *The Constituent Museum.* Here the central problem is how the museum might be reconstituted as relations rather than objects. As Yaiza Hernández Vélazquez puts it, this is "collective task of committing to a constituent process without claiming any authority over it, an assembly from below that slowly undoes the one that stands above."[76] The museum in this mode is not about audiences and top-down exhibitions, but the interplay of active constituents. Such a museum is not centered on a building, but as Raúl Sánchez Cedillo puts it, "a network of practices, affinities and encounters."[77] The constituent museum comes into being and sustains itself "on the basis of the promises [museums] have broken and not those they have kept."[78] And it makes of those promises the work of connecting, serving to encourage and enable the "joining of lives through knotting, weaving and binding."[79] As the ropes, GIFs, and protests I've gathered here attest, such connective work is by no means easy or guaranteed, nor is it always desired. Perhaps aesthetic assembly in the reconstituting mode can offer a means of testing out exactly these risky and contested approximations of museums (and anti-museums) in a new key.

Of Basalt, To Decarbonize

Art is not a "magic bullet" capable of reorganizing "our critical and moral faculties without effort," writes Olivia Laing. "It's work. What art does is provide material with which to think: new registers, new spaces. After that, friend, it's up to you."[80] Among the richest materials aesthetic assembly can provide are those that arrive as disruptive constituents, or what Arlette Farge, in a passage on archival research, calls "distracting documents" that are "breaths of fresh air," the things that defy the "preselected field" and are "gossipy, suggestive, or just different."[81]

Static artworks are one context for such assembly-based disruption. As though shifting a conversation, a once marginal or unseen element of the work offers an affect or an impression that runs against those already in play, making for a more lively and intensive experience or interpretation than had existed a moment before. In the contexts of open-ended and participatory works, new constituents arrive to disrupt the existing interpretive or perceptual order. Sometimes these disruptions are quite visible, as in Douglas Davis's *The World's First Collaborative Sentence* (an early internet-based project that is exactly as it sounds). Other times the disruptions work in unrecognizable, aggregate fashion, as in a piece by Ian Cheng centered on a snake-like algorithmic consciousness called *BOB (Bag of Beliefs),* whose movements shift based on the contributions of the distributed assembly of participants, trying to give precooked offerings of sentiments to the mercurial BOB. And still other times, as in the movements to contest and rework the accumulated wealth and hegemony of art museums, it is a flood of interconnected disruptions—actions, ideas, and movements—that aims to politically and perceptually overwhelm.

Plural reading is likewise subject to such generative intrusions. Newly introduced terms and ideas make for unexpected questions. Additions to the suite of examples suggest an unexpected constellation, the opening of new registers and new spaces. As a case in point, as I consider how to close this chapter, I look back at Serra's list, and I find the second to last entry seizes my attention: "of car-

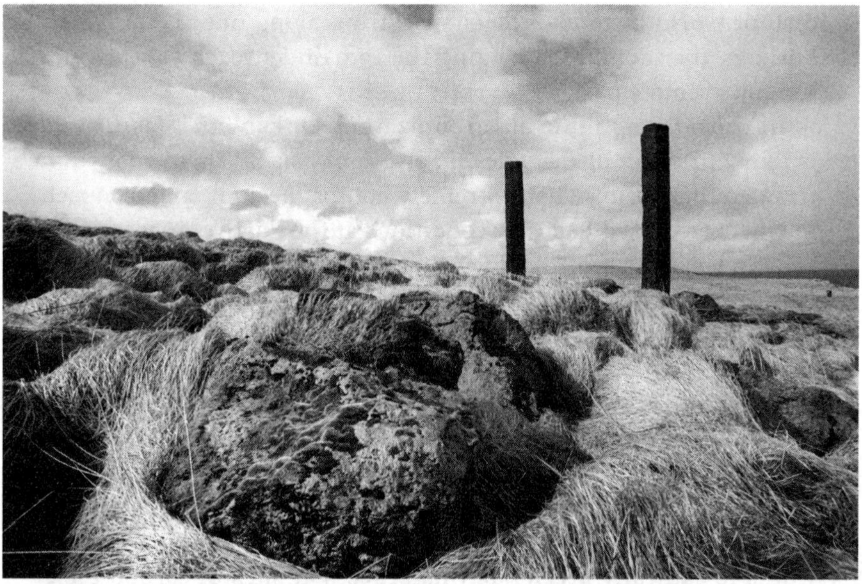

Figure 2.9. A document of Richard Serra's configuration of paired basalt columns on an island off Reykjavík, Iceland. Dirk Reinartz, "Richard Serra, Afangar, Island." Copyright Estate of Dirk Reinartz. Courtesy Galerie m, Bochum, Germany.

bonization." What Serra is referring to is the process by which organic materials are transformed into carbon or a carbon-containing residue, as in the production of charcoal and fossil fuels. In an insightful essay that likewise draws inspiration from *Verb List,* Lynne Cooke is also drawn to the term, linking carbonization with Serra's response to a 1988 commission by the Icelandic state.[82] For what would come to be called *Áfangar,* meaning a stopping point or a stage in a journey, Serra proposed to partly alter the landscape of a small island near Reykjavík called Viðey (Figure 2.9). "Onto this historic ground," Cooke summarizes, Serra "introduced nine pairs of basalt columns in a loose circle that rings the coast and straddles the narrow isthmus."[83] Because Viðey's protected status precluded any mining, the basalt pieces were drawn from elsewhere. As much a distributed apparition as a rocky engine of perception, the mineral constellation serves to quietly intensify viewers' experiences of the already transformative place. In Cooke's words, the "coupled elements" function as "portals through which viewers scan the distant world beyond—the city nestling along one sector of the horizon, the mountains ringing the remainder, each evocative of Iceland's remote past."[84]

In considering how "of carbonization" links with *Áfangar,* one is likely to think of the volcanic origin of basalt. This widely distributed rock forms when extremely hot magnesium- and iron-rich magma is exposed to cooler conditions at the Earth's surface, typically in the deep sea.[85] And yet there are other, more urgent links. Based only some 30 km from *Áfangar,* a business venture called Carbfix was, as of 2020, a business venture aimed at mitigating the effects of global warming.[86] Under the right conditions, basaltic rocks will naturally undergo carbonization, meaning they will form solid carbonate substances through reactions with carbon-containing gases and liquids. Seeking to sequester carbon in a solid state (as opposed to confining it in gas form in deep chambers that can leak, a method favored by the oil and gas industries), Carbfix works to radically accelerate this process at sites of carbon dioxide emission, with the geothermal Hellisheiði Power Station as the original test location. Tim Smedley explains: "Waste CO2 is captured from the power plant's steam, is dissolved into large volumes of water and injected into the basalt below." The basalt comes to look "like a black sponge, filled with air holes that the CO2 settles in" and with which it "forms calcite—or mineralized carbon—within just hundreds of days, not hundreds of thousands of years."[87]

The hope is that this sequestration process can be widely applied. At the same time, the Carbfix project is also not free from skepticism. There are questions about the quantities of water required, the availability of basalt, and the dangers of seismic activity that injection can induce. More incisively, there is concern that carbon sequestration distracts from the root causes of the climate emergency, serving to grease rather than interrupt the extractive logics that perpetuate the impacts of fossil-fuel economies.[88] My reasons for invoking it by way of conclusion are neither to criticize nor to champion this form of sequestration as such. (Efforts at mitigation, however helpful in the short term, cannot replace the coconstruction of just and livable "mutual relation" at a planetary scale, a condition of actual, sustained, equitable thriving that violently market-dominated political economies cannot and will not deliver.[89]) Rather, I find that two important things emerge for this book's theory of assembly when *Áfangar* and the practice of corrective carbonization come into contact.

The first is a provocation toward a revision of this chapter's typology. In using Serra's *Verb List* as my departure point, I have argued it performs an open-ended gesture toward the realm of the artistically possible. However, lingering on the material fact of basalt air holes filling with calcite, I am pushed to think yet further. While Serra's list is open-ended, it is also layered, and one of the most important layers is an insistence, time and again, on material processes, from folding and creasing to shaving, hooking, felting, tightening, wrapping, hinging, and diluting. From where I sit, this emphasis in Serra's assembly (and across his career) serves to provoke questions of redirection. Could it be that this typology is overly weighted toward the visual and the verbal? What would an emphatically material dynamic of assembly involve? For initial answers to these questions, one could look to artistic practices in which, as Wu Hung puts it, generic, natural, and artificial materials are "'adopted' by artists, given agency, and become their private means of making art over a significant period of time." Such was the case in an exhibition at the Los Angeles County Museum of Art in 2019 and 2020 called *The Allure of Matter: Material Art from China.* In moving through the exhibition, it was often difficult to disentangle the constituents of the many works that seized on assembly, as in a pile of paper fragments by Huang Yong Ping that engages in direct disfiguration of art historical taxonomies, *The History of Chinese Art and A Concise History of Modern Painting Washed in a Washing Machine for Two Minutes.*[90]

The other thing that emerges between *Áfangar* and carbonization is not conceptual, but political and ecological. More than situated near the ocean, the work is keyed to it, as among the choices Serra made in arraying the columns was to set all but one at the same elevation: 10 meters above sea level. As greenhouse gas emissions persist at catastrophically high rates, the global average sea level creeps ever higher. In Iceland, rising sea levels have been observed in certain areas (including Reykjavík), but the country has also seen another consequence of global warming known as postglacial uplift. The melting of glaciers—the island now loses billions of tons of ice each year—means a tremendous reduction in mass and therefore a lifting of the land. The future is unknown: the basalt columns could remain well above the ocean, or they could eventually become subject to its reach. Either way, they will continue to be bound up with the effects of climate change.[91]

Perhaps this relationship between an artwork and an unfolding disaster can be understood to embody a demand for reversal. While companies like Carbfix continue to explore measures to mitigate the effects of carbon-based industries, more and more entities, from activist collectives to cultural institutions to states, small businesses, corporations, and consortia, must add something to their own implicit lists of actions and themes: decarbonization. At issue here is a different kind of carbonization: the profit-driven entrenchment of systemic reliance on fossil fuels across many human societies. Historically speaking, carbonization began to take hold in the century before Denis wrote on color; it picked up steam over and above an artist composing an alternative typology in the late 1960s; and it continues through to the reterritorializing movements of the 2020s. Carbonization has been global; its effects are radically widespread; and the internet by no means portends a magical release from its operations and effects, given the reliance of networked machines on carbon-intensive mining and manufacturing, not to mention energy production via coal and natural gas.[92] At the same time, the distribution of carbonization's negative effects has been far from even, disproportionately impacting poor, Black/Indigenous/People of Color and global-south communities.

How exactly could safe and equitable decarbonization unfold? By what means could the grip of the industries that pushed carbonization be loosened or severed? What would it take, as Ben Tarnoff puts it, to simultaneously "decarbonize and democratize the internet"?[93] These are not questions that any single artwork or museum exhibition can or should answer. And yet, through mobilizing the available means of communication, expression, and provocation in art and beyond, and through reworking the available indexes of artistic options, the many constituents of art worlds can help to augment the expressive and imaginative resources available to those who strive for intersectional climate justice. While museums have begun to divest from fossil fuels (whether in good faith or begrudgingly), artists and art collectives have begun to fuse methods of assembly-based and assembly-infused art-making with demands to decarbonize and conjectures around the shapes that alternatives might take, or already do. Among the key drives for a theory of art qua assembly is to provide further scaffolding and impetus toward such undertakings, whether through analogy, reconstitution, or still other vectors of artistic possibility. As the next chapter will show, the need for this work has become all the more urgent as memes and other highly portable engines of perception command increasing quantities of sight and mind.

3

Memes, Assembly, and the Internet

To many people in the early 2020s, memes are funny images with a bit of text on them. These kinds of images don't just pop up on your social media feeds occasionally. They're always there. Maybe you scroll past most of them, but maybe there are also some that end up earning a pause, either because they make you (literally) laugh out loud or because they're relatable, or maybe just because they gather a thought you've had but never quite expressed (much less memed). From this presently quite common perspective, in other words, memes are best understood as little packages of connection. They're humorous pictures quickly shared to grab some likes and comments, not likely to yield much in the way of critical inquiry.

For another (and maybe somewhat smaller) subset of people, there's a partial truth in that perspective, but to treat image memes as the be all and end all of memes would do a major disservice.[1] Take, for instance, that thing people do when they trick someone into clicking on a link to a ridiculous eighties music video in which a man in a trench coat insists he will never give you up—when people "rickroll" each other. Or that old trend in which one person after another laid themselves flat on odd spots like street signs and fast-food counters, or "planked." Or that obsession with the Shiba Inu dog/"Doge" who managed to become the face of a type of cryptocurrency. In each of these cases and thousands more, including many that didn't go mainstream, what was going on was not the sharing of an amusing combination of words and images. It was the suddenly (and sometimes enduringly) popular reworking of a theme, format, action, or idea.

One of the first academics to take memes seriously, Limor Shifman, helps put language to what is going on here. For Shifman, a meme isn't an individual piece of media, much less just an image with some words on or around it. A meme is a "a group of digital items."[2]

These groups of items are not like art exhibitions, with all the exhibition's components gathered in single places, like the rooms of museums. Rather, these groups, these memes, have a special ability to be in many different places at once, from platforms and accounts to screenshot folders, or even just people's minds. Binding the members of these memetic groups are their "common characteristics" (like the act of planking or the presence of the lovable dog), the fact that they "were created with awareness of each other" (people don't rickroll in isolation), and finally the fact that they've been "circulated, imitated, and transformed via the Internet by many users" (it's a collectively done internet thing, or what Gretchen McCulloch calls "in-joke replication"[3]). From this perspective, any inclusive account of memes must harken back to Richard Dawkins's coining of the word, when he (and other eventual adherents of "memetics") sought to demonstrate how pieces of cultural information like songs (or even something as large as democracy, a "memeplex") manage to reproduce and transmit themselves like genes do. Take a look at one bastion of memetic invention, the subreddit /r/Memes, and you will find Dawkins's vision of culture and society put to creative reuse. According to this collective's self-description, a meme is "an element of a culture or system of behavior that may be considered to be passed from one individual to another by nongenetic means, especially imitation."[4]

Of course, if you take the time to linger in not just this but many other subreddits, or if you ask people who have grown up with memes (such as a large majority of students in a class on memes I've taught several times), even Shifman's and /r/Memes's more plural distillations of this vast cultural domain can seem sorely lacking. This is because of a whole suite of further memetic examples that don't quite fit. There are, for instance, those "challenges" that arrive and thrive, then fade. There are those oddly alluring (and often disturbing) images deemed "cursed." There is that purposely baffling meme of a blue frog on a leaf with the label "Arson." There is that meme of a meme from the future that you'll inevitably not understand, and that in 2021 created a minor stir when someone used it to pretend to have predicted the rise of the popular video game *Among Us*. There is Bugs Bunny become Big Chungus, a meme once used in "wholesome" ways but eventually deployed toward offensive and aggressive ends by "shitposters."[5] There is that use of a jovial comic book frog (Pepe, created by Matt Furie), first for relatively benign reasons, then for the sake of racism and hate speech, then as an expression of solidarity among left-wing protesters in Hong Kong. There are numerous further memes of a hateful kind to which I will not give the benefit of attention. There are yet other memes that, in my not mentioning them, appear to reveal something about me (i.e., hopeless "normie"). And there are still others I can signal for knowing audiences through the simplest of gestures. (For example, for anyone who remembers 2019 anyway, I need only write: "Ugh, analyzing memes is tiring. Kyle needs a Monster.")[6]

In one iteration of the memes class, I asked the students to join me in confronting this memetic ferment with a new definition. About 130 of us all together, we started by comparing what's already out there. We looked at those that keep it simple, like Amanda Brennan's "pieces of content that travel from person to person and change along the way." We also looked at more encompassing attempts, such as Ryan M. Milner's summation of memes as "linguistic, image, audio, and video texts created, circulated, and transformed by countless cultural participants across vast networks and collectives."[7]

The definition we ended up with built on Shifman, Brennan, and Milner's, but with some key modifications. A meme is *a piece, series, or recognizable use of media, typically humorous, that is easily shared, transformed, or performed via the internet, and that is collectively embraced by specific communities or subcultures.* Part of what has been added here is a nod to the double uses of "meme": it speaks to memes as both individual items ("check out this meme") and groups of items or actions ("it's a meme now"). The definition also incorporates the trait of humor without making that trait universal, considering that (as several students pointed out) some memes are downright weird, absurd, or depressing. Finally, unlike most other quick glosses on memes we encountered, this definition emphasizes the elements of reception and belonging. (In insisting on this feature, the class echoed Lauren Michele Jackson, who, among other things, speaks to what she calls the "blackness of meme movement," as well as the degree to which memes rely on Black language and expressivity.[8]) For the students in my class, especially BIPOC (Black/Indigenous/

People of Color) and LGBTQIA+ students, any definition worth its salt must speak to the lives and deaths of memes across the "networks and collectives" that make and spread them. It must also speak to the joy and investment many memes elicit, and hence the inclusion of the word "embrace," a term I initially worried was too imprecise, but eventually came to appreciate, given the intensities of glee and even defensiveness students displayed around certain memes.

In any case, the point of this exercise was not that everyone ought to finally agree on one definition to rule them all. (After all, ours was far from perfect.) The point was that, when proposing to study this unruly domain in an inclusive and intersectional way, one does not simply "define" meme.[9] Instead, one will do what Jackson, Shifman, Milner, and others do, which is research and report in an avowedly pluralist mode. That means venturing into the ever-expanding memescape with a taste for analogies and disanalogies. It means accepting that the memescape undergoes constant revision (and that there are, in fact, many memescapes, and these memescapes might one day face their own kind of heat death). Finally, it means remaining attentive to the frequent but not necessarily universal features that make memescapes hum, from speed, spread, and mutability to referentiality, remix, and relatability to Blackness, absurdity, antagonism, and humor.

The upshot of my own plural reading of memescapes is an argument for a lens switch. This lens switch is embodied in a meme that saw widespread use in 2018 and 2019. The image comes from the 1990s anime show *Brave Fighter of Sun Fighbird.* In one episode, a yellow butterfly passes by. The android asks, "Is this a pigeon?" For several years, the image was something to reference among a knowing few. But eventually it became a widely used "template." The android stands in for the person or group or institution perceiving something. The butterfly stands in for what that something actually is. And the pigeon is whatever silly or misguided possibility the android entertains (Figure 3.1). My argument isn't that there's been a silly misrecognition with respect to memes (much less that we should focus on image memes). It's that we who see fit to interpret and study the cultural domain, whether academically, critically, or creatively, need to shift the premises through which we conceptualize what memes are, how they work, and ultimately what they do. The dimension of memes that needs attention (the

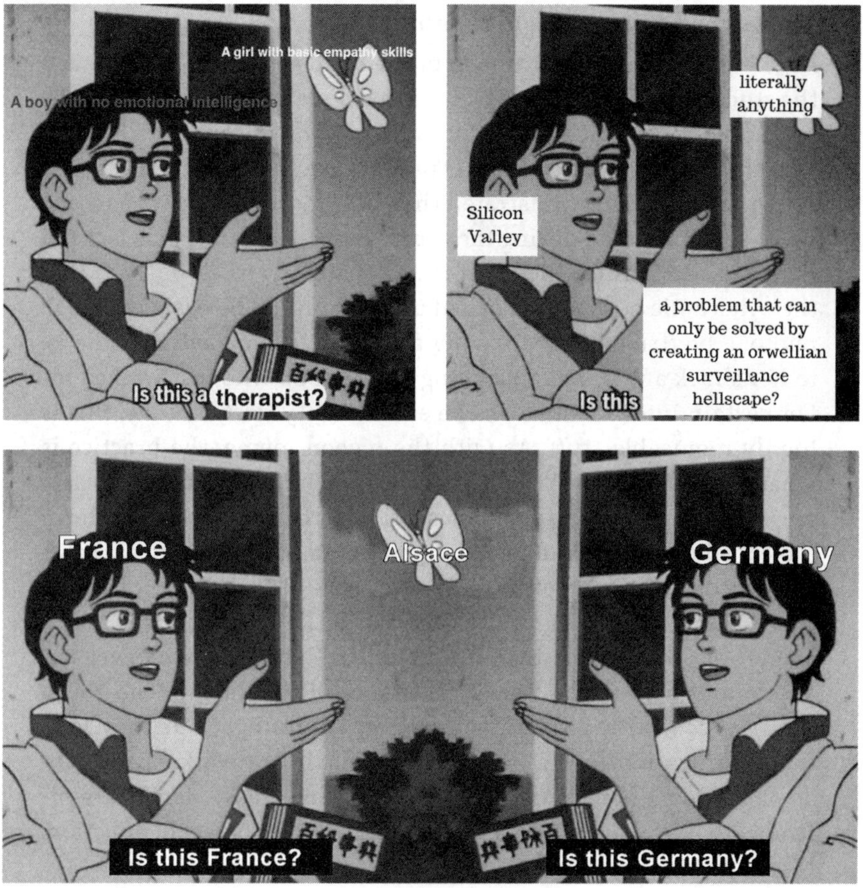

Figure 3.1. Examples of the "Is this a pigeon?" meme. Collected in 2021.

butterfly) is the dimension of assembly. Not quite conversation, folklore, or street art (as other scholars have helpfully framed them), memes are sometimes quite delightful, sometimes quite boring, and still other times quite corrosive uses of media assembly at both small and extremely large scales. Part of the value of this lens switch is that it will help us make sense of the success, stakes, and ongoing potentials of particular memetic modes and strategies. Another is that it will help us better name and interpret (and hopefully also mitigate and oppose) their increasingly evident capacity to do harm.

Memes as Expressive Folksonomy

At one point in the first version of the memes class in 2017, I asked the students how you could be sure that a meme is dead. "When it's on Facebook!" yielded a healthy share of knowing snickers. I asked why this was. "Because then our parents are sharing it."

Perhaps no meme illustrated the point more that year than one that began to spread during the course before eventually (as Jackson puts it in her "unified theory of meme death") "retreat[ing] back into the cybernetic ooze unless called upon again."[10] The basis is a stock photo: a boyfriend is not paying attention to his girlfriend; he is, to her shock and dismay, gawking at a woman who just walked by. For certain internet users in the early twenty-first century, this is highly memeable stuff. As with the pigeon meme, the practice is what editors at Know Your Meme (a commercial website that categorizes and summarizes memes usefully but imperfectly[11]) term "object labeling."[12] What you do is position media constituents (usually words) over each of the relevant parts of the image, of which there are most commonly two or three. In so doing, you make something funny, relatable, enlightening, biting, or whatever the case might be. To take a classic instance of this meme, The Youth are in a committed relationship with Capitalism, but they look with admiration to the enticing Socialism that walks away. (Or, as one student generously worked up for my class, Memes are offended to find that Students now look to another object of affection, Metadata.)

The so-called "distracted boyfriend" meme might have retreated into the cybernetic ooze, but the core practice of object labeling has not, as all manner of scenes and subjects now become the stuff of labeled expression, from fine art photographs as maps of states of mental health to dams that embody claims that one is definitely not racist (Plate 6). In fact, object labeling has become a kind of expressive commonplace, not just across more normie spheres like Facebook, but across subreddits, message boards, chats, channels, and DMs throughout the many insider and outsider haunts of the internet. In helping contextualize the practice, editors at Know Your Meme reach into histories of Western political communication, citing Benjamin Franklin's famous configuration of the American colonies as a cut-up snake. For her part, Heather Schwedel frames object labeling as "a recyclable meme format for our endlessly memeable times . . . Saying such complicated things in a way that manages to be both strictly literal (hence the labels) and totally metaphorical at the same time (your depression is not actually a little boy with a trumpet) is what keeps us coming back."[13]

My own take on object labeling accords with the argument of this chapter, which is the need to recalibrate our understanding of memes by way of assembly. In one sense, object-labeling memes embody the degree to which assembly has itself become memetic. While far from the only form memetic assembly can take, image and object-labeling memes vividly embody the accessibility and expressivity in the use of mutually informing elements that act like expressive citizens, or what I call "constituents." With little effort (apparently little, anyway), selected words and images become the stuff of metaphor and analogy, or of contrast and overlap. Meanwhile, as is evident in "meme queen of depression Instagram"[14] @aidenarata's take on quarantine group chats, the very act of reusing material from a known memetic source—in this case the previously (and subsequently) memed cartoon Little Bear—imbues the assembly with the implied presence of distributed aggregates of other people, not just those who can relate but also those who might yet respond, whether in likes, comments, or yet further memetic assemblies (Figure 3.2).

The other part of my take on object labeling is more involved. It is one thing to focus on a named and known use of memes (like object labeling). It is another to look across many different types of memes for distinct patterns that haven't been articulated as such. One virtue of this work is disclosing something that people know in practice but that often tends to elude critique and analysis. Another is to stir up thinking where it has otherwise become settled, such that a host of potential categorizations and conceptualizations stand open for pursuit. It's not that object labeling is the only way to do this. It's that object labeling is a rich departure point for an especially widespread and consequential use of memes, one that I argue deserves close attention.

The use of memes I have in mind is on display across this trio:

(a) Starting in earnest in the early 2010s, it became possible and interesting to respond to statements and situations with GIFs. In early instances, these looping moving images filled up custom websites, each of them sitting beneath statements

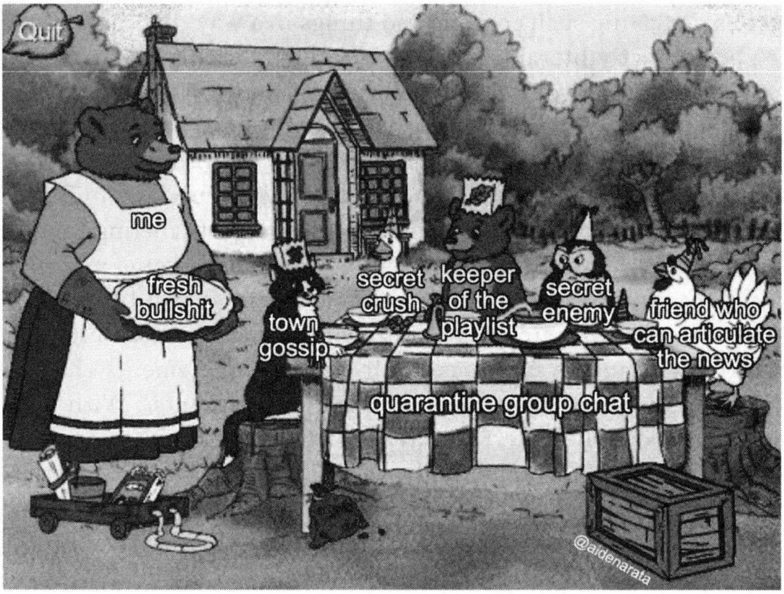

Figure 3.2. Object-labeling meme and exemplary use of constituents and positions by Aiden Arata / @aidenarata. Posted to Instagram, April 15, 2020.

like "my face when my boss . . ." or "when a guy starts to explain . . ." As time went on, GIFs were possible reactions to posts and texts. The thing one created with a reaction GIF was the union of the provoking content with the response, often as though one were taking on the facial expression of someone else, like shock at error or delight at achievement. (Jackson shows how reaction GIFs can also become the means through which non-Black users engage in "digital blackface."[15]) The use of these reaction GIFs has tended to rely on dedicated web libraries or repositories of options available to smartphone users in the midst of typing. Someone (or something, an algorithm) has organized responses that match terms, like "excited," "concerned," or "impatient."

(b) In January 2017, an image of a black and yellow frog overlaid with the phrase "hippity hoppity get off my property" appeared on the meme page "There's a War on For Your Memes." Various people posted image memes in response, such as a black and red frog with "hippity hoppity seize the property," or later, "hippity hoppity you're now my property" spoken by a frog wearing suspenders and aiming a gun, this image meme fused with a "when" meme: "When you see a fire meme that has a poorly placed watermark you can crop out before stealing" (Figure 3.3). Over the coming years, with varying levels of seriousness, people posted comments, tweets, and YouTube compilations with or about people doing "hippity hoppity you're now my property," taking and reusing songs, dances, and memes. Meanwhile, the phrase, having become a well-known "snowclone" (a phrase that can be reused and reapplied), also appeared within various TikToks, such as someone pretending to tell cops knocking at the door to leave the property. The phrase also appears in usernames and profiles, such as one female-presenting user with the handle @hippityhoppity2929. By using the name "WomenRproperty," this person fuses the "hippity hoppity" meme with a patriarchy-laden second one.[16]

(c) Finally, on TikTok and YouTube, it has become common to walk viewers through the presenter's take on one or another thematic list. Typically, what you do is react as the pieces of your list come on screen. Maybe you're dancing or maybe you're shifting your eyebrows. In any case, one among the many examples of this practice of the performed list in 2020 was "fashion through the decades." In many cases, there wasn't a great deal of imagination to the choices of costume, as fashion history corresponded with prevailing images from white-dominated Hollywood. But certain TikTokers worked differently. For @itsmayart, for instance, fashion through the decades meant donning headwear as worn across different Muslim majority countries at different times, doing so with facial expressions that appear to match both the clothing and the context, but that also had the TikToker acting toward the camera in a manner recognizably their own (Figure 3.4).[17] In other words, in responding to the relatively simple meme, various TikTokers assembled the obvious but oddly overlooked fact that the history of fashion is not the same for everyone.

The mix of examples will seem quite disparate at first blush, mixing not only types of media but also registers and stances.[18] The question is whether there are family resemblances here, not just minor

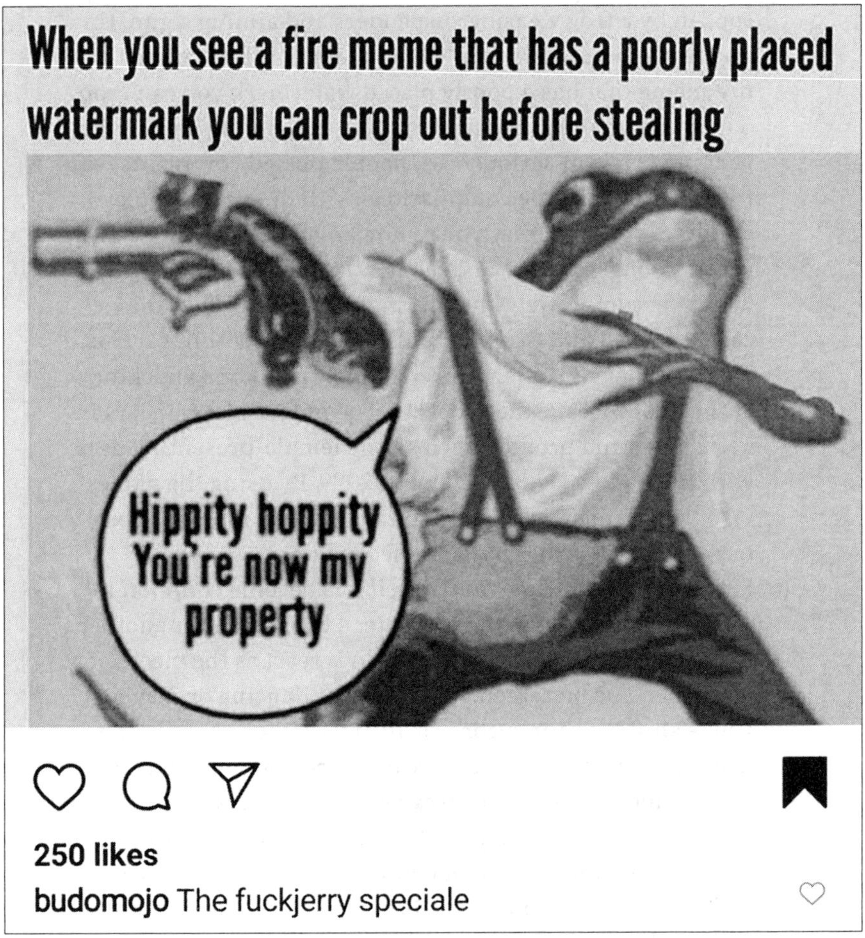

Figure 3.3. Example of the "hippity hoppity" meme. Collected in 2020.

or arbitrary things, but rich, repeatable, and socially and psychically consequential things.

I see several. The use of the meme makes or performs some kind of take, usually but not exclusively humorous, on a subject the reader/viewer can recognize if they're in the know. The take is not shared in the form of a definitive verbal truth claim, nor is it made in the form of a definitively posed mirror of reality. Instead, there is a visual, aural, or performative presentation of the subject in question as a particular coordination, arrangement, compilation, juxtaposition, or fusion of media. It is often, but not always, funny

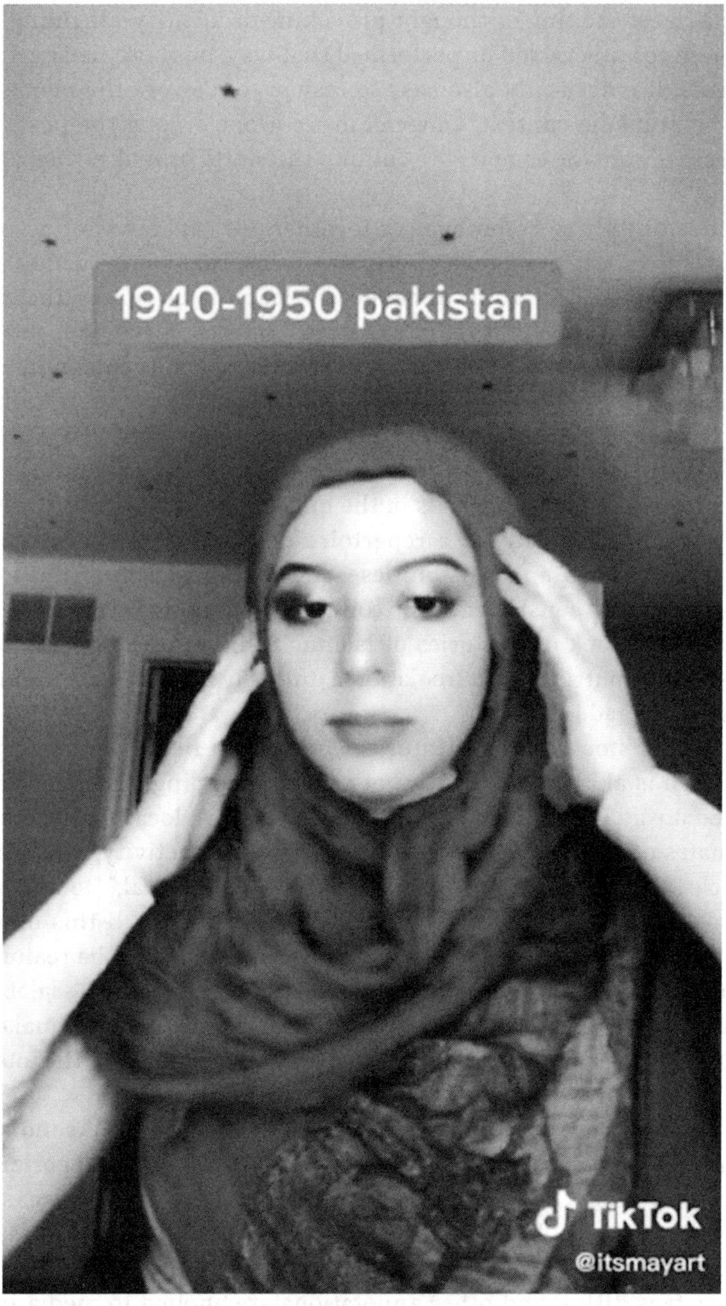

Figure 3.4. Example of the "fashion through the decades" meme in a 2020 TikTok post by @itsmayart.

(or at least exciting or thought-provoking or identity-affirming) to see things assembled or performed that way, by those means, in a meme. It is typically also easy to reshare or rework the meme in a social-media context. One can make it one among the posts or messages or stories one puts out into the world or makes visible to others.

Reading these resemblances together, we can say we find one widespread use of memes: a form of a form. That use of memes assumes, whether in ironic or believed or habituated senses, that the world is reducible to a set of situations and scenarios. This use of memes seizes on that premise by presenting constituents (phrases, screenshots, gestures) in memetic labels and arrangements, rather than baldly stating something (or saying nothing at all). Meanwhile, one is not set apart from the world scene in presenting the microproject. Instead, one is in the midst, with others, both drawing from and adding to a repertoire of memetic constituents—materials, ideas, and sensibilities—and ways of selecting and configuring those constituents. (By contrast, imagine a graphic novelist crafting a book on histories of Islamic fashion in their signature style, thus putting into circulation a uniquely rendered account for others to read.)

Taking stock of these features, it can seem like the underlying pattern is akin to the practice of concept mapping, as there is indeed a way in which these examples all involve locating the coordinates of something, whether an emotion, an activity, or a piece of clothing. (For similar reasons, terms like "positional," "temporal," and "locative" also come to mind.) But subsuming all this under concept mapping would risk confining the analysis to the realm of object labeling alone. The more appropriate and indeed "scalable" way of understanding what is going on here is to join meme makers in venturing a new coinage, building on a term distinct to the internet era: "expressive folksonomy."

A term coined by Thomas Vander Wal in 2004, "folksonomy" doesn't refer to memes.[19] It refers to the labeling and categorizing people perform across social and participatory media. Whereas in the context of a library or digital archive, tags and other metadata would be applied to media in a controlled manner, with folksonomy, tags, titles, and other annotations are applied to media in a more or less open way. It is the "folk," which is to say the users, who perform these unsystematic labors. The results of these labors are not hierarchical category schemes based on agreed principles, but rather user-generated descriptions and classifications. As is explored in the extensive literature on the topic, the values of folksonomy are several: ease, flexibility, variety, community connection. At the same time, at least from the perspective of the more traditional classification practices of institutions, there are drawbacks. Lack of top-down control can mean redundancy, misspelling, esoteric tags. The fruits of these labors can be largely unusable. (Some projects, such as Rhizome's VocabWiki, manage to enrich the metadata around certain collections by mixing folksonomy with top-down processing and curating.)

The use of memes I am putting on the table is folksonomy by other means and toward other ends. Although there might be literal tagging going on, that is mere excess activity surrounding the crux of the matter, which is the memetic act or expression itself. Consider again what these memetic examples are. They are assemblies of media among groups of related media (and mediated performance) made within and for provisional and distant network-based groups of meme makers, viewers, and sharers. That tells us something about the "folk" aspect. (In line with the recent coinage of "folx," which aims at a more inclusive and in some cases specifically queer rendering of "people generally," I'll also put "expressive folxonomy" on the table.[20]) But further consider that these memetic examples are, in one way or another, partly or nearly entirely, instances of publicly performed labeling, classifying, and taxonomizing. That work of labeling, classifying, and taxonomizing is a cascade. There is the response to something that, for whatever reason, deserves attention and categorization. This is something that is being brought into view (like a type of experience or action) or responded to (like an influencer's viral post). There is then an attempt at categorization and organization, not always the same (not like always adding a hashtag to an image), but in different modes and to different ends, from the presentation of an image to the use of a phrase to the selection of certain sartorial signifiers. And then there is the actual address of the subject matter in question. As several of these examples indicate, this folksonomic cascade isn't always so obvious and clear as a visual assembly like the pigeon or boyfriend meme. In the "hippity hoppity" case, for example, someone can memetically annotate something as an appropriation by means of a title (a compilation of "hippity hoppity" TikToks). Alternatively, in the fashion TikToks, someone can *imply* annotations with what they do and don't choose to do in response to what they're showing: a simple, subtle facial expression that indicates how something, like a particular style of hijab, should be classified. In still other cases, the work of expressive folksonomy won't even be "in" the meme. It will be in the choice of meme, or the timing of the presentation (such as in implicit response to a recent pop culture event), or the accompanying comment.

Of course, this way of talking about memes can feel quite divorced from their actual, dynamic presence, which is so often ironic or cutting (or weird) in nature. (I think, for instance, of a nonfolksonomic instance, like the cats with prosthetic hands meme, which was nothing less than people sharing pictures of cats with small prosthetic hands where their paws should be.) Hence the need for the qualifying adjective: this is *expressive* folksonomy that we are talking about. At one level, what is expressive is the choice of material. As looping reaction GIFs and high-energy TikToks make evident, these uses and inventions of memes are not about the dry establishment of reliable terms for items of potential and mild interest. They are about using (and sometimes mocking or abusing) categories for humor, provocation, and exclamation. At another level, just as essential, what is expressive is the mode of delivery. What is occurring is textured and perceptual: the act of classification is "clinched," as it were, only when the viewer has made sense of (or even reused) the artifact or performance that does the classifying and arranging. A reaction GIF might embody a sense of something surprising; it might connote confusion; or it might connote some subtle mix of reactions. But the interpreting audience has to have a read on how the situations or subjects in question are being positioned in a constantly shifting world of reference, and that read happens only through scanning the constellation of terms in an image, or reading the codes and citations across the media, timing, and terms in a performance. (As I frequently experienced in teaching my class, there is a kind of oral cultural dimension to memes; you know what you're encountering through exposure, repetition, and memory, and no amount of archival searching will get you all the knowledge you need unless someone in the know shows you the way.)

One consequence of this more indirect expressiveness through visual, verbal, and performative assembly is that expressive folksonomy leaves the interpretive process out there in the open, such that new interpretations or creative reuses are possible. The classification also has the virtue of being something shared and often "insider," rather than something official and verbal. Because it's by the folks (or folx) themselves, this appropriation belongs, as it were, to the internet, or more precisely, it belongs to a particular subculture, collective, or identity category.[21] In short, the work of using memes for the sake of rapid assemblies of classifications and categorizations is an increasingly intuitive form of communication and expression. People know in practice that they can take advantage of this expressive mode across genre, subculture, format, time, and geography. They live and breathe this heterogeneity toward various ends, from absurdity and insight to relatability and aggression.

But that is just one way to think through expressive folksonomy. Another is to map its consequences in contexts of enduring importance. Gender, that most contested of categories, is one such context. What we see between expressive folksonomy and gender, at least in many modern European and North American contexts, can be conceived as follows. On the one hand, there are numerous premises in circulation that affect how people live and understand gender. On the other hand, there are certain uses of media and culture that work variously to confirm, contest, or reshape those premises. In other words, we can consider what processes of thinking and categorizing are in place around gender, and then we can consider how expressive folksonomy might affect those processes. To adopt one among many possible and valuable framings of struggles around gender, there is what Judith Butler calls "the coercive hold of norms on gendered life."[22] These norms exercise a coercive hold, in that they function to negatively constrain possible gender performances, how people might live and act upon the genders (or the refusals of gender) they know and desire. That constraint is quite frequently cisgender, patriarchal, and binary (biologically male and biologically female), but there are many ways in which the "coercive hold" can operate, including stances on gender packaged as "critical" that propound aggressively exclusionary, transphobic schema.

The role of expressive folksonomy in these dynamics is, along one track, reinforcement. Coercive gender norms find further entrenchment by way of a new means of attack. Looking across the memescape, examples of the more binaristic and misogynistic variety are frequent and predictable, from snowclones like the aforementioned "women are property" used without irony (or with inadequate or misplaced irony[23]), to subreddits that "actively antagonize feminist perspectives and women in general," to 4chan boards where, as Milner puts it, "racism and sexism are memetic ideas themselves."[24] And indeed the image and object-labeling memes that address millions of eyes on a daily basis are rife with these dynamics. (As an example of their frequent simplicity but maximal portability, in one case, an image of Adam and Eve as two white people is overlaid with "God Created Man and Woman" at the top and "Democrats Created All the Other Genders" at the bottom.) What matters is the way expressive folksonomy adds to the mix. They do so by offering visual and performative consolidations fused with postures of belonging and ease of transmission. The consolidation is often a binary before one's eyes and in one's device, one that is set among other expressive acts and artifacts. The belonging is the sense of familiarity with the meme. It can also be familiarity with the person sharing or performing the meme, or with the subcommunity in which it is shared. Whoever engages these memes finds a cheap and highly transmissible materialization of an oppressive schema, an attempt to "reclaim forms of identity that have been rightly challenged."[25] Readily saved, liked, and shared, the oppressive media assembly stands ready to join in and encourage further oppressive media assemblies, including those that gather regressive notions around other dimensions of life, including race and ability. Premises are reinforced; new premises take hold; aggressively restrictive and hierarchical stances are reenergized. Expressive folksonomy helps tighten the already tight grip of coercive gender norms.

At the same time, in accordance with the Janus-faced nature of memes, the practice of expressive folksonomy can also participate in what Butler—who, as of 2021, would place themselves in the category of "nonbinary" and has been "enjoying the world of 'they'"[26]—calls the "relaxing" of the coercive hold of said norms.[27] In Butler's writing, which is not focused on cultural expression as such, this is a matter of a radical realignment in the premises people (and the law) hold around gender, sexuality, and their many intersections with other categories and contexts, as well as around the "kind of analysis or alliance needed to realise ideals of radical justice."[28] As Butler points out in their book on precarity and popular assembly, they could be misread as saying gender is utterly open.[29] They could also be misread as saying gender is somehow quite established and unshakeable. Butler responds with an assertion of the overall project of "performative" framings of gender. What is sought is not everyone's total transcendence of any gendered character whatsoever, nor a yielding to insistent, habituated norms. Instead, it is a release from the tight grip of expectations and disciplinary measures that enforce unacceptable constraints.[30] It is also a procession into gender thriving and gender abundance and gender evasion, all of this in unpredictable, situation-specific variations that play out in different ways for different bodies in different places, circumstances, and intersections, all under the assumption of a basic right to live and breathe "in public, freely, and with protection from violence."[31] If there is a central norm in this vision, it is to "safeguard breaks with normality, and offer support and affirmation for those who make those breaks."[32]

Like the rich array of critical stances around gender, including those not centered in the West and those that critique aspects of Butler's evolving work, the instances of expressive folksonomy in this vein are many and various, some with wit, some with tenderness, some with venom. For instance, should a group of young friends find their way to the bevy of reaction GIFs tagged with "nonbinary" in a readily available GIF library like Tenor, they will find themselves confronted with a suite of joyfully performed categorizations and anticategorizations: neither boy nor girl but an experience; "gender free" as something to dance to; beauty and gender as things that are "infinite"; and bodies in motions and costumes that materialize the refusal. Alternatively, should those same friends venture into the written or spoken debates around transphobia across social-media channels, they will find the speakers posting GIFs and memes (and emojis and other free-floating constituents) that grant further energy and inspiring ornament to their assertions, or that work to humiliate the speaker whose thoughts stand to be opposed, uses of a kind of internet rhetoric, not so much ethos, pathos, or logos, but what we might venture to call "memos," a rhetorical appeal by way of references and reuses you'll know if you're in the know. Still further, should those same friends venture into /r/ShitRedditSays, they will find a context of "counterpublic contestations," in which the people posting "employ the aggressive adversarial humor that characterizes lulz and trolling in order to push against the white, male centrality prevalent in participatory media collectives."[33]

And then there are those projects that are not quite memes, but meme-proximate and meme-infused, and that creatively combine narrative, representation, performance, and assembly. I think, for instance, of the account of Schuyler Bailar, the first trans Division I NCAA athlete. Bailar's posts feature questions and aphorisms around trans lives and trans politics in prominent letters; the videos are suffused with a consciousness of internet tropes, idioms, and aesthetics; and the account is accompanied by introductions to terms and orientations Bailar and others see as essential to supporting the rights and thriving of trans people (Figure 3.5). It is not really possible or necessary to say which of these uses of expressive folksonomy qua gender is most ascendant or influential. The point is that a particular distinguishing potential of memetic expression joins the world of mediating and regulating gender in consequentially distinct ways. Expressive folksonomy plays a competitive role in the redistribution of assembled premises around the gendered dimensions of contemporary life. It also provides a means of refusing the isolation of those premises to gender alone, linking up these dynamics of thinking and categorizing with a host of others across the social field.

Recognizing the mixed roles of expressive folksonomy around gender is one way of seeing its importance. Another is to take a step back. There is, for instance, Jonathan Crary's idea that the content of digital communications is far less consequential than the structure that is reinforced. (Quite often, or so he contends, acts of digital expression and communication only further validate one's participation in the flows of capital and exchange, regardless of the content.[34]) There is also, on the opposite end of the spectrum, Hito Steyerl's concept of the "poor image" that has the virtue of ease of travel and, in that capacity, serves the function of forming and enacting bonds between those who might never meet.[35] Through lenses like these, one addresses what is being performed or enacted.

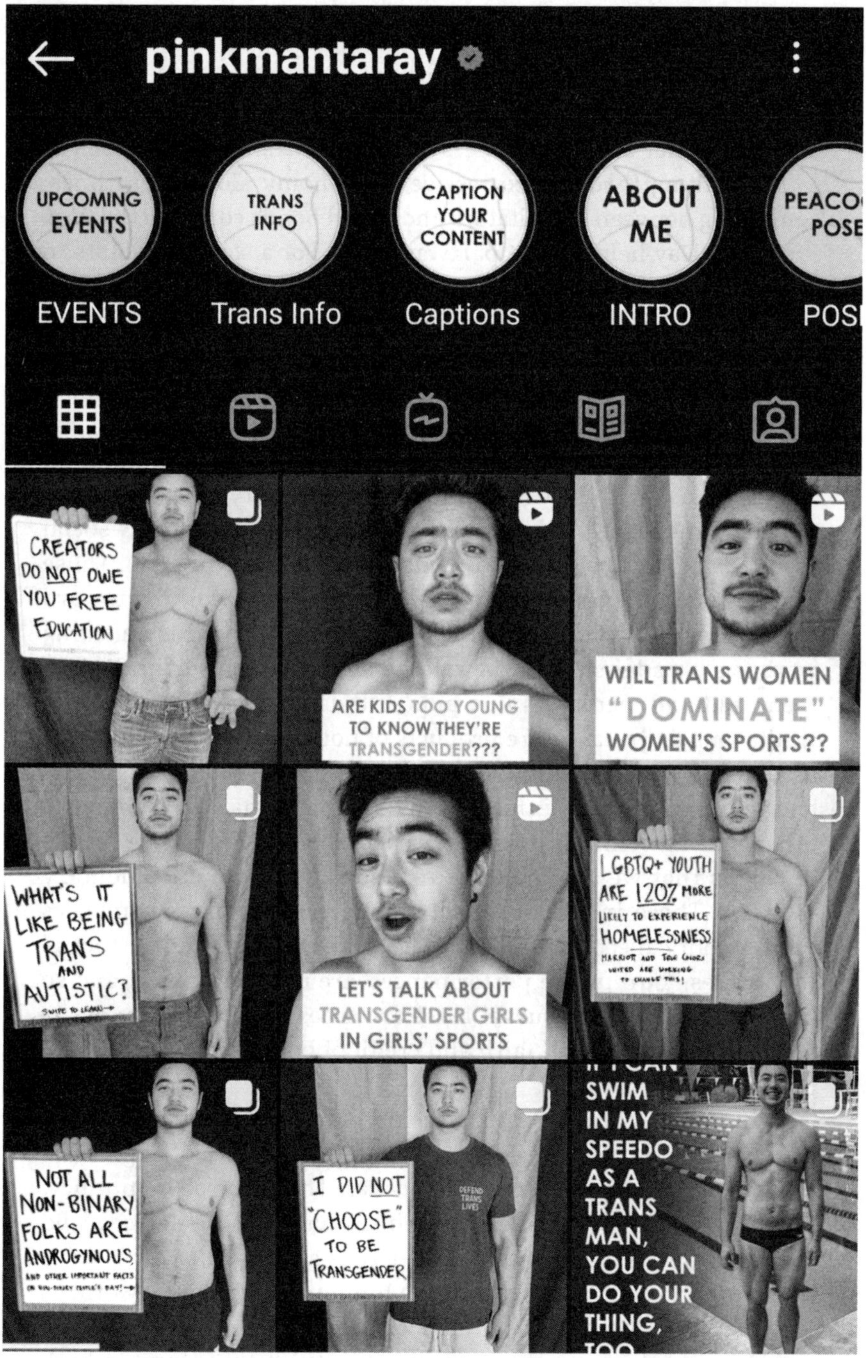

Figure 3.5. Schuyler Bailar, Instagram account @pinkmantaray. Screenshot from 2021.

These enactments are the characteristics of media activity that do not depend on specific content, communities, themes, or trends. They are things that occur regardless of whether one knows or likes it.

In thinking through expressive folksonomy along these lines, something between exploitation and visual bonds comes to the fore. Ronald E. Day helps us get partway there. For a start, he points to something that precedes and exceeds the particular: various kinds of "indexes." For Day, "index" refers to an ongoing process of tracking and recording "places, searches, expressions, and actions" by way of cookies, metadata, and other means. It's not just that these indexes exist in the background for no reason. Rather, they are "reinjected back into social and documentary systems," often through direct means, as in the use of assessed "personality characteristics" to determine what kind of content and advertising to show social media users, and when and in what quantities (Figure 3.6). Those systems and indexes are then readjusted in turn, working toward "further predictable expressions." The context for this indexing work is a broader shift in the relationship between self and document, self and media. As Day puts it, today those who use digital media on a daily basis "are products of not even whole documents, as they were once known, but rather of documentary fragments and representations—'information'—in communication with each other and in communication with ourselves." The consequence of this is that we are "mediated by sociotechnical documentary indexes." These indexes connect and direct "us to performances within political economies." And the stakes are high. "Like stocks," Day writes, "our 'future performances' are not guaranteed, and so both market and state surveillance are necessary for the system as a whole to have the full faith and credit of both the governors and the governed."[36]

What can be drawn from these observations is the position of the subject who would create or engage any instance of expressive folksonomy and any meme whatsoever. That subject is in a new position because of new devices and the habits those devices (and their architects) tend to support. There is a widely manifest drive to "attempt to continuously propose him- or herself to the world as the subject of documentary representation" (and, I would add, assembly), and there are systems and structures that stand to both benefit from and manipulate how those proposals work.[37] In other

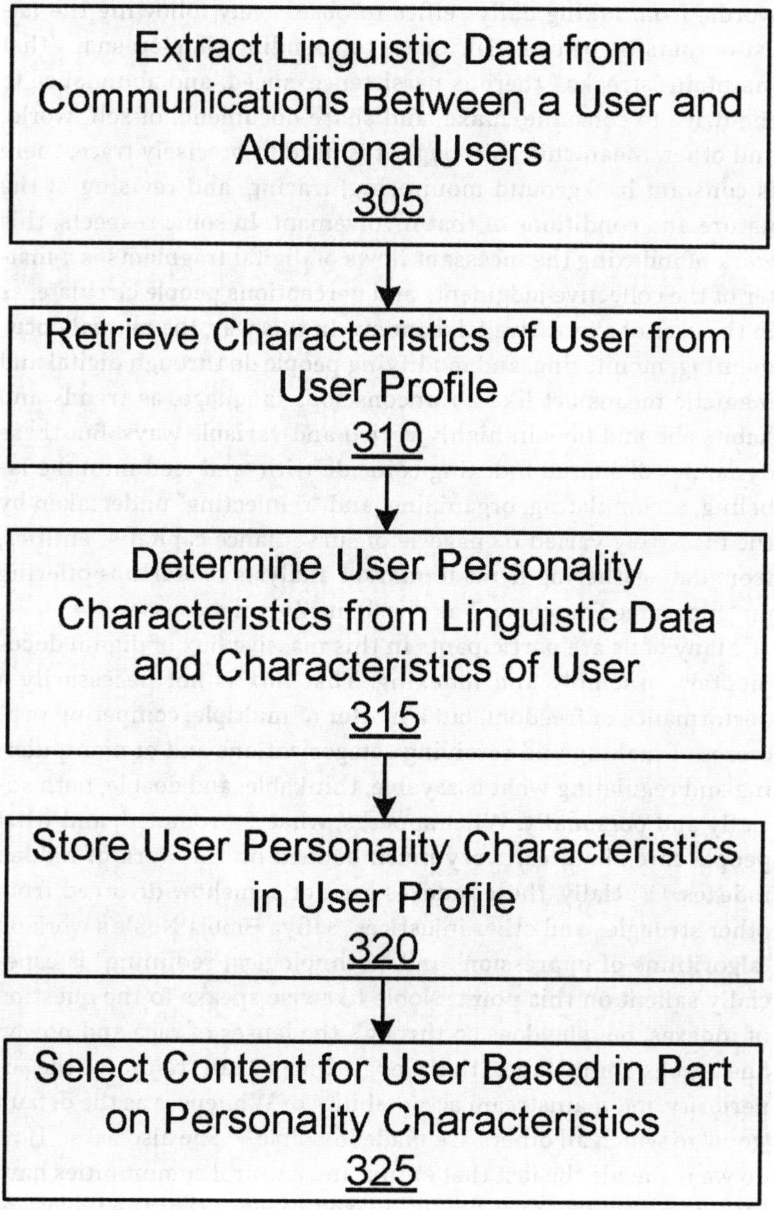

Figure 3.6. A "flow chart of one embodiment of a method for determining user personality characteristics." Michael Nowak et al., on behalf of Facebook, Inc., United States Patent 9,740,752 B2, August 22, 2017.

words, from taking daily selfies to obsessively following the latest outputs by beloved TikTokers to spending time on snaps that maintain "streaks," there is persistence, speed, and abundance to the drive to consume, make, and share documents of self, world, and other. Meanwhile, although it is hard to precisely trace, there is constant background monitoring, tracing, and revising of the nature and conditions of that involvement. In some respects, this work of indexing the incessant flows of digital fragments is a matter of the collective judgments and perceptions people circulate, as in the uses of expressive folksonomy. In this way, the mutual documenting, monitoring, and modifying people do through digital and memetic means act like an unconscious language, as trends and habits ebb and flow in highly varied and variable ways. But these dynamics of shared indexing coincide with (and feed into) the labeling, accumulating, organizing, and "reinjecting" undertaken by the massively varied menagerie of surveillance capitalist entities, from data gathering firms to market analysts to startups offering up "guaranteed outcomes," as Shoshana Zuboff discusses.[38]

Many of us are participants in this massive flux of digital documentary assembly and indexing. That flux is not necessarily a performance of freedom, but a matter of multiple, competing processes of making and receiving categorizations and of manipulating and regulating what is sayable, thinkable, and doable, both socially and personally. What appears, what is promoted, and what people care about can very much depend on the work of hidden indexes. Crucially, these indexes are not somehow divorced from other struggles and other injustices. Safiya Umoja Noble's work on "algorithms of oppression" and "technological redlining" is especially salient on this point. Noble likewise speaks to the question of indexes, but she does so through the lenses of race and power. She argues, for instance, that Google Images can "reinforce the superiority and mainstream acceptability of Whiteness as the default 'good' to which all others are made invisible."[39] She also asks: "How do we reconcile the fact that ethnic and cultural communities have little to no control over being indexed in ways that they may not want? How does a group resolve the ways that the pubic engages with Google as if it is the arbiter of truth?"[40]

Taking these observations to heart, the situation can look dire.

The indexes that most inform and discipline the expressive and communicative lives of digital subjects are those of corporations and states dedicated to advancing their own interests. Quite often, as in the case of Silicon Valley, these indexing institutions are compromised by not only the lack of what Noble calls "a diverse and critically minded workforce on issues of race and gender" but also what Wendy Hui Kyong Chun identifies as a spurious and often discriminatory commitment to sticking people and content together based on perceived similarity and therefore helping to make "segregation the default."[41] The shared practice of expressive folksonomy could be seen as a performance and validation of these very conditions. Yes, one is interested, amused, or informed by whatever is undergoing expressive folksonomic treatment. But one is also reinforcing and extending one's enmeshment in the broader array of forces that would have acts of indexing and categorizing and clustering dominate the everyday, the intimate—anything.

And yet it would be wrong to adopt a strictly pessimistic perspective here. As the enumerative manifestoes of movements like Strike MoMA embody, and as Noble's pointing to "public noncommercial search" implies, index does not always equal bad.[42] Indexing by other means and toward other ends can be empowering, even transformative. Day says that critique "is an event that attempts to alter social and personal indexes and how they are composed, accounted for, and valued."[43] Expressive folksonomy can be exactly such an event, an assertion of redefinition by expressive rearrangement. I think of the words of Aria Dean, for instance, who works to "scribble a line from memes to blackness to the poor image, encircling them all together with a perforated line labeled 'circulation.'" For Dean, liberation won't take place on "corporate platforms, where Mark Zuckerberg profits directly" from the reproduction of images of violence against Black people. Nevertheless, there might yet be "some power in the readily made, readily unmade, ever shifting, ever distributed meme—power in a 'poor image' that slips through borders for those of us who are heavily policed, whom the state and other forces would like to make fixed."[44] I also think of reflections by Eloghosa Osunde in a more literary vein. "Seeing as many of us are alive on the outskirts of definitions," she writes, "seeing as that's the address that saved some of our lives, the place where we watch our safeties spring out of the ground, it's clear that whatever was defined can be redefined. Whatever was written by a person for a people, can be edited by a person or a people. We're proof. What is society, anyway? It's an anthology of someones. We make it up. We have always made it up."[45]

There might yet be ways that memetic folksonomy can help contest and rework the world's "anthologies of someones" while also foregrounding the problems Day and Noble note and putting them front and center for others. Perhaps it can do so in more local instances, with memetic assemblies that manage to evade (or mock or clarify) coercive indexes while helping disseminate more emancipatory ones. Perhaps memetic folksonomy can also support revisions and reimaginations at wider scales. Whether through reaction GIFs, snowclones, classificatory performances, or still other memetic uses, many different people engaged in the practice can recompose shared indexes of possible actions, possible thoughts, or even possible subjectivities over long periods of time. Unsystematic, imperfect, and partial, this would be expressive folksonomy in a distributed and democratic mode. Chun helpfully frames these paradoxes through the lens of capture: "The desire to capture and to draw connections, maps, and models can open a future that defies what is captured, but only if we dwell in the disconnect between map and action, model and future—only if we occupy the collective chimera we are offered and become characters, not marionettes, in the ongoing drama inadequately called Big Data."[46]

Of course, we would be neglecting the daily realities of memes on the internet if we didn't *also* label expressive folksonomy this way: "frequently just for the lulz."[47]

Memes as Hyperdistributed (and Sometimes Corrosive) Media Assembly

Toward the end of the 2019 class, I asked the students what hashtag they would apply to life on the planet in the year so far. (This was June.) As part of the last session, I projected their responses as a sliding cascade, like a credit sequence. It struck a chord. Maybe this was because the brief moving-image assembly hit on deeply felt themes. (The first four entries were #panic, #absurd, #climatechange, and #meh; the last four were #bitcoin, #abortion,

#GetThatBread, and #BLM.) More likely, it was because of the memes, from #yeet (twice) and #oof (twice) to #thanosdidnothingwrong and #BTSFESTA2019 to #worsttimeline.

As I think back now, I see that this wasn't just a fun way to end the class. It was also a way of engaging in a scale shift, from the particulars of many individual memes to the larger evolutions of memescapes, the unruly fact of what has come before, as well as the wonderment (and maybe also dread) around what might come next. (I say this while recognizing that someday this whole thing might die in the Jackson sense—the idea of an "internet meme" as quaint-sounding as "surfing the web.") This is exactly the kind of shift I now undertake. If the theory of assembly can lead us to expressive folksonomy, a concept that can be applied to many other spheres of digital media, how can it also help disclose the workings and implications of an even larger data set, even a data set as vast as all memes ever and everywhere?

One place to start is a relatively undercited article in the history of discourse on memes, Mike Godwin's "Meme, Counter-meme," published in *Wired* in 1994, just as access to the World Wide Web was beginning to expand in the United States. The article is a short reflection on something Godwin did in 1990 that turned out to be quite consequential. "I set out," Godwin recounts, "to conduct an experiment—to build a counter-meme designed to make discussion participants see how they are acting as vectors to a particularly silly and offensive meme . . . and perhaps to curtail the glib Nazi comparisons. I developed Godwin's Law of Nazi Analogies: As an online discussion grows longer, the probability of a comparison involving Nazis or Hitler approaches one. I seeded Godwin's Law in any newsgroup or topic where I saw a gratuitous Nazi reference. Soon, to my surprise, other people were citing it—the counter-meme was reproducing on its own!"[48] The concepts here are as significant in the twenty-first century as they were in the twentieth. Internet memes spread among minds and machines by way of horizontal repetition. Which memes circulate, and to what degree, matters. And hence the need for agile and effective counter-memes.

How this article relates to memes as media assembly is not immediately evident. If anything, it seems like a departure, because Godwin seems to construe memes in a strictly Dawkinsian vein, as singular organisms that can be seeded, take hold, and yield new, individualized memes in turn. By contrast, I've been trying to get at the patterns across many memes, and I am now zooming out to the entire, dispersed history of internet memes.

The crucial move is to pluralize. Take the various examples of memes I have floated in this chapter. Set them alongside others you might know. Set those alongside still others you don't know because you haven't seen them. And set these alongside the Godwin counter-meme. What we can trace is a constellation of which any maker or sharer of memes is a part. That constellation is dimly discernible in the early years of Godwin's Law. Over time, the more elements that enter its formation, the brighter, more pronounced, and more detailed that formation becomes. This is the collective performance, in and through memes, of digital, visual, verbal, and gestural assembly at the speed and scale of the internet. This is assembly that is both highly distributed and highly generative, a persistent and (eventually) seemingly pervasive ferment of actions, affects, ideas, and responses. This is memes as hyperdistributed, hyperparticipatory, and sometimes corrosive media assembly.

The fundamental notion here is relatively simple. Whether as images, acts, animations, or speech, memetic instances gesture outward in the directions of their constitutive references. Memes make coordinates and arrangements in a world of relational and expressive possibility. When someone produces or participates in a meme, they engage in an act of media assembly that recombines existing constituents and positions, whether from prior memes (prior assemblies) or a myriad of other sources. These acts of assembly are not isolated and authorial, but collective and derivative. These acts of assembly can serve to inform and alter other assemblies in turn, everything from the meme (or memes) in which it participates to the dispersed and contested assembly of all memes everywhere. Part of what makes the Godwin example useful is its function as a kind of microcosm of this fundamentally decentralized process. (Followers of Timothy Morton might call memes, construed this way, a "hyperassembly" or a "hyperpractice."[49]) For instance, those who created new "laws" in response to Godwin's Law were collectively sketching a virtual version of the constellation that would become internet memes: Danth's Law, Skitt's Law, Wheaton's Law—these were assemblies among assemblies, new fusions of Godwin's Law with whatever contexts and constituents were under consideration, or whatever humorous or other goal was at stake. In the years to come, countless other memetic assemblies would take their positions within the elusively defined but collectively imagined super-constellation of all internet memes. Fast forward some three decades later, and these kinds of performances of hyperdistributed and hyperparticipatory media assembly have taken place among more and more people around more and more contexts with more and more references in play. The drive to "add a new bit of creativity to a fixed premise"[50] is persistent and widespread, from blends of words and emojis for "reasonably hostile laments"[51] (a form of memetic political dissent in Oman) to Gen Z teens roasting millennials for their side parts and skinny jeans.[52]

I say this notion is relatively simple because it accords with what I have been saying in this book. There is a specific and increasingly widespread cultural form that deserves the name "assembly" and that takes place across widely varying scales. My name for assembly at the broader end of the scale has been "distributed assembly," as in the examples of the virtual lives of Jenny Holzer's art or the visualization and mediation of the Mexico–U.S. border. Now we see that this distributed assembly need not be based around an artist or even a common concern. Instead, it can be performed in and for the nodes, clusters, and paths of digital networks. Memes are a shared, hyperdistributed, and hyperparticipatory practice that undergoes constant revision and reconfiguration through new additions and new performances. In a networked world, "meme" is no longer just a noun. It's also a verb. A meme isn't "anything that goes viral."[53] A meme is an assembly. To meme isn't to represent or even (quite) to remix. To meme is to reassemble.

What *is* more elusive is how such a perspective on memes contributes to accounts of memes already in circulation. There are increasingly many rich ones from which to choose, including (but by no means limited to) Shifman's and Lynne McNeill's notions of memes as "folklore"[54] (in Shifman's case, "(post)modern folklore"), Jackson's notion of the "blackness of meme movement," and An Xiao Mina's vision of memes as the "street art of the social web" that can become part of the imaginative scaffolding of political movements (or become movements in themselves).[55] With respect to the notion of hyperdistributed assembly, the most extensive overlap is with Milner's account in *The World Made Meme*. It doesn't take long into reading this book to see family resemblances between world-made-meme and memes as hyperdistributed media assembly. Those resemblances are most evident in Milner's metaphor of weaving. That metaphor, Milner writes, "casts individual participatory media texts as strands that intertwine into threads of interaction, eventually forming whole tapestries of public conversation."[56]

Strands and tapestries for Milner's book and constituents, positions, and assemblies for this one—we seem to encounter something quite unflattering, not a case of family resemblances, but a case of needless conceptual cloning. And yet there is one key difference here. Milner's book is not, in fact, centered on weaving, but on conversation. Memes are, in his estimation, occasions for public discourse and responsive interaction. "At the smallest level," Milner writes, "the messages we spread are of our choosing. Even if we can't control collective sentiment—even if we can't control culture industries—we can decide what resonates with us and what bit of conversation we'll contribute. We have the power to weave our own strand into the tapestry. It's a small power, but it's ours, and it's more vibrant when it intertwines with the vibrant strands all around us."[57] As is evident in this call to responsive and ethical memetic production, conversation is not just a dimension of memes; it is their lifeblood. And it is even the lifeblood of participatory media more generally.

The central difference I have with Milner, who has written an essential and extremely useful book on which I have relied throughout this book and in my courses, is that I avoid placing conversation at the center of my comprehensive take on the unwieldy phenomenon that is memes. One reason is basic: there are myriad instances of memetic production in which little to no direct interplay with others is occurring. It is instead about performing a certain custom or arrangement, or even just putting things together in a way they haven't been put together before. Calling these instances conversational denies them their aesthetic and performative specificity. The other reason I do not put conversation at the center runs deeper. It is the same reason I do not place things like street art or postmodern folklore at the center of the analysis. Doing so places value on acts of cultural combination when those acts appear to overcome combination, or when they appear to reach toward a higher level of coherence. We have seen how, in other contexts, the assumed means of transcending or cohering is a compelling narrative or a successful mimesis. In the text in question, it is conversation that does this work. This is the larger and more stable thing, the tacit emergence to which all the chaos of memes points. Their powers and their perils turn on the (indeed quite real and abundant) impacts they have on these manifestly important things we call public conversations.

It is not, therefore, just saying something necessary to suggest that the history of internet memes is a history of hyperdistributed media assembly. It is also saying something, as it were, protective. (I smirk a bit in writing that word; of all things memes seem least in need of protection, but what we are talking about is protecting certain ideas.) What an assembly-based approach to memes ultimately does is work to maintain, rather than exceed, the fundamentally combinatory and open-ended nature of this dramatically widespread and influential phenomenon. Showing how memes are acts of evolving, collective conversation is illuminating; asserting memes as street art is valuable; framing memes as postmodern folklore does good work. But these generalizations also risk enacting tacit erasures. Crucial realms of meme cultures are obscured; potentials for further impactful inquiry become harder to see. My response is to suggest that an emphasis on media assembly better suits us to negotiate these generalizations while seeding terms and taxonomies more acutely responsive to memes as acts and artifacts of selection and reconfiguration within a vast collective performance of assembling and reassembling across all manner of technical, social, and cultural differences.

The significance of this intervention will feel more tangible when we find ourselves better suited to address specific examples, and this ought to include examples that embody the fact that Godwin, Milner, Jackson, Dean, and several others emphasize: certain memes do harm. One meme that comes to mind along these lines (and that already seems like the distant past) can be labeled via its constitutive phrase: "jobs not mobs." In the lead-up to the 2018 midterm elections in the United States, a self-styled "meme warfare consultant" sought to encourage widespread use of the phrase as a hashtag and rallying cry. The near-term sources of the meme were left-wing protestors being labeled "mobs" and the coincident critique of the use of this term from various corners. (Also in circulation was an idea that a flood of migrants was making its way to the U.S. border.) The meme warfare consultant's notion of turning these derogatory (and often racist) renderings of current events and politics into fodder for memetic production gained momentum as the phrase inspired a myriad of tweets, image macros, comments, and columns. The exclamatory version "jobs not mobs!" eventually made its way into the Twitter feed of then-President Trump. From there, the meme reached a perverse culmination by becoming an official Republican talking point. Candidates and pundits were encouraged to invoke the phrase wherever possible.

Because this meme is repugnant, it could be difficult to accept it as an instance illuminated by the theory of media assembly. It might even be difficult to accept the idea of granting this microhistory analytical attention, particularly as doing so allows its "memetic payload" another avenue.[58] (I am reminded of the words of Toni Morrison: "Oppressive language does more than represent violence; it is violence; does more than represent the limits of knowledge; it limits knowledge."[59]) And yet it is valuable to see how this meme embodies the hyperdistributed and sometimes corrosive character of memetic assembly and exchange, a character that would be seized on for regressive ends many times over in the years to come.

We can see this first by way of a special project of the *New York Times* (Plate 10).[60] What the developers of this visualization have done is to plot the meme. Starting from the top of the page and traveling down, a central spine gathers dots that signal instances color-coded for the contexts in which they appear, like Reddit and YouTube. The number of memetic instances correlates with the width and quantity of the individual circles. Along the way, particular instances are highlighted for their distinction or importance; in addition, there are section breaks narrating new developments. The visualization is not a perfect mirror of what took place out in the world (nor, unfortunately, does it offer an open data set that others could examine or reuse). It is a distinct way of exhibiting the actual situated unfolding of the meme as an event of distributed assembly within a history of hyperdistributed assembly (and not, it seems to me, a visualization of conversation, folklore, or street art as such).

This event of distributed assembly began with an instance of discrete assembly. This was two words that rhyme ("jobs" and "mobs"), these words linked by a single negating term ("not"). Although it clearly uses a well-established Republican and right-wing trope, the way that negation works is still not fully prescribed. It could be mobs stand in the way of jobs. It could be that one ought to support the people who support jobs rather than mobs. Or it could be that attention ought not to be given to mobs (or to critiquing the misuse of that term), but rather to people and affiliations "jobs" is meant to signal. In any event, the key observation to make here is that the link between assembled words is productive. It is not productive in the socially ameliorative sense, but in the sense of yielding and provoking across networks and collectives. Part of what makes it productive is the ease of utterance and remembrance. It fits within limited spaces; it implies further binaries, like Black–white and capitalist–communist. Fused with other catalyzing factors—including political advertising, echo chambers, and Trump's Twitter account—these qualities are consequential for just how quickly the meme spread, for how much memetic material was produced, and for how many people and accounts found themselves exposed to each other in the process. That the hashtag was not the singular locus of media assembly around which the meme turned is evident in the original video that intercuts journalists critiquing the use of mobs with scenes of left-wing protest (Figures 3.7). Here it is not as simple as two elements brought into expressive union. It is a more complex array. What we see includes narratives but is not itself a narrative. What we see includes conversations but is not itself a conversation. The memetic video is an act of selecting and arranging that implies an indefiniteness to the type of material that might be produced (and a mockery of the harm done by oppressive language). It also encourages the production of further examples along these lines. These, too, tend to take the form of reductive and corrosive assemblies, with forcible mythologies of racial and intranational warfare at their hearts. These assemblies stand ready for redistribution into the reservoirs of other topics. And they provide testing grounds for the assembling that can take place in the future, in even more extreme terms.

Although observing the distributed workings of "jobs not mobs" provides a useful initial illustration of memes as distributed and hyperdistributed media assembly, it is not enough. It is also necessary to put this meme in dialogue with other memes and with

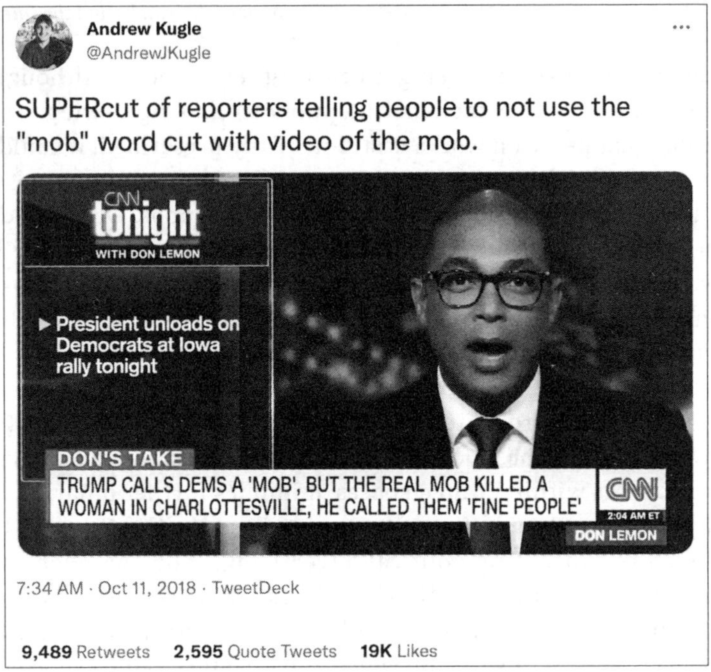

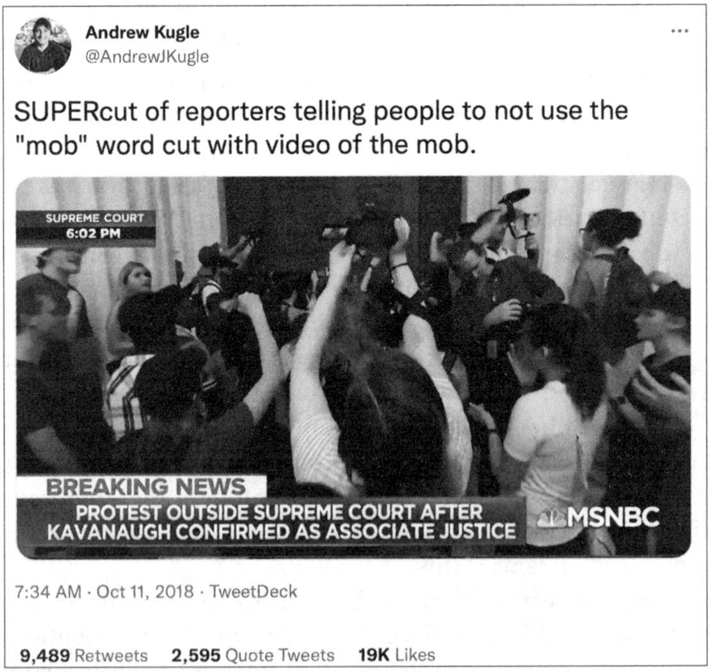

Figure 3.7. Screen captures from "SUPERcut of reporters telling people to not use the 'mob' word cut with video of the mob," posted to Twitter by @AndrewJKugle on October 11, 2018.

dynamics of communication and interaction in social media more generally. Three examples stand out for present purposes:

(a) The first is one I alluded to at the outset: a widely studied meme based not in a phrase, but in the comic-book character Pepe created by Furie. The frog first entered into hyperdistributed assembly in relatively benign instances of expressive folksonomy. (His signature phrase is "Feels good, man.") Starting in 2015, however, first 4chan shitposters, then affiliates of alt-right and white-supremacist movements began to appropriate the image for their own purposes. Pepe became Donald Trump standing at a podium. Pepe stood alongside Trump and his cabinet, all of them "deplorables." Pepe killed liberals and feminists in a video game. A #savePepe campaign was started by Furie and the Anti-Defamation League. And then, in 2019, Pepe appeared during protests against extradition and diluted autonomy in Hong Kong. He now stood for the injury to a protestor, and his image began to appear repeatedly, an image of unity that appealed to the youth of the movement (although there remained concerns about the possible import of white-supremacist and other tropes through its use). And hence a third meme within a meme came to be: from Pepe as play to Pepe as hate to Pepe as protest.[61]

(b) The second example is both a meme and a parafolksonomic tactic in use as of the time of writing of the present book. So-called "Trump trains" are, as artist and researcher Erin Gallagher summarizes, "tweets that contain nothing but a list of usernames, some emojis, and usually a meme or a gif. It's a social media growth hack that's been around for a while . . . but has been enthusiastically adopted by pro-Trump Twitter users since the 2016 elections."[62] Gallagher goes on to explain: "Each tweet is referred to as a 'train car' and sometimes the train cars have numbers. Users included in each train car tweet are called 'riders' and there are 'conductors' that organize each train and dedicate a great deal of their time on Twitter to this activity." There is, therefore, a network of trains: "Because they are all different trains but they're participating in the same activity, each of the trains is interwoven with other trains, which is probably normal in networks like this." The upshot is more followers for pro-Trump accounts and wider distribution of pro-Trump memes, hashtags, GIFs, videos, faces, images and voices.

(c) As a final example, there have been active efforts to weaponize memes and deputize meme-infused communities.[63] As Stephanie Mencimer reports, "well-funded conservative groups" worked to "train young internet-savvy right-wingers in the art of meme-making, enlisting a growing army in what they see as the coming meme war of 2020."[64] Along similar lines, there are more distributed efforts among far-right groups to seed and support meme accounts aimed at spreading extremist ideas and furnishing ideological interpretations of unfolding world events.[65] Furthermore, as observed by Jacob Davey, "troll armies bring themselves together in almost semi-military style hierarchies" aimed at activists and politicians.[66] Meanwhile, on platforms like Discord and Steam, "online harassment of minority groups is treated as a form of real life game. This acts as a potential vector to bring young people into contact with extreme right wing activity."[67]

Four instances of distributed assembly are set side by side, then: "jobs not mobs"; Pepe the frog (one of many memes to undergo such transformations[68]); Trump trains; and widespread training and trolling.

An obvious family resemblance here is the advancement of Trumpian agendas through networked means. But that is a mere surface characteristic shared by too many things on the internet to warrant attention as such. What we are looking for is something more particular and indeed repeatable: a crosscutting use of distributed, memetic assembly for which counter-memes (or other tactics) become necessary. We have a memetic event, a memetic appropriation, and two memetic methods. The novel family resemblance that links these disparate instances is what I think of as distributed *dis*assembly. An article that shares much with Godwin's provides essential means toward the elaboration of this concept. Matt Goerzen puts on the table the use of memes (including Pepe the Frog) by extreme right-wing groups.[69] For Goerzen, the crucial variable is attention. The various memes dominate what is seen and circulated. In finding their way to eyeballs, social media feeds, and tracking software, they transmit their "memetic payloads." In so doing, they impact the spectrum of what is thinkable and discussable. Ideas that would have otherwise never made their way into wide public discourse now do so (a phenomenon called, as Goerzen points out, the "Overton window," named after policy analyst Joseph P. Overton). The subdomain of hyperdistributed media assembly that is alt-right memeing thus serves the nefarious end of affording wider circulation to bigoted, hateful, and violent speech, thinking, assembly, and practice.

The fashion in which instances of distributed disassembly work is not identical, but analogous. What is similar is the effect of circulating ideas that would not otherwise travel well through various media over time. What is distinct is an unacknowledged, shared trajectory. In each of these examples, by one means or another, two dynamics are feeding each other. One is the active assault on various democratic norms. The other is both directly and indirectly collaborative expansion of means and sites for this assault. Together these dynamics make for a shared practice, distributed over space and time, of working to variously corrode, undermine, or pervert what are otherwise well-established and essential habits of democratic speech, behavior, and practice. In other words, what we have is a disturbing paradox. Acts of media assembly, such as making memes and consolidating followers, are also acts of social and political disassembly. This is a contribution to what has been called "democratic erosion" by dispersed consolidation and toxic aggregation, sometimes through false equivalences (e.g., Trump's notion of "very fine people on both sides" after the deadly 2017 Unite the Right rally in Charlottesville, VA), other times in the refusal of any side but the right one. It is slow (but sometimes fast), digital (but also embodied), discursive (and performed) political corrosion.

These acts of disassembly are not mere media noise, nor are their impacts and success measurable only in election wins and losses. They concretely alter what is thinkable, sayable, and doable. The events of January 6, 2021, were a sharp illustration of how this is so. On the one hand, this was not, as scholars of democratic erosion emphasize, pure aberration.[70] There have been many instances across the world of protest "subverted for antidemocratic ends," and it is often the case that a leader who performs "contempt for established norms" manages to mobilize those "radicalized by political sectarianism, truth decay, and conspiracy theories" into "antidemocratic disruption," effectively making fascist and antidemocratic sentiment and behavior into something memetic. On the other hand, there was something distinct (if not entirely unique) about the severity of the event's memetic and configural dimensions. In the days leading up to the event, another phrasal meme that emulated the "language of prodemocracy activism" ("Stop the Steal!") was weaponized by those in power as both a rallying cry and a viral, memetic constituent. Then, as I discuss in the Conclusion, the insurrection itself unfolded like some surreal multistage performance of many existing and emergent memes and other media assemblies, shifting back and forth between media and popular assembly. This was an intense and violent consolidation of distributed disassembly in real time. It also persists in memory as an available, assembled repertoire of antidemocratic affects and tactics.

I started this section with Godwin's article. I'll close with it as well. "If it's possible to generate effective counter-memes, is there any moral imperative to do so?," Godwin asks. "When we see a bad or false meme go by, should we take pains to chase it with a counter-meme? Do we have an obligation to improve our informational environment? Our social environment?"[71] To some degree, these questions are symptoms of their moment. This was 1994, a time when the internet and the web were not seemingly everywhere you go, but rather occasionally accessed portals to somewhere else, "cyberspace," that "notional environment" populated by websites, chat rooms, and newsgroups. In such a time, it was clearly reasonable to pose the idea of informational stewardship. The internet could be seen as a closed space of shared cultivation in which users had ample say and share. Now nearly three decades removed, with the internet (at least in many places) quite pervasive and increasingly enmeshed with the nondigital, this way of separating out the internet as a distinct space seems strange. (Meanwhile, the term "internet" has itself taken on multiple meanings.[72]) Information and environment overlap and intersect.[73] Not only that, but the digital and the ecological are increasingly yoked by way of elaborate media infrastructures, structures for monitoring and disaster response, and the waste stream.

All this to say that Godwin's proposition has taken on unexpected meaning. Among the consequences of distributed disassembly has been the undermining of what new norms, institutions, and practices might develop for the sake of variously local, regional, national, supernational, Indigenous, and intersectional climate justice. The science of the climate emergency is questioned. The rationale for action is rejected. The people affected are dehumanized. In other words, as W. J. T. Mitchell puts it, in response to "the most consequential *imagetext* in our time [i.e., climate change], . . . a whole industry of climate change denial has emerged, grounded in populist ignorance and the short range interests of predatory capitalism, especially the fossil fuel industry. The plain evidence of the senses, the shrinking of the polar ice caps, rising sea levels, expanding deserts and wildfires are dismissed and denied. What we see, and what they say are completely at odds."[74] Given the role of this variation on memetic assembly, it seems essential to continue to confront the apparently unflagging ecological force of memetic production. The many creatures and entities and processes we gather together under "environment" can live and die in part because of the hyperdistributed media assembly pulsing through the networks of undersea cables that crisscross the globe. The call to generate effective counter-memes takes on a new urgency. This is a call that both echoes *and* exceeds the longstanding tasks of the critical arts, a persistent calling toward, in Mitchell's words, "making the truth visible, exposing lies, revealing contradictions, and providing new paradigms for the imagination."[75] Memes on biodiversity and environmental racism? Memes that facilitate climate optimism? Maybe. But the heart of the call is this: memetic production must afford new, crosscutting techniques that overwhelm in their power and persistence. Hyperdistributed repair, ever wider capacity for reassembly, networks toward reparations, collectives for defensive and reparative counter-memes—I'm not sure what these techniques would be. But this much seems fair to say: assembly in the media sense must evermore actively interact with assembly in political, ecological, technological, and still other senses.

Assembly as a Property of the Internet Era

In first teaching and now writing about memes, I have found there is an unavoidable paradox looming over the whole operation: one always ends up saying both too much and too little. Too much is said because, as the "explains the joke" meme testifies, the move to translate (not to mention seriously analyze) memes is humorously out of step with the actual acts of making, liking, and sharing them. Too little is said because there is always more that could and should be addressed with respect to this insistent, complex, and enduringly significant phenomenon: more about the latest trending topics (as I finish revising this chapter, these topics include meme coins, meme stocks, the metaverse, and NFTs); more about race and appropriation; more about capitalism; more on the question of warfare and propaganda; more on the sense of how, on a daily basis, memes figure in collective diets of joy, perspective, and distraction. Nevertheless, between the too much and the too little sits the necessary and the possible, and one last line of questioning concerns the internet era as a whole. What can memes help us see about cultural forms at scale? Does the rise of digital and networked technologies tend to favor certain dominant cultural forms? Does it unleash otherwise dormant forms?

As things stand, at least in English-speaking and English-translated scholarship, there are at least three dominant frames for the internet as a context of cultural form. One of the earliest is Janet Murray's vision of the internet as a place in which the cultural forms of narrative and representation thrive. "The human urge for representation, for storytelling, and for the transformational use of the imagination," Murray writes in 1997, "is an immutable part of our makeup, and the narrative potential of the new digital medium is dazzling."[76] Murray sees storytelling as an endemic potential, not just in individual artifacts but as a collective practice, and she reasserts as much in a 2016 update to the book: "We have not yet fully exploited the potential of digital representation to exchange kaleidoscopic, transformative stories, but we are assembling the building blocks of this emerging medium artifact by artifact, maybe even tweet by tweet."[77]

Not long after Murray circulated this representational and story-centric view of the internet, Lev Manovich introduced its apparent inversion, suggesting that, with the rise of digital and networked media, narrative had ceded its longstanding dominance to its correlate (or even its "enemy"[78]), one defined by a lack of temporal sequencing and instead marked by an equality among its component elements, a cultural form he dubbed "database." For N. Katherine

Hayles, writing in 2012, Manovich's account of a cultural form that "see[s] the world in terms the computer can understand" is both persuasive and flawed. On the one hand, it is indeed the case that expressive and rhetorical uses of data proliferate and that they do so through features of sorting, cataloging, and querying that narrative cannot muster. On the other hand, it is, in Hayles's view, more useful to think of database as narrative's "symbiont," rather than its enemy, the two forms in a "mutually beneficial relation."[79] For Hayles, in other words, while the "position narrative occupies in the culture" can shift, and while the cultural form of database has been largely responsible for such a shift, narrative remains an evolutionary and everyday fundamental. In their ubiquity and adaptability, narratives can, she writes, "transform to accommodate new data and mutate to probe what lies beyond the exponentially expanding infosphere."[80]

Finally, for one last perspective on the internet as cultural form, the fact of the "infosphere" is of especial salience. From various corners, writers emphasize the emergence of remix and mashup cultures, on the idea that a signature feature of networks is cutting, pasting, and modifying, taking and appropriating, creative reuse.

So, to which of these, or to what else, does a theory of memes as assembly point? It isn't to some new and overly reductive story of cultural formal warfare in which a longstanding binary battle (between database and narrative) has been triangulated (now among assembly, database, and narrative). Nor is it (as I emphasized at the end of chapter 1) to the understandable but nonneutral and ultimately deceptive notion that "everything is a remix." Rather, it is a vision of cultural form inspired by the weed-like qualities of memes, the way they appear, spread, and survive like a kind of profligate, "spontaneous vegetation." Call it "assembly as a property of the internet era." This is the idea that assembly is not only something particular and separable, as in the artifacts of expressive folksonomy that people make, or as in the distinct, historically specific, and ongoing exercise of making and sharing memes in the vein of hyperdistributed assembly. Assembly is *also* a part of the very "physics" and "ecology" of networked life. In other words, *one can scarcely avoid doing assembly when participating in networked life.* This is because of the relational, configural, and accumulative dimensions of so much of this participation.

Whether I tap out my next text or compose my next post or make my next meme, I am at least partly in the business of configuring elements and aggregates of elements. I select certain elements (numbers, letters, pixels, emojis, punctuation, etc.); I also position and reposition them. No doubt, there are other, nondiscrete operations at work as well, operations that produce "analog feelings, rich in continuous input and gradations of the sensory," such as the feel of tapping my phone.[81] And no doubt other cultural forms are in play, most often acts of representation ("look at what I saw") or storytelling ("you won't believe what they did") or argumentation ("let me tell you why you're wrong"). Nevertheless, time and again, I seize on a drive to variously encounter, select, assemble, and disassemble constituents. This requires at least some awareness of the rhetorical dynamics I put in play by going with one version of a configuration over another—what these choices of arrangements say or do that others don't, or don't quite. Furthermore, many everyday acts of communication (appending emojis to a question to try to temper its effects by way of contrast, or choosing trendy annotations to layer on a video) consist of generating, however minutely, assembly-infused and assembly-like effects (Figure 3.8). Still further, the large aggregates I build by intention (such as an elaborate slideshow) or by course (such as my expanding social media profile) are also exercises in assembly, both because of the form in which they are made and because of their openness to being read as selective gatherings of materials, thoughts, and references. Moreover, most anything I share will be received by my loved one or my acquaintance, or the unknown stranger or quarantine group chat or whomever else, within and alongside the presence of other pieces or aggregates of media. Nothing appears alone; everything appears within a network of possible and often interlinked alternatives. There is always this and that in enduring or temporary configuration with other things.

Finally, not always but quite often, the format through which I engage in networked interaction with others allows them the opportunity to have a partial say in the composition of the assembly of constituents I have already produced. They can, for instance, alter the count of likes, or they can add to the lineup of replies, or they can make my assembly a constituent of theirs. Tech companies and advertisers (rather than users) can also try to guess at (or even adjust) my own needs and desires. These prescriptive guesses af-

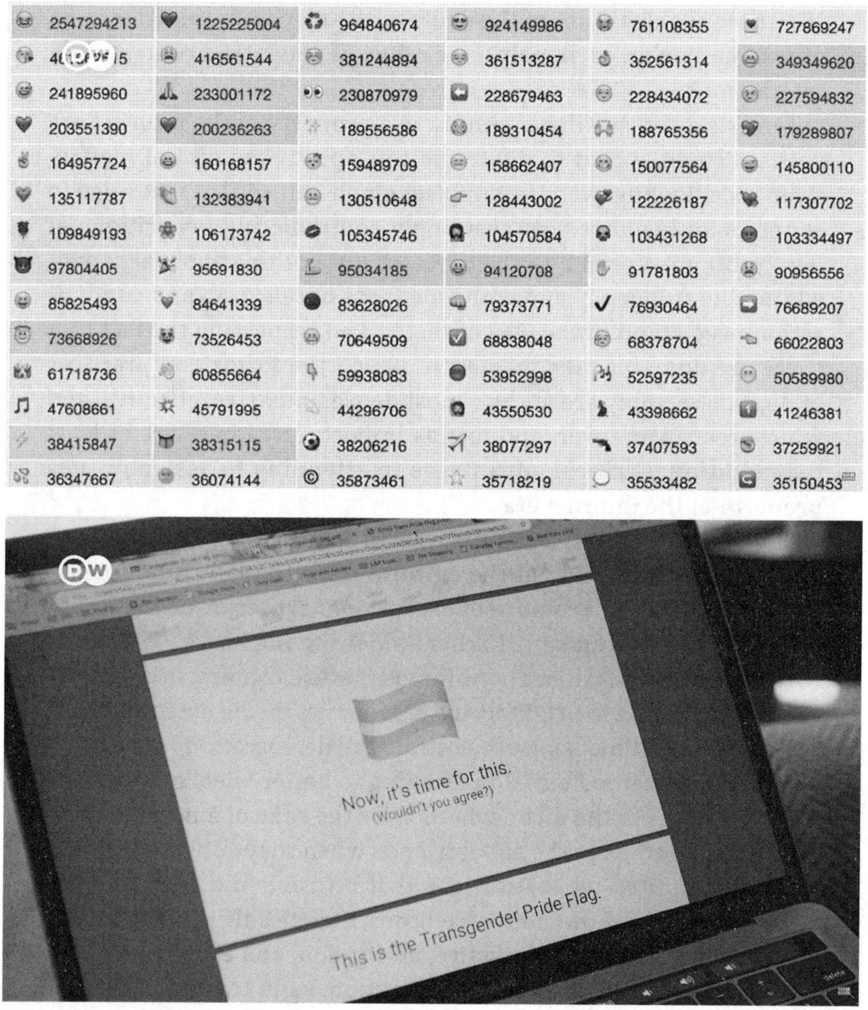

Figure 3.8. Traces of assembly as a property of the internet era: an animation of emoji uses (several billion are used per day as of 2020) and a subset of slides arguing for the addition of a Transgender Pride Flag emoji. Screen captures from "Have you ever heard of the 'Emoji Commission'?" Deutsche Welle documentary, May 4, 2020, YouTube video, 49:52, youtube.com/watch?v=Fr9L27V337E.

fect what populates the feeds and "For You" pages through which I scroll (or to which I am beckoned by notification), for better and (quite often) for worse. For all these reasons and still more (an alternative sketch of assembly as a property centers on "we" rather than

"I"), there is a quantum of the expressive and communicative form of assembly in an extremely wide range of networked contexts and interactions.

One risk of asserting assembly as a property of the internet era is that I could appear to dilute the concept to the point of ineffectiveness, allowing even the simplest emoji-infused text message to count as an instance (and seemingly contradicting my critique of "everything is a remix" in the process). But nothing about acknowledging the frequency and embeddedness of selection and configuration need stand in the way of seeing and respecting the fact that there are domains, like memes, in which the forms and practices of digital assembly are at their most dense, intensive, effective, and widespread. Moreover, and just as importantly, there are at least two additional critical advantages in attending to assembly as a property of the internet era.

For one thing, I can avoid the impression that this book's theory of assembly assumes that the cultural form is really, underneath it all, the exclusive province of exceptional artists or in-the-know, tech-savvy meme makers. Rather, one thing the history of memes reveals is the persistent room for, as it were, agency in assembly (and in exercising the right to and freedom of media assembly). It is a fundamental dimension of the strategy's democratic appeal. There is still unrealized potential in learning to better wield and support the better uses of the form, whether for the sake of a more humorous life, or to come to the aid of friends when they suffer, or to work to abolish oppressive institutions that refuse to die. It is a matter of building know-how: networked constituents cultivate these relational literacies through practice, discussion, and exchange. Those literacies do not pertain only to reception, as in the broadcast era. They extend to making, influencing, sharing, critiquing, and reconfiguring. As Osunde put it: "We make it up. We have always made it up."

The other critical value in emphasizing assembly as a property of the internet era is of a different order. It pertains to those exercises of compiling and rearranging that take place in the shadows. As in Day's notion of "indexing it all," networked interactions don't just feed into the visible and interpretable assemblies people can see and share. They also feed into invisible and calculable quasi-assemblies of data, metadata, and automated analysis that remain widely inaccessible. From posting a photo to sharing a new meme, the exercises of digital agency one pursues literally produce constituents of characters, such as numbers like geolocations, terms like keywords of interest, "data exhaust" like the frequency with which we charge our phones, and these enter into all manner of corporate and state databases, or what Zuboff calls the "shadow text."[82] There the constituents of our electronic interactions join other constituents drawn from other places, whether those associated with you or those associated with others deemed your analogues by virtue of one or the other demographic category. With "experience . . . dragooned as raw material to be accumulated and analyzed as means to others' market ends,"[83] the aggregates of data about you (or those deemed like you) become the stuff of money exchanged (this profit-driven entity buying that profit-driven entity's knowledge) or power wielded (this power-driven entity using that power-driven entity's knowledge to try to alter behaviors, or at least to sell others on the idea that they can alter behaviors[84]). And, quite often, as Noble's work helps us see, the various processes into which the constituents of your networked life have fed will end up impacting the life you and others (classified as) like you can live, from something as seemingly banal as the advertisements you see to something as obviously consequential as the resources that accrue to your demographics or the likelihood that you will be the subject of state scrutiny, political propaganda, or even state and extra-judicial violence.

Perhaps this feels like a jarring way to end this chapter: from a recognition of the agency and often the sheer joy in seizing on memetic and configural literacies to a sobering recognition of the extractive accumulations of data assemblies in which most people have little say. But until there is deep and democratic structural change—change that includes figuring out how, as Salomé Viljoen puts it, our "data relations" can become not "oppressive, exploitative, and even violent" but mutually "empowering and supportive"[85]—such will be the prevailing conditions of networked life: the uplifting then the harrowing, the beautiful between the awful, the profitable over the generative, the real against the fake.

4

Generative Assembly after Disaster

Among the most successful uses of assembly in the early days of social media was neither a meme nor an artwork; it was an urgent, low-resolution comparison (Figure 4.1).[1] The impetus for the comparison was one of the largest storms of the 2005 Atlantic season: Hurricane Katrina. The venue was the recently launched photo-sharing platform Flickr. The author of the assembly, working under the username dustin3000, compares two recent news photographs, both of them framing citizens, goods in hand, wading through floodwaters.[2] The difference in captions is hard to miss: one, for the Black person, uses "loot"; the other, for the pair of white people, uses "find." The author's own caption and title ("Racism") clinch the implication: as a blogger at the *Daily Kos* blog would put it: "It's not looting if you're white."[3]

The potent juxtaposition went viral. It provided means and motivation for discussions of discrimination and violence across mass media and blogs. Kanye West would cite the comparison in his famous rebuke of the Bush administration during a televised fundraiser.[4] In fact, so remarkable did this example of virality appear at this media-historical juncture that a *New York Times* story traced the juxtaposition's circulation and impacts, as well as the responses of the photographers and news organizations.[5] Though the original Flickr post eventually became inaccessible, copies of the visual-verbal assembly have persisted.[6] One was added to the Hurricane Digital Memory Bank (HDMB), a participatory digital archive of some twenty-five thousand items, discussed below.[7] Another circulated across social media channels in advance of the landfall of Hurricane Harvey in 2017. The now historical comparison served as a warning.

Part of what makes the comparison important is what it emphasizes. Like any environmental or technological disaster, Katrina

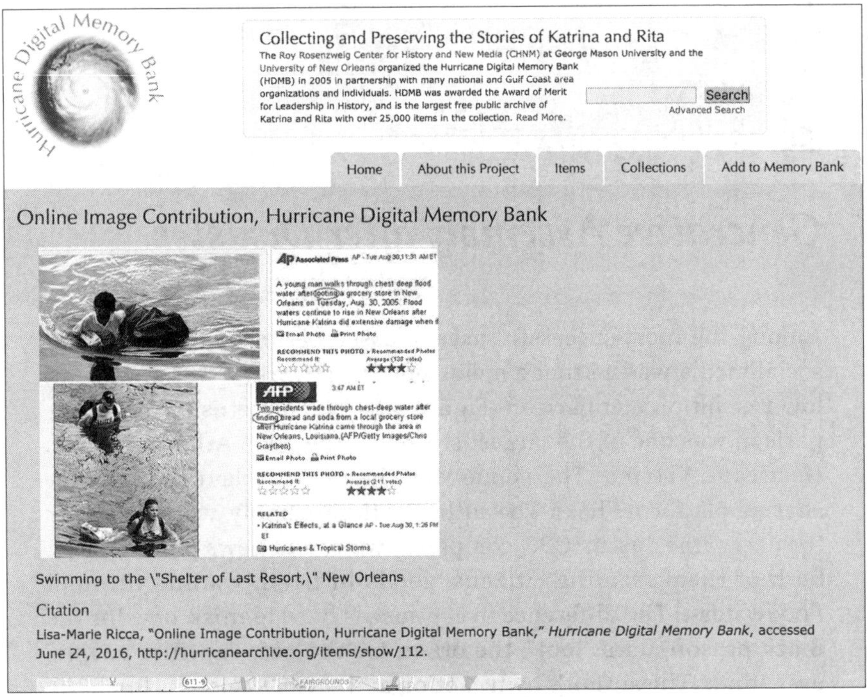

Figure 4.1. One generative assembly joins another. Lisa-Marie Ricca's contribution of dustin3000's "Racism" to the Hurricane Digital Memory Bank (2005).

was neither natural nor neutral. Race, bias, and perception mattered from the first. This was certainly the case with respect to the world of journalism and television, a significant subset of which struggled to report the unfolding scenes without falling into stubborn racial tropes. Valorie Thomas contrasts the "Black Creole cityscape," its "diasporic disidentifications with mainstream U.S. narratives of racial purity," with the frantic "hyperessentialism of the moment," the latter embodied in CNN host Wolf Blitzer's comment that the people wading through floodwaters were "so poor" and "so Black."[8] But it was also the case with on-the-ground decision-making about rescue and policing.[9] Indeed, although not at the same scale, disproportionate effects and race-inflected media framing extended to Vietnamese American, Latinx, Indigenous, and Arab Muslim communities in New Orleans and the larger Gulf Coast region.[10]

Another key valence of "Racism" is of a different order. (I am referring to it by the author's apparent title.) Many of us have grown used to thinking that the best uses of media in response to disaster are those that move audiences with the power of a story or that inform and persuade politicians and publics through the evidentiary force of representation. While there is ample reason to continue to pursue these cultural forms, the considerable success of dustin3000's intervention helps call that implicit premise into question. Viewed through this book's lens of media assembly, the contribution is neither a story about nor a strict mirroring of that reality of differential framing understood as pervading government and media response to Katrina. Rather, it is a cogent documentary configuration that speaks of and through the evidence in the form of a transmissible unit—an assembly. Zooming out from this single example to the wide array of cultural responses to Katrina and still other disasters, what one finds is not a handful of analogous uses of media, but numerous important ones. The thought that opens is simple but consequential. Instances like "Racism" belong to their own category of communication and cultural expression undertaken in response to disaster. Projects in this mode deserve more than passing mention. They deserve equal attention.

This chapter defends and elaborates the thought. The name I propose is not "media assembly after disaster," but rather "*generative* assembly after disaster." What sets the practice apart is the work of assembling records and signifiers related to disasters into particular kinds of media artifacts. Like other instances of assembly examined in this book, those artifacts characteristically maintain the active appearance and interactive potential of selection and arrangement. They do this in formats as varied as comics, photobooks, paintings, films, exhibitions, memes, and multithousand-item online archives. These assembly-based artifacts might involve moving accounts of characters and events, and they might well make absent scenes and subjects present. But this is neither the full extent nor the sole strategy at work in most of these cases. Instead, instances of generative assembly seize on the expressive potentials of compilation and configuration. In so doing they tend to support various articulable and often highly effective kinds of what I call (in conversation with other writers) "generativity."

The crucial question in these pages is what this generativity entails, or what assembly can *do* in response to disaster. The varieties and intensities of the strategy's uses after Katrina suggest one key thing: generative assembly can constitute especially powerful means of intervening in prevailing conditions of mediation and remembrance around events of environmental and social violence. Generative assembly can do crucial cultural work where those prevailing conditions are somehow limited, biased, lacking, or misdirected, and where stories and representation might not suffice. Assembly can also help frame the crucial question of what comes next: regeneration, repair, and as is often needed, reinvention. At the same time, as the last chapter emphasized by way of memes and distributed disassembly, uses of assembly can also act as engines of deception and entrenchment, and this is often (though not exclusively) the case in digital contexts. In developing terms and taxonomies for generative assembly after disaster, we can more adequately address the wide spectrum of cultural possibility in the wake of large-scale ecological, social, and technological upheavals, events that seem poised only to increase in an era of multiple, intersecting, pathological, economic, and climate disasters.

Disaster Media beyond Image and Narrative

"Katrina" refers to a massive hurricane; it also refers to the fatal, preventable flood of over eighty percent of New Orleans that followed.[11] A tragic and violent technological catastrophe, the flood was also a social and ecological disaster many years in the making. The levees meant to protect the city from exactly such a hurricane had not been properly constructed or maintained: Douglas Brinkley calls them "ugly monuments to shoddy engineering," "a lot of poured concrete, on swishy sand and peat soil, that wasn't properly maintained."[12] And it was Black residents, poor residents, and residents of color who died and suffered the most. Despite heroic efforts by many residents and first responders, over eighteen hundred people lost their lives across New Orleans and the larger Gulf Coast region; hundreds of thousands more were displaced, many of them permanently. The Federal Emergency Management Agency (FEMA) was woefully underprepared, and the administration of then President George W. Bush failed to act quickly enough. It has been widely recognized that there was a "color" to this unnatural disaster, the slow and militarized response to which only further laid bare the widely embedded devaluation of Black lives.[13]

Between the severity of these events, their openness to imaging, the need for reflection and reform, and the usual appetites for spectacle and suffering, there emerged what Michael Mizell-Nelson (a key leader of the *HDMB*) characterized as a documentary impulse not seen since the Great Depression.[14] Much of this impulse played out in the immediate unfolding and aftermath, from the work of traditional reportage in radio, television, and newspapers to contributions across blogs, message boards, and (only recently) emerging platforms like Flickr and YouTube. (Facebook had barely gotten its start, and Twitter had not yet come on the scene.) But the impulse also persisted in the months and years ahead. Various cultural producers from within and beyond the Gulf Coast devoted time and energy to these events, their implications, and their ongoing consequences, including multivenue biennales. Meanwhile, Katrina persisted in memes, metaphors, and movements. As Jamelle Bouie argues, "Black collective memory of Hurricane Katrina" played an informing role in the emergence and evolution of Black Lives Matter. The events of 2005 and beyond "sowed the ground for a reckoning," and integral to this reckoning was the "deep sense that America is indifferent to [Black Americans'] lives and livelihoods."[15] Along these exact lines, iconic images of Katrina, including those of suffering crowds at the Superdome, have continually been mobilized in support of racist tropes of blame and apathy by meme makers, many of them working in the modes discussed in the last chapter, the rapid reclassification of expressive folksonomy and the corrosive work of distributed disassembly.

In terms of the nature and distinction of generative assembly in all this, two further selections out of Katrina's media landscape can support an initial encounter, acting as bridges to a more detailed mapping of projects that directly address both Black collective memory and white indifference around Katrina, whether by artists like Kara Walker and Mark Bradford or by distributed publics.[16] The first selection is Josh Neufeld's 2009 comic *A.D.: New Orleans after the Deluge.* The assembly-infused comic is distinct from the "Racism" comparison along multiple lines: it appeared several years after the storm; it is not digital but physical; its imagery is not photographic but drawn; and it takes longer than a few moments to experience

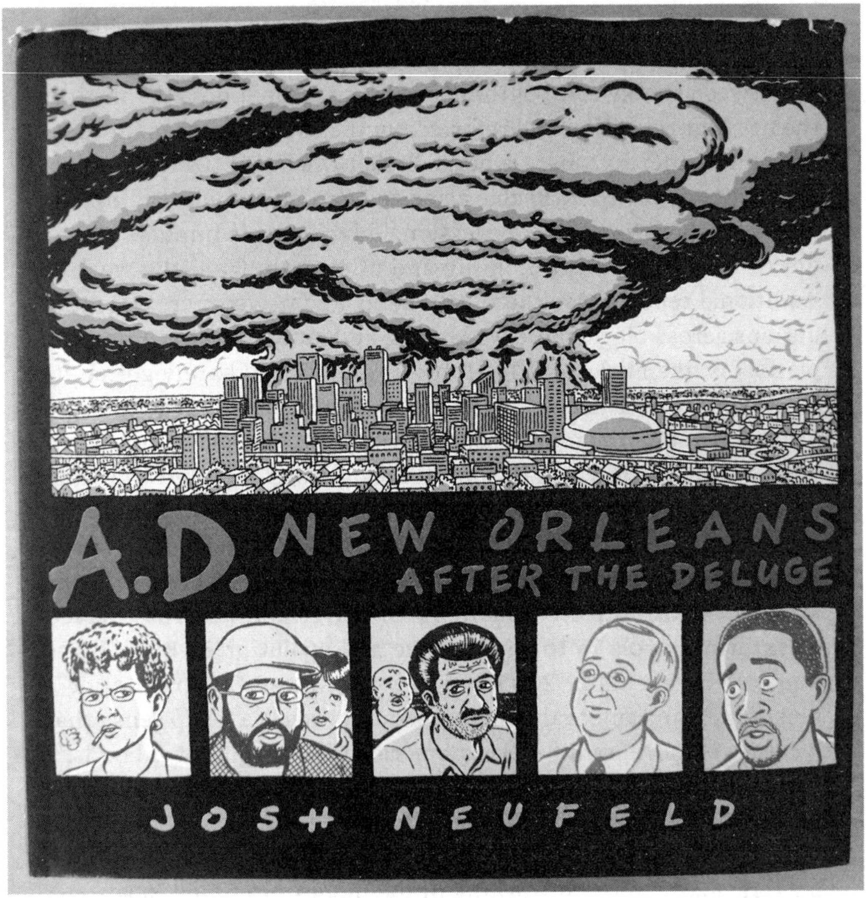

Figure 4.2. *A.D.* convenes moving stories of loss and heroism in response to Katrina. The book is also a paradigm (and partly flawed) instance of generative assembly. Cover of Josh Neufeld, *A.D.: New Orleans after the Deluge.* Copyright 2009 by Josh Neufeld. Reprinted by permission of Pantheon Books, an imprint of the Knopf Doubleday Publishing Group, a division of Penguin Random House LLC.

(Figure 4.2).[17] Alongside renderings of the storm and the flood, some of them derived from iconic news photographs, Neufeld arrays drawings of interviewed citizens' stories and reflections, starting before landfall and concluding a year later. Richard Misrach's 2010 photobook *Destroy This Memory,* the second, assembly-infused selection, has other distinguishing features: it emerged in the con-

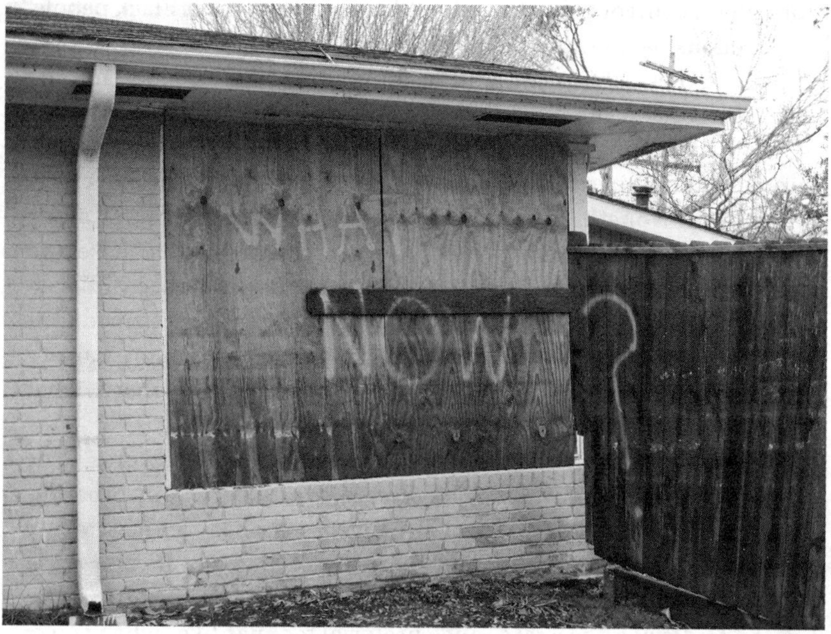

Figure 4.3. The back cover of the photobook adds one last statement to the photographer's configuration of spray-painted messages. Richard Misrach, *Destroy This Memory,* 2010. Copyright Richard Misrach. Courtesy Fraenkel Gallery, San Francisco.

text of contemporary art, and it nearly entirely devalues narrative in favor of the consolidation of affecting photographic imagery (Figure 4.3).[18] Shortly after the storm, Misrach traveled around New Orleans and the Gulf Coast region compiling several thousand images of devastated landscapes with a consumer-quality digital camera. Ahead of the five-year anniversary, Misrach selected sixty-nine of these images for an exhibition and a book. The book's images were printed in vertical rather than horizontal succession, each over a foot wide. All of them frame spray-painted messages on buildings as well as boats and cars, but absent any people. The last of these messages, visible on the back cover, asks, "What now?"

This chapter isn't about assessing the usefulness of a particular medium, such as comics or photography, around Katrina. It also doesn't focus on the problems of position and privilege that must be taken into account when (as in these and other cases) white outsiders confront events that predominantly impact Black people, Indigenous people, and people of color. (To be crystal clear, though: I believe these are essential lines of inquiry; they are just not my focus in these pages, and there are other writers who have pursued them in depth, including with reference to the flood of outside volunteers and nongovernmental organizations to New Orleans after the storm. Nonetheless, I do engage with critiques of *A.D.* along these lines below.[19]) My question is what can be said of these and comparable media instances in terms of the confluence of disasters and cultural forms. At stake is the shared index of medium-nonspecific expressive and communicative forms across responses to Katrina and other disasters—what forms are out there, what they can do especially well, and how they can go wrong.

As things stand, there are two ready-at-hand answers.[20] The first is that *A.D.* and *Destroy This Memory* are, like so many other instances of media after disaster, effectively instances of the strategy of narrative. As much is evident across books like *Narratives of Crisis: Stories of Ruin and Renewal,* articles like "Why Do We Turn to Stories in the Midst of a Disaster?," and curatorial taglines like "when you're rebuilding community, every story matters."[21] The predominant notion is that disastrous events tend to induce spaces of narrative invention and even competition. "Humans by their very nature are storytellers," Matthew W. Seeger and Timothy L. Sellnow write: "Disasters, tragedies, and crises are powerful and disruptive forces that change the course of lives, families, institutions, communities, and societies. As such, they become the stuff of stories."[22] This point is echoed in texts and discussion surrounding Katrina. For instance, for John O'Neal, who facilitated reparative, cross-racial story circles in post-Katrina New Orleans, "if we get enough people engaged in telling enough stories, and if we get enough artists and teachers engaged in using those stories, analyzing those stories and the dynamics they reveal, then we'll find ourselves in a position to make stronger, more deeply rooted plans."[23] Along similar lines, Kate Parker Horigan argues that narrative proves fundamentally necessary for mourning, reflection, debate, and policy reform in the wake of disasters. "[The] personal narratives that describe Katrina in public contexts shape how it is remembered," Horigan writes. "As the memorialization of Katrina in monuments and anniversary celebrations reveals, the themes of those narratives get taken up in published texts and in material and customary culture."[24] In Horigan's compelling account, as in so many others, storytelling is the natural and essential activity of individuals and communities grappling with the material, medial, and mnemonic consequences of catastrophes.[25]

The second ready answer to the question of disaster and cultural form favors narrative's frequent corollary: representation. In his 2015 *Flood of Images: Media, Memory, and Katrina,* for instance, Bernie Cook argues that fictional and documentary moving-image media offer more robust means of recalling and interpreting the disaster than could the established archive of television media. In a different vein, James Johnson emphasizes the problems of visibility and apprehension that face publics who would assess the nature and the consequences of disasters and their aftermaths.[26] Johnson calls attention to the mass migration caused by Katrina, then he points to artistic projects (including Misrach's *Destroy This Memory*) that attempt to bring that migration into visibility through the representative work of multiple documentary photographs. In other articles on and beyond Katrina, we see repetitions of the same core idea: to respond well to disaster is to undertake the longstanding communicative strategy of accurately and compellingly presenting faithful copies of how things were. Such a perspective pervades critical and scholarly literature on the cultural lives of disasters throughout the modern period, not just in discussions of photography, but across studies of reportage, graphic narrative, social media, and beyond.

Although they certainly rely on the cultural forms of narrative and representation, *A.D.* and *Destroy This Memory* are not strictly defined by them; they rely also on a form of media practice that does not fall into either of these umbrella categories. In line with the broader argument in this book, analyzing that practice requires more than recourse to terms that have been associated with accumulation and organization around memorialized events, terms like archive, database, or curation.[27] On the one hand, acts of purpose-driven assembly of expressive constituents define these projects' coming into being: in producing "Racism," dustin3000 encountered the two captions and arranged the provocative visual-verbal unit; in putting a comic into circulation, Neufeld recorded interviews and subsequently interwove drawn renditions of scenes and stories;

in building toward an exhibition and a book, Misrach constructed archives of imagery that cohered around event and scene before devising an affecting sequence. On the other hand, the meanings and implications of these assembly-based and assembly-infused artifacts depend on their audiences' willingness and capacity to read visual and verbal languages of spatiality and arrangement. With "Racism," citizen users judge based on scanning and juxtaposition; with *A.D.*, citizen readers follow diegetic developments while also engaging the poetry in arrangements of word, image, and frame; and with *Destroy This Memory,* citizen viewers interpret the analogies and differences in spray-painted messages and scan those messages' landscapes of loss and absence. Importantly, such acts of reception also take place in dialogue with larger configurations: the vast array of material events gathered under the name "Katrina"; the actual, evolving media landscape of that event; and the various prevailing conditions of seeing, saying, and sharing that impact, without determining, the disaster's interpretation and remembrance.

Why analyze these media practices through the lens of not just assembly but also generativity? At one level, the term provides a way of calling attention to the capacity to produce or to beget; it implies fecundity; and it has a corollary in the term "regenerative," thus pointing toward efforts at repair. The term is also indicative of openness and invention. In multiple invocations of generativity in modern thought, we learn that, out of certain structural conditions come novel or transformative acts, whether through language, behavior, technology, production, or algorithm.[28] We also find that generativity can be lively and even threatening. As Fred Moten observes, the generativity of people, music, texts, and ideas can cause fear; institutions can be "freaked out over the generativity that destroys order," and so persistently attempt to preempt and smother generative movements, stories, and sounds. Meanwhile, perceptions around race and other categories can inform what generativity is deemed too generative by those who would attempt to arrest its workings.[29]

Finally, generativity orients us toward the manifold productive nature of assembly. Circulating artifacts generate the bulk of effects for assembly, but the process of production might matter as much as the artifact, which is to say that there may be socially ameliorative (or richly disruptive and disordering) effects in the very practice of gathering and convening signifying entities, effects that exceed the actual specificity of what is shown or how it is arranged.[30] In digital and networked contexts, this dimension of generativity expands. Certain technological formations, such as the photo-sharing groups or participatory digital archives produced after Katrina, afford the generativity of distanced collaboration (or conflict). What others add generates new additions of material and metadata. These assemblies can also undergo generative reassembly. They can also decay or disappear.

Among the crucial reasons this is specifically *generative* assembly, then, is that the drive to assemble is activated, not just in a single way or at one scale, but in many ways and at multiple intersecting scales. The meaning and implication of any instance of generative assembly depends partly on audiences' and users' production of something—of interpretation, imagination, affect, a new concept for a contribution, a new plan of action—out of some subset of documentary, informational, and architectural arrangements. That something can manifest in consistent ways, as with the takeaway that dustin3000 sought. Other times there are unanticipated or esoteric ways of reading generatively, such as recognizing and valuing idiosyncratic associations within and among the frames of comics, or finding patterns that link scenes and writing across divergent sequences of photographs, or opting to share or remix fragments across social-media platforms. The point is that generative assemblies present, at least in part, structured and conditioned fields of open interpretation. As much is true of nearly any media form, but the architectures and features of generative assembly especially encourage the coincidence of guided attention and inventive response. In this way, assembly can serve as a generative force against the failures of memory and discourse and toward the ends of justice, recovery, and reform, particularly amid the very circumstances that viral assemblies like "Racism" seek to oppose.

From Prevailing Conditions to Key Dynamics

The crucial question is what generative assembly can *do*. To answer this question well, one must be willing to confront a potentially overwhelming heterogeneity of mediums, scales, and registers. Somehow the critical arrangement of historical images in an exhibition context such as Walker's 2008 *After the Deluge* at the Met in New York must productively compare with the sequencing of contemporary photographs of place in a digital platform, such as Christopher Kirsch's photo collection I call *Floodlines*, and these, in turn, must compare productively with distributed assembly in a digital archival repository (such as the *HDMB*).[31]

A first step is establishing the larger frame. The projects in question respond to Katrina, but they also respond to what I have been calling "prevailing conditions" of mediation and remembrance around Katrina. In heuristic fashion, we can separate these conditions into two broad classes. For one, there is the familiar notion of collective or social memory, elaborated in the work of thinkers like Maurice Halbwachs, Pierre Nora, Michel Rolph-Trouillot, and many others.[32] What gets remembered of public violence and by what means? To what degree does spectacle reign over discourse? How and why do certain historical "silences" (to use Trouillout's term) persist, and how might those silences be overcome? How do networks shift the terms of collective memory such that, as Andrew Hoskins puts it, the "media–memory relationship" becomes both "more intense" and "diffused and dispersed"?[33]

With respect to Katrina, several scholars have identified such questions as integral, analyzing the ways in which the event has been retrospectively reduced or rationalized. For instance, Diane Negra argues that, "after an initial frenzy of media coverage, efforts to impose conservative representational discipline over an event deemed ideologically problematic have played out over a sustained period of time."[34] Cook, on the other hand, argues that "television news formed the foundation for the memory and understanding of Katrina" and that "documentary film and video both built upon that foundation and attempted to destabilize it by offering contrasting information and interpretation."[35] Still other scholars emphasize local conditions in New Orleans and the broader Gulf Coast region. I think, for instance, of the "profane archaeology" of Shannon Lee Dawdy, who approaches any given city as a "churning assemblage of human and nonhuman elements" and who argues that "New Orleans is an especially archaeological place," where "residents are keenly aware of dirt and debris, of the processes of decay, burial, and demolition" as well as of "the creation of new landscapes."[36]

A second set of prevailing conditions to which assembly re-

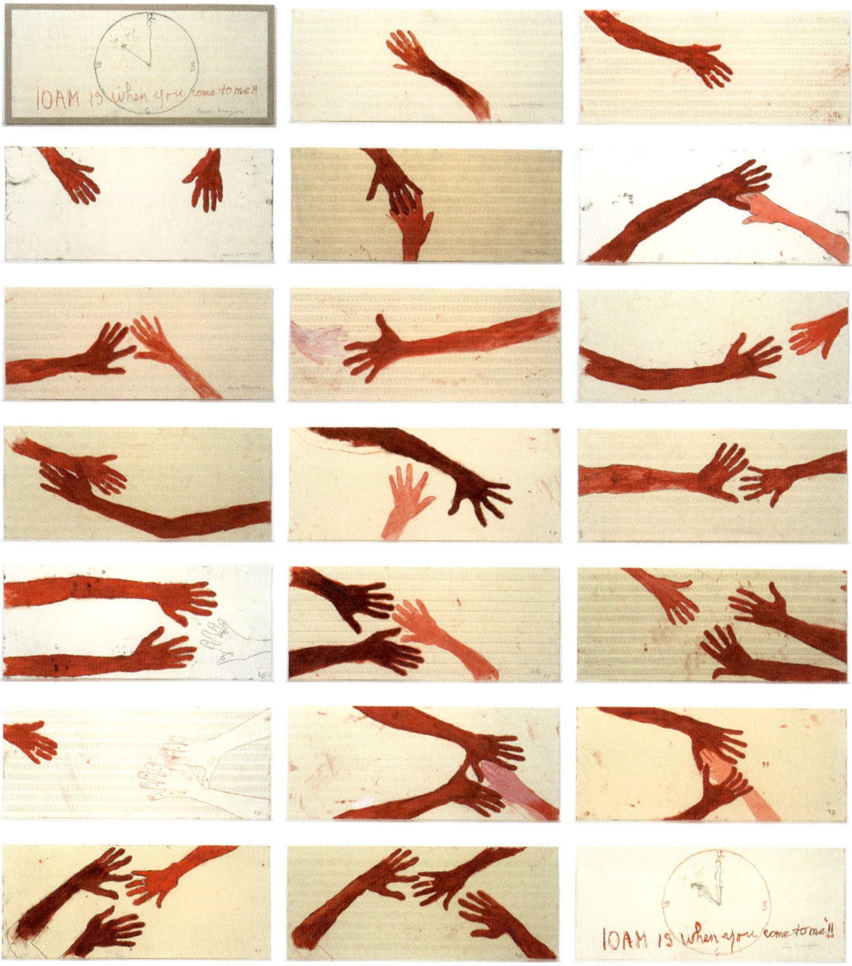

Plate 1. A moving testament to work with an assistant—and a member of a provisional subfamily of assembly based in the expressive configuration of hands. Louise Bourgeois, *10 AM IS WHEN YOU COME TO ME,* 2006. Etching, watercolor, pencil, gouache on paper, 20 pages, each sheet 14 ⅞ × 35 ⅝ inches (37.8 × 90.5 cm). Collection Artist Rooms Foundation. Copyright 2021 The Easton Foundation / Licensed by VAGA at Artists Rights Society (ARS), New York.

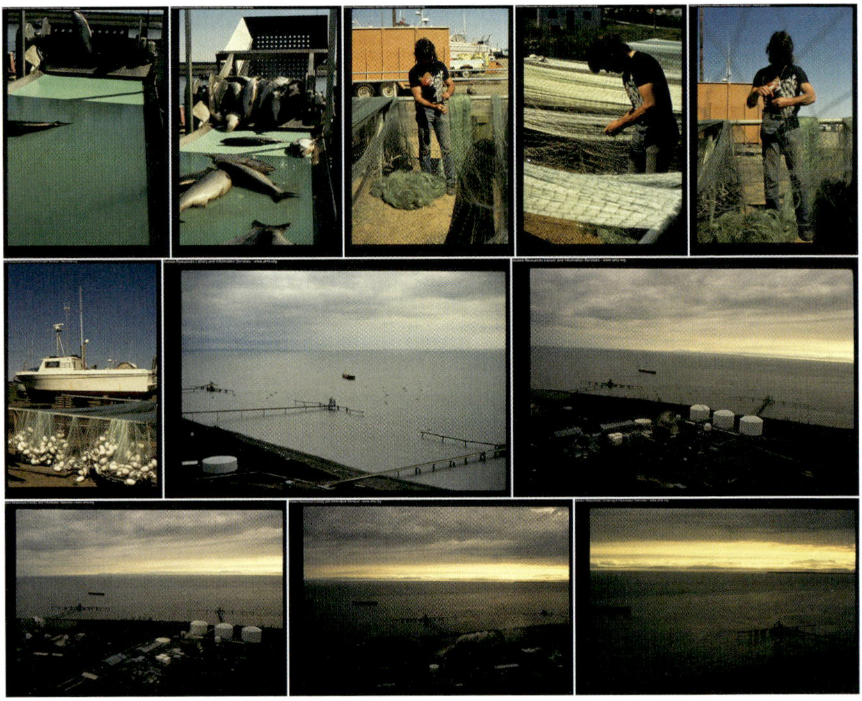

Plate 2. An unintentional expressive assembly: careful work on a fishing net abuts a flotilla of fishing boats attempting to block an oil tanker from docking, in protest of preventable oil spills. Screenshot of digitized slides related to the *Exxon Valdez* oil spill held by the Alaska Resources Library and Information Services (ARLIS), as posted to Flickr.

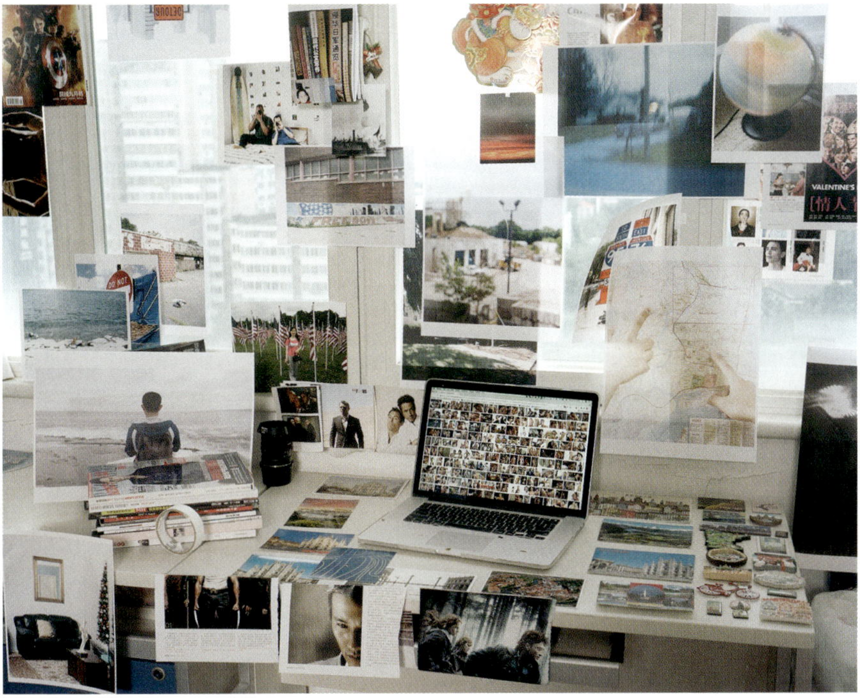

Plate 3. The assembly on the artist's computer comes in and out of resonance with the assemblies that surround it. Guanyu Xu, *My Desktop,* 2018. Archival pigment print, 24 × 30 inches. Copyright Guanyu Xu. Courtesy of the artist and Yancey Richardson, New York.

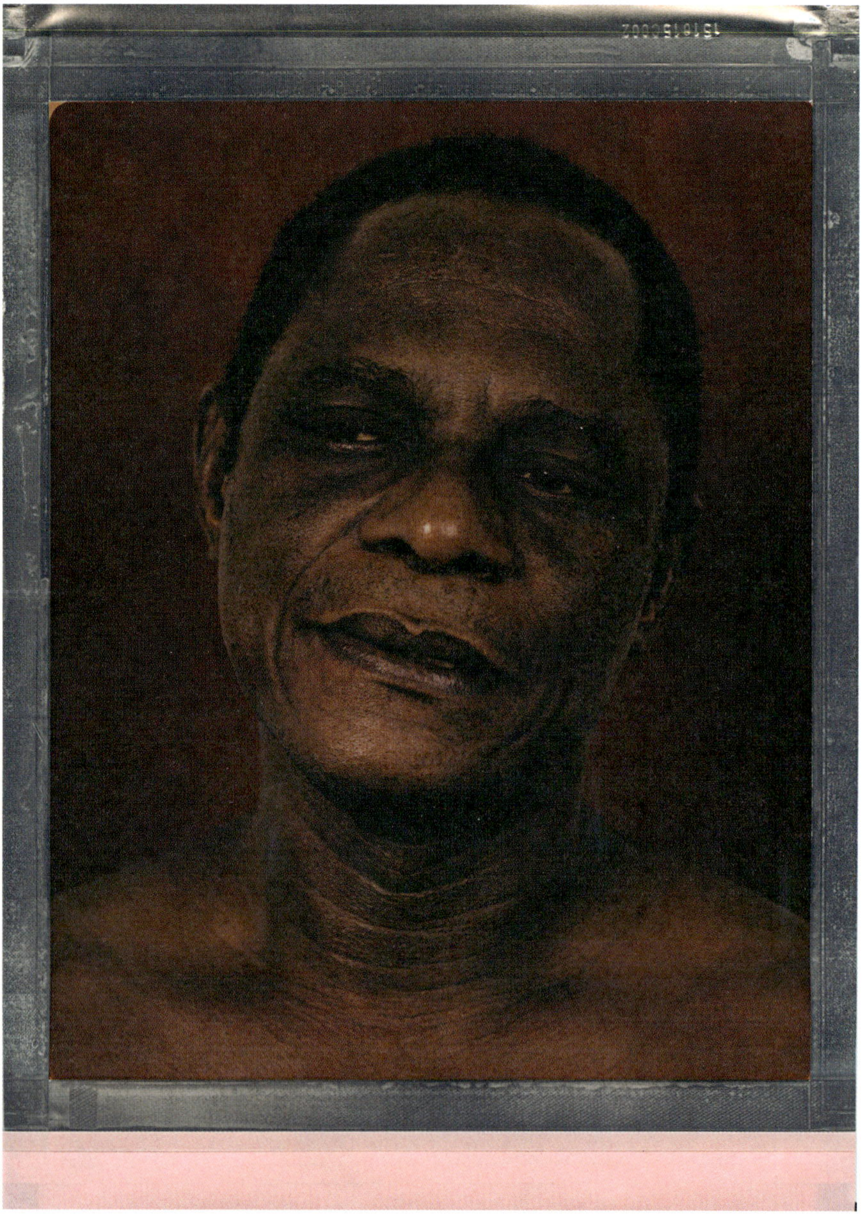

Plates 4 and 5. The drive to assemble as the drive to read juxtaposed photographs. Samuel Fosso makes two of 666 facial expressions in *SIXSIXSIX,* 2015. Copyright Samuel Fosso. Courtesy of JM Patras, Paris.

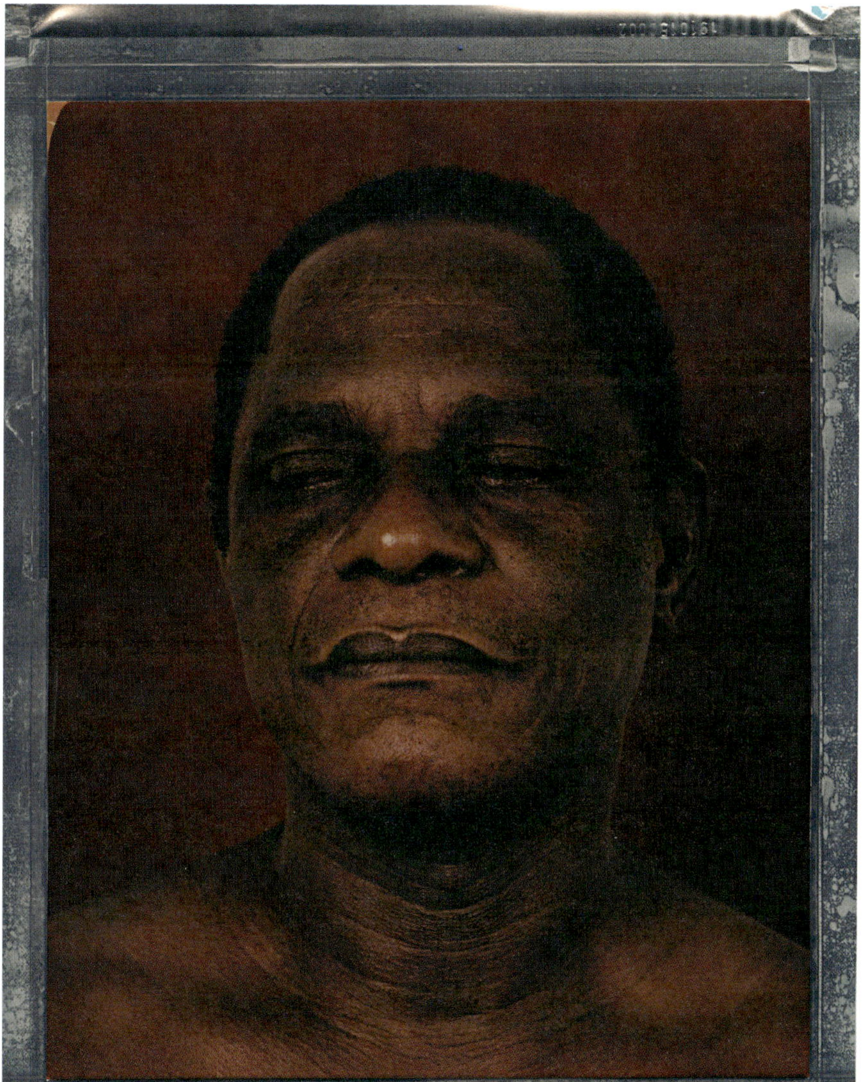

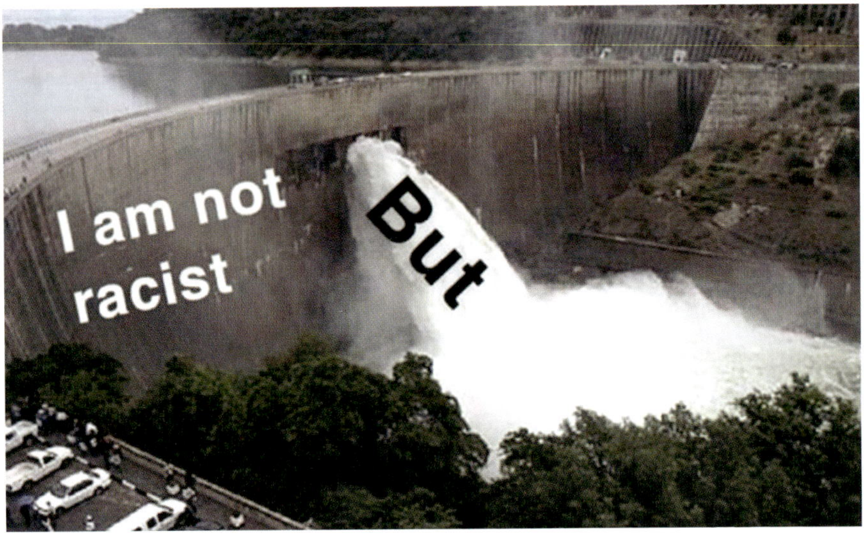

Plate 6. "I am not racist But." Image meme. Collected in 2020.

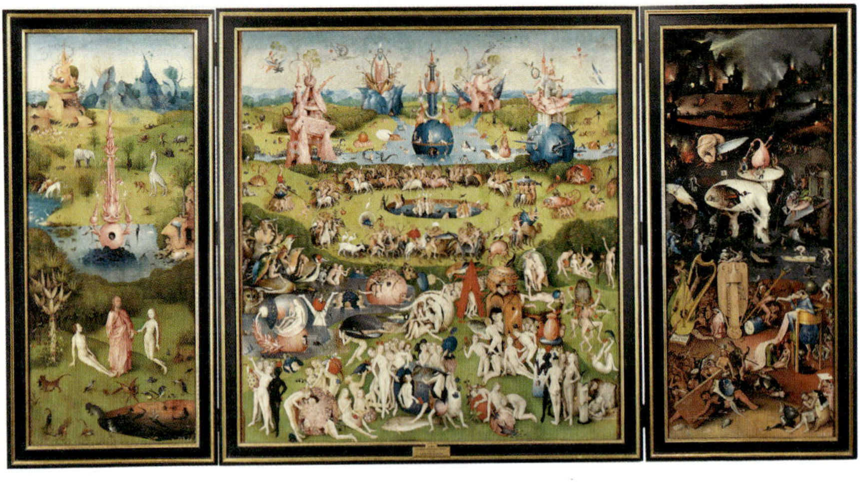

Plate 7. Flesh, flora, and fauna in one configuration after another. Hieronymus Bosch, *The Garden of Earthly Delights,* 1490–1500. Grisaille, oil on oak panel, 81 × 152 inches (205.5 × 384.9 cm). Copyright Photographic Archive Museo Nacional del Prado.

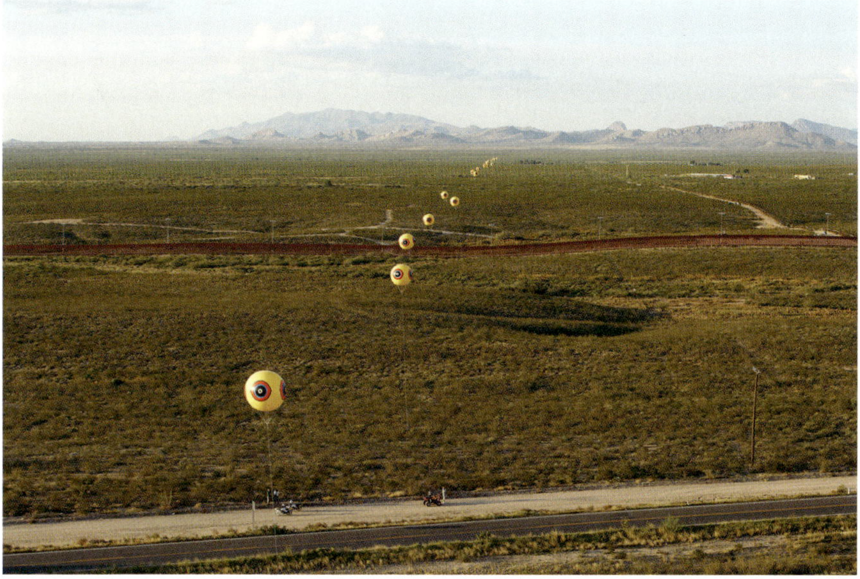

Plate 8. Lofted balloons as the work of analogy and the occasion for generative dialogue. Postcommodity, *Repellent Fence / Valla Repelente,* 2015. Land-art installation view. Photo credit: Michael Lundgren. Copyright Postcommodity. Courtesy of Postcommodity and Bockley Gallery.

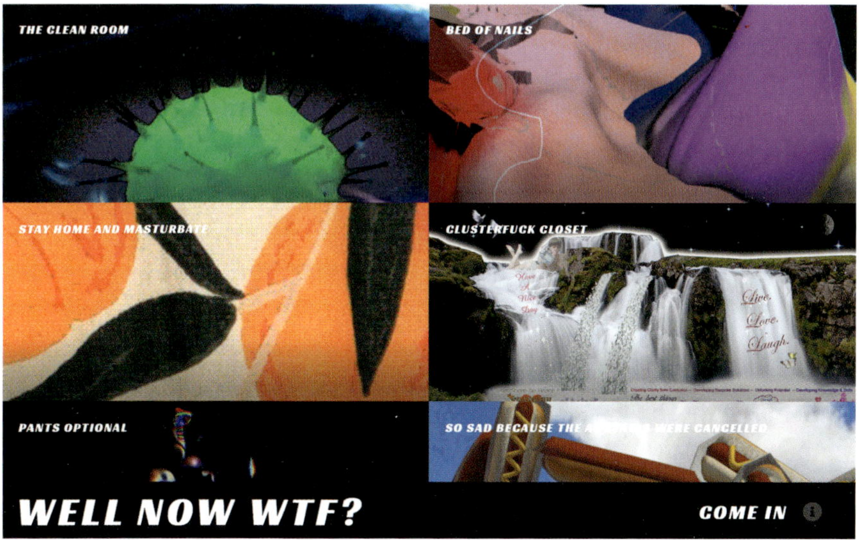

Plate 9. Rapid, disjointed, experimental, and exploratory media gathering in the midst of "social distancing." *Well Now WTF?* (2020), curated by Faith Holland, Lorna Mills, and Wade Wallerstein. Hosted on Silicon Valet (siliconvalet.org).

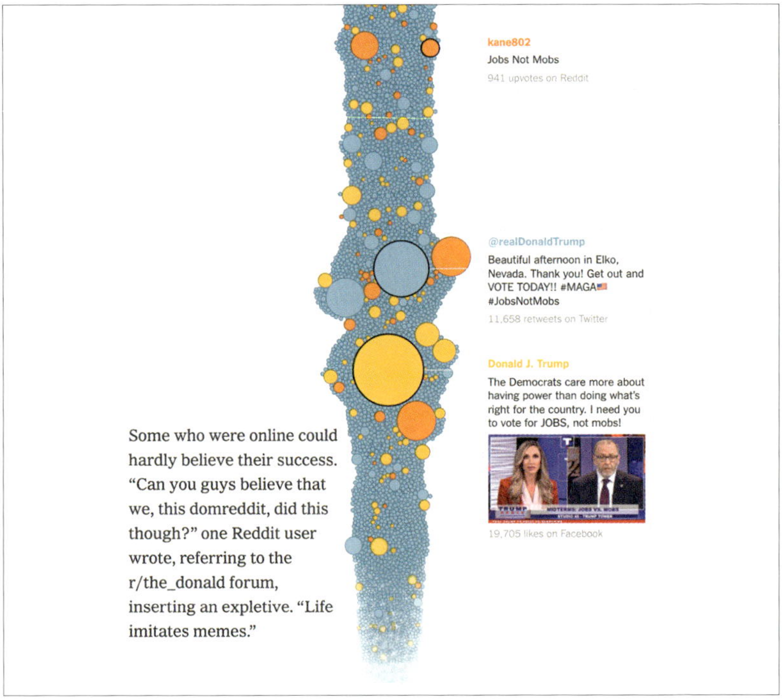

Plate 10. Excerpt from visualization of "jobs not mobs" meme. Keith Collins and Kevin Roose, "Tracing a Meme from the Internet's Fringe to a Republican Slogan," *New York Times,* November 4, 2018. Screenshot. Licensed by PARS International Corp.

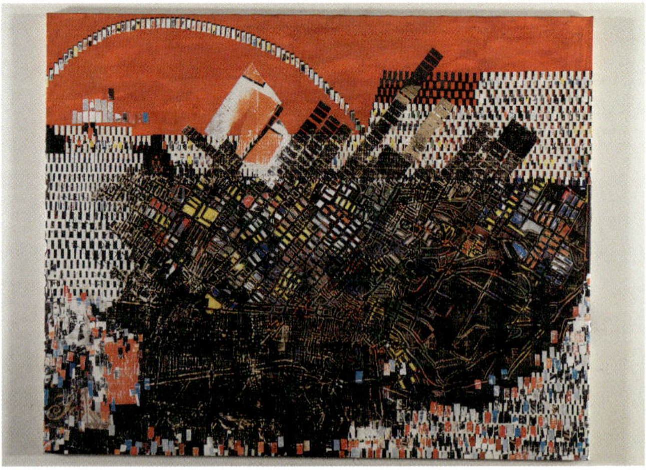

Plate 11. Remapping and reconfiguring the 1921 Tulsa Race Massacre. Mark Bradford, *Scorched Earth,* 2006. Mixed media on canvas, 94.5 × 118 inches. Copyright Mark Bradford. Courtesy of the artist and Hauser & Wirth. Photograph: Bruce White.

sponds is defined by capacity. How do acts of communication and expression like recording, writing, and arranging either manage or fail to address the reality and complexity of their subject matter? Once again, there are important precedents.[37] Hayden White, for instance, asserts our basic limitations before all histories, arguing for our dependence on genres of storytelling. White also marks certain events as especially resistant to cognition, imagination, and discourse.[38] Along similar lines, Saidiya Hartman speaks to the difficulty of working to "recast the past," but she also argues for the "political utility and ethical necessity of historical fiction" for the task.[39] Disasters of radical breadth and intensity constitute one extreme manifestation of these basic conditions of cognitive-imaginative struggle. At least two writers have expressed such sentiment around Katrina. For Johnson, as I have already alluded to, "photography, exemplified by the work of [Robert] Polidori and Misrach, amplifies our ability to imagine both the disorienting situation confronting New Orleans after Katrina and the ways that people approached that situation."[40] For Aric Mayer, "while the documentary and photojournalist accounts were troubling to viewers, they were in fact more comforting than the reality of the city, which seemed to defy and elude the available means of media representation."[41]

With these overlapping senses of the frame of prevailing conditions established, it is once again the methods of plural reading and critical typology that prove most effective. I highlight resemblances of form, function, and effect that are variously widespread, common, and rare. The question is how these dynamics bear on the conditions of representation, mediation, and remembrance that have come to dominate, conditions that are constantly evolving and only ever partially gleaned.

Elemental Witness

The first dynamic is what I call "elemental witness." This is a particular kind of "historiographic experience," to use Okwui Enwezor's term.[42] It involves reading, watching, perceiving, and feeling—doing so in response to transmitted histories of disaster, malfeasance, and recovery.[43] Crucial to this dynamic's conceptual interest and interruptive power, elemental witness does not take forms we might readily imagine. It might involve fragments of stories, but it is not the structured engagement with an unfolding narrative. It might involve instances of viewing or listening, but it is not oriented toward mediating presence. Instead, elemental witness takes place alongside, prior to, and among such actions, and it thus has a distinct place in the broader ecology of citizen witnessing practices. One crucial conceptual precedent is the notion of "constellation" in the work of Walter Benjamin and Theodor Adorno. Martin Jay summarizes constellation thus: a "juxtaposed rather than integrated cluster of changing elements that resist reduction to a common denominator, essential core, or generative first principle."[44] A general definition of elemental witness echoes Jay's summary: elemental witness is the reading and exploring of assemblies of minimally narrated and highly heterogeneous media elements such as images, words, and interfaces together with the diverse things these elements communicate, such as sensations, dimensions, facets, and perceptions, all of these interpretable pieces borne of and alongside given disasters and their aftermaths.

Three projects are especially appropriate for elaborating what elemental witness involves and why it matters. The first we have already encountered: Misrach's photobook *Destroy This Memory.* The second example is Walker's 2008 *After the Deluge.*[45] Already under a commission to assemble holdings of the Met into an exhibition, Walker reconfigured her project in response to Katrina (Figure 4.4). Both Walker's exhibition and the subsequent book convene historical visual material from the Met (paintings, ephemera, etc.) related to themes of muck, fluid, race, and failures of containment with selections from her own work and a single photographic image of an African American woman wading through oily floodwaters. The third example does not have a title; I will call it *Floodlines.* At the two-year anniversary of Katrina, New Orleans musician and artist Christopher Kirsch uploaded to his Flickr photostream images of scenes in the city, many of these presenting sites where the high-point of floodwaters remained visible. A selection of these entered the *HDMB.*[46] The subsequent assembly is a photo sequence embedded within the overall archive. Should visitors find their way to this sequence, they will click from one image to the next, each appearing on its own page, each with the tags and captions from Flickr.

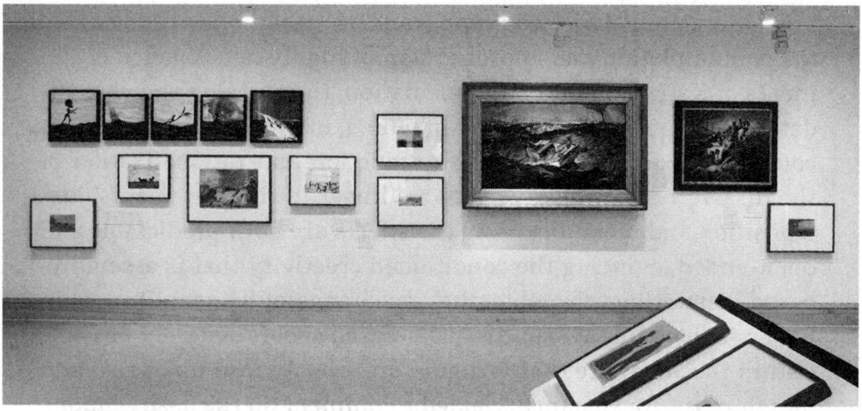

Figure 4.4. Kara Walker responds to Katrina with selections from her own work interposed between historical emanations of racist pathology, fluidity, and failures of containment. "Kara Walker at the Met: After the Deluge." The Metropolitan Museum of Art, The Lila Acheson Wallace Wing, The Gioconda and Joseph King Gallery, March 21 to August 6, 2006. The Metropolitan Museum of Art, New York. Image copyright The Metropolitan Museum of Art. Image source: Art Resource, N.Y. Artwork copyright Kara Walker.

Kirsch's visual-verbal configurations are variously emotive, argumentative, and pedagogical.

Together these artifacts suggest that elemental witness takes at least two forms. The first, instanced by Kirsch and Misrach's projects, is epiphenomenal; the production of such experience occurs alongside whatever other primary effects and ambitions of the work. With *Destroy This Memory,* a progression through its wide pages is a progression through tragedy, humor, and anger; it is also an encounter with indirectly preserved voices that might have otherwise fallen from attention. With *Floodlines,* a progression through the images is a progression through overarching themes like memory, environment, and loss, as well as consistently indicated subcomponents and alternative paths; hyperlinked tags lead outward to other fragments and facets, such as private, rescue, water, watermark, or waterline. In both projects, any given image contains a radical density of information and sensory data (substories and subexperiences of the larger disaster) and given pairs or subsequences can expand and divert, or images removed from each other come into relationship through the contingencies of spectators' interests and idiosyncrasies.[47] The two photographers' assemblies thus enable the contemplation and apprehension of highly heterogeneous elements of Katrina's reality and mediation; they catalog and consolidate ways of knowing and ways of telling, many of them things that could fall away in retrospective reduction and rationalization of the disaster. As witnessing viewers linger in those elements' juxtaposition and recombination, the effects are both predictable and open-ended, evincing the conditioned creativity that is assembly-based generativity. Notably, the appearance of Kirsch's images in Flickr enabled further social-media-based generativity not possible within the structure of this digital archive. A close-up of rust and marsh grass, for instance, yielded a comment on the desire among residents to preserve flood lines as "magic katrina symbols,"[48] arguably an instance of "Katrina patina," in which, as Dawdy puts it, remnants serve as the "material archive of [residents'] historical experience."[49] Also preserved in the comments for Kirsch's post is a request to use the image, apparently for the post-Katrina HBO series *Treme*; there the image joins a new visual assembly, in the form of the opening credits' photographic montage.

The second version of elemental witness is integral. Compilers of elements put into circulation sensory-semantic apparatuses that directly facilitate and thematize element-driven questioning. This is the case with Walker's project. Consider the following selections from her introductory remarks:

> The story that has interested me is the story of muck. At this book's inception, the narrative of Hurricane Katrina had shifted precariously away from the hyperreal horror show presented to the outside world as live coverage of a frightened and helpless populace (relayed by equally frightened and helpless reporters) to a more assimilable legend. Lately, the narrative of the disaster has turned to "security failures," or "the question of race and poverty," or "rebirth." And always at the end of these tales, reported on the news, in newspapers, and by word of mouth, always there is a puddle—a murky, unnavigable space that is overcrowded with intangibles: shame, remorse, vanity, morbidity, silence. . . . I have asked the objects in this book to do one more thing. Instead of sitting very still, "staying Black," and waiting to die, I have asked each one *to take a step beyond its own*

> *borders to connect a series of thoughts together related to fluidity and the failure of containment.*[50]

Evident across Walker's reflections is a concern with prevailing conditions of mediation and remembrance and the particular problem of reduction. Joining a rich history of artists (like Fred Wilson) who act as disruptive curators (an "open-ended" and "self-reflexive, performative act of interpretation"[51]), her project's generative intervention is that of critical, element-driven historical connection. The "elements" here are both the individual objects and all that those objects carry with them, from their visual or verbal contents to the histories they reference and embody. There are, on the one hand, works by Walker herself, some in the mode of drawings, others in silhouette, including Black minstrels dancing in the blood of a murdered enslaved person, and a young girl surrounded by flames, a can dropping from her hand, suggesting she has set the fire. On the other hand, there are objects selected from the Met; these include examples of the eighteenth- and nineteenth-century silhouettes of white Americans Walker's work frequently references and reworks, as well as iconic works like Joseph Turner's 1840 *Slave Ship (Slavers Throwing Overboard the Dead and Dying, Typhoon Coming On)* and Winslow Homer's 1899 *The Gulf Stream.* Moving through this complex and intensely undecided assembly builds up a well of references and feelings while also opening well-known phenomena to renewed address, such as the remarkably and insidiously varied manner in which visual culture has not just reflected, but helped maintain and multiply this country's racist "muck."

At the same time, Walker's act of documentary-aesthetic configuration offers the means for problematizing typical ways of narrating, remembering, and visualizing histories of environmental and social violence, particularly those marked by what she calls "racist pathology."[52] The book's table of contents most acutely actualizes this duality of facilitation and critique: here is a semilegible arrangement of themes and events like "Murky," "Middle Passages," "Inundation," "Superdome," and "Portents," and yet there is failure built into the very proposition, with no subsequent image in the book quite matching the ostensive categorizations.[53] As Michael P. Bibler suggests, even as it makes forceful historical connections, such as between *Slave Ship* and the murderous flooding of the Lower

Ninth Ward, Walker's project does not ultimately seek to assert pure repetition or parallel.[54] Instead, the assembly addresses an "irregular"—but actual, real, consequential—"historical continuum" across which its visual and material manifestations (and refusals) of racist pathology came into being. In so doing, *After the Deluge* seems to call on viewers to address what is "wholly new and unknown about Katrina," even as they "acknowledge the seeming repetition of events from slavery to the present."[55] Making the material elements of muck and water integral, seizing on the uncertain and indeed risky aesthetic acts of analogizing and reconstituting, it insists on the "importance of finding new ways to look at the historical in order to envision change."[56] Somehow, Walker suggests, the transit among traces, dimensions, and impressions has a place in witness as reparative work, while also being necessarily insufficient.

Of course, what that transit looks like and whether and how that witnessing and reparative work unfolds will depend on readers' positions in relation to these histories. And indeed, for the many people who *ought* to engage in the elemental witness Walker posits, those positions include that most persistent of pathological intersections: white privilege. To take Walker's assembly seriously as a white person in the United States is to see entrenched orders posed and undone. It is also to pick up where things might be remade, including (or even especially) by way of the digital networks where memory is "perpetually open to present and future amendment."[57] I think of the words of Roger Simon, for whom there can be "practices of remembrance within which an assembled testament of words and images" does more than bear witness to violent histories.[58] Those assembly-infused practices also allow one to "experience a questioning of and transformation in one's own unfolding stories and the frames on which one might argue for a possible future."[59] Walker's elemental testament radically elaborates these potentials. It also persists as an open invitation to their generative pursuit in the turbulent seas of social and popular media. "In this book's analogy," she writes, "murky, toxic waters become the amniotic fluid of a potentially new and difficult birth, flushing out of a coherent and stubborn body long-held fears and suspicions."[60]

Present Blankness

While elemental witness is an individual and collective experience facilitated through generative assembly, a second dynamic of assembly is a formal feature available to practitioners and engaged (and in some cases remade) by audiences. We can establish an initial perspective through that "sequential art" that richly fuses storytelling and picturing with configuring and convening: comics.[61] There the formal dynamic of "present blankness," a term I derive from comics scholar Hillary Chute, is fundamental.[62] Consider, for instance, a page from Neufeld's *A.D.* (Figure 4.5). The author establishes a scene of intense heat through the top left and top right panels; the succeeding middle panels indicate the sound of a vehicle; and the largest panel presents pleas and outrage at the arrival of policing over and against desperately needed supplies. Present blankness manifests in the gaps of white space between these frames; these gaps are instances of what gets called the gutter. Two things the gutter achieves are immediately evident. For one, it marks the passage of time, in this case an unspecified duration from waiting to arrival. Second, it indicates unseen action, action that the reader can imagine with varying levels of consciousness and intensity. Were we to stop at these functions for the gutter, we would have this to say of present blankness: within the broader field of concern about engaging Katrina, present blankness is an architectural feature in support of experience and communication; intensive, book-length mobilizations of present blankness scaffold assembly-saturated narrative; present blankness thus supports visual-verbal modes of disseminating histories of violence and responses to violence.

Per the account of Chute in *Disaster Drawn,* however, there is more going on here. In any given comic, the interplay of frames, gaps, drawings, and words will yield other effects. The gutter, Chute tells us, provisions space on which the reader can "connect and project"; the gutter cues an alternative "psychic order" to narrative; and the gutter foregrounds the uncertainty of storytelling, that prevailing condition of limited access, a condition that Chute demonstrates the work of drawing centrally negotiates.[63] In disaster-centered comics of quality and scope, these various functions will run together. Any given instance of present blankness can support an array of intersecting, even competing kinds of generativity: narrative, affective, elemental, representational, and what I call configural. I present this example for its accessibility but also because it displays the affecting and memorable recursion of emergency and media assembly and because it advances an emphatic memory of injustice in need of mnemonic return while also implicitly acknowledging the inability to fully convey that injustice's realities and effects. As Chute poignantly puts it, comics circulate as "dynamic texts inclined to express the layered horizon of history." They do so in ways that favor both "visual efficacy and limitation."[64]

With this example, the word limitation takes on extra meaning. Neufeld's project began as a serial web-comic in the online publication *SMITH Magazine.* There the project could redouble its already rich uses of media assembly. It linked outward to audio interviews and various Katrina-related "simulations, archived news reports, and YouTube videos." It also acted as a waypoint to glimpses of the depicted residents' lives, from the MySpace page of a band to cocktail recipes. Furthermore, and most suggestively, it included a comments section, where "readers could not only offer their reactions, but . . . engaged with the author and even the subjects of the text."[65] The distributed assembly of readers often critiqued or corrected what they were reading, and they engaged in sometimes quite extensive conversations, including around race and representation. As Horigan points out, this relative openness of the web version disappears in the printed text. "Gone are 'the epitexts and peri-texts that carry the traces of complex textual histories,'" she writes, quoting Gillian Whitlock and Anna Poletti, "and in their place, are comic characters who become static stereotypes as they are consumed without the benefit of dynamic contextualization."[66] The generativity that had once flowed freely became canalized, and the difference between *response* to racial pathology and *reinforcement* became difficult to see. (I find myself wondering how the generativity of the digital original might have been maintained in the modality of the book, or how it might yet be recovered.)

More difficult to articulate, and likely to receive less attention, are the roles of present blankness in formats other than the paper comic and the web-comic. Another medium that richly invites uses and infusions of assembly, the photobook, offers an especially important site. Among the many produced after Katrina, an especially relevant example is *Still Here: Stories after Katrina* (2008) by Joseph

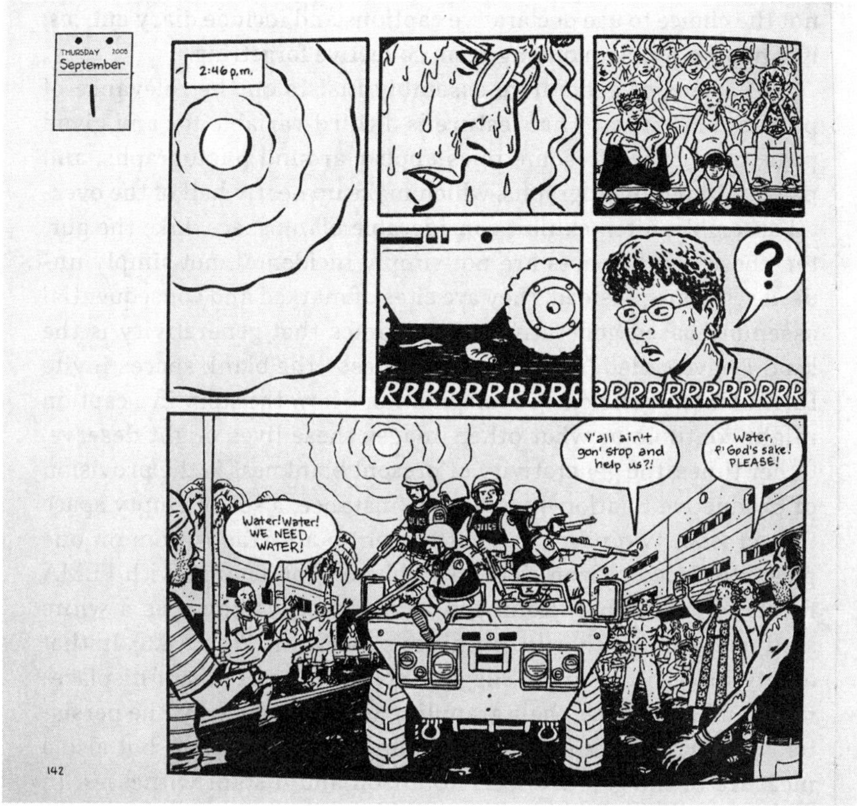

Figure 4.5. An example of the author seizing on the dynamic of "present blankness" in *A.D.* Graphic-novel excerpt from Neufeld, *A.D.: New Orleans after the Deluge.* Copyright 2009 by Josh Neufeld. Reprinted by permission of Pantheon Books, an imprint of the Knopf Doubleday Publishing Group, a division of Penguin Random House LLC.

Rodríguez. Broadly speaking, the book presents several dozen black and white photographs that document the lives of African American people displaced by Katrina as they try to rebuild their lives, primarily in distant Denton, Texas. The images range considerably, although a marked quality of what the introduction calls "grit" persists throughout: there are intimate renderings of faces; there are scenes of life together at home; there are death and mourning; and there are glimpses of work and community.[67] From one perspective, any role of present blankness will seem beside the point: it is not the realities of suffering and perseverance these images assert; it is not the choice to use declarative captions and include diary entries; it is not the problem of long-term collective forgetting.

But a lens of generative assembly insists on the relevance of present blankness. That feature is a third variable for any given page; gaps of white sometimes appear around photographs, and pages without photographs, which make up nearly half of the overall assembly, often exhibit considerable blank space. Like the gutter, these blank spaces are not simply incidental, not simply unused segments; instead, they are sites of marked and consequential assembly-based generativity. Sometimes that generativity is the kind I have called "structured openness": the blank spaces invite further interpretation and imagination—how the story in a caption might continue or what other images these lives might deserve. Other times, the generativity of present blankness is the provision of productive relationships. In one instance, a sea of empty space that crosses two pages calls attention to a juxtaposition: on one page, displaced citizen Katrina Robinson contending with FEMA forms; on the other, Robinson again, now watching as a white staff member of a charity examines paperwork (Figure 4.6). In that empty space is, one might suggest, Robinson's and others' displacement and resistance, their grappling with bureaucracy, the persistent precarity, the simple fact of being and responding, but also a measure of the gap between Robinson and distant witnesses. In still other instances in *Still Here,* the generativity of present blankness is precisely the lack of growth, production, and meaning. The emptiness is the reality of absence; it is all the care not provided. It is also the basic insufficiency of watching over acting. Such is the multivalence of generative assembly that no one effect of present blankness necessarily predominates.

Between these different examples, an important and open question emerges, which is whether meaningful "blankness" is possible in the digital sphere. The example of *A.D.* as a web-comic suggests part of the answer inasmuch as the present blankness wasn't just the gutter in the actual drawings, but the open field for commentary in the participatory web format. In this way "blankness" can be conceived as the space beneath an assembly of comments, or the space that awaits in a new post. There is what hasn't yet been added to the superassembly of Katrina-related art and media, and there is what ought to be added. Perhaps there is also a remaking of digi-

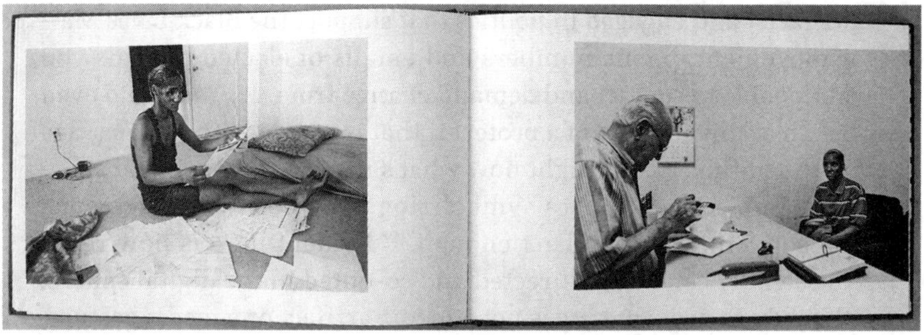

Figure 4.6. In the mode of generative assembly, the gap between photographs can be as significant as the photographs. Pages 82–83 of Joseph Rodríguez, *Still Here: Stories after Katrina* (New York: powerHouse, 2008). Licensed by Great Bowery Inc.

tal space such that it isn't just empty and unformed, but maintains certain qualities and is itself open to revision, the digital as in some ways "smooth" rather than "striated," to use the terms from Gilles Deleuze and Félix Guattari.[68]

Maybe digital present blankness can work both ways at once, as reading and response. A recent example was undertaken in the names of George Floyd, Breonna Taylor, Ahmaud Arbery, and countless other Black citizens murdered by police. At one level was a call by two Black women music executives, Jamila Thomas and Brianna Agyemang, for a day of refusal of business as usual in and beyond the music industry under the hashtag #TheShowMustBePaused. This was to be something like present blankness as concerted action: the absence of certain habits and images pointing up the abiding presence of racism, inequality, and exploitation. At another level, however, there was the distorted and "misassembled" version of this day, in which thousands of people, many of them seeking to express solidarity, combined the hashtags #blackouttuesday with images of black squares. The assumption that one was refusing to post content missed the mark, and the frequent use of the #BlackLivesMatter hashtag hindered access to resources and conversations thereby. What *was* to remain as empty as possible that day was the normal accumulation of the habitual; what was to be present, full, even overflowing, were resources and conversations, protest, and planning. As Brooke Marine put it that same day, one could better focus on "how to become actively anti-racist and engaged in politics that support the Black Lives Matter movement; phone numbers and emails of elected officials you want people to contact and demand change from. . . . You could even post an archival photo of a protest if that is in line with the message you're sending, . . . but right now what's needed is action, and sharing a simple black square symbolizing your position as someone who condemns racism isn't enough."[69] Evident here is how readily assembly can be misdirected and co-opted in the digital sphere. Often what needs making is not a media artifact or a media gesture, but a decision, a donation, a change.

Emergent Archiving

Of course, the intensive production of media artifacts is itself also a kind of action, and that is the case with the third and last dynamic, *emergent archiving*. This modality involves, as its name suggests, acts of assembling that deserve to be identified as archival. This can mean something more familiar and conventional is at work, like acts of official memory, aimed at preservation, following normative protocols, whether analog or digital. But instances of emergent archiving can also take other forms: they can lack a mission of preservation while nevertheless keeping and maintaining; they can lack systems of official description while nevertheless invoking appearances of systematicity; and they can act as apparatuses based in citation and juxtaposition, even if their organizing principles are unclear or numerous.[70]

I look to the work of Mark Bradford as exemplary of emergent archiving at the individual level. Here is an artist who, until the storm and flood in 2005, had developed a pioneering practice at the intersection of abstraction, representation, and assembly. Many of his works, paintings largely produced without paint, are built with merchant posters gleaned from his Los Angeles neighborhood. Katrina changed things. Bradford's practice became, as he describes it, more "confrontational."[71] Relative to Katrina, two of Bradford's works are especially relevant, as both permute the archival and the emergent. In building the first, *Mississippi Gottdam* (2007), named for Nina Simone's forceful 1964 protest song, Bradford compiled comic-book pages, billboard paper, and other debris from the streets of New Orleans, attached them to his canvas in a grid structure, then placed a layer of silver leaf on that grid. He then enacted a method for which he has become well-known, sanding those materials partly back into appearance in the manner of décollage. What remains is a series of black, white, and grey flows, reminiscent of a "dilapidated wall," a "seascape," and "oncoming waves," and the fragments of colorful paper like "flotsam and jetsam after the deluge" (Figure 4.7).[72] The second is the massive ship *Mithra* (2008), named for a god of truth and light with etymological roots in binding and contracts. For this work Bradford further relied on the assembly of found paper, but he also amplified his material and aesthetic ambition. The paper adhered to an imposing ark, built of storm-resisting plywood boards and three sea containers shipped from Los Angeles, planted in the middle of the Lower Ninth Ward for Prospect.1 New Orleans in 2008 (Figure 4.8).

With *Mississippi Gottdam,* we witness the archival qua preservation (the found paper), arrangement (the overall grid and the comic book's archive-like frames), and citation (the titular protest song), and we witness the emergent in the typical marginality of those preserved things, in the lack of systematic organization, and in Bradford's subtractive revelation of some but not all of those constituent holdings. (Some of the words in the comic seem to speak in oblique ways of circumstances after the disaster. For example, a character in one asks, "What if all these weirdos don't like people just dropping in?") With *Mithra,* we witness the archival in the preservation and arrangement of found things but also in the figuration of the ark, which serves to rescue and preserve against the flood.[73] We witness the emergent in ways similar to the painting, with the sides of the ship partly displaying and partly obscuring found materials; but we also encounter the quality of provisionality and urgency: the ark occupies a place undergoing uncertain processes of change. The kinds of generativity these two assembly-infused works enable are both shared and divergent. With *Mississippi Gottdam,* it is the provision of reflective experience, a kind of partial elemental witness suffused by fields and subfields of present blankness. It is also, in conjunction with the song, an act of protest aimed at the "slowness of recovery efforts in low-income communities after Katrina."[74] The ark amplifies and elaborates this act of protest. It is an emphatically resistant assembly—a massive body in space—and it is of further significance that the project

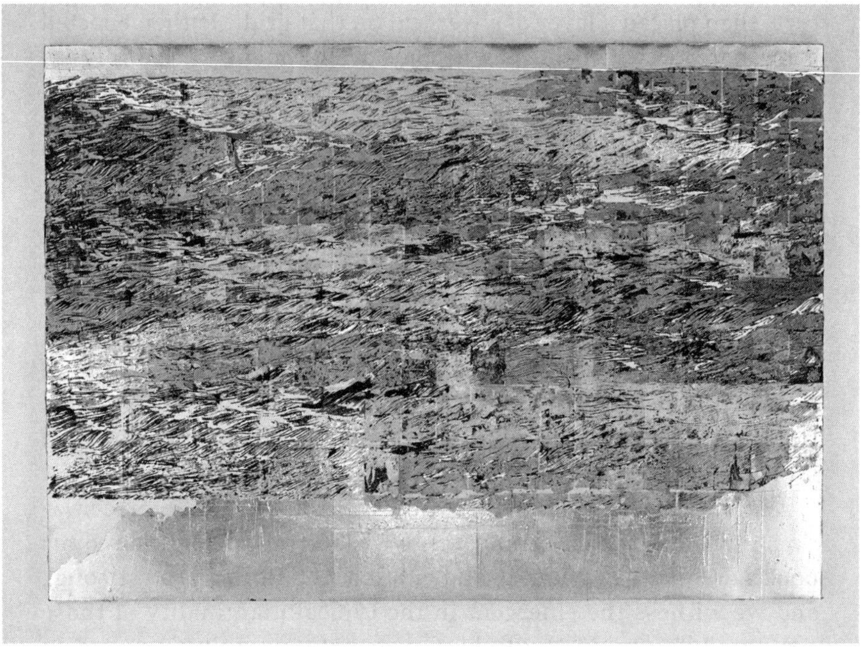

Figure 4.7. A closer view of the work reveals its basis in generative assembly, including layers of found comics subject to décollage. Mark Bradford, *Mississippi Gottdam,* 2007. Mixed media on canvas, 102 × 144 inches. Copyright Mark Bradford. Courtesy of the artist and Hauser & Wirth.

wove Bradford, for whom arts education is a deep commitment, into the communities of the Lower Ninth Ward, including sustained work with a nonprofit organization. As Bradford himself puts it, the paper-laden ark constituted "material" in the process of "making some political gesture." That political gesture, which served to place a "material archive" of plywood and found materials in figurative motion, aimed to be forceful. "I really wanted to make it feel like that 'boom, boom, boom, boom,'" Bradford recalls. "I almost wanted it to feel like a battleship."[75]

The second example has a considerably more ambiguous status. As the contributions to the digital version of *A.D.* attest, generative assembly can also take place in distributed fashion, with diverse actors working at largely anonymous remove; it can also be highly virtual, dependent on code, database, and pixel; and it can involve emphatic concern for normative ends of preservation. The tag cloud

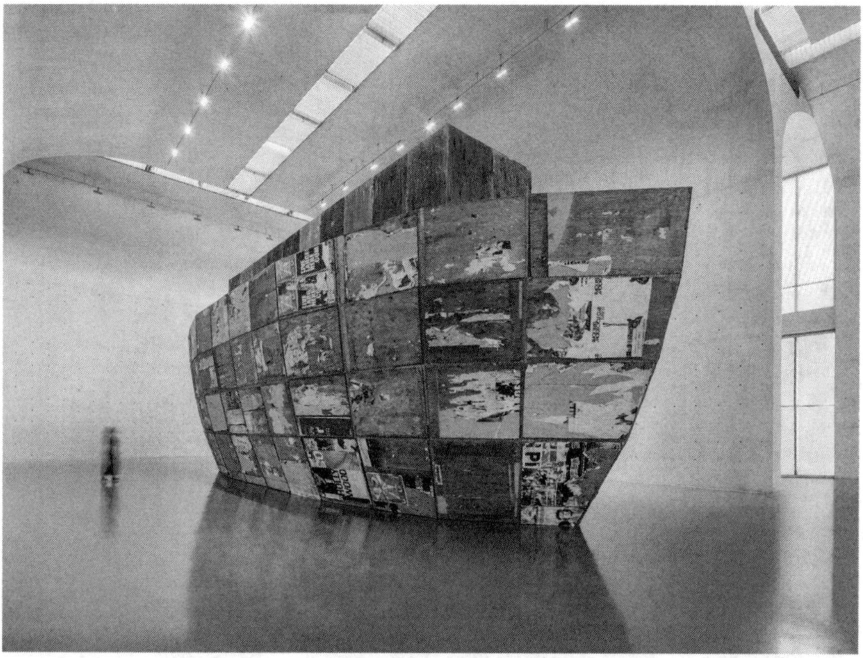

Figure 4.8. The ark was originally sited in the Lower Ninth Ward during the first Prospect biennale. Mark Bradford, *Mithra,* 2008. Mixed media, 286 × 773 × 250 inches. Copyright Mark Bradford. Courtesy of the artist and Hauser & Wirth. Installation view, "Mark Bradford: Los Angeles," Long Museum West Bund, Shanghai, 2019. Photograph: Joshua White / JWPictures.

of the *HDMB* presents an especially poignant, if also fraught, example of what such forms of emergent archiving can produce and perform (Figure 4.9). In a basic sense, the tag cloud serves as one among multiple means of access to the materials in the online repository of twenty-five thousand items, the other means being keyword search and a Google map. Like much of the material making up the archive, the tag cloud's constituent tags are user-generated and folksonomic: they have not been subject to a controlled vocabulary, and the project leaders have not enforced a specific menu of terms based on newly established or preexisting standards. Are we to immediately accept such an assembly as a welcome expansion of access to histories of Katrina? Or should we follow the lead of some interpreters in establishing a basic skepticism of projects of distributed emergent archiving like *HDMB,* and thus by extension

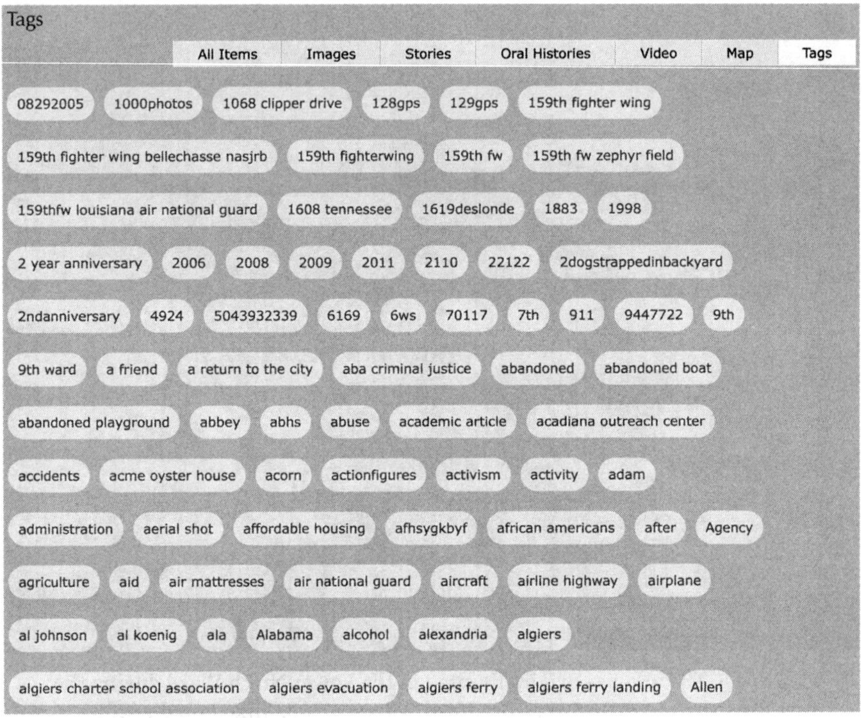

Figure 4.9. A hyperlinked legacy of distributed assembly after disaster. Detail of tag cloud of the Hurricane Digital Memory Bank (2016).

dismiss this constituent artifact? As with any instance of generative assembly after disaster, it is necessary to adopt a nuanced approach. Like all the projects addressed so far, the tag cloud is a multivalent, multiformat, multimotivated media artifact addressing complex, mediated histories and open to numerous situated engagements, uses, and reuses. In short, it is variously and precariously generative.

Critiques might go something like this: the tag cloud is of a piece with reduction; it serves only to further abstract; it turns the disaster into so many discrete topics; it supports neoliberal tendencies toward social atomization; it favors documentation over discourse; it fails to mitigate fault lines of belonging, or maybe even exacerbates them.[76] More optimistic assessments would vary considerably. This is a generative subassembly, or a machine for provocation and redirection. There is a peculiar force to the gathering of element after element, humor alongside suffering, the familiar alongside the eccentric: action figures, affordable housing, air national guard; death, dedication, democratization; web dubois, website, web-comic. For all its functions in serving research toward determined ends, the tag cloud also suggests a lack of knowing and of paths not taken. It is also an expressive visualization. That visualization affords a sense of vastness, as one scrolls through an impossible quantity of potential concerns, issues, realities, and perspectives. The subassembly also embodies something essential: the potential for reassembly and redistribution. The *HDMB* is constituted by schemes of transmissible data and media. Though there would be ethical, technical, and other challenges, an intervention in both this archive's contents and its architectures of display and dissemination could take place. Such a project, critically conceived, would self-consciously negotiate prevailing conditions of representation, mediation, and remembrance. It would also look to legacies of smaller-scale, discrete assembly for the kinds of dynamics it aimed to actively facilitate.

The Work Still to Be Done

Elemental witness, present blankness, and emergent archiving are three among a variety of ways in which media assembly can enact and enable retrospective interpretation and witness. In mapping them, my point has been both to grapple with Katrina in particular and to think about the mediation of disaster more generally. I have argued that compilation and configuration take place in convergent fashion across diverse media, that such practices can generatively intervene in prevailing conditions of mediation and remembrance, and that the legacies of these endeavors exist productively, if also sometimes precariously, in the broad and still-evolving ecology of witnessing and interpreting Katrina.

If this account has been sufficiently generative, then it will be clear that other lines of inquiry are possible, and that certain questions remain open, around both Katrina and other disasters. Rather than zoom out to consider other events and other forms of violence, which is part of the function of the next chapter, it seems more fruitful to close by asking how this account of generative assembly after disaster might look different were we to address practices of disaster-centered assembly undertaken at a very wide scale.

For one thing, we would have to consider hyperdistributed media assembly as it occurs in relation to a single event. Were we to focus on Katrina, for instance, we might contemplate something like the massive configuration of interpretable cultural material about the event across various evolving media over time, but we might also undertake a reversal. With each dynamic and example I have addressed in this chapter, the direction has been outward to inward; practitioners and participants assemble around this central subject of Katrina. Taking distributed assembly into account, we could shift to think about assembly that takes place from Katrina outward. What I mean is various documentary and expressive constituents emerging from or around Katrina—data, images, sounds, ideas, dimensions, phrases—that come into assembled relationship in other contexts where Katrina is not the center of concern or attention. Instead, there is a redistribution of this event's media manifestations. Many questions arise. For instance, what does it mean when an extraordinarily famous and influential pop star (Beyoncé) performs from the top of a submerged police car in clear reference to Katrina? Is this an instance of opportunistic appropriation that co-opts the culture and suffering of New Orleans, as several Black feminist critics argued, or is it an instance of redistributing and consolidating attention, meaning, and power around these events, or even, as Mari E. Ramler suggests, a "reclamation," a "baptism," and a summoning of the past toward the forming of the future?[77] In a different vein, what would it mean to consider all the repetitions of racist and white supremacist interpretations of Katrina in the assembly-based domain of memes? By what means could such repetitions be opposed, whether through "counter-memes," expressive folksonomy, or still other avenues?

The second way I respond to the question of hyperdistributed media assembly after disaster is quite different. I look to Benjamin's oft-cited reading of Paul Klee's oil transfer drawing *Angelus Novus* in "Theses on the Philosophy of History," the same essay in which Benjamin famously observed: "There is no document of civilization which is not at the same time a document of barbarism."[78] Faced with Klee's rendering of "an angel looking as though he is about to move away from something he is fixedly contemplating," Benjamin sees someone who sees differently. "Where we perceive a chain of events," Benjamin writes, this angel of history "sees one single catastrophe which keeps piling wreckage upon wreckage and hurls it in front of his feet." In other words, for the angel of history, the human past is no steady story, as we may think; it is instead a maddening accumulation; it is a grotesque and ill-starred assembly. Benjamin does not clarify this configural claim, nor does he say here whether all of this might someday flip, whether the whole thing might not yet get rearranged into something utopian, or at least more livable. Klee's monoprint does not appear to offer an answer either, despite Benjamin's feeling of deep kinship with it; the artist responsible for a reworked version, Ken Aptekar, observes that the print can seem to bear "little relationship" to the essay, presenting "an almost gleeful, goofy, alert figure, centered in a bright clearing" (Figure 4.10).[79]

In light of the passionate efforts of cultural actors in response to disasters like Katrina, it is worth lingering on the elemental sense in which Benjamin figures distributed catastrophes as the endless accumulation of their traces and refuse. Is it possible for projects of generative assembly to slightly enhance the possible emergence or endurance of the better arrangements of our vulnerable, war-torn worlds? Can the ways we configure media correspond to the ways we would hope to configure ourselves, even amid conditions of seemingly endless disaster?

In a recent essay, Jesse McCarthy writes that the task of the "artist, writer, and revolutionary anarchist" is to "find a way to make the Angel's wings beat again." I read McCarthy's words as an act of critical and speculative reconfiguration. This reconfiguration speaks to the power of the figure of the Angel of History, but it also wrests the Angel from Benjamin's orbit in a manner the thinker might well have appreciated.[80] First, McCarthy suggests that the Angel is not fixed and singular, but many places and active: "We have to be on the lookout for her. We have to take notice and speak up when she passes by."[81] Then McCarthy suggests another figure for the Angel: Walker's installation, made of foam and forty tons of sugar, water, and resin, or what Doreen St. Félix calls "a Sphinx creature with the kerchiefed head of a mammy figure, her breasts naked, her vulva prominent,"[82] and which Walker titles *A Subtlety,* or the *Marvelous Sugar Baby*: an Homage to the unpaid and overworked Artisans who have refined our Sweet tastes from the cane fields to the Kitchens of the New World on the Occasion of the demolition

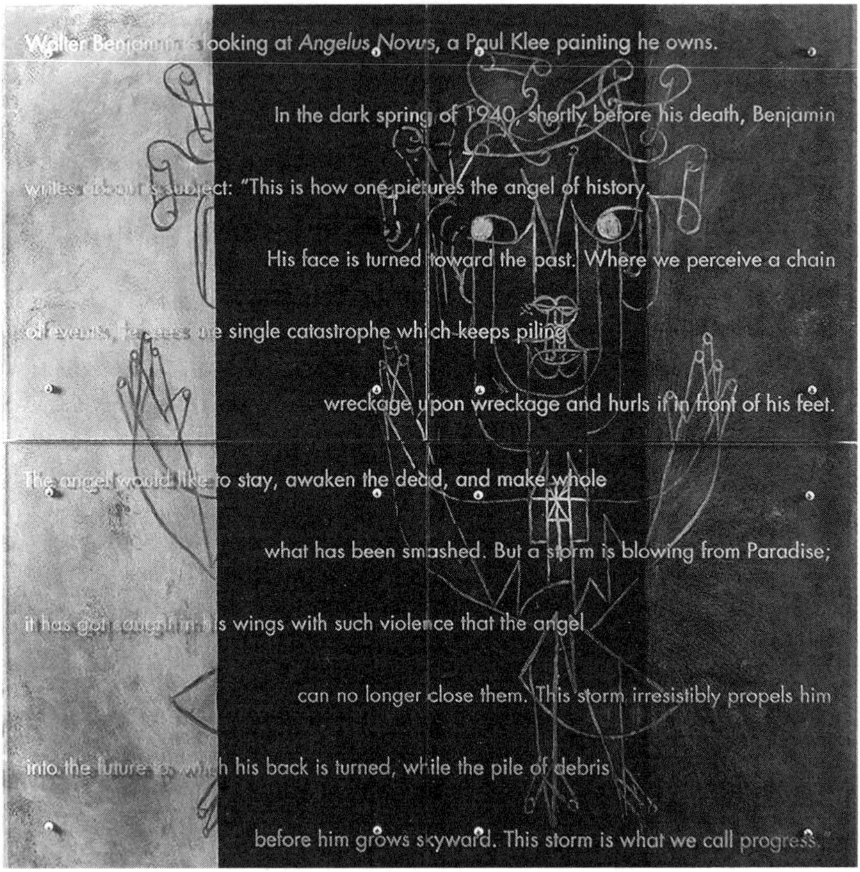

Figure 4.10. Ken Aptekar, *Walter Benjamin is looking,* 2000. Four panels, oil on wood, sandblasted glass, bolts, 60 × 60 inches. Courtesy of the artist.

of the Domino Sugar Refining Plant. For McCarthy, this Angel of History "emerges as a towering work that looms for us to see, to look up from our daily routines and interrupt them if only for the space of a visit."[83] *A Subtlety* also looks back upon not just any world—much less an implicitly white, European, and cis-male-dominated world—but a world "made by the black woman, . . . the one who makes possible the work still to be done."[84] Perhaps, to return to Walker's notion of a "new and difficult birth" after Katrina, acts of generative assembly, from the simplest to the most complex, can help to gather energy and resources for the "work still to be done," especially in circumstances where that work seems otherwise impossible to see or to narrate or to perform.

Of course, as I read McCarthy's reworking of Benjamin as a white person born and living in the United States, I also see that generative assemblies must do something else, something like demanding a revision in the thinking and acting people do not just about, but also from within (and in evasion of) whiteness, not toward a Black–white binary, but toward qualities places like New Orleans live and breathe: intersectional, plural, and vibrant. In the face of violent disassembly, people assemble again, in both new and proven ways, toward more just and more livable worlds.

5

The Powers and Perils of Media Assembly

Wealthy, white, and global-north disasters tend to receive more attention and more resources than poor, BIPOC, and global-south disasters. Although it remains essential to attend to events of sudden mass casualty, the long and complex aftermaths of disasters, such as the vast "racial disparity in resources available to rebuild" after Katrina, must also remain in the spotlight.[1] Although violence is often unexpected and shocking, it is also often distributed, habituated, and invisible.

Among insights into issues of violence, injustice, media, and activism in recent decades, few have matched the above in their importance and reach. What has been at stake is an enduring dynamic, one that becomes increasingly pressing as the world gets both hotter and more connected: how instances of collective and nonindividualized harm, destruction, and fatality are framed, understood, and disseminated significantly impacts who and what get to matter. Aided in part by a media landscape that favors the obviously awful, situated within societies riven with division, discrimination, and domination along the lines of race, gender, sexuality, class, and ability (among other categories), the conception of violence that tends to hold favor, and therefore to command eyeballs, minds, and bank accounts (at least in many European and North American contexts), is the conception of violence as sudden, unexpected, visible, and purposeful. It is not that such a conception is incorrect according to writers committed to an expanded account of violence. It is that it is consequentially incomplete. To favor certain forms of violence over others is to undermine possible responses to those other forms of violence, such as the impacts of past housing discrimination on life expectancy or the distributed and ongoing consequences of climate change for Indigenous subsistence practices. These are forms of harm that are not sudden, but "slow, routinized, and banal,"[2] or that are spread out rather than spectacular, or that disproportionately fall on populations of people who do not tend to receive equal standing as visible and valuable within dominant channels of discourse, debate, and policy-making.

Over the last several decades, these moves to expand intellectual and political accounts of disaster and violence have made waves across the many scholarly contexts in which these topics come under study, from geography and policy studies to sociology and feminist studies. Thanks in part to Rob Nixon's *Slow Violence and the Environmentalism of the Poor,* this web of concern has grown to include contexts like literature, art history, and media studies.[3] (Although it neglects to mention as much, Nixon's book is, as Jenna Marie Christian and Lorraine Dowler observe, indebted to a "long line of feminist scholars, as well as critical race, queer, and postcolonial and decolonial scholars."[4]) Of primary interest here is whether and how certain cultural projects might meaningfully respond to the inequitable treatment of nonsudden, distributed, and, as it were, "poor" violence. To use Nixon's idiom, if certain forms of slow violence tend to occur frequently and out of sight, and if they tend to disproportionately affect poor, minority, and micro-minority communities, then anyone concerned with the intersections of disaster, media, and culture necessarily confronts "representational, narrative, and strategic challenges" that have themselves remained undertheorized.[5] "How can we convert into image and narrative," Nixon asks, "the disasters that are slow-moving and long in the making, disasters that are anonymous and that star nobody, disasters that are attritional and of indifferent interest to the sensation-driven technologies of our image-world?"[6]

The question has been taken up by numerous artists, critics, and scholars, and this seems likely to continue, as the same complex of issues persists, as technical means to document and disseminate forms of violence only increase, and as doubts persist about whether the underlying issues of indifference and differential mattering are open to meaningful modification through expressive means.[7] Given the gravity of these matters, it is well worth pausing to consider whether the various terms and assumptions in play deserve one's full trust, or whether it might be necessary to engage in critique and renovation. While certain scholars have done so relative to the theorization of violence, there has not yet been, at least as far as I'm aware, an effort to question Nixon's specific and persistent appeal to better narratives and better images.

Toward a New Roster of Media Possibilities amid Slow, Structural, and Other Modern Violences

The notion that criticism and scholarship would go wrong in continuing to maintain both explicit and tacit emphases on narrative and representation in response to slow, structural, and other "modern violences that work at varied scales and speeds" (to use Lindsey Dillon's helpful terms) becomes apparent from within Nixon's project itself. [8] This is because some of Nixon's richest examples do not match up with this reduction of the strategic palette. Instead, they point to the concrete workings of other cultural forms and expressive strategies, with at least one carrying particular relevance and promise, what this book calls "media assembly" and "generative assembly."

One of the most instructive examples along these lines is an example of mediated resistance to slow violence that appears in Nixon's epilogue. There Nixon frames the ambivalence of the digital, which, for all its promises of democratization and access, would seem to exacerbate long-standing problems of inattention in one direction and excessive absorption in another. As an example of possible strategic response to this challenge, he cites an underwater cabinet meeting held off the coast of Maldives, an island nation subject to catastrophic flooding amid rising sea levels. In 2009, the first democratically elected leader of the country, President Mohamed Nasheed, led his cabinet on a scuba dive. The group proceeded to gather "behind a conference table anchored to the seabed, a Maldivian flag planted behind them. Oxygen mask in place, the president signed into law a national commitment to becoming carbon neutral within ten years."[9] Documentation spread through mass and social media (Figure 5.1).

Nixon's book is powerful in its emphasis on concrete strategies, and here he sees the strategies his book favors. Relative to narrative, Nixon writes: "Through the compensatory realm of symbolic activism, President Nasheed sought to distill a narrative of planetary urgency from a crisis so attritional and so seemingly far-off that it might appear a causeless threat to an already invisible nation

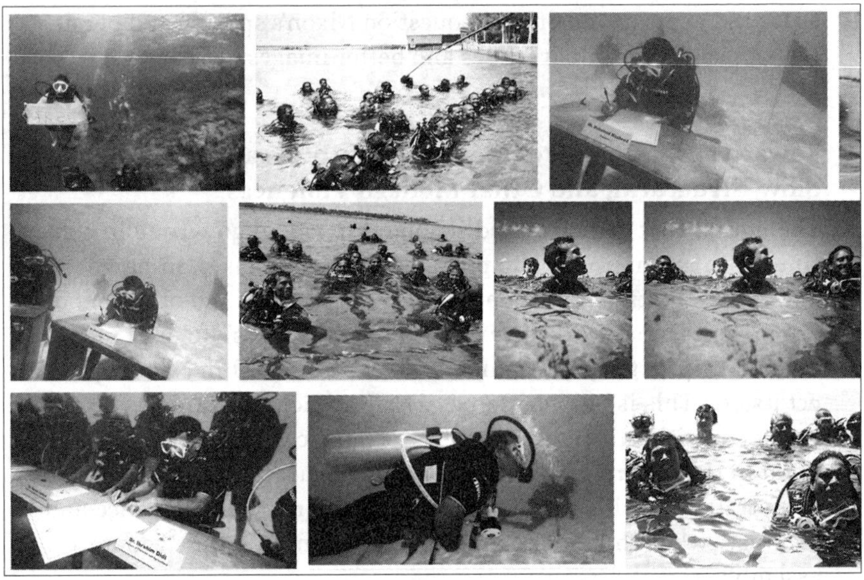

Figure 5.1. Performative, embodied assembly occasions distributed, expressive assembly. Image search results for "maldives underwater protest nasheed" using Microsoft Bing. Screenshot, September 2021.

of no apparent consequence."[10] Relative to image, Nixon writes: "President Nasheed's underwater cabinet meeting offers an image of reverse inundation that speaks directly to the environmentalism of the poor. Here it's not brown immigrants threatening to 'swamp' the neoliberal fortresses of the still predominantly white rich, but rather poor brown people confronting the threat of having their national territory swamped as a result of a 200-year experiment in hydrocarbon-fueled capitalism whose historic beneficiaries have been disproportionately rich and white."[11]

These are compelling assessments. But it also doesn't take much to see other expressive strategies are at work. One of these is well-known: Nasheed and the others are seizing on the strategy of performance, and maybe even what Carrie Lambert-Beatty calls "parafiction" (partly plausible, just outside of the fictional, an unusual, governmental paraficitional performance).[12] But a second expressive strategy at work here is infrequently named. The president and cabinet members made themselves into media constituents. As constituents, they enacted an unusual mix of representative and quasi-popular, demonstrative assembly. This was an evocative mix of both familiar and unfamiliar postures and comportments undertaken underwater, and this mix yielded a distributed assembly of images, statements, gestures, affects, and ideas in turn. (Another unexpected product was a second dive in a memetic vein, only this time in yellow T-shirts that read "Free Nasheed," as a subsequent government had imprisoned the former president after a politically motivated conviction under the antiterrorism act.[13]) Both in its moment and in subsequent reference, this complex and dispersed set of configurations—neither a single story nor a single image, nor a single performance, but many of these mixed with assembly and other cultural forms—does the work of provoking and informing. It can also persist as a model for other actions in the future. As movements like the United Farm Workers, ACT UP, and Black Lives Matter have repeatedly demonstrated, and as any number of more emergent and less widely known efforts have elaborated, there can be considerable force in the work of convening and configuring people, pictures, and performances as the constituents and catalysts of activist media assemblies.

Other examples are less blatant in their uses of assembly, and that includes a book of great importance to Nixon: Rachel Carson's *Silent Spring*. Here Carson documents the catastrophic impact of pesticides on plants, nonhuman animals, and people in the United States. She calls out the disinformation of chemical corporations; she also helps establish new paradigms for environmental protection. The book's influence was and remains considerable (albeit not without critique, founded or not[14]). Nixon's analysis this time is trained on a piece of writing rather than a performative assembly, and is once again in keeping with the narrative/image scheme. "In struggling to give shape to amorphous menace," Nixon writes, "both Carson and reviewers of *Silent Spring* resorted to a narrative vocabulary: one reviewer portrayed the book as exposing 'the new, unplotted and mysterious dangers we insist upon creating all around us,' while Carson herself wrote of 'a shadow that is no less ominous because it is formless and obscure.' To confront slow violence requires, then, that we plot and give figurative shape to formless threats whose fatal repercussions are dispersed across space and time."[15]

Reading these remarks, it can seem like the critical discussion should end there and that one ought to go out and start crafting and sharing stories capable of transmitting these kinds of events into movable minds (including the not slow but "fast" floods and fires catalyzed and exacerbated by climate change) while also plotting means toward overcoming them. But that impulse forgets a dimension of Carson's book that is essential to its power and distinction. Take the oft-excerpted first chapter of *Silent Spring,* "A Fable for Tomorrow." On the one hand, that chapter has considerable staying power because of its presentation of not just information but story. This story starts with an anytown; this anytown is then hit by a mysterious blight, then another, and then another; and for the first time the spring is silent, without birds. As the short chapter ends, a fable of hubris and harm has been established, and the book appears set to unravel the stories of which the fable is metonymic. The human story Carson tells could end in unresolved tragedy, or there could be a remarkable recovery and resolution.

None of this is wrong per se; it is simply insufficient. Like many other projects responding to slow violence, *Silent Spring* makes use of methods of expressive gathering that sometimes fly under the radar. There is the town that is thriving; there is the town that is suffering. There are the beautiful rhythms; there are the compounding disasters. As Karin Reisinger puts it, "Carson assemble[s] fragments of silence to show the ubiquitous future of pollution." In other words, "A Fable for Tomorrow" isn't just a memorable story; it is also a memorable composite. And just like the strategy of storytelling, the strategy of generative compositing at work in the first chapter repeats and transforms throughout the chapters that follow. As she "assembles a wide range of domains and sites," from "tobacco plantations" to a household "where the 'housewife' dies of acute leukemia after spraying spiders with DDT," Carson brings data, imagery, insight, anecdote, and analogy into novel and affecting arrangements. Seeking to "compose an image of a future yet to come," Carson weaves an "assemblage [that] unfolds a conjunction of situated stories and transformations, territories, substances and applied practices and their effects: assembled voids and absences."[16] As much as this is an environmentalism animated by story and image, it is also an environmentalism infused with a kind of writerly reassembly. As the discussion of Katrina showed, part of the power of this kind of work can be that it leaves open the potential for a different kind of account, not only emphasizing single, guilty actors or attempting to trace strictly linear chains of cause and effect, but rather arraying many variables and valences, not toward petrified reckoning with the insurmountable, nor toward absolving those responsible for perpetuating harmful conditions, but toward more informed and more imaginative thinking and mobilizing amid the difficult complexity (and the often straightforward malfeasance).

Far from being absent from Nixon's account of slow violence, then, assembly is there from beginning to end as an unseen third player subsumed under the dominance of the two main players, narrative and image. Indeed, just as Nixon's point is that disasters possess "unequal heft"[17] but are not less real and consequential as a result, we can say that modes of expression, communication, and mediation also possess unequal heft but are not any less useful or necessary as a result. Like performance, abstraction, and other forms, assembly is there with image and narrative, and it has been for a long time.

The question is what to do. It isn't that we ought to forget image and narrative. It's that we ought to avoid repeating the same tendency toward hierarchy and reduction that necessitated the intervention in the first place, particularly as the circumstances of both media and preventable harm grow ever more entrenched and vast. The value in challenging this conceptual situation isn't merely intellectual. Newly deploying assembly against modern violences will also be enabling for the very strategic, interruptive, and reparative practices Nixon's project rightly and powerfully emphasizes.

What is at stake in this chapter, then, is a new index of media possibility to which artists, critics, scholars, and others can look when considering the use of data, image, word, and other media in responding to slow, structural, and other forms of violence. Just as in response to large-scale disasters and just as in the realms of art and memes, assembly in response to modern violences does not take just one form or do just one thing, nor does it exclusively yield positive effects. At the same time, the most effective uses of assembly do tend to exhibit certain patterns. With all this in mind, I follow the approach in other chapters, tracing a critical typology of certain discernible sectors of these potentials. The big picture point is to refuse the limitation of a strictly representational and narrative approach. The further advantage is the construction of a reservoir of assembly-based and assembly-infused potentials (and awareness of misuses and abuses) for the sake of future practices.

Conceptual Reassembly and the Continuum of Violence

"Violence," write Nancy Scheper-Hughes and Philipe Bourgois, "is a slippery concept—nonlinear, productive, destructive, and reproductive. It is mimetic, like imitative magic or homeopathy. . . . Violence gives birth to itself. So we can rightly speak of chains, spirals, and mirrors of violence—or, as we prefer—a continuum of violence."[18] We should not understand violence "solely in terms of its physicality—force, assault, or the infliction of pain—alone," they continue here: "Violence also includes assaults on the personhood, dignity, sense of worth or value of the victim. The social and cultural dimensions of violence are what gives violence its power and meaning. Focusing exclusively on the physical aspects of torture/terror/violence misses the point and transforms the project into a clinical, literary, or artistic exercise, which runs the risk of degenerating into a theatre or pornography of violence in which the voyeuristic impulse subverts the larger project of witnessing, critiquing, and writing against violence, injustice, and suffering."

Among the things one finds in these remarks is a commitment to recognizing the surprisingly open and contestable nature of the concept of violence. By rights, such a concept should not be a concept at all; it should be simple, brute fact—to inflict violence is to inflict violence, end of story. Nevertheless, as these anthropologists insist (as do so many others devoted to this terrain of concern), nothing but a fundamentally pluralist approach can hope to suffice for problems of public harm. Violence does not happen in isolation; violence repeats itself. Violence is not strictly physical; it is also social and cultural. Violence is never delineable into strictly separated categories. Rather, there is a "continuum of violence,"[19] which is to say that there is considerable variation in how violence emerges and unfolds, and yet the many different kinds overlap and interrelate to the point of appearing, at times, indistinguishable.

The first strategic use of assembly I address has played an indispensable role in making both the continuum of violence and the continuum of possible responses to violence more tractable. Among the earliest and most cited instances of this mode of assembly-based response (here examples precede the definition and analysis) is Johan Galtung's "Violence, Peace, and Peace Research," a 1967 essay that Nixon and countless others cite. Galtung calls attention to forms of violence that are not necessarily tied to a specific individual, nor even to a collective actor like a military brigade. In instances of such "structural violence," there is still killing or mutilation or manipulation, but there "may not be any person who directly harms another person." Rather, "the violence is built into" a social structure and "shows up as unequal power and consequently as unequal life chances."[20] As Paul Farmer puts it with reference to examples like the global AIDS epidemic, structural violence follows from "social arrangements that put individuals and populations in harm's way. The arrangements are *structural* because they are embedded in the political and economic organization of our social world; they are *violent* because they cause injury to people" who are most often "not those responsible for perpetuating such inequalities."[21]

Comparable examples of the assembly-based dynamic likewise involve appending otherwise unexpected terms to the "slippery" concept of violence. In a 1983 book, for instance, Michael Watts explores what he calls the "silent violence" of famine induced by precarious market structures in northern Nigeria.[22] Some years later, having lived and worked among impoverished Brazilians contending with starvation, humiliation, and despair, and having documented instances of mothers hastening the deaths of their sickly children, Scheper-Hughes coined the term "everyday violence."[23] As we have already seen, Nixon's coining of the term "slow violence" consolidated a history of conversation around what Carson had called "death-by-indirection." Nixon's term emphasizes the question of time and duration in a way that Galtung's concept does not and has corollaries in yet further notions like "letting die" and "creeping environmental change."[24] More in the realm of political theory, Jacques Derrida entered into a long line of political thinking about "the violence involved in the formation of political orders"[25] by foregrounding "foundational" violence: "the allegedly originary violence that must have established [a state's] authority and that could not itself have authorized itself by an anterior legitimacy."[26] For Joan Cocks, the emphasis on structural violence, valuable as it is, risks overshadowing the ongoing consequences and enactments of such foundational violence, which tends to involve the "eradication of one set of meanings animating a way of life to clear the ground for another set," and which tends to induce a "lack of a sense of loss of what has been erased" for the people "whose sensibilities have been molded within a new order of things."[27] As a final example, in a 2018 post to the software development website Github (a significant gesture in itself), the artist Mimi Ọnụọha argues for the category of "algorithmic violence," which she defines as "the violence that an algorithm or automated decision-making system inflicts by preventing people from meeting their basic needs."[28]

What one witnesses across such cases isn't just the practice of neologism; it is a mode of critical practice. Refusing to see violence as strictly a matter of guilty subjects harming innocent subjects, instead aiming to call attention to the structures, rhythms, and mechanics of violence, critics and researchers introduce new locutions that do crucial conceptual and attentional work.[29] This is specifically an exercise of reassembly (and not, for instance, re-narrating or re-representing), because it consists in producing a readily circulatable reconfiguration of existing terms. There are dominant, unrevised understandings of what violence is possible and actual, and those understandings serve in the exclusion and occlusion of economic, social, ecological, and other forms of harm. These semantically charged pairings of words help consolidate the project of contesting and reworking those understandings by combining familiar terms in unfamiliar ways. Newly armed with these terms, then, citizens, scholars, and activists can see things that otherwise went unseen, or articulate problems in ways not possible before, or draw connections that might otherwise have been lost. Furthermore—and this is especially true in the digital era—certain assemblies of terms become "sticky" or even memetic in the sense that they bind together further examples, references, hashtags, images, and other media. They thus help foster networks of interrelated material in protoassembled form, a partly configured reservoir of possibility to which thinkers, actors, writers, activists, and others can respond through further acts of expression and communication. Conceptual reassembly feeds distributed assembly.

If one use for conceptual reassembly is helping make modern violences more thinkable and circulatable, another is a matter of forging practicable conceptual counterweapons. A paradigm instance is Kimberlé Crenshaw's argument for the existence and importance of what she terms "intersectionality." In a 1976 federal case, five Black women sued General Motors, arguing that their being subject to layoffs was an extension of earlier discriminations, as Black women in particular had only begun to be hired from 1964 onward, making them disproportionately subject to layoffs in a scheme based on seniority. The Court's ruling, which did not go in the plaintiffs' favor, characterized their suit (with a notably derisive emphasis on legal recombination) as an attempt to "combine two causes of action into a new special sub-category, namely, a combination of racial and sex-based discrimination," and it bemoaned what it framed as the "prospect of the creation of new classes of protected minorities, governed only by the mathematical principles of permutation and combination."[30] In reviewing this case and others like it, Crenshaw witnessed a legal instantiation of a truth long known and expressed by Black women: that their and others' oppression (and the violence of and from such oppression) tends to be subsumed under a single umbrella, like race or gender, when it is, in fact, multidimensional and "interlocking."[31] Crenshaw responded by coining "intersectionality," a term she thought of as an "everyday metaphor that anyone could use."[32] Here is an early characterization:

> Consider an analogy to traffic in an intersection, coming and going in all four directions. Discrimination, like traffic through an intersection, may flow in one direction, and it may flow in another. If an accident happens in an intersection, it can be caused by cars traveling from any number of directions and, sometimes, from all of them. Similarly, if a Black woman is harmed because she is in an intersection, her injury could result from sex discrimination or race discrimination, . . . But it is not always easy to reconstruct an accident: Sometimes the skid marks and the injuries simply indicate that they occurred simultaneously, frustrating efforts to determine which driver caused the harm.[33]

As the passage makes evident, intersectionality is, as a conceptual lens, a generative arrangement: a familiar term ("intersection") combines with familiar concerns (driving, accidents, threats, harm), questions (directions, variables, causality), and actions (reconstruction, investigation, redress). This convergence offers a means of resisting legal and conceptual roadblocks that have become otherwise habitual. Crucially, it is also built to encourage recombination and reuse beyond the legal context. In an article from 1994, for instance, Crenshaw points to intersectionality as "a way to articulate the interaction of racism and patriarchy generally," and as a means of describing the "location of women of color both within overlapping systems of subordination and at the margins of feminism and antiracism."[34]

Intersectionality has seen ample, significant, and widespread citation and use (as well as, in more recent years, some earnest critique, as well as ample politically motivated derision). It has also spurred yet further conceptual reassembly. A recent example of the latter is Leah Thomas's concept of "intersectional environmentalism."[35] In a May 28, 2020, Instagram post, Thomas presents an assembly of four images, one of which says, sixteen times over, "Environmentalists For Black Lives Matter."[36] Thomas's caption introduces the project: "It is unfair to opt in and out of caring about racial injustices when many of us cannot. These injustices are happening to our parents, our children, our family and our friends. I'm calling on the environmentalist community to stand in solidarity with the black lives matter movement and with Black, Indigenous + POC communities impacted daily by both social and environmental injustice." The police murder of George Floyd in Minneapolis happened just days before Thomas's post. In the protests, actions, and organizing activities that followed from this event, intersectional environmentalism proved highly generative, even memetic, altering not just how people framed their political organizing but also linking people, movements, and ideas that would otherwise not be linked.

Unabashedly networked and expressive, Thomas's work of reassembly built on Crenshaw's project of "mediating the tension between assertions of multiple identity and the ongoing necessity of group politics."[37] Along exactly these lines, intersectional environmentalism wasn't without skeptics, as Cameron Oglesby relates, from questions about Thomas's status as an influencer working with corporate sponsors to deeper questions around the nature and value of the movement. For the person often referred to as the father of environmental justice, Robert Bullard, the notion "doesn't signify anything different than what we have already developed and institutionalized in the work," nor does it have a proven value for communities fighting environmental racism on the ground. Moreover, Bullard says, intersectional environmentalism risks overlooking and even overwriting the difficult and ongoing efforts of the last several decades to redefine the who and the what of environmentalism such that it would be, as Vernice Miller-Travis recalls, far larger and more inclusive "than what traditional groups and folks were about." (Among other things, this has meant newly centering advocacy and policy of consequence for Indigenous and people-of-color communities, including around structurally unequal subjection to environmental hazards and the expropriation of land, water, and forest.) From another perspective, voiced by Taylor Morton of WE ACT for Environmental Justice, intersectional environmentalism and environmental justice are effectively the same thing, but they provide "different points of access" to concepts and problems people have historically found difficult to understand (or accept), making any rifts between the two unnecessary and unproductive. For those most moved by intersectional environmentalism, however, Thomas's work of reassembly was real and consequential. In John Paul Mejia's more restrictive read, for instance, environmental justice largely focuses on "how environmental degradation affects oppressed peoples," and it has effectively unfolded as an "insider game in D.C.," sympathetic to market-based solutions. Among the things distinguishing the alternative, intersectional approach is the effort to "bring our struggles to different places."[38]

As these clashing perspectives make evident, the assembly of new terms in response to the continuum of violence is an imperfect and contested effort. Activists can create provisional scaffoldings on which to build up sharper or more accessible understandings. They can also put those scaffoldings into circulation more quickly than ever before. At the same time, violence remains too habituated, intersectional, and pervasive to either traffic in strict essences or refuse to modify viral innovations. It seems activists of all stripes must be willing to shift their assemblies' applications and arrangements in response to new (and overlooked) perspectives. If the goal is meaningful and responsive witnessing, critiquing, and organizing, then one of the most important strategies is the deceptively simple operation of reordering conceptual words, and thus, when it works, concrete worlds.

Thematic Countermapping

What concepts like "slow violence" and "intersectionality" open and consolidate, further activist and expressive labors must extend and elaborate. The gap between what ought to be and what is remains wide, and part of what helps narrow this gap is the perceptual, interpretive, and rhetorical work of artistic, mass, and social media intervention.[39] Narrative and image are possible modes, but to focus only on these is to miss the power of others, with assembly as an essential one among them.

For those who would turn to mapping, which is frequently though not always assembly-based or assembly-infused, the exercise is inevitably fraught. Far from neutral reflections of the world, maps are selected and arranged for particular purposes, and among the most prevalent purposes has been to aid and unleash destructive enterprises. Whether for the drive to imperial conquest, the mineral-hungry demands of industrial capitalism, or the policing and segregation of populations, map users have long derived significant advantage from the exercise of placing the world onto flat planes. More recently, mapping has become a constant and widespread, but also markedly ambivalent, performance. Even as mapping "deterritorializes" and "opens new avenues and multiplicities," it also tends to amplify precarity; indeed, the latter is, in Wendy Hui Kyong Chun's reckoning, the "dominant network condition, and mapping follows and amplifies networks."[40] Still, in spite of these strong headwinds, critical mapmakers have forged alternatives, using acts of cartography to insist on the persistence of other worlds and on better, as yet unrealized worlds over and against the worlds claimed by those in power.

The variously assembly-based and assembly-infused version of this practice is what I call "thematic countermapping." The basic features of this practice are embodied in a map with a title: *Poison/ Palate: The Bay Area in Your Body* (Figure 5.2).[41] The map appears in *Infinite City*, a counteratlas of the unceded ancestral homeland of the Ramaytush Ohlone, now called San Francisco, California, as well as the larger region now known as the Bay Area, conceived

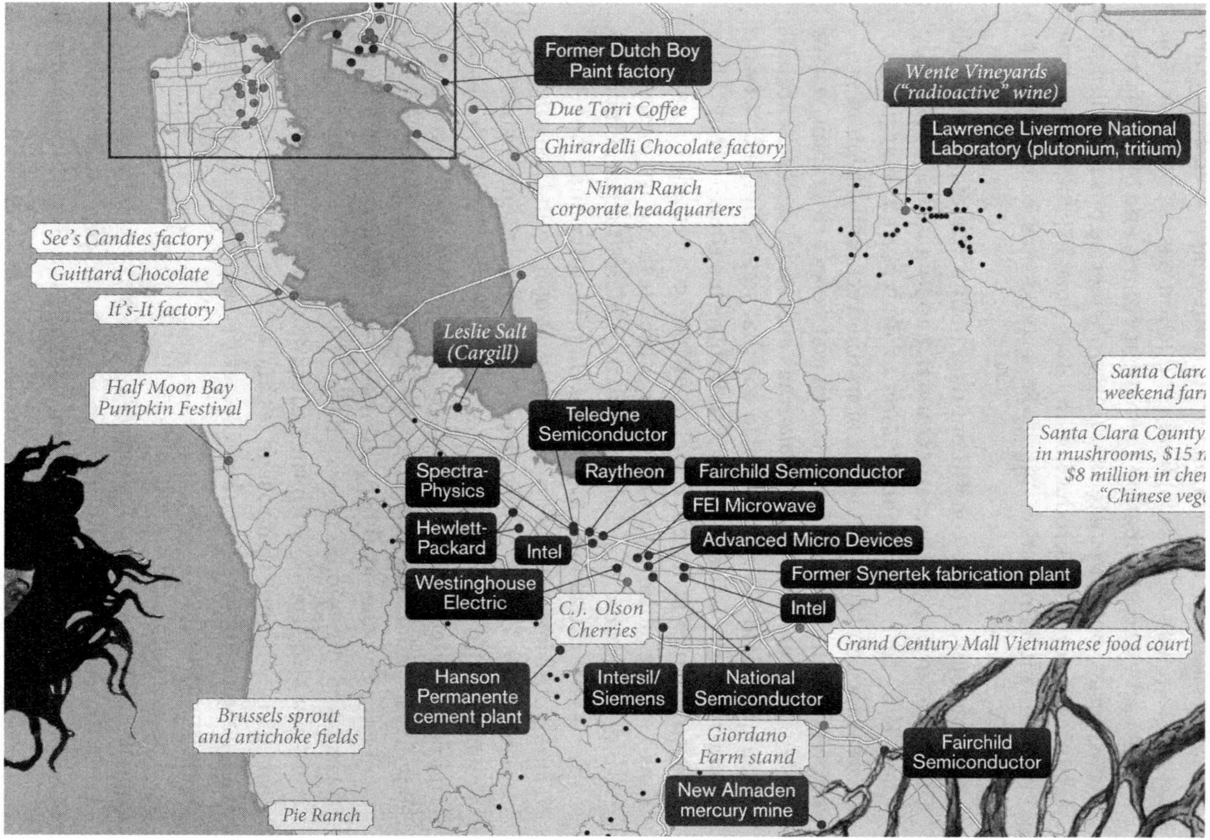

Figure 5.2. A first version of thematic countermapping—a provocative data assembly. Amid the "palate" and "poison/palate" spots of the larger Bay Area are multiple highly contaminated Environmental Protection Agency Superfund sites, concentrated in Silicon Valley. Detail of *Poison/Palate: The Bay Area in Your Body* from Rebecca Solnit, *Infinite City: A San Francisco Atlas* (Berkeley: University of California Press, 2010). Licensed by Copyright Clearance Center / Rights Link.

and curated by Rebecca Solnit. One major conceit of the atlas is that everyone carries with them idiosyncratic maps of the sites in which they live, work, and play. With *Poison/Palate,* Solnit and her collaborators redouble the perspectival potential of mapping by assembling five kinds of sites in the Bay Area: the "palate" sites, where everyday (dairies or an Ohlone shell mound) and specialty (markets or famous restaurants) food production has occurred; poison sites, beset by contamination from oil, mercury, and other materials; wineries; poison/palate sites (certain wineries or salt and sugar factories) where food production involves poisons; and full-fledged Environmental Protection Agency Superfund sites, concentrated in Silicon Valley.

In convening these constituent data points, the map does what this first version of thematic countermapping characteristically does. It undertakes a mobilization of unexpected, marginal, or untested assembly for the sake of partial reconfiguration of well-known worlds. This is a familiar, normatively cartographic way of looking at the planet (*Poison/Palate* has a classic, Western, cardinal orientation, laid flat), but it is also one that seizes on the otherwise eccentric work of dissident data assembly. One contribution of this particular map is its configuring of interconnectedness, as the slow violence of the supposedly immaterial tech industry coincides with the contradictions and complexities of military and industry in areas that ostensibly gain part of their identity and importance from opposition to those things and part of it from the delightful concentration of both noncorporate agricultural enterprises and signature culinary brands. An additional power here is the spatial and open-ended mode. While a story on the contradictions of the Bay Area's industries would also be fruitful, the dissident data assembly in the classically spatial mode manages to exercise a rhetorical and mnemonic power that words struggle to match. The work can also "speak" with the other constituents of the atlas, not least of all with one that assembles and locates the names of places and peoples "before the names"—before colonial settlement and state-sponsored genocide.

The more striking digital versions of this mode work to intensify opportunities for the reader/viewer to explore and compare. I think, for instance, of Brian Holmes's browser-based project *Petropolis.*[42] Centered on Chicago, the interactive map is powerful in part because neither the city nor the petroleum industry can continue to seem like isolated entities. Instead, they are part of a massive network of networks (some might say an assemblage) of material and economic processes, and the nodes and pathways that make up these networks extend far and wide. Holmes doesn't just trace petroleum's toxic avenues. He also gathers and locates responses by assembled activists. Battle is made with the siting of hazardous materials, like petroleum coke, and with the institutions responsible for that siting. Meanwhile the overall cycles of oil production and consumption continue apace, as do the flows of "living rivers" Holmes assembles in a second, eponymous thematic countermap.

Whereas the first version of thematic countermapping takes shape in artifacts that maintain (typically Western) cartographic norms, a second version involves their simultaneous embrace and refusal. Alongside Julie Mehretu, Joe Hamilton, and Layla Curtis (to name a few), Mark Bradford stands out as an artist who has most creatively explored this union, what Claire Reddleman calls "cartographic abstraction."[43] A pair of works included in a 2015 solo exhibition at the Hammer Museum called *Scorched Earth* is especially salient. Among the central themes of the show is what Anita Hill, in an interview with Bradford, calls the "transformation caused by AIDS at the cellular, community and global levels."[44] For Bradford, who lived through the height of the crisis in the United States as a gay, Black man, what was an essential recognition was the structural and fatal role of policy. "You look past your personal story to policy," he tells Hill. "Why are certain areas the way they are? Why aren't there more services in certain areas?" Policy, Bradford continues, can be both action and nonaction. "It can be active aggression. It can be the silent killer in the room."[45]

In producing art in response to such histories of structural (but also painfully visible and often quite rapid) violence, Bradford (who observes that maps are "nothing but the biggest lies on the planet") opts for rich variations on cartographic abstraction suffused with assembly. For *Finding Barry*, Bradford and assistants sanded away layers of paint on a wall in the museum long dedicated to displaying artists' projects, including one by Barry McGee, for whom the work is named (Figure 5.3). The emergent shape of the sanded lines is a map of the United States with statistics on the U.S. population per one hundred thousand diagnosed with AIDS in given states

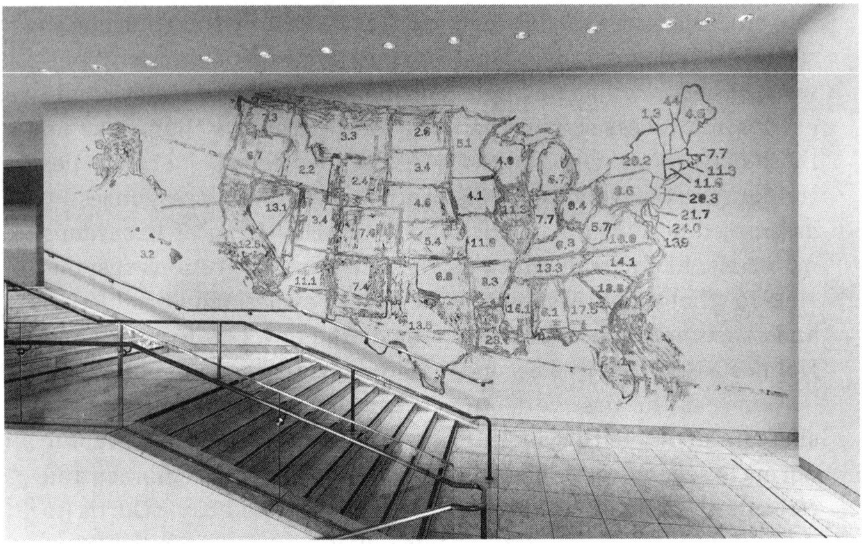

Figure 5.3. Bradford's combination of assembly, mapping, and décollage presents statistics on the population per 100,000 diagnosed with AIDS in California and other states as of 2009. Mark Bradford, *Finding Barry,* 2015. Excavated wall painting, 254 × 568 inches. Copyright Mark Bradford. Courtesy of the artist and Hauser & Wirth. Installation view, "Mark Bradford: *Scorched Earth,*" Hammer Museum, Los Angeles, 2015. Photograph: Joshua White / JWPictures.

as of 2009. In removing layers and thus excavating the accretions of decades, Bradford both metaphorizes enduring illness and visualizes variance across different geographic contexts. Bradford also assembles something that became familiar during the Covid-19 pandemic, the differences that state-specific policy makes: the configurations of polities, the assertions of identity, the refusals of full-fledged public health measures that make for deadly circumstances and often unequal exposure to harm. The constitutive layers of color, which themselves carry physical traces of the time period in question, insist on the reality of these histories of harm, as well as on their endurance in memory.

A second work, called *Scorched Earth,* veers further into the relational potential of sanded layers. In this case, it is an event of rapid and sudden violence that forms the focal point (Plate 11). Over May 31 and June 1, 1921, two years after the spate of murderous attacks against Black people during what came to be called Red Summer—events that sparked "a new era of black resistance to white injustice"[46]—yet another incident of brutal violence against Black communities unfolded in Tulsa. This time the catalyst was the threat to lynch a Black man accused of assaulting a white woman in an elevator. (He likely tripped as he walked in.) Over several hours, aided by an all-white police force that passed out weapons, white assailants gunned down Black residents of Tulsa's Greenwood district while looting businesses and setting buildings ablaze. Thousands were left homeless; dozens were left with gunshot wounds and burns; and the Red Cross estimated at the time that the number killed was three hundred, though the exact total is still not known. Bradford recalls reading about assailants dropping incendiary devices from aircraft. Against the idea that "America's never dropped a bomb on American soil," Bradford sought to emphasize that it had (and indeed it happened again in 1985 in Philadelphia). "A hugely dynamic center" of Black commerce and culture "was becoming too strong and too big and powerful," Bradford recalls, and this attack tried to intervene through extreme and direct violence.[47] As Scott Ellsworth documents, the violence was also archival, as white-run institutions in Tulsa attempted to erase the events from the city's memory, with records destroyed, images confiscated, and a long-time refusal to include the massacre in local curriculum.[48]

In *Scorched Earth,* representation and abstraction fuse with a compelling use of generative assembly. The structure of serial repetitions of constituents in mutually informing positions across the top and middle layers of the work has figured in Bradford's practice since early in his career. Here those assembled repetitions serve to configure the sheer dynamism of the district. They also contrast with the scorched earth below, and with the layers' and grids' implications of enduring consequences. The event did not really end. Nor did the structurally violent consequences of a myriad of discriminatory policies and the persistence of racially motivated violence against Black communities. Ample research has documented the persistent and widespread legacies of this and numerous other events of racial violence that involved the systematic eradication of accumulated wealth.[49] As noted by Dreisen Heath, who makes a persuasive case for reparations in Tulsa, "compounding inequalities stemming from the massacre led to lower life expectancy, increased need for mental health services, loss of economic opportunity, and other harms to community members over decades," and indeed into the present.[50] In other words, not only did traumatic memories of this event of sudden (though habituated) violence persist, but so too did multiple forms of policy and structural violence, including refusals to invest in the community. What also didn't end, of course, was the vibrancy, invention, and solidarity of Black communities perceived as a threat to white hegemony. Descendants of victims of the massacre fought to rebuild "despite the hostility of powerful sectors of the city and state," and they continue "to press their claims for justice."[51]

Bradford's work presses that claim in its piercing rearrangement of those days in Tulsa. The arrangement is especially generative in the sense that this fusion of abstraction, cartography, and assembly makes for no strict, predetermined meaning. In this case, that openness proves especially important.[52] "In the discourse surrounding the massacre," Robin D. G. Kelley tells an interviewer, "it seems like the fate of those few blocks in and around 'Black Wall Street' is all that matters." In fact, Kelley points out, the vast majority of Black people in Tulsa were "not getting rich." A large majority of Black men were employed as "porters, janitors, gardeners, chauffeurs, etc.," and "93 percent of employed Black women cleaned, cooked and cared for children in white households." Those who did purchase property were typically forced to use salvaged materials for houses without underground sewage lines. The consequences of this selective mapping are vital:

> If we only remember the loss of property and wealth and the evisceration of a Black elite, then we only imagine a potential future in which someone like J. B. Stradford could have been the Black "Hilton," where the wealthy are wealthier, and projected "reparations" payments are calculated based on accumulated property at the time of the violence. Despite recognizing that the entire community suffered, "compensation" would be differential, mirroring the very system of racial capitalism that structured enclosure (segregation), violence, deep inequality and poverty for most, and premature death. We will also forget what might be the most impactful response by the community: mutual aid, a caring culture, and the impulse toward self-defense and protecting one another. And if our memories begin and end in 1921, we are stripped of a full accounting of the process of displacement and dispossession—which begins with the inaugural theft of Indigenous lands and still hasn't ended.

Seen through a lens of media assembly, Kelley's intervention does more than insist on the full continuum of violence in and before and after this event. It also recalls Crenshaw's work of conceptual reassembly via intersectionality. An intersectional accounting of histories of displacement and dispossession coincides with an intersection of approaches: conceptual intervention, countercartography, and critical conversation. Reading Kelley in this way, seeing these events differently as a result, the confluence of realism and abstraction in Bradford's assembly appears in a new, sharper, and more encompassing light. Like social and cartographic abstraction, reassembly changes what people read, see, care about, know, and remember. An open question is whether and how people can use social networks to amplify and democratize rather than exploit and undo this transformative power to reconfigure. This is a question of special urgency in a country beset by what Eric Foner, reflecting on the events in Tulsa, calls "legally mandated amnesia."[53]

If part of the power of configural and abstract cartography is the insistence that violence is countered not only at the level of power but also at the level of perception, a third version takes that proposition further by centering on premises rather than places. I think, for instance, of a chart by Kyle Powys Whyte that resonates with Kelley's spoken intervention (Figure 5.4).[54] What Whyte assembles here is a comparison of two accounts of the "same" historical period. For U.S. settlers like the leaders, entrepreneurs, soldiers, and citizens that devastated Indigenous lands and lifeways, history was strictly linear, and Indigenous histories were little more than a dimly perceived precursor from which settler time was strictly segregated. "Indigenous Time" refuses these premises: Indigenous history and U.S. settlement coexist; what appears as a linear progression is actually a sequence of cyclical times; settler history is minimized while Indigenous history is a dramatically longer span. "Imagine if you understood time differently," Whyte proposes, "forgetting about the clock, the days and months, but think about organizing yourself through environmental changes and longer term trends. The qualities of relationships are the generators of fluidity, not just with climate, but with gender identities, sexual lifestyles, and all the aspects of who we are."[55]

Another feature of the premise shift is, as Whyte explains, a relationship to the remarkably casually discussed notion of the end of

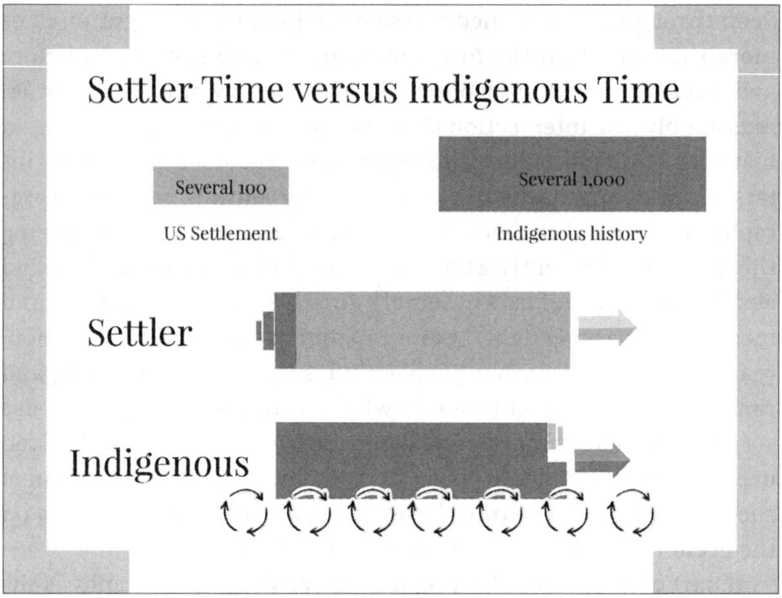

Figure 5.4. Kyle Powys Whyte, "Settler Time versus Indigenous Time," from "It's Too Late for Indigenous Justice: Problems with Climate Change Advocacy" (2019). Prezi. Courtesy of the author.

the world. His carto-temporal assembly frames the situated nature of that perspective. One can only claim the end of the world if one's cultural and geographic world has not already undergone catastrophic undermining: "As Indigenous peoples, we do not tell our futures beginning from the position of concern with the Anthropocene as a hitherto unanticipated vision of human intervention, which involves mass extinctions and the disappearance of certain ecosystems. For the colonial period already rendered comparable outcomes that cost Indigenous peoples their reciprocal relationships with thousands of plants, animals, and ecosystems—most of which are not coming back."[56] For Whyte, no approach to ongoing catastrophes like climate change can hope to persist without the noncoerced consent of Indigenous peoples. His chart is both an intervention in this struggle and a model for exercises going forward. Premise-altering reassemblies of fundamental categories have an essential role to play. These aren't just representations of violence. They are catalytic reorderings of the actual and the possible.[57]

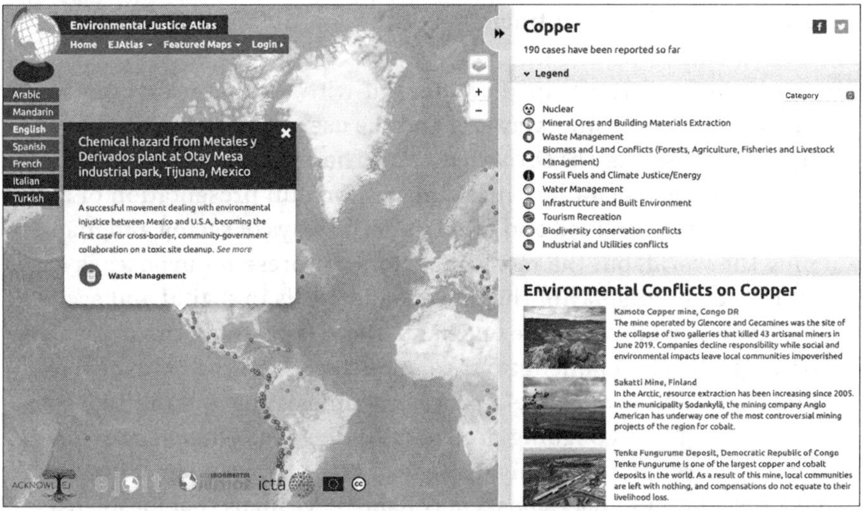

Figure 5.5. One among multiple thematic countermaps in a large digital assembly. *Environmental Justice Atlas.* Screenshot, September 2021.

A final version of thematic countermapping is not centered on individual maps, but on many maps made to accumulate and circulate. On the more data-driven side is a digital assembly called the *Environmental Justice Atlas.* Presenting points on the map where environmental struggles take place, filterable by type, and with certain thematic maps curated for direct access, the site has many functions and missions in one. It plays a role of gathering the sheer abundance of struggles around environmental justice, while also making the "mobilizations" communities undertake toward environmental justice "more visible." The atlas works to "highlight claims and testimonies and to make the case for true corporate and state accountability for the injustices inflicted through their activities." Finally, the atlas acts a waypoint not only toward information, but also to finding others who might work in the same area, connecting struggles across problems and processes that are often purposely kept separate.[58] A map of struggles around copper is especially instructive for the way it both lacks and exceeds the qualities a narrative (like a book or an article) might offer (Figure 5.5). The connections between the different events are undecided. One can look very quickly, not paying much attention. But one can also gain a potentially much-needed view of multiple ongoing struggles, a view of use for recruitment or for the coordination of actions already underway.

Also informational in character but with emphases on creative design, disruptive intervention, and the use of nonnormative mapping modalities is *The Decolonial Atlas.* There are many reasons the project deserves citation, including its forceful presentation of alternatives to ingrained and often imperial ways of seeing and mapping the world, but the most important for present purposes is its simultaneous display of the powers and perils in digital and accumulative assembly. On the one hand, there is power in the project's driving goals to "challenge our relationships with the land, people, and state," and to support "a process of unlearning and rediscovering," as well as an ongoing project of "indigenous language revitalization" through toponymy (the use of place names). There are, for example, Jordan Engel's posts of collaborative maps that locate, list, and translate Indigenous place names (and that includes a map of the lands upon which the present book's press are situated).[59] There are also maps that provide informative angles on current events and topics and histories undergoing widespread discussion, such as a map of America's "suppressed histories" of anti-Black massacres, presented one hundred years after the one in Tulsa. Still others combine his timely approach with the signature, toponymic commitment, as with a collaborative map produced in collaboration with Dakota Wind in response to the defiant actions of water protectors at Standing Rock, combining Lakota/Dakota place names for local rivers with the proposed pipeline route (Figure 5.6).[60] Finally, from a map of anticolonial resistance movements in Africa to a cartographic catalog of music of the African diaspora, Engel also undertakes a near-daily practice of posting that is both against the grain and highly engaged, making and echoing many different, interlocking calls for justice and reparation.

At the same time, there are instances when the project points to the perils in thematic countermapping, even when intentions are good. An especially illustrative instance is "Tribes Spanning the U.S.–Mexico Border," produced and posted by Engel in 2017. At the top of the map is a long-standing refrain: "We Didn't Cross the Border, the Border Crossed Us / No Cruzamos La Frontera, La Frontera Nos Cruzó a Nosotros." The map itself attempts to visualize the ancestral lands of native peoples bisected by the border: Kumeyaay, Cocopah,

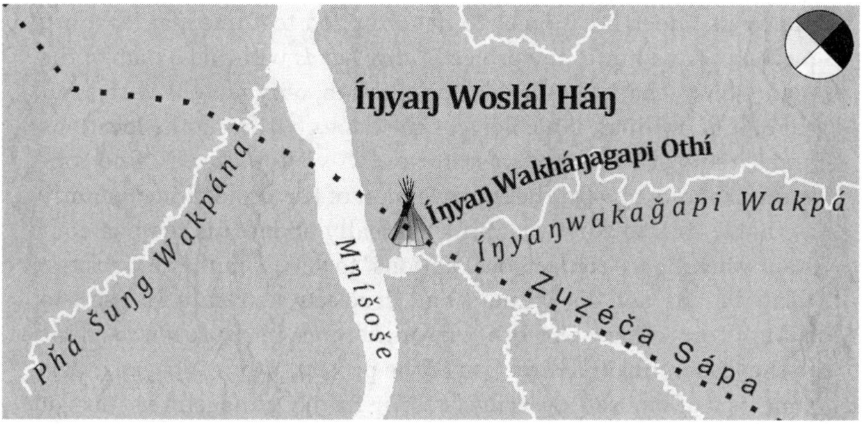

Figure 5.6. Jordan Engel and Dakota Wind, "Dakota Access Pipeline Indigenous Protest Map," from *The Decolonial Atlas* (2016). Decolonial Media License 0.1.

Quechan, Tohono O'odham, Yaqui, Tigua, and Kickapoo. The sense of critique comes through first with respect to exclusion; a user named ApachePunk comments that the map doesn't include the Lipan Apache. The critique then expands by way of a comment by "indigifem," the username for poet, researcher, and activist Margo Tamez. While Tamez appreciates the post's overall intentions, she also finds the map serves to erase "the current-day lived, experienced and understood Indigenous World of the bordered-walled territories." Against its intentions, the map serves to "re-endow the state with power to name and shape realities for social, political and economic purposes." Furthermore, it neglects the fact that "US federally recognized 'Indian' nations are only a slice of the larger whole of the US-MX region when it comes to the diversity of continuing, surviving, and self-determining Indigenous peoples, nations, and tribes." Tamez suggests a more fruitful and properly decolonial approach would address current-day political realities by way of "cartrographic 'truths'" drawn from Indigenous social organizations. In other words, in political and formal terms, Tamez has worked to disassemble through words what the map gathers in pixel.[61]

At least one other project of thematic countermapping shows how the dimension of critique can be taken as a given rather than confined to the comments. (Engel, who is to be credited with supporting ample conversation and connection-building across media platforms, does not appear to have replied to Tamez, at least not publicly.) A visitor to the project *Native Lands* will find a map of the planet in normatively Western orientation, only not one with typical boundary lines, but color-coded shapes outlining the locations and extents of Indigenous territories.[62] A visitor *also* will find constant prompts toward the imperfection of the project: a constantly available link to ways to "think critically about this map"; a constant warning to "contact local nations" to verify; multiple websites, related maps, and disclaimers; and, crucially, a prompt for users to submit corrections. One other key difference in approach pertains to the leadership and direction of the project. While it began as the endeavor of one self-described settler from Okanagan territory, it has since become an Indigenous-led not-for-profit organization. In short, the project's decolonial dimensions extend to the very constitution of the project itself. The digital assembly informs the organizational one.

The question of the constitution of boards points to one last example of the digital and accumulative mode of thematic countermapping that bears mentioning: Josh On's *They Rule.* Started in 2001, the project was an "interactive visualization of the interlocking directories"—who sits on which board of directors—of the largest companies in the United States.[63] In an innovative move for its time, visitors could actively participate in reassembling the project by arranging, annotating, and sharing the connections they discovered or wished to highlight (Figure 5.7). For On, this was partly a matter of doing political battle through art, data, and code, showing just how consolidated power was in a few hands. It was also an exercise in conceptual remapping. This was a time when the future of participation on the internet looked wide open and potentially highly emancipatory, a place where "millions of potential social relations . . . can be formed," but where "the formats for these communications has only just begun to develop."[64] In revealing the interlocked nature of corporate entities through his custom, free, and participatory platform, On could implicitly sketch the coordinates of an alternative internet populated by projects like the aforementioned atlases. Indeed, with each map of the networks of the powerful, including several of considerable visual and configural creativity, the potential for alternative modes of arranging both expressive and economic worlds found new outlet. As I write, a new

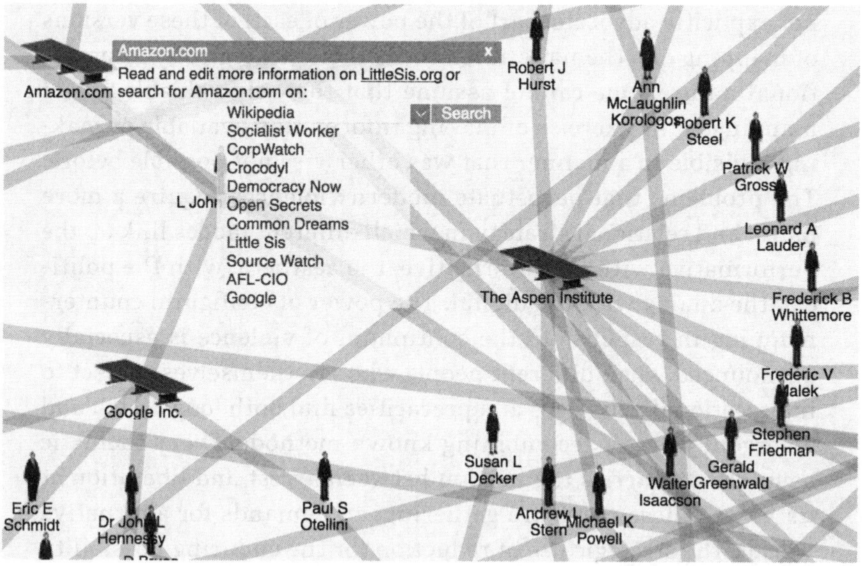

Figure 5.7. A map produced with Josh On's *They Rule* (2001–18). Courtesy of the artist.

iteration of *They Rule* is in the works. No doubt among the companies the new iteration will include will be those that have continued to finance and profit from the extraction of fossil fuels, like J. P. Morgan Chase & Co. and ExxonMobil. But there will also be new players, and that includes Facebook (now "Meta"), a corporation and social-media platform that derives profit from distributed assembly, and that has played no small role in supporting and expanding networks of public harm.

One could look at this transmedia catalog of thematic countermapping and argue that its constituents are all instances of arresting images or moving stories à la Nixon (perhaps even noting the use of "story" in many cases). But such characterization misses the degree to which they involve exercises of selection and configuration, and it further fails to account for the drive to be seen and engaged as relational and relationally expressive acts, whether in terms of reading the rhetoric and aesthetics of arrangement or in terms of recognizing the powers and perils of gathering, recombining, resharing, and contributing.

Although it is an extension of intersectionality Crenshaw does not explicitly advocate, part of the power of each of these versions of mapping qua thematic assembly is their strategically intersectional nature. One cannot assume that the only valuable use of mapping is the exercise of making information available or making it visible in a manner that was otherwise not possible before. The problems that perpetuate modern violences require a more plural and relational strategy in which different modes link up the performative with the informative, the aesthetic with the political, the analog with the digital. The power of configural countermapping in response to the continuum of violence is especially pronounced when different people who are themselves subject to intersectional privileges and precarities find both long-tested and emergent ways of recombining known methods. Every thematic countermap carries the tension between arrest and liberation at its heart. These maps are gatherings of demands for alternative worlds, the strategic use of reduction for the enduring possibility of emancipation.

Memetic Drip, or The Ambivalent Incrementality of Social Media

With the rise of digital and networked media, the varieties of possible media-driven responses to violence grow exponentially. This is partly because of ease of access: there are fast and cheap technologies with which to document events and processes of harm, response, and recovery. The digital expansion is also (arguably) a matter of expanded capacity to label and learn. Manipulation, deception, and censorship aside, different forms of violence are, by and large, more readily seen, taught, and debated in a time of web searches, hashtags, Wikipedia articles, vloggers, and influencers. Not only is it increasingly possible to encounter violence as a topic (or to make it a topic); it is also increasingly possible to attach particularizing language, context, and imagery to events, circumstances, and perceptions of violent occurrence. One can often find not just the conceptual means but also the contexts and communities (and shared drive) necessary to participate in efforts to variously reveal, heal, or forestall forms of public harm (or, to be frank, to perpetuate them). Meanwhile, the legacies of these efforts in storytelling, image-making, and assembling are quite often mere seconds away (for many people, most of the time, anyway).

In contemplating these conditions, it is tempting to adopt an extreme response. On the one hand, in an Enlightenment vein, one might suggest that digital-cultural abundance stands to radically lessen violence by way of constant revealing and informing. On the other, one might argue that digital-cultural abundance largely distracts from the necessary and difficult work of organizing against the very systems and structures that bring about differentials of violence in the first place. Although I find value in such debates, I also see them as of a piece with a long-standing tendency in which the arrival of new media forms—from the telegraph in the nineteenth century to tweeting in the twenty-first—yields utopian and dystopian and, therefore, polar thinking. As Mark B. N. Hansen puts it: "Any Promethean step forward is, so it seems, necessarily accompanied by fears that we have overstepped, that we have introduced something detrimental to our 'natural' life."[65] What seems to me more urgent is the development of other, more plural and intersectional modes of critique and analysis, particularly as time goes on and as so-called "new" media become "old" and effectively immanent.

My accounts of conceptual reassembly and thematic countermapping leaned toward the more empirical and taxonomic modes. My final addition to the chapter's critical typology is more openly speculative. I start by momentarily stepping out of the digital (and the assembly) frame, instead looking to the question of time in activism, media, and politics. There is, for instance, Chloe Ahmann's fieldwork in Baltimore, Maryland, where activists fought a "four-thousand-ton-per-day trash incinerator," one that would "release thousands of pounds of lead, mercury, and fine particulate matter into Curtis Bay, already Maryland's most polluted neighborhood."[66] There Ahmann came to recognize that, "when faced with the challenge of gradual industrial incursion and its often inconclusive effects on human health, residents subject to the vagaries of delayed destruction learned to *work* slow violence and its machinery of perceptual confusion," ultimately defeating the project when the state determined the permits had expired.[67] Among the examples Ahmann cites are efforts to induce time lags and delays in that industrial incursion, "pouring energy into catching the company on a technicality."[68] As "students, environmentalists, and social-justice workers mined the minutiae of construction regulation," Ahmann explains, they "transformed sluggishness (a perceptual block) into a frame for noticing the project's inadequacies."[69] In other words, time was a problem (too little of it, the urgency that things ought to change, the waning of interest) but time was also a means of defense and counterattack. And one of the crucial, strategic uses of time (the concept I am drawing on here) was what Ahmann ventures to call "incrementality." In its typical meaning, incrementality "describes a gradual buildup that sometimes coalesces into something (an event, a reform, a disease)." Incrementality is also about what persists and remains: "While many toxics are regulated as though they are benign beneath a given threshold, they tend to linger in the human body and build with the passage of time, accruing in bodies exposed to multiple, continuous releases."[70] It's not that Ahmann wants to suggest "a direct link between how toxics behave and how toxic developments are resisted." Rather, she says, there are "striking resonances between slow attrition and incrementality as a political strategy." Working time by way of incrementality, the residents found ways of "weakening an opponent through small, successive victories," or they managed to make "progress toward controversial ends while no one [was] watching."[71]

Very much related to incrementality, a second relevant concept is "drip." Instances of scholars employing it ("drip" is also a word for sexy or fashionable style) are many: the "drip, drip, drip of ideology";[72] the "drip effect"; the "drip campaign";[73] and "stalagmite theories."[74] For David Roberts, the way to meaningful change concerning climate "is not through any particular way of writing stories. It's through a relentless drip, drip, drip campaign—just like the one the Right has waged. It's about nagging, becoming national nags. . . . For thirty years, every time the Right saw a news story that didn't take their concerns seriously, they would nag the journalists. They would invoke liberal media bias over and over and over—drip, drip, drip—and eventually the media became conditioned like a puppy. You smack it on the nose enough times, it will do what you ask."[75] In other words, the accuracy of Roberts's take on dog training aside, drip is a way of working media that forgoes a Nixonian emphasis on arresting stories and images in favor of an incremental and persistent approach to engagements with both mass-media players and politicians.

My speculative question is not whether incrementality or drip is better. It is whether and how incrementality and drip take place in and through digital assembly in analogous fashion. My sense is that they do, and not just in one or two instances, but widely and often. The following, purposely dense (and nonexhaustive) aggregate of examples is meant to say as much. These are initial summaries ahead of a synthetic comparison:

(a) One is already on the table: @intersectionalenvironmentalist (Figure 5.8). As the core concept continually reasserts itself by way of the account (and Thomas's associated advocacy work), followers learn, for instance, of the work and strategies of Indigenous and Latinx activists; they see updates on places (like state parks) where intersectional environmentalist work is being done; and they bask in energetic reposts, like collaborator and queer environmentalist @pattiegonia dancing in imitation of *The Sound of Music,* only to insist on the capitalist origins and perpetuation of climate change. Meanwhile, a growing number of other people use the concept as a lens for their actions and media contributions. In other words, intersectional environmentalism has become memetic. Its varied expressive outlets serve as waypoints to established concepts like decolonization and as venues to amplify intersecting voices, including Indigenous voices like @queernature cofounder @queerquechua.

(b) Other accounts directly use memes to address modern violences. For example, @climemechange regularly shares original memetic material produced by an unnamed person with widely used templates (Figure 5.9).[76] A similar but lesser known account is called "Rare and Endangered Memes for Edgy Environmentalists." Representative posts include: a reshare of a *Decolonial Atlas* map of Indigenous blockades in 2021; a link to efforts to establish an "agrihood" in Detroit; and a Spongebob Squarepants image meme stating "80% of the world's remaining biodiversity is on indigenous land" and labeled with "'Humans are a disease' is colonizer shit." That same image meme might well appear on a third

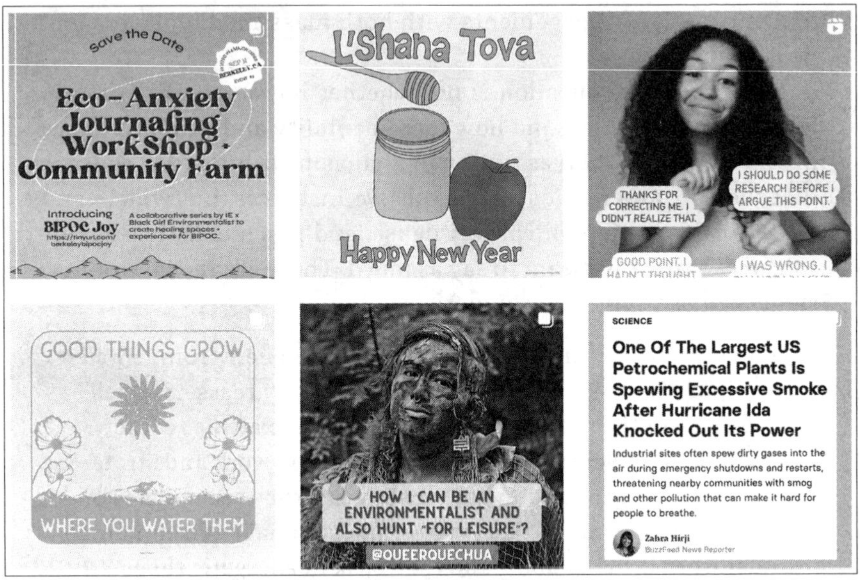

Figure 5.8. The vibrant and varied posts of @intersectionalenvironmentalist. Screenshot, September 2021.

example called @indigenous_fememeisms. Here the account owner describes themselves as: "rez rat going 🦅 university 🦅 now DC | Anishinaabe and also a Cree grandpa for some reason | this is not the place to project ur insecurities." Among other things, the account's memes sharply oppose settler states; they mock things like Instagram infographics that would teach you how to "decolonize thanksgiving"; they self-consciously adopt memes that have gone mainstream but toward insider humor about life on the rez; and they quote from critical literatures like Philip J. Deloria's *Playing Indian.*

(c) In stark contrast with the above examples is a distinct continuum of artifacts, projects, and practices that direct skepticism and aggression toward premises, people, and supposed character types associated with environmental and social justice. Quite often these efforts rely on fallacious comparative assemblies (as in a fake comparison of *Time* magazine covers on a "coming ice age" shared by an official with Trump).[77] Other times they involve memes and meme-

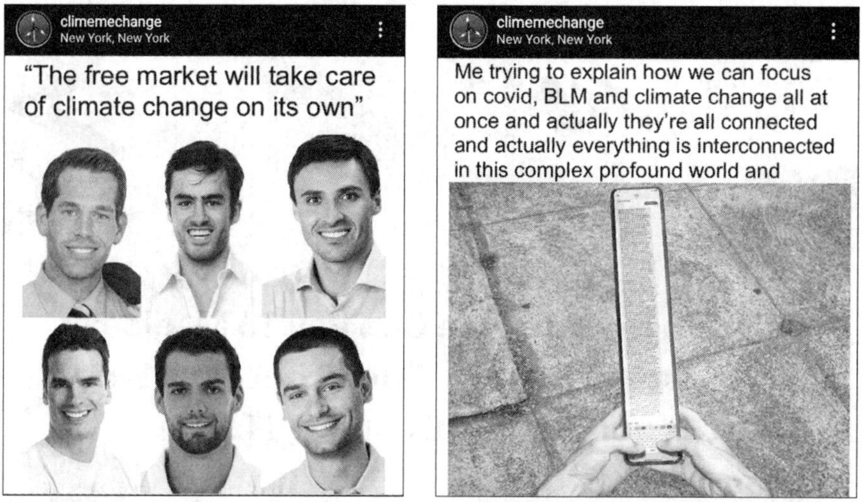

Figure 5.9. Memetic assembly as satirical intervention in the era of climate change. Selections from the Instagram account @climemechange. Collected in 2020.

infused comments (as in mocking reporter Aura Bogado for linking the high death toll in Haiti during Hurricane Matthew with environmental racism[78]). These memetic responses also find pathways through mainstream media. Such was the case, for instance, with a cluster of memes and memetic statements in the United States and Australia mocking efforts to address the climate emergency during the Covid-19 pandemic (Figure 5.10).[79] These memetic instances combine with posts of news and videos—continuous messaging built around the same underlying premises.

(d) Quite divergent from (c) is the work of environmentalist "content creators." An example getting its start amid writing for this book is EcoTok, a group that directly cites intersectional environmentalism. Over a dozen young people of varying ethnic backgrounds, genders, and styles post videos to TikTok with varying senses of humor, seriousness, and purpose (Figure 5.11). The shared emphasis is action: ways to advocate and organize; events to follow and organizations that need donations; reasons for optimism and ways to act on that optimism. Furthermore, the videos share in the use

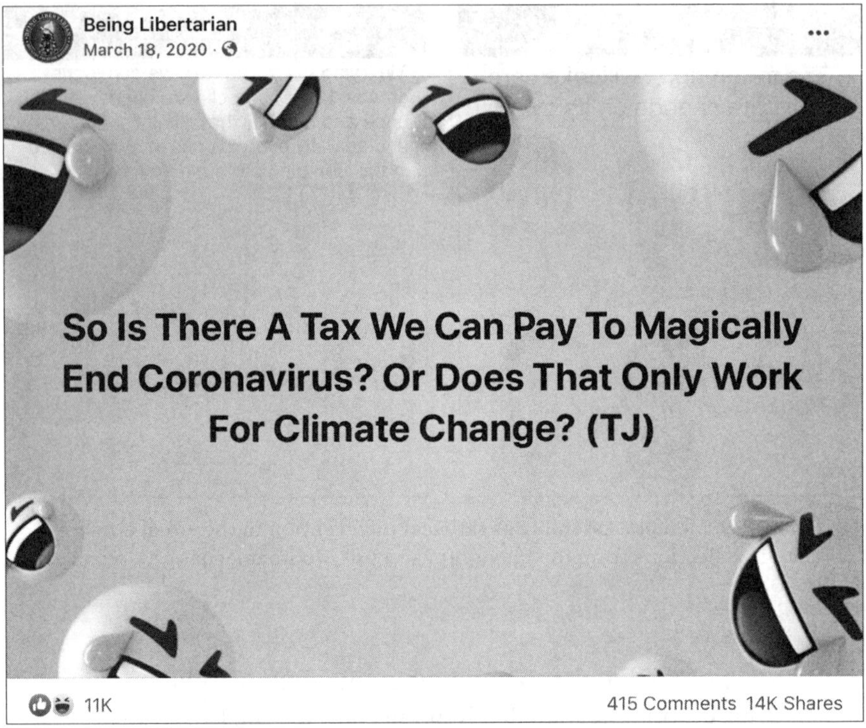

Figure 5.10. One of many memes mocking climate action as part of an unending assembly of further media in this vein. From Facebook page of Being Libertarian, LLC, as cited by Cameron Wilson, "Climate Deniers Are Making Memes about the Coronavirus to Argue against Urgent Climate Action," *BuzzFeed,* April 1, 2020, buzzfeed.com/cameronwilson/right-wing-coronavirus-climate-change-memes-denier.

of memes and memetic references, as well as a basic ease with digital modes of expression.

(e) Finally, there is a multi-platform project called *The Nap Ministry*. Founded by artist, activist, theologian, and healer Tricia Hershey, the project argues that "rest is a form of resistance" and works to "name sleep deprivation as a racial and social justice issue."[80] Consistently calling for "unraveling from very deep and violent systems via rest," the project's social-media presence is rich and varied in its messages and images around white supremacy and hypercapitalist "grind culture." It also consistently emphasizes structural violence at the level of the body, as when Hersey observes "Black women

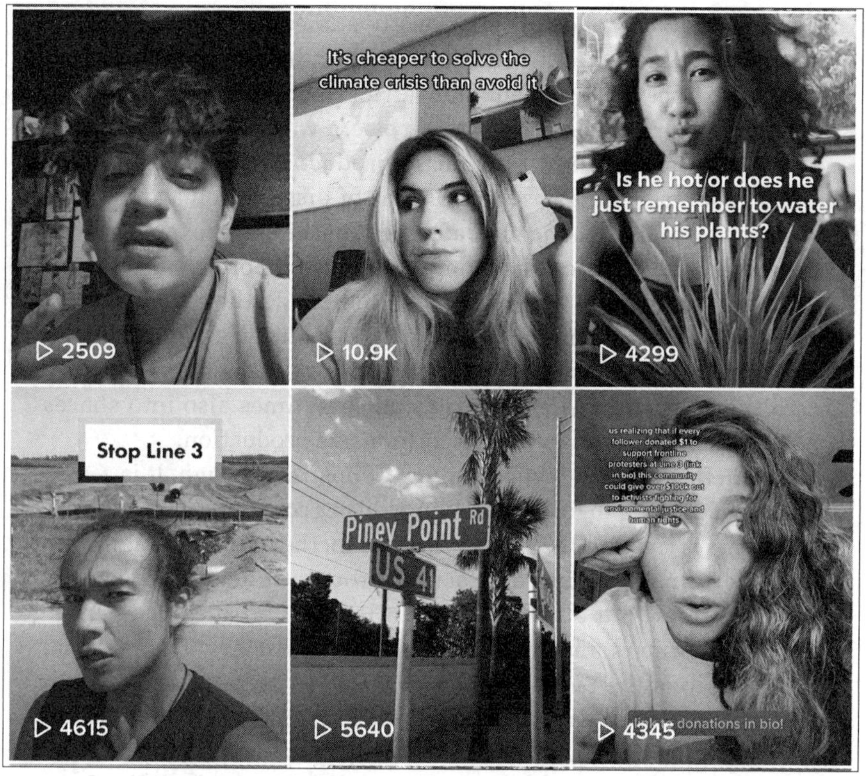

Figure 5.11. Short-form environmentalist videos as memetic drip on @eco_tok. Screenshot, September 2021.

> and women of color who are dying while they're having babies because of the healthcare system rushing them and not caring for their bodies and not listening to them."[81] Not strictly memes, the project's posts are nevertheless frequently quasi-memetic in their consistency of shape and portability, and that includes the use of the phrase "lay down," as with a post with the call to "DIVEST FROM CAPITALISM LAY YO ASS DOWN" (August 23, 2021), to which Hershey added an annotation that begins with "Our bodies are a site of liberation."

As ever throughout this book, the point is not that these different examples are somehow secretly the same, much less that they are adopting the same premises, as indeed each involves importantly divergent (and in one case manifestly antagonistic) assumptions, stances, values, and strategies. The point is that they mutually embody a distinct strategic bent I now map, what I call "memetic drip."

Memetic drip is, before anything else, a way of naming the constancy and persistence of memetic production in general. In the third chapter, I emphasized questions of distribution around memetic and quasi-memetic media. In light of the above examples, it is repetition and duration that come to the fore. In other words, none of these examples is an expressive one-off. Rather, they release images, stories, assemblies, performances, and memes (or quasi-memetic material) with regularity. Those releases find their way into thousands of feeds and eyes and sometimes also into shares and citations, or even in further responsive production.

Memetic drip isn't just constancy of posting, though. It is a constancy of posting in direct relation to other constants. One of these constants is the drip that Roberts refers to: the multisite campaigns to undermine thinking and action around climate change (and other matters). But another constant is much broader: the persistence of disasters and the effects of those disasters. The material fact of drip is the fact of liquids released in small but persistent amounts. Slow violence and environmental racism can manifest in this mode. There is, for instance, the drip (and increasingly also the flood) of water from melting glaciers, or the dripping (and the flowing) of harmful industrial waste into watersheds, and there is the drip-feed of intravenous therapy for patients consigned to hospital beds. It is not that these material drips are the same as memetic drip. It is that there is, to use Ahmann's term, "resonance" at the level of their constancy. Part and parcel, there is the crucial sense in which these exercises in memetic drip—those in (c) notwithstanding—are, for all their flatness and digital aesthetics, keyed to disasters that don't go away. They seek a slowing and an undoing of toxic flows through bodies, neighborhoods, and ecosystems. And several seek a hastening of the work of not just mitigation, but transformation and undoing. They are strategic and necessarily imperfect projects aimed at suspensions and reversals by means of persistent media production. Very much a product of the fast pace of social media, they are also deliberate efforts to make speed into accumulation, connection, and return. (Of course, as projects dependent on the raw materials and energy production of the

"Anthropocene," they are also suffused by paradox. Simone Browne speaks to this point: "When the supply chain of the digital technologies we use to witness and cultivate dissent, as [Aliyyah Abdur-Rahman] put[s] it, starts and ends in spaces like Agbogbloshie, what role is played by this garbage imperialism and its colonial underpinnings? This is seemingly where the discarded and disregard meet in ways that necessitate reparative work."[82])

Alongside these broader strategic overlaps, there are tactical specificities that don't necessarily cut across the whole group. As sites of incrementality, rather than incrementalism, the political strategy dedicated to small changes over time, these accounts are potentially, in however humble a measure, timekeeping and disciplinary devices. Take @climemechange. For all its emphasis on humor and irony, it is also a repetition of commitments. It is an assertion of positions over time, an assembly extending out into time. To the slow (and also sudden and quite visible) violence that occurs in conjunction with climate change (and differential exposure to its effects), the account offers a consistent infusion of perspective and humor. Maybe, as these releases go out to thousands of followers, they do little or nothing. But maybe they can also serve a modest reminding and binding function, helping to maintain avenues of attention and attitudes toward action, particularly in moments when energy and optimism are low. The consistency of those releases might, for instance, manage to continually configure climate change as part of the digital cultural now, as something urgent, current, and addressable, not far off, forgettable, and intractable. That's not the same as saying memetic releases in this vein will manage to furnish the "resilience all movements need to survive and thrive in the long term," nor as suggesting they will solve the organizational challenges faced by fragile social and ecological alliances.[83] It's saying they can serve as one among hundreds of devices: little bundles of imaginative scaffolding, brief respites from cynicism and fear, random cracks in the ways we have things arranged.

Continuing in this more speculative vein, the other functions qua memetic drip to which these examples point are a matter of distribution and recruitment. While it might well be the case that most followers of these accounts are already sympathetic, informed, and active, that doesn't preclude the possibility of transit in other directions. In other words, the liquidity of "drip" suggests a possible move through the cracks and fissures of echo chambers and algorithmic tunneling. A brief encounter can become a follow, and a follow can become a source of ongoing flows, such that one begins to make (or perform) memes of this kind (not to mention the flows of related accounts and content they might invite by way of algorithm, a part of their own and potentially friends' and followers' digital, visual, and cognitive circulation). Of course, the vast suite of memetic media I refer to in (c) are a part of the constant drip, too. These accounts and their memetic payloads can likewise perform their own disciplinary and distributive functions, courting followers who might not otherwise have listened, helping (however partially) shore up ideological commitments that might not otherwise have calcified, media constituents binding political ones. Practices and processes of memetic drip compete at the level not only of content and commitment, but also of quantity, dispersal, recruitment, and retention.

Another way of construing memetic drip finds an anchor in EcoTok. Go to this account and pursue the kind of quick scrolling through bursts of song and reference that TikTok invites, and you will not find memes in the image meme vein. You will find numerous memetic behaviors and performances, which is to say ways of acting or performing that are familiar and repeatable for particular (and often large) sets of people, such as mouthing the lyrics of a depressing song along with a few overlaid words to suggest a sense of being depressed about certain activities (like climate pessimism). This is working time via memes, but it is also working in a time of memes (and influencers and "content creation"). Accounts like EcoTok work within and around and in dialogue with a world in which memetic reference and memetic reconfiguration are (for now, anyway) givens. They perform the incrementality of creating and posting in a manner that mines and maneuvers the general drip, working their way into the diets of the everyday but also doing the work of signaling affiliation by way of know-how. With all the complexities and imperfections memes carry, this is an attempt at relational communication about what people can concretely do in a manner that aims to compel emulations and repetitions.

Although doing so as (apparently) one person, @indigenousfememeisms likewise performs the work of incremental (and in this case, fundamentally intersectional) production in a time of memes. Doing so allows given issues and problems (such as the habits of reporting on Indigenous people and policies in the United States) to circulate within the memetic landscape. Perhaps primarily built for the enjoyment and affirmation (and provocation) of Indigenous folx, the memes of this account also compete against other memetic and quasi-memetic assemblies in the mode of counter-memes, all the while refusing followers the uncritical comfort of believing watching and listening are actual concrete affiliation, instead insisting on difference and divergence. The continuous release of assembled premises alternative to the structures that differentially harm (themselves subject to humorous derision) counters the continuous circulation of the media (and the people behind those media) that tend to favor (and benefit from) those structures.

And then there are those sources of drip, like *The Nap Ministry,* that work through indirection and incrementality by constantly assembling the right to and the need for refusal and release. This isn't for just anyone. It is for those who have been (and remain) widely and disproportionately subject to modern violences and systemic racism. (The ministry notes its work has been co-opted by "white wellness folks.") Ahmann speaks to the aspect of exhaustion in battles against slow violence. Jonathan Crary speaks to the necessity of sleep amid domineering landscapes of pervasive electronic transactions and behavioral modification.[84] And here, repeated time and again, is the always-on state of social media yoked to the ministry's reverence for the fragile rhythms of bodies. This is constantly speaking and assembling near and alongside those bodies, such that the people who live in and through those bodies, especially Black people, might be restored. This might be restoration into the punctuation of a day's fight against the structures and willing agents of systemic and structural harm, but it is also, as the ministry repeatedly emphasizes, not about being productive. It is about "rest as reparations"; it is about rest as a "divine and human right." It is also about the regular enactment of this right, not just in theory, but in physical fact. That enactment can be as simple as putting away one's phone or refusing to answer an email outside business hours. It can also be rejecting the premises of grind culture and 24/7 capitalist striving.

It can also be out in the open. In 2019, the ministry undertook a moving and embodied assembly in Atlanta, one that had "Black people on a rest altar sleeping for 3 days in a row" while "a soundtrack of healing music played." Called *A Resting Place,* this intervention unfolded over three days. As @thenapministry recalls beneath a cluster of images of the installation two years later, "thousands of people passed by to encounter and engage with the power of rest."[85] Thanks to the ministry's memetic drip, thousands continue to regularly encounter—and, one hopes, act on—that power.

Fast Violence and Inventive Vigilance

In July and August 2019, it seemed like the whole world was on fire. Global average temperatures approached the hottest on record, leading to deaths from heatwaves and the (then) largest known loss of ice in Greenland. Meanwhile, massive fires overtook large stretches of Siberia, Indonesia, and the Amazon. Amid these and still other disasters (including unprecedented floods along the Mississippi River), conversation raged around the impacts of climate change, with many insisting (rightly so) that the effects of this ongoing disaster were by no means hypothetical, but present, urgent, and extremely violent. Among the people weighing in on Twitter was the philosopher of ecology Timothy Morton. "Rob dude," Morton wrote, referring to Nixon, "it's time to retire the meme. This is extremely horrifyingly fucking fast violence, especially for non-white people."[86] Someone soon commented: "Suddenly-increasingly-not-so slow-at-all-violence is kind of a mouthful though." Morton shot back, "That's why I didn't say it." Morton then clarified their position: "We should say fast violence. Fire and hurricanes and melting are fucking fast. I'd go so far as to say that seeing violence against non-white people as slow is really really problematic."

I can recall the odd mix of shame and skepticism I felt reading this exchange. Although I had long seen the concept of slow violence as unusually underquestioned, I had not sufficiently considered the potential problems in casting violence against people of color as slow. At the same time, I could not shake a series of questions about this set of utterances. Why does Morton address Rob as "dude," and why do they characterize the concept as a "meme" that one might put to rest? Even while granting that Twitter favors quick, abbreviated, and often aggressive speech, is the suggestion that no violence of any kind should be seen as slow, or is it that slow violence is of less urgent concern when manifestly fast violence is occurring? Finally, is it Morton's suggestion that Nixon effectively favors a harmful and presumably self-serving meme rather than effective and inclusive critical thinking, and that, whether he likes it or not, he frames violence against poor people and people of color as always slow, distant, and diffuse?

Having sat with these questions by way of fellow writers on the subject, I find two thoughts demand articulation by way of closing. The first is not about assembly per se. It is about the critical tension inherent in the concept of slow violence. On the one hand, it seems valuable for one act of conceptual reassembly (the move to theorize "slow violence") to give way to further reassembly in turn (the move to emphasize "fast violence"). On the other hand, the substance and the delivery of Morton's critique undermine the project they purport to support (and that their writing and podcasting do actively support), which is naming, interpreting, and undoing the conditions that enable "modern violences that work at varied scales and speeds." An article by Naya Jones points to why. For one thing, Jones, who identifies her roots as Blaxicana, does what Morton indicates is problematic, which is to frame certain forms of violence against people of color as slow. For instance, for Jones, "affective pressures of whiteness and racial surveillance can act subtly on the body as emotional slow violence, with implications for Black well-being and healing." Furthermore, "microaggressions maintain a delayed and attritional impact; they are chronic and wearing, subtle and often denied."[87] But Jones also critiques the concept as originally conceived, pointing to the way it embodies a dominant mode of geographic looking. That mode of looking assumes—and here Jones quotes Katherine McKittrick—that "we can view, assess, and organize the world from a stable (white, patriarchal, heterosexual, classed) vantage point." For Jones, in other words, Nixon's account of slow violence overlooks its own locatedness. It also overlooks the way that being out of sight can itself be the context for violence: "in the context of racial surveillance, to be considered out of place can be lethal."[88]

In presenting this powerful rejoinder to the implicitly white vision of slow violence as violence out of sight, Jones both parallels and exceeds Morton's reactive refusal. Jones is explicit about this plural and nuanced mode: "How might I write about Black food geographies and slow violence, without (re)presenting these geographies and violence(s) as lost-and-found, as McKittrick puts it?"[89] For Christian and Dowler, one answer is to risk a relational approach that can acknowledge overlaps and intersections among modern violences while also emphasizing the fact of the fast, the brutal, and the manifestly terrifying. For instance, they write, the "slow march of economic and political exploitation can incite explosive and violent responses, like an act of terrorism, and an act of terrorism can then be used to justify a generation of oppressive changes to immigration or policing policy with violent impacts that stretch across time. . . . Slow forms of violence imbricate with the fast, and the fast inescapably shapes the slow." Seeing and reading in this flexible and multiscalar way "helps us to link the causes and consequences of violence," and in that sense to forge "pathway[s] to challenge impunity."[90] Concrete reparative interventions often require paradoxical conceptual ones.

My other thought in response to Morton's tweets is a provocation to anyone who would take up the project of analyzing (and doing) generative and media assembly. In this chapter, I have tended to emphasize the durationally intensive end of the spectrum of media, from concepts developed through creative research, to thematic countermapping that tends to take ample time to produce (and relatively long to appreciate), to a vision of memetic production in its unfolding and persistence rather than its speedy veneer. But there must also be other times and rhythms to justice-driven, assembly-based, and assembly-infused media practices, including the very fast, the highly ephemeral, and the repeating. In fact, Jones suggests an even more intriguing proposition: the creative *mixture* of rhythms and times, the speedy with the slow, the looping with the progressing, the short with the long. In the midst of her research, Jones found herself turning to an assembly-infused medium that reaches back to the early days of the internet (and to the optical toys of the nineteenth century): the animated GIF. For Jones, making GIFs based on informants' testimonies (such as exaggeratedly keeping her hands visible while shopping) became a means of "feeling and thinking through" and of "embodied bearing witness." Making GIFs also pointed to another potential: in contrast to "flat images sans reanimation, the GIFs disclose how slow violence can surface again and again, in testifiers' everyday experiences, memories, and bodies."

In other words, among the many things I hear in Jones's project is a broader lesson about expressive strategies. Although they can indeed fail and deceive, creative uses of what Jones dubs "evolving media" have a key role to play in efforts to mitigate and undo the realities and consequences of modern violences. As Jones puts it, quoting Nixon, these uses of media can function as "'a potential resource of hope' if 'deployed with inventive vigilance' for environmental justice."[91] As the many practitioners gathered in this book have shown, the need for such inventive vigilance is more extreme than ever.

Conclusion

From Paranoid to Reparative Assembly

Whether it takes a few seconds, an hour, or a whole decade, more and more people find ways to seize on the cultural form of assembly. Not only are there increasingly many would-be constituents in circulation (data, words, images, sounds), but there are also increasingly widely accessible means through which to add to, reshape, and distribute the assemblies that host those constituents. As the drive to assemble expands its reach, so do the visible and available potentials in this transmedia form. From an amusing pairing of facial expressions made for followers to an elaborate Venn diagram that provokes a few hundred thousand strangers, these potentials suffuse many people's cultural worlds, so much so that media assembly manages to feel increasingly intuitive while also remaining wide open for further invention.

Collating and arranging, selecting and configuring—the things people do with assembly can sound cold and abstract at first blush, as though they enjoyed nowhere near the appeal and obviousness of following characters through events (narrative) or making scenes and subjects present (representation). And yet, from a nurse on a smoke break reinventing a trending meme to a venture into configural aesthetics for a famous artist, the daily churn of cultural production reveals the capacious allure of this distinctly relational way of using media. The activities of assembly can yield everything from a momentarily diverting image macro calling out a politician's bullshit, to a connective colloquy of GIFs in a pandemic, to the collective, evolving, motley, wonderful, awful world of memes. At the same time, people who work with nondigital materials do not somehow miss out on the dynamic powers of assembly. They, too, take advantage of the form, whether through the analogical invention of balloons crossing a border, the interruptive power of newly organized museum holdings, or yet further expressive effects in mixes of people, symbols, and things no one has attempted. Crucially, the work people do with assembly does not so much mirror or narrate the world as rearrange it. Sometimes quite easy to read, other times requiring a great deal of effort (or insider knowledge) from those who encounter them, these acts of rearrangement can be highly generative. Assemblies are open-ended interpretations of the shapes the world might yet take. One assembly begets another.

At the same time, in spite of the form's accessibility, vibrancy, and reach, and perhaps because of the historical dominance of other expressive strategies or the form's overlaps with montage, collage, database, and other modern and contemporary forms, or for still other reasons, direct studies of media assembly remain relatively rare. *A Theory of Assembly* has argued that this should change. After all, if it is indeed the case that, across art, memes, disaster, and slow and structural violence, there are not just the odd handful of instances of assembly, but many significant ones, even a widespread explosion of instances, then it will mean an unnecessary shortcoming in criticism, scholarship, and curating to let that form remain undertheorized and underrepresented. This would mean continually misreading a vast array of cultural instances through dominant lenses that aren't quite appropriate, seeing an attempt to rework an existing narrative when there is really an attempt to form a novel and restorative constellation, or seeing an effort to challenge dominant representations when there is really a risky effort to combine what hasn't yet been combined. Ignoring assembly would also mean denying the kaleidoscopic inventiveness of the internet era its due, allowing that inventiveness to remain more out of reach and comprehension than it ought to be. Schemes for rhetorics and maps of strategies toward rich and needed things such as the beauty of arrays, the wonderment of patterns, and the amusements and critiques in unexpected comparisons would continue to elude those who might otherwise make good use of them. Humans have long been storytelling animals. Now we see they are also assembling ones.

So, part of the work here has been to establish terms and taxonomies for a cultural form that no properly intersectional account of contemporary European and North American art, media, and communication should ignore. I have offered a vision of what assembly is and does. It is selecting constituents, configuring them into positions and platforms, and it is often configuring the viewer or would-be participant in turn, leaving to them what they will do with their drive to perceive or participate in assembly. I have also offered a vision of assembly in its more complementary and unconscious guises, from an enigmatic painter's uses of assembly in a hallucinatory rendering of utopia and dystopia to assembly as part of the physics and ecology of the networked era, something one often can't help but do when interacting through digital means, however partially or however rapidly.

I've also emphasized the intellectual binds that assembly presents. Right here and elsewhere, time and again, the idea of reading assembly across not just art, but all manner of media, whether fine or vulgar, whether hard-won or quick, can induce a feeling of conceptual vertigo (or perhaps, for some, just skepticism). And yet, as these chapters have shown, the interpretive problem is not intractable. Making sense of a cultural form that joins narrative and representation (and allegory, visualization, database, and others) in cutting across numerous contexts is not just manageable, but fruitful, at least if we are willing to dispense with certain dominant habits of seeing, saying, and interpreting. We recompose and redirect our conceptual lenses, finding and welcoming strangely overlapping family resemblances both obvious and subtle, both widespread and uncommon. Ferreting out elusive but actual linkages and overlaps, engaging in speculative recategorization—the interpretive practice of plural reading is crucial to the work of contesting and revising the known and valued palette of cultural forms.

But the plural reading of assembly isn't just intellectually generative. It is also urgent. This is because of the pronounced *ambivalence* of assembly. I don't mean ambivalence in the sense of indifference or wishy-washiness. I mean ambivalence in the sense of simultaneous, interconnected, and yet ultimately divergent states.[1]

At one level, assembly works its magic as a strategy toward humor, delight, and reflection, the fact and the joy of expressive freedom. It is also a tool for political communication: a necessary, powerful, well-tested, and effective mechanism toward progress and possibility. The exercise of meaning-making through consolidation and arrangement has force; so, too, does the practice of organizing images and ideas in a manner that retains open-endedness. The labors of rearrangement can be vital and transformative, particularly in the

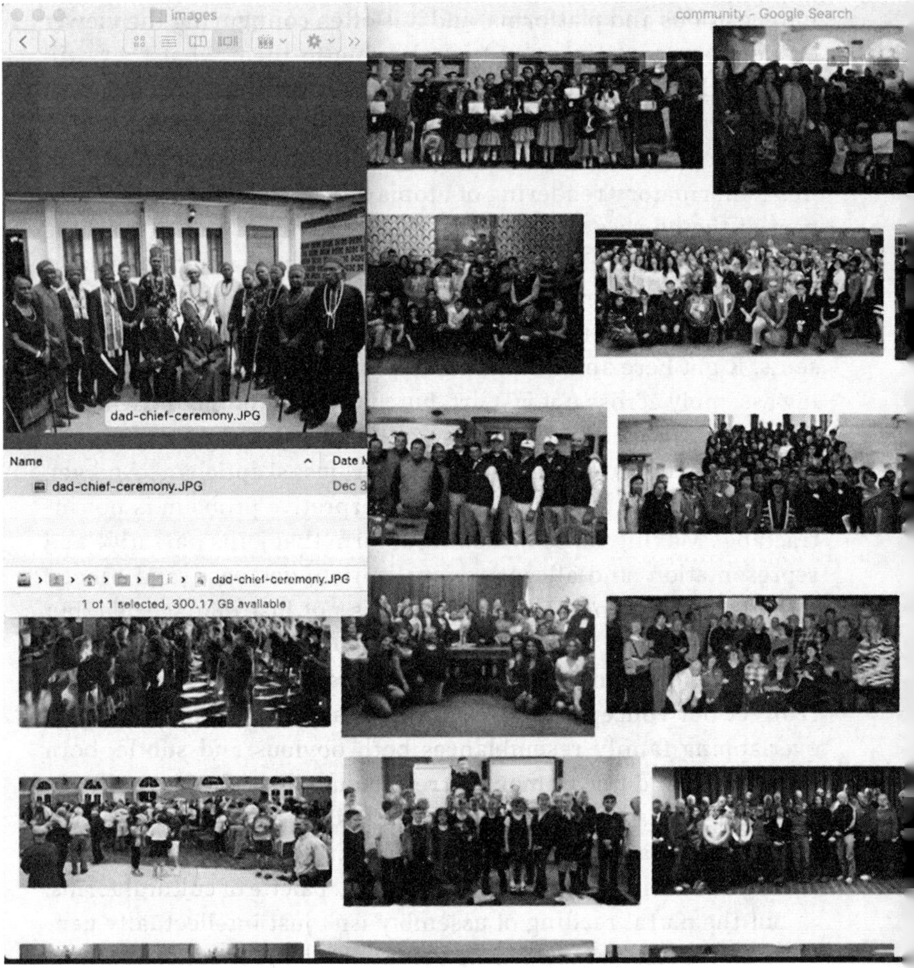

wake of disastrous events and their all-too-common remediations through oppressive lenses. To read and study assembly is to know something effective and useful in ongoing struggles for social and ecological justice and thriving, whether a means of making perceptible that which eludes perception or a means of maintaining hope amid so little that might give one hope. To read and study assembly is also to know something Mimi Ọnụọha explores in her multipart project *Us, Aggregated.* For the third installment in the series, Ọnụọha sets photos from her family's collection with names like

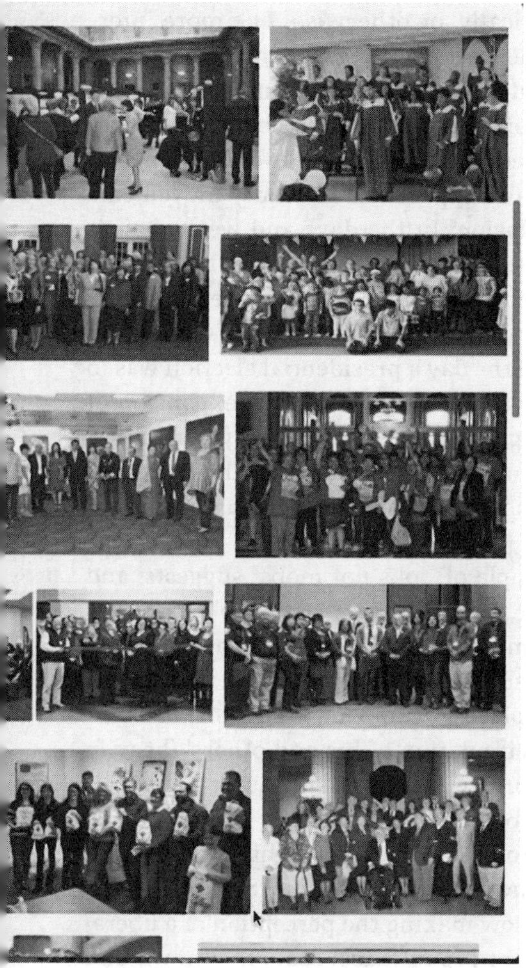

Figure C.1. "... a manufactured aggregation of 'us' that remains an 'us' nonetheless." Mimi Ọnụọha, *Us, Aggregated 3.0,* 2019. Courtesy of the artist.

"animal" and "dad-chief-ceremony" alongside those deemed algorithmically similar via Google's reverse image search (Figure C.1). The assembled images manage to "evoke a sensation of community and similarity" while they also belie "the fact that the subjects are randomly assorted, a manufactured aggregation of 'us' that remains an 'us' nonetheless."[2] In other words, to see and value exercises of media assembly is also to see and value persistent exploring and questioning around how "we" (or, really, the many instances of "we" that we each inhabit) have been constituted and arranged, whether willfully, algorithmically, or otherwise. The more interconnected and algorithmic the world becomes, the more necessary these exercises in analogy and reconstitution become.

And yet, all these powers of assembly are matched by misuses and abuses. The ability of assembly to aid in causes of freedom and thriving parallels an ability to support and intensify movements based in regression and exclusion. In the days and weeks before January 6, 2021, in the hours during which the so-called "Stupid Coup" unfolded, in the enduring aftermath in which people wrestled with how the Capitol could have been overrun by a violent and manifestly racist assembly on the day a presidential election was to be certified, this harrowing valence of the dramatic expansion of the cultural form came through with remarkable and vexing force. This was a variation on assembly's perniciousness I had not myself imagined, but one that I now see a theory of media assembly at least partly anticipates.

For one thing, as the example of "jobs not mobs" suggests, and as the more insidious practice of distributed disassembly presages, instances of assembly both minor and widely writ played crucial roles in making such an event thinkable and practicable. Those roles included memes that placed Trump in a position of obvious power, or that sped the circulation of his and others' (heavily funded and algorithmically prioritized) messages asserting the illegitimacy of the election. Working in conjunction with podcasts, long-form YouTube videos, and mass-media punditry, uses of assembly also supported conspiratorial fantasies like "Stop the Steal!" and false comparisons, somehow making the perception of a liberal conspiracy to put an end to the republic feel real and known and legitimate. Racist and anti-Black and anti-"lib" perspectives held well before the focus on the election also found themselves readily shored up in the accumulating fragments of social media feeds or in the compendia of disinformation racing through group chats and comment threads. (As Lisa Nakamura pointed out in 2002, the internet consistently "propagates, disseminates, and commodifies images of race and racism."[3]) Meanwhile, the conspiracy theory of QAnon, that most thoroughly paranoid of configurations, played a crucial additional role. This was a memetic assembly of extraordinary reach, its crowd-sourced stories and images already sufficient to harness the imaginations of thousands of adherents with fantasies about secret, satanic crime among a deep-state cabal. Now the social connections and mental and emotional investments of those adherents proved extraordinarily helpful in spreading theories of voter fraud and election conspiracy into and out of extreme right-wing, white-nationalist and other "similarity-based 'neighborhoods'" across profit-driven media platforms.[4] These connections and investments also recruited participants for the insurrection.

As the anticipation of the event in threads and memes gave way to the flesh and blood convergence of thousands of people immersed in boisterous speeches and feverish costume, the uses and operations of assembly expanded into territory that eludes linear description. I find some sense begins to emerge when I engage in something between narrative and assembly, excerpting passages from journalists' accounts of the day, arranging them more or less chronologically:

(a) Face-painted and brightly festooned pilgrims bearing banners—snarling Trump straddling a tank, pumped-up Trump-as-Rambo brandishing a machine gun, grimacing Trump as motorcycle gang chieftain—milled about the archaic hulk of the Washington Monument looking like the remnants of a postapocalyptic cult, with beefy bearded men in camo pants and Harley jackets, and women wearing red, white, and blue sweatshirts and draped in red "Make America Great Again" flags like Roman togas.[5]

(b) Lauren Boebert—a newly elected Republican, from Colorado, who has praised QAnon and promised to wear her Glock in the Capitol—had tweeted, "Today is 1776."[6]

(c) After he had read out once more all the discredited claims about all the dark doings in inner-city Detroit and Philadelphia and Atlanta—adding ruefully that the wily Georgians had now succeeded in *stealing the election again*—the president came to the point of what lay before us this day: "We're going to have to fight much harder. And Mike Pence is going to have to come through for us. And if he doesn't that will be a sad day for our country. . . . We're going to walk down, and I'll be there with you, we're going to walk down to the Capitol and we're going to cheer on our brave senators and congressmen and women, and we're probably not going to be cheering so much for some of them. Because you'll never take back our country with weakness. You have to show strength and you have to be strong. We have come to demand that Congress do the right thing. . . . We fight. We fight like hell, and if you don't fight like hell, you're not going to have a country anymore."[7]

(d) To the strains of "Tiny Dancer" and then "YMCA," the mass began to loosen and separate.[8]

(e) A woman in a kind of red, white, and blue pajama suit gazed down at her phone and shouted, "Pence just threw Trump under the bus!" A blond-haired woman in a woolly Trump hat said to no one in particular, "The courts won't help. The Supreme Court won't help. The only one left is us."[9]

(f) "It was amazing to get to see the president talk," Babbitt said afterwards, in a Facebook video obtained by TMZ. "We are walking to the Capitol in a mob. There is a sea of nothing but red, white and blue patriots." She was grinning. At the Capitol, Babbitt would be among the crowds of Trump supporters who pushed and fought their way past the Capitol police and into the building itself, forcing lawmakers to flee or hide, and temporarily halting the certification of Biden's election victory. . . . Widely circulated videos show Babbitt hopping up to push herself through one of the door's glass panels, towards the legislators at the other end of the hallway, as a man shouts "Bust it down!" The footage shows a shot ringing out, and Babbitt falling to the ground.[10]

(g) The America Firsters and other invaders fanned out in search of lawmakers, breaking into offices and revelling in their own astounding impunity. "Nancy, I'm *ho-ome!*" a man taunted, mimicking Jack Nicholson's character in "The Shining." Someone else yelled, "1776—it's now or never." Around this time, Trump tweeted, "Mike Pence didn't have the courage to do what should have been done to protect our Country . . . USA demands the truth!"[11]

(h) As captured in the video, prosecutors said, Jensen "led the crowd toward [Police Officer Eugene Goodman] in a menacing manner" and repeatedly ignored his demands to stop. He later told police that he purposely jumped to the front of the crowd because he wanted his QAnon T-shirt to be prominently seen on TV, so that "Q" would "get the credit" for the insurrection.[12]

(i) Inside was proceeding a peculiarly contemporary coup. Some attackers wielded pipes or hockey sticks or flagpoles, some wore helmets or gas masks or bandanas, but in this "second 1776" cell phones and cameras were the vital weapon in every revolutionary's hand. "Needing to have reality confirmed and experience enhanced by photographs," as Susan Sontag observed, "is an aesthetic consumerism to which everyone is now addicted." January 6 seems likely to be the most photographed coup in history. Amid the awful violence, what still more awful things might have been done if more revolutionary image junkies had spent their time to some purpose other than selfie-taking, videoing, and live-streaming?[13]

Together, these fragments suggest a variation on assembly that well exceeds the essential but also more readily narratable picture of many political actors buoyed in their belligerence by imaginative infrastructures of media assembly. In the unfolding of this event, which was both in one place and in many places—on the ground, on television, on the internet, in chat channels, in the White House, in millions of people's imaginations—the fully mediated versions and the "real" version were so fused as to become at times indistinguishable.

It is tempting to say that the people gathered there in absurd but actual defiance functioned like a motley "assemblage." That would mean saying they constituted an aggregate of technics, rhetorics, affects, and bodies, an aggregate amorphous in appearance and ideation that nevertheless managed to act and destroy, however stupidly or gallingly, possibly with coordination, possibly without, maybe thought through by the narcissistic lame-duck president himself, maybe by people around him with more capacity for seditious planning. But that configuration of things won't quite do, because it doesn't speak to the events in their simultaneously surreal, physical, virtual, and destructive unfolding. More helpful is an analogy used by Peter Galison in a very different context:

> Imagine an ocean covered by a confined atmosphere of water vapor. When this world is hot enough, the water evaporates; when the vapor cools, it condenses and rains down into the

> ocean. But if the pressure and heat are such that, as the water expands, the vapor is compressed, eventually the liquid and gas approach the same density. As that critical point nears, something quite extraordinary occurs. Water and vapor no longer remain stable; instead, all through this world, pockets of liquid and vapor begin to flash back and forth between the two phases, from vapor to liquid, from liquid to vapor—from tiny clusters of molecules to volumes nearly the size of the planet. At this critical point, light of different wavelengths begins reflecting off drops of different sizes—purple off smaller drops, red off larger ones. Soon, light is bouncing off at every possible wavelength. Every color of the visible spectrum is reflected as if from mother-of-pearl. Such wildly fluctuating phase changes reflect light with what is known as critical opalescence.[14]

For Galison, critical opalescence approximates the "fluctuations back and forth between the abstract and the concrete" in the efforts to coordinate and understand time in the late nineteenth and early twentieth centuries.[15] With respect to January 6, the analogy speaks to a condition of violent phase shifts between expressive and political modes. This event wasn't just a popular assembly partly enabled by exercises of media assembly in the lead-up. It was popular assembly *as* media assembly and media assembly as popular assembly in turn.

Whether on the ground or at a distant remove, what you saw or felt or heard were "wildly fluctuating phase changes" between multiple modes of collective expression and action. Bodies became media constituents; media constituents and media assemblies flowed out of mouths and phones, and extensions of memetic assemblies like a QAnon shirt or new fodder for memes such as feet on Representative Nancy Pelosi's desk seized hold of cameras and feeds. The propagandistic assembling of the election lie mixed with much larger assemblies of ideology and anti-Blackness built over centuries all found expression in the fact of a gathering of bodies both loosely and tightly coordinated in the violent exercise of overrunning the sanctioned, habituated democratic exercise of postelection transition. It was an equally physical and virtual performance of a destructive and assembled threat to the event of democratic procedure set to occur within the Capitol building. The effect of this was the bloodshed, the loss of life, the traumatic fear; it was also that more abstract but still palpable and consequential sense of damage to the health and legitimacy of democratic institutions and norms. The corrosive powers of distributed disassembly were both consolidated and widespread, stretching their expression across the planet. Meanwhile, these constituents, in these positions, indeed these constituents overrunning and shirking established, normative positions—this aggregate of "insurgent collective actors" had managed to tangibly assemble itself, to make itself and see itself and disseminate itself in the mode of "popular manifestation," as some embodiment of a supposed "people," this arrangement, this reservoir, this form, this assertion of who and what gets to matter.[16]

For a theory of assembly, these variations on human interaction toward violence and division are malevolent uses of expressive tactics that can otherwise be the stuff of tremendous emotional and cognitive liberation. They are awful examples of the digital ascendancy of the cultural form in spirited faux-democratic use, not as some outside document or media ornament, but as playing an active role in the conditions and unfolding of an egregious, bloody, destructive enactment. This was a violent political performance aimed at asserting a vision of a country absent people and communities that have continued to live and thrive within and across its borders, people and communities who have done so in spite of insidious, widespread, willed, and intersecting forces, from white supremacy and white nationalism to heteronormative patriarchy, settler colonialism, and market fundamentalism.

As I write this conclusion in the summer of 2021, some four hundred people have been arrested in connection with these events, but it is by no means assured that many will see convictions, and it's least sure for the main instigators and abettors, who still walk freely. It is said that nearly half of Republicans agree that Trump was "called by God to lead," and seven in ten believe that the election was stolen and that Joe Biden is an illegitimate president.[17] Meanwhile, the person who cites these statistics, Mark Danner, reports: "Republican elites, frightened by and pandering to their base, are feeding its resentment and grievance by doubling down on Trump's Big Lie that the election was stolen. Even as they weaponize the Big Lie—using it as a rationale to pass legislation that will make it harder for certain overwhelmingly Democratic constituencies to cast ballots—they are bolstering it through widely covered 'pseudo-events' like the Arizona vote 'audit' and other spurious recounts to come."[18] Danner asks what lies ahead when fantasies like these dominate a significant minority of the country's political horizon. He suggests it is not unreasonable to assume that "at least some will respond with violence" and that this violence could "feed the radicalization of Republican policy in a fervid feedback loop." Perhaps, as Danner and others suggest could be the case, these concerns will prove unfounded, and the events of January will remain an awful anomaly. But a theory of assembly suggests that a "fervid feedback loop" is precisely the kind of thing pernicious practices of expressive gathering can enable, sustain, and amplify, especially when they are aligned with well-funded (and algorithmically amplified) stories, images, and advertisements. Urgent and incisive counterassemblies seem at this moment like indispensable measures.

I feel pangs of dread as I write this. And yet I also find myself remembering the words of thinkers whose work both evades and opposes the premises convened at the Capitol that day.

I think, for instance, of an article written by Toni Morrison in 2015. Morrison starts by recalling the hopelessness and creative paralysis she faced in the aftermath of George W. Bush's defeat of John Kerry in 2004. She recalls how, the day after Christmas that year, she relayed her experiences to a friend, who promptly responded: "No! No, no, no! This is precisely the time when artists go to work—not when everything is fine, but in times of dread. That's our job!"[19] Writing eleven years later, Morrison builds on her friend's sentiments. She speaks to a double condition long known: artists and writers who have lived in harrowing conditions like the flourishing of "oppressive power" and "terrified populations running for their lives," but who have nevertheless found ways to persist and even thrive. This isn't Morrison invoking some version of an insidious ideology of neoliberal resilience; nor is it some airy call to focus on one's own work and life path. No: this is the same person who would write, a year and half later, when Trump was elected, of "a collapse of white privilege" to which many Americans have responded by "flock[ing] to a political platform that supports and translates violence against the defenseless as strength."[20]

What Morrison is speaking to is a fiercely plural belief in action and expression in spite of ongoing "demonstrations of weakness" by the privileged, the powerful, and those who fall in line with them. This is an exhortation toward defiant thinking and making. "There is no time for despair, no place for self-pity, no need for silence, no room for fear," Morrison writes. Though it is surely the case that "the world is bruised and bleeding," and "though it is important not to ignore its pain," it is also imperative that we "refuse to succumb to its malevolence." And a crucial way we (not just artists and writers, but anyone) engage in that refusal is by speaking and creating and assembling amid the maelstrom. It is also, as I think Morrison is implying, adopting an intelligent and critical orientation toward the analogies the world constantly exhibits, not conveniently pretending that all things and everyone are the same, much less that differences don't exist or matter, but maintaining the wit and the willingness to see and appreciate and act on partial and sometimes elusive connections. "Like failure," Morrison concludes, in a manifestly analogical mode, "chaos contains information that can lead to knowledge—even wisdom. Like art."[21]

As I think back to Morrison's refusal of malevolence, I also remember a distinction laid out by the queer theorist Eve Kosofksy Sedgwick in 1990 and elaborated by Griselda Pollock, Olivia Laing, and others in subsequent years. On the one side is "paranoid reading," a mode of reading Sedgwick finds across critical and queer theoretical literatures, and that Laing identifies as characteristic of the domain of social media. This is a mode of interpreting (and posting and commenting and liking and sharing) that can be quite necessary and powerful, particularly in response to circumstances of injustice, but in which one can also be caught up, becoming, as Laing puts it, "addicted to the ongoing certainty that the next click, the next link would bring clarity."[22] In the paranoid mode, Laing writes, there is a "faith in unveiling hidden acts of violence, believing if the awful truth is only revealed, it will automatically be transformed,"[23] as though, in Sedgwick's words, "to make something visible as a problem were, if not a mere hop, skip, and jump away from getting it solved, at least self-evidently a step in that direction."[24] The alternative to this is what Sedgwick calls "reparative reading." This is a mode of interpreting (and of posting and commenting and liking and sharing) that is "more invested in finding nourishment than identifying poison."[25] Not somehow avoiding disaster and tragedy, and actually not "any less attentive to the grim realities of loss and oppression,"[26] the reparative mode seeks to "organize the fragments and part-objects she encounters or creates."[27] Reassembling in this way, the reparative reader works to "find or invent something new and sustaining out of inimical environments."[28]

In other words, like Morrison's knowing refusal of malevolence, reparative reading doesn't imply running from the atrociousness of assembly in the regressive mode. Nor does it point to overly blunt takes on the inherent malice of digital technologies. Nor is it somehow a complete replacement for criticism in its more subversive and venturesome modes. Rather, adopting a stance of repair means accepting that nothing will be repaired well or sustainably when both the root causes and the sustaining structures and strategies go ignored. It means maintaining the openness and flexibility of seeing and thinking that figures like Morrison, Sedgwick, Laing, and others demand, shuttling between the sacred and profane, the high and low, the linear and nonlinear. And it means not just interpreting, but making and contributing, building and organizing.

Finally, I recall a graduation speech by Judith Butler, whose book on performative and political assembly helped me find the path to writing this one. "An active and sensate democracy requires that we learn how to read well," Butler says, "not just texts but images and sounds, to translate across languages, across media, ways of performing, listening, acting, making art and theory."[29] In ideal conditions, they further reflect here, we will "lose ourselves in what we read, only to return to ourselves, transformed and part of a more expansive world—in short, we become more critical and more capacious in our thinking and our acting." If my book has been successful in its aims, then it will hardly seem like a leap to add assemblies to Butler's list of what we must learn to "read well." It will also seem right and good to assert the further necessity of learning to assemble well, doing so not toward violent regression but toward emancipatory endurance and fervor, pragmatism and outrage, the physical-virtual pursuit of restitution and reconfiguration: democracy in a state of generative opalescence.

Not far from the Capitol building, visible within the Rotunda of the Charters of Freedom at the National Archives Museum, is (as of 1952 and still now as I write some seventy years later) a crucial, handwritten phrase: “the right of the people peaceably to assemble.” It is the obvious but necessary move to end this book by invoking the need to nurture and reimagine the exercise of this right—this power—in its different and contested guises across cultural worlds, not only in the vital terms of embodied political gathering but also in the plural modes of reparative media assembly, doing so in defense of everything from quick laughs to astonishment to the future of mutual and equitable thriving.

Acknowledgments

The first person I must thank is the person to whom this book is dedicated: my wife, Natalie Kleefeld. Her roles in this project are too deep and too many to try to encapsulate. Suffice it to say the book wouldn't exist without her, and that includes the many times she bravely and incisively waded through first drafts while I played with our daughter, Aada, in the other room. In ways I'll tell her about someday, Aada nourished my heart and fed my imagination throughout the last three years of this project, and for that (and so much else about her) I feel immensely fortunate.

The project took root well before I had ever thought about assembly, when I found the Department of Rhetoric at Berkeley as an undergraduate. I owe special thanks to Kaja Silverman for making me believe that my ideas could matter, for her mentorship and example, and for the many ways she has encouraged my life of the mind. I'm also grateful to Judith Butler, Felipe Gutterriez, and Trinh T. Minh-ha for the support they offered, both in seminars and in the transition to graduate school.

The Film and Visual Studies program at Harvard University was a rich and wonderfully open-ended intellectual home, and I extend my thanks to the many people connected with the program, especially Giuliana Bruno, Lindsey Lodhie, and Robb Moss. I owe a debt of gratitude to my advisor Peter Galison for his consistently rich questions, provocations, and guidance. I also appreciate the time Jimena Canales, Carrie Lambert-Beatty, and Jeffrey Schnapp dedicated to my work. I must also thank Jeffrey and the founders of metaLAB for welcoming me into their likewise wonderfully open-ended design lab. It was through work with the lab that my dissertation on digital archives of disaster and what I then called "archival assemblage" came into being. I am especially grateful for the many illuminating conversations and collaborations around data, museums, and ecology with my colleagues Matthew

Battles, Yanni Loukissas, Cristoforo Magliozzi, Sarah Newman, and Jessica Yurkofksy. I am also grateful to the people of the Reischauer Institute of Japanese Studies for the opportunities they offered in connection with the Japan Disasters Digital Archive.

I had the fortune of starting an early version of this project during a CLIR/Mellon postdoctoral fellowship at the University of Rochester. Nora Dimmock led a vibrant and welcoming environment in the Digital Scholarship Lab. Rachel Haidu and Jacob W. Lewis of the Department of Art and Art History provided crucial feedback on my first stab at this book's core ideas.

On a Sunday drive from Buffalo back to Rochester I made a last-minute decision to apply for a job with the History of Art and Visual Culture Department at the University of California, Santa Cruz. I'm deeply grateful that I did. I owe special thanks to Stacy Kamehiro for her wisdom and friendship and to Jennifer González for her insights into the research process. My gratitude also extends to the undergraduate and graduate students I have had the extraordinary privilege of teaching and advising, and without whom I wouldn't have had either the opportunity or the inspiration to write these chapters. I also appreciate the support provided by the Arts Research Institute, which helped make the plates possible. I must also thank the many artists and media practitioners who allowed me to include their work in these pages.

My parents and stepparents—Lynette Brasfield and Tom Parry, Bill Brasfield and Patty Leavitt—supported and celebrated this whole undertaking, and for that and so much more I am extremely grateful. I am also extremely grateful to Peter Morrison and Elaine Rubenstein for their constant encouragement and for showing me (among other things) how humor and thought can go hand in hand. My deep thanks also extends to my friend Colin Kielty, who has long been the first person I turn to when I'm stuck or need to try out a new idea.

The book came into its own only thanks to Leah Pennywark at the University of Minnesota Press. I owe Leah my gratitude for her belief in the project and for a wonderfully genial and generative revision process. I am also grateful to Anne Carter and everyone else I have worked with at the Press. I can't thank them enough for allowing the book to include such a wide variety of images and for inviting Heng Wee Tan to design the cover, which I love. Finally, I must thank the people who offered generous feedback on this book, including readers of my earlier work, Ryan M. Milner, and several anonymous reviewers. I hope you see your ideas and questions reflected in these pages.

Notes

Introduction

1. I'm referring to a story about a neighborhood cat jumping out of an oak tree told by my daughter, Aada, when she was a toddler.

2. I'm referring to an article on striking agricultural laborers published with two photographs, one by Rodrigo Rentería-Valencia, the other by Terray Sylvester; see Carl Segerstrom, "Coronavirus Concerns Revive Labor Organizing," *High Country News,* June 18, 2020, hcn.org/issues/52.7/north-labor-coronavirus-concerns-revive-labor-organizing.

3. I'm thinking of instances of "generative art on the blockchain," as at artblocks.io.

4. Examples of "storycentrism" are legion. It has become "commonplace to describe humans as storytelling animals" (Hanna Meretoja and Colin Davis, *Storytelling and Ethics: Literature, Visual Arts and the Power of Narrative* [New York: Routledge, 2017], 1). Ken Plummer writes: "As we find the world troubled by failing democracies, authoritarianism and the new digital risk, so it becomes important to think how human beings retain their humanity as narrating animals" (*Narrative Power: The Struggle for Human Value* [Cambridge: Polity, 2019], 108). On narrative as a transmedia form, see Marie-Laure Ryan, *Avatars of Story* (Minneapolis: University of Minnesota Press, 2006). I'm not saying claims of storytelling as essential ought to be wholly dismissed, but debated and nuanced, particularly in light of sociotechnical shifts. I appreciate, for instance, Sylvia Wynter's rejoinder to "the West's hitherto secular liberal monohumanist conception of our being human." Wynter speaks to the emergence in Africa of *homo narrans,* "a hybridly auto-instituting, languaging cum storytelling species" (*Sylvia Wynter: On Being Human as Praxis,* ed. Katherine McKittrick [Durham, N.C.: Duke University Press, 2015], 31). Also relevant are debates around anti-narrative stances, as in Tyler Bradway, "Queer Narrative Theory and the Relationality of Form," *PMLA* 136, no. 5 (2021): 711–27.

5. My inclusion of representation could strike some as odd. From this vantage, representation isn't so much a cultural form as what underlies any cultural form. But that assumption is historical and rhetorical rather than timeless and ontological. Socrates emphasizes "mimesis" in Plato's *Republic,* and Aristotle frames art as mimesis in his *Poetics* (for translations, see Plato, *Republic,* trans. Robin Waterfield [Oxford: Oxford University Press, 1994], and Aristotle, *Poetics,* trans. Malcolm Heath [London: Penguin, 1996]). Also see the entries on "mimesis" on The Chicago School of Media Theory website, lucian.uchicago.edu/blogs/mediatheory. Notably, for Wynter, "'the central mechanism at work' in processes of colonization—and even decolonization—'was

and is that of *representation*'" (Nandita Sharma, "Strategic Anti-Essentialism: Decolonizing Decolonization" in *Sylvia Wynter,* 169, italics original).

6. See Lev Manovich, "Database as Symbolic Form," *Convergence: The International Journal of Research into New Media Technologies* 5, no. 2 (1999): 80–99; Manovich, *The Language of New Media* (Cambridge, Mass.: MIT Press, 2001); *Database Aesthetics: Art in the Age of Information Overflow,* ed. Victoria Vesna (Minneapolis: University of Minnesota Press, 2007); and N. Katherine Hayles, *How We Think: Digital Media and Contemporary Technogenesis* (Chicago: University of Chicago Press, 2012). Engagements with Manovich's claim that the digital-era "database" is supplanting narrative are too many to cite. They include mixes of critique and application, as in Hayles, *How We Think,* and as in Jessica Pressman, *Digital Modernism: Making It New in New Media* (Oxford: Oxford University Press, 2014). For earlier uses of "symbolic form," see Erwin Panofsky, *Perspective as Symbolic Form* trans. Christopher S. Wood (New York: Zone, 1997 [originally 1927]), and Ernst Cassirer, *The Philosophy of Symbolic Forms,* trans. Ralph Manheim (New Haven, Conn: Yale University Press, 1957 [originally 1928]). Panofsky recalled extending "Ernst Cassirer's felicitous term to the history of art" (*Perspective* , 40–41). On Cassirer and Panofsky, see Allister Neher, "How Perspective Could Be a Symbolic Form," *The Journal of Aesthetics and Art Criticism* 63, no. 4 (2005): 359–73, and Emmanuel Alloa, "Could Perspective Ever be a Symbolic Form?," *Journal of Aesthetics and Phenomenology* 2, no. 1 (2015): 51–71. Also relevant is Hiroki Azuma, *Otaku: Japan's Database Animals,* trans. Jonathan E. Abel and Shion Kono (Minneapolis: University of Minnesota Press, 2009).

7. See Carolyn Dean, *A Culture of Stone: Inka Perspectives on Rock* (Durham, N.C.: Duke University Press, 2010). Certain examples of *apachita,* or "miniature mountains of stone" (97), can be understood as "representational" because they look like mountains, but to stop there would be to maintain "the Western preference for figural imagery" (44). Dean shows how these artifacts are also "presentational"; they embody—they *are*—mountains (60–61). Also see *De-Westernizing Visual Communication and Cultures: Perspectives from the Global South,* ed. Guo-Ming Chen, Maria Faust, and Thomas Herdin (Baden-Baden: Nomos, 2020), and Catherine Grant, Dorothy Price, et al., "Decolonizing Art History," *Art History* 43, no. 1 (2020): 8–66.

8. Another symptom of the dominance of certain cultural forms is reduction. For example, Marco Frascari asserts that "non-trivial" architecture requires storytelling ("An Architectural Good-Life Can Be Built, Explained, and Taught Only through Storytelling" in *Reading Architecture and Culture: Researching Buildings, Spaces and Documents,* ed. Adam Shar [New York: Routledge, 2012], 224–234). Also see Douglas Crimp's suggestion that "sequential images, regardless of their ambiguity, will inevitably elicit a narrative" in his important catalog essay for "Pictures," republished in *X-Tra* 8, no. 1 (2005): 17–30.

9. Although I refer to the digital and internet eras in this book with relative fluidity, I acknowledge that they're not coextensive and that the notion of an "era" is nonneutral. I agree with W. J. T. Mitchell's call "to exert some pressure on the commonplace notion that we live in a 'digital age'" (*Image Science:*

Iconology, Visual Culture, and Media Aesthetics [Chicago: Univeristy of Chicago Press, 2018], 140). On the politics of time, see Judith Butler, "Sexual Politics, Torture, and Secular Time," *British Journal of Sociology* 59, no. 1 (2008): 1–23.

10. I use "transmedia" to indicate a phenomenon not confined to any one medium. For Marsha Kinder, it "suggests a deliberate move across media boundaries—whether it's referring to intertextuality, adaptations, marketing strategies, reading practices or media networks" ("Transmedia Networks," *Marsha Kinder Legacies*, marshakinder.com/concepts/o11.html). Also see *Transmedia Frictions: The Digital, the Arts, and the Humanities*, ed. Marsha Kinder and Tara McPherson (Berkeley: University of California Press, 2014).

11. Hayles, *How We Think*, 40. I use the terms "cultural form" and "expressive strategy" interchangeably. For Anne Hartman, cultural forms knit "disparate elements of the social and political fields" ("Doing Things with Poems: Performativity and Cultural Form," *Victorian Poetry* 41, no. 4 [2003]: 481–90, at 484–485 and 483). Other uses refer to things like hip-hop, television, magazines, sports, Russian rock music, the public, and hosting. Expressive strategy is used for things like religion, parody, education, opera, and allegory. Also relevant are Bernard Siegert, *Cultural Techniques: Grids, Filters, Doors, and Other Articulations of the Real*, trans. Geoffrey Winthrop-Young (New York: Fordham University Press, 2015), and Liam Cole Young, "Cultural Techniques and Logistical Media," *M/C Journal* 18, no. 2 (2015), journal.media-culture.org .au/index.php/mcjournal/article/view/961. Young describes cultural techniques as "the means by which humans and tools assemble basic categories of space, time and being."

12. As Caroline Levine shows, "form" needn't only refer to the composition of a cultural object; it can also refer to "all shapes and configurations," "all ordering principles," and "all patterns of repetition and difference," from a poem to a social movement (*Forms: Whole, Rhythm, Hierarchy, Network* [Princeton, N.J.: Princeton University Press, 2015)], 3). I join Levine and others in exploring these more flexible uses of the concept. See, for instance, Anna Kornbluh, *The Order of Forms: Realism, Formalism, and Social Space* (Chicago: University of Chicago Press, 2019). Also relevant is Sianne Ngai's expanded account of aesthetic categories, all of which "are experiences of a particular kind of form," in *Our Aesthetic Categories: Zany, Cute, Interesting* (Cambridge, Mass.: Harvard University Press, 2012), 23.

13. Kurt Vonnegut, *A Man without a Country* (New York: Random House, 2007), 133.

14. W. J. T. Mitchell, *Picture Theory: Essays on Visual and Verbal Representation* (Chicago: University of Chicago Press, 1994), 89n9.

15. See *Before-and-After Photography: Histories and Contexts*, ed. Jordan Bear and Kate Palmer Albers (New York: Bloomsbury, 2017).

16. I use "media artifact" to mean both whole projects and parts of projects. See Yi Zhao's entry on "artifact," on the Chicago School of Media Theory website.

17. Melanie Bühler, "(Re)Discovering Art History's Philosophical Foundations—An Interview with Hanneke Grootenboer," in *The Transhistorical*

Museum: Mapping the Field, ed. Eva Wittocx, Ann Demeester, Peter Carpreau, Melanie Bühler, and Xander Karskens (Amsterdam: Valiz, 2018), 45.

18. E. H. Gombrich, *Art and Illusion: A Study in the Psychology of Pictorial Representation* (New York: Pantheon, 1960), 286–87.

19. Marta Gili, *Milagros de la Torre: Photographs 1991–2011* (Barcelona: RM, 2012), 128.

20. W. J. T. Mitchell, "Image," in *Critical Terms for Media Studies,* ed. Mark B. N. Hansen and W. J. T. Mitchell (Chicago: University of Chicago Press, 2010), 35–48, at 39. The term "firstness" comes from Charles Sanders Peirce, referring to, in Mitchell's words here, "inherent qualities such as color, texture, or shape that are the first things to strike our senses." With respect to secondness, Mitchell here notes the "double take that Wittgenstein called 'the dawning of an aspect.'"

21. Gili, *Milagros de la Torre,* 132.

22. Art can even remake, as Jacques Rancière puts it, "the distribution of capacities and incapacities" (*The Emancipated Spectator,* trans. Gregory Elliott [New York: Verso, 2009], 49). Davide Panagia casts Rancière's writing in assembly-like terms, saying it aims not so much to present a definitive argument as to "display an arrangement of perception and sensation" [*Rancière's Sentiments* (Durham, N.C.: Duke University Press, 2018], 15).

23. Áine Cane and Shana Lebowitz, "26 Signs You're a Great Boss, Even If It Doesn't Feel Like It," *Business Insider,* October 16, 2019, businessinsider.com/signs-you-are-a-good-boss-2017-6; A. C. Lura, "Top 10 Bloody Histories Behind Common Surgeries," Listverse, March 12, 2020. listverse.com/2020/03/12/top-10-bloody-histories-behind-common-surgeries.

24. I draw this metaphor from Maria Evangelatou, who speaks to the kaleidoscopic potential of "continuous transformations in the eyes of different people" (*A Contextual Reading of Ethiopian Crosses through Form and Ritual: Kaleidoscopes of Meaning* [Piscataway, N.J.: Gorgias, 2018], 338).

25. Umberto Eco, *The Infinity of Lists: An Illustrated Essay,* trans. Alastair McEwen (New York: Rizzoli, 2009).

26. Alan Liu, *Friending the Past: The Sense of History in the Digital Age* (Chicago: University of Chicago Press, 2018), 169–72.

27. Eco, *Infinity of Lists,* 321. Eco characterizes chaotic enumeration as the "delight in introducing the absolutely heterogeneous."

28. Snyder's list recalls asyndeton and parataxis. Words and phrases sit side by side without coordinating clauses or subordinating conjunctions.

29. artandfeminism.org.

30. André Brock Jr. speaks to this paradox in his book on "distributed Blackness"; it was inspired by "millions of Black people interacting through networked devices . . . at once separate and conjoined," what he thinks of as the "online aggregation and coherence of Blackness online, absent Black bodies" (*Distributed Blackness: African American Cybercultures* [New York: New York University Press, 2020], 1).

31. Zeynep Tufekci, *Twitter and Tear Gas: The Power and Fragility of Networked Protest* (New Haven, Conn.: Yale University Press), xiii.

32. On the way assembled bodies say things "even if they stand silently," see Judith Butler, *Notes Toward a Performative Theory of Assembly* (Cambridge, Mass.: Harvard University Press, 2015), 18.

33. See Shoshana Zuboff, *The Age of Surveillance Capitalism: The Fight for a Human Future at the New Frontier of Power* (New York: Public Affairs, 2019).

34. Ruha Benjamin, *Race after Technology: Abolitionist Tools for the New Jim Code* (New York: Wiley, 2019), 83.

35. Trevor Paglen, "Invisible Images (Your Pictures Are Looking at You)," *The New Inquiry,* December 8, 2016, thenewinquiry.com/invisible-images-your-pictures-are-looking-at-you; Joanna Zylinska, *Nonhuman Photography* (Cambridge, Mass.: MIT Press, 2017).

36. Manovich, *Language of New Media,* 218.

37. I note the potential to connect this thought with theoretical investigations of relation, as in Éduoard Glissant, *Poetics of Relation,* trans. Betsy Wing (Ann Arbor: University of Michigan Press, 1997 [originally 1990]).

38. My thanks to Brock Stuessi for introducing me to *Over the Edge* and the film *How Radio Isn't Done* (2017).

39. Hayles, *How We Think,* 176, 182.

40. Hayles, 176.

41. In the eighteenth century, Gotthold Ephraim Lessing asserted the need to conceptually separate poetry and painting (Gotthold Ephraim Lessing, *Laocoön* [1766], trans. Edward Allen McCormick [New York: Bobbs-Merrill, 1984]). Clement Greenberg argued for what has become known as "medium specificity" ("Modernist Painting," Forum Lectures [Washington, D.C.: Voice of America, 1960]). The concept has been taken up by numerous critics, including Rosalind E. Krauss, who sees a commitment to the features and histories of given mediums and "technical supports" as essential, enabling artists to avoid complicity with flows of images and capital (*Under Blue Cup* [Cambridge, Mass.: MIT Press, 2011]).

42. Distant reading is often attributed to Franco Moretti, "Conjectures on World Literature," *New Left Review* 1 (January–February 2000): 54–68. Ted Underwood traces a longer history ("A Genealogy of Distant Reading," *Digital Humanities Quarterly* 11, no. 2 [2017], digitalhumanities.org/dhq/vol/11/2/000317/000317.html). Surface reading emphasizes the "complexity of literary surfaces," seeking out "patterns that exist within and across texts" (Stephen Best and Sharon Marcus, "Surface Reading: An Introduction," *Representations* 108, no. 1 [2009]: 1–21, at 1 and 11). As for "plural reading," I have found uses in linguistics, briefly with respect to Roland Barthes, and in the work of Daniel Shore, who introduces a computer-aided method for scanning and comparing "sentences plucked from many different texts," seeking to remain attentive to their "form, use, and context" ("Plural Reading," Theorizing the Digital Archive, theorizingthedigitalarchivesaa.wordpress.com/about/daniel-shore; see also *Cyberformalism: Histories of Linguistic Forms in the Digital Archive* [Baltimore, Md.: Johns Hopkins University Press, 2018]).

43. On philosophical approaches to art through family resemblances, see: Noël Carroll, "History and the Philosophy of Art," *Journal of Philosophy of History* 5 (2011): 370–82. Also see: Morris Weitz, "The Role of Theory in

Aesthetics," *The Journal of Aesthetics and Art Criticism* 15, no. 1 (1956): 27–35; Maurice Mandelbaum, "Family Resemblances and Generalizations Concerning the Arts," in *The Philosophy of Art: Readings Ancient and Modern,* ed. Alex Neill and Aaron Ridley (New York: McGraw Hill, 1995), 193–201; Haig Khatchadourian, "Family Resemblances and the Categorization of Works of Art," *The Journal of Aesthetics and Art Criticism* 28, no. 1 (1969): 79–90; Robert McGregor, "'Art'—Again," *Critical Inquiry* 5, no. 4 (1979): 713–23; Carlo Ginzburg, "Family Resemblances and Family Trees: Two Cognitive Metaphors," *Critical Inquiry* 30, no. 3 (2004): 537–56.

44. See Sheldon M. Cohen, "Family Resemblance in the Thirteenth Century," *Philosophy* 48 (1973): 391–94. Several modern thinkers invoke similar concepts, including Friedrich Nietzsche. See Marcin Mizak, "Why Wittgenstein?: Family Resemblances," *Lingua ac Communitas* 15 (2005): 51–70.

45. Organized as a nonlinear sequence of loosely affiliated sections (and written on index cards), *Philosophical Investigations* is a kind of philosophical assembly. Wittgenstein framed philosophy as recombination: "The work of the philosopher consists in assembling reminders for a particular purpose" (*Philosophical Investigations,* trans. G. E. M. Anscombe [Oxford: Blackwell, 1953], §127). Jorge Luis Borges makes a similar contention: "It is venturesome to think that a coordination of words (philosophies are nothing more than that) can resemble the universe very much" ("Avatars of the Tortoise," *Labyrinths: Selected Stories & Other Writings* [New York: New Directions, 1962], 207).

46. Ian Bogost, *Persuasive Games: The Expressive Power of Videogames* (Cambridge, Mass.: MIT Press, 2007).

47. Wittgenstein, *Philosophical Investigations,* 32.

48. Carole L. Palmer distinguishes between shared "basic features" and "variable characteristics" ("Thematic Research Collections," in *A Companion to Digital Humanities,* ed. Susan Schreibman, Ray Siemens, and John Unsworth [Malden, Mass.: Blackwell, 2004], 348–65).

49. Wittgenstein's work has been influential on several artists; see, e.g., *Paolozzi and Wittgenstein: The Artist and the Philosopher,* ed. Diego Mantoan and Luigi Perissinotto (London: Palgrave Macmillan, 2019).

50. Among the more incisive arguments for an expansive approach to media is Wendy Hui Kong Chun, "Did Somebody Say New Media?" in *New Media, Old Media: A History and Theory Reader,* ed. Wendy Hui Kyong Chun, Anna Watkins Fisher, and Thomas Keenan (New York: Routledge, 2004): 1–10. See also Mark Hansen and W. J. T. Mitchell, "Media" in Hansen and Mitchell, *Critical Terms for Media Studies,* vii–xxii, and John Durham Peters, *The Marvelous Clouds: Toward a Philosophy of Elemental Media* (Chicago: University of Chicago Press, 2015).

51. I appreciate Sarah Kember's observation that her use of the collective pronoun "does not assume or imply any consensus" but is preferable to "more awkward indirect modes of writing" ("Ubiquitous Photography," *Philosophy of Photography* 3, no. 2 [2012]: 331–48, at 331n1).

52. See Robert S. Nelson, "The Slide Lecture, or the Work of Art 'History' in the Age of Mechanical Reproduction," *Critical Inquiry* 26, no. 3 (2000): 414–34.

53. See Trevor Fawcett, "Visual Facts and the Nineteenth-Century Art

Lecture," *Art History* 6, no. 4 (1983): 442–60, and Anne Bordeleau, *Charles Robert Cockerell: Architect in Time* (Farnham, UK: Ashgate, 2014).

54. Tina M. Campt, *Listening to Images* (Durham, N.C.: Duke University Press, 2017), 43.

55. Mark Silverberg refers to family resemblances and a "web of similarities" in *The New York School Poets and the Neo-Avant-Garde: Between Radical Art* (Farnham, UK: Ashgate, 2010), 11. Mitchell speaks to an Aristotelian approach that can "link a number of specific entities together by family resemblance" (*Image Science,* 17).

56. Mieke Bal, "Towards a Relational Inter-Temporality," in Wittocx, Demeester, Carpreau, Bühler, and Karskens *Transhistorical Museum,* 48–63, at 61.

57. Campt, *Listening to Images,* 22.

58. See Christopher D. Johnson, *Memory, Metaphor, and Aby Warburg's Atlas of Images* (Ithaca, N.Y.: Cornell University Press, 2012).

59. Griselda Pollock, *Encounters in the Virtual Feminist Museum: Time, Space and the Archive* (London: Routledge, 2007), 11.

60. Pollock, *Encounters in the Virtual Feminist Museum,* 11.

61. Eve Kosofsky Sedgwick, *Touching Feeling: Affect, Pedagogy, Performativity* (Durham, N.C.: Duke University Press, 2003), 146. I should note that Aubrey Anable, Kris Cohen, and Patrick Jagoda also richly engage with Sedgwick's reparative approach.

62. Olivia Laing, *Funny Weather: Art in an Emergency* (New York: Norton, 2020), 4.

63. Leah Singer, "Louise Bourgeois," an interview of Jerry Gorovoy, *Apartamento* 27 (Spring/Summer 2021): 88.

64. Allan Madden, *10 AM IS WHEN YOU COME TO ME* (2006), *Tate,* November 2014, tate.org.uk/art/artworks/bourgeois-10-am-is-when-you-come-to-me-al00345.

65. Singer, "Louise Bourgeois," 102.

66. See Ryan M. Milner and Whitney Phillips, *The Ambivalent Internet: Mischief, Oddity, and Antagonism Online* (Malden, Mass.: Polity, 2017).

67. Jasmine Johnson and Alice May Williams in collaboration with MoreUtopia!, "A Glossary of Gestures for Critical Discussion," criticalhandgestures.tumblr.com.

68. Michael Andor Brodeur, "That Hand Symbol You're Seeing Everywhere? Not OK," *Boston Globe,* September 21, 2018, bostonglobe.com/arts/2018/09/20/that-hand-symbol-you-seeing-everywhere-not/6NXpp9PHsEKiunjypIFjDJ/story.html.

69. Campt shares a photograph by her husband, who is Jewish, using his hands to frame a pair of photos of Meyer Gluckman, a Jewish inmate at Breakwater Prison in South Africa who was compelled to display his hands for the camera. For Campt, the gesture transforms the "convict album . . . into what it sought to distance itself from all along: a family album" (*Listening to Images,* 99).

70. Benjamin Peters, "Digital," in *Digital Keywords: A Vocabulary of Information Society and Culture,* ed. Benjamin Peters (Princeton, N.J.: Princeton University Press, 2016), 93–108, at 105.

71. Ariella Aïsha Azoulay, *Potential History: Unlearning Imperialism* (New York: Verso, 2019).

72. John O. Havard, *Disaffected Parties: Political Estrangement and the Making of English Literature, 1760–1830* (Oxford: Oxford University Press, 2019), 66–69.

73. Kelly Wisecup, *Assembled for Use: Indigenous Compilation and the Archives of Early Native American Literatures* (New Haven, Conn.: Yale University Press, 2021).

74. My thanks to Ryan M. Milner for pointing out this connection. See Nicholas A. John, *The Age of Sharing* (Malden, Mass.: Polity, 2017), and Yves Citton, *The Ecology of Attention,* trans. Barnaby Norman (Malden, Mass.: Polity, 2017). My title is partly inspired by a book that approaches aphorisms "transhistorically and transculturally" (Andrew Hui, *A Theory of the Aphorism: From Confucius to Twitter* [Princeton, N.J.: Princeton University Press, 2019], 21).

75. Manuel DeLanda, *Assemblage Theory* (Edinburgh: Edinburgh University Press, 2016), 51.

76. *Oxford English Dictionary Online,* s.v. "lens (n.)."

77. On different types of lenses, see Rudolf Kingslake, *A History of the Photographic Lens* (San Diego: Academic Press, 1989).

78. See Ariella Azoulay, "Aïm Deüelle Lüski—Cameras for a Dark Time," *aperture* (Winter 2010): 34, and Azoulay, *Aïm Deüelle Lüski and Horizontal Photography* (Leuven: Leuven University Press, 2014).

79. John Phillips discusses the difficulty of translating the term "assemblage," which includes senses of arrangement, fitting, and fixing, in "Agencement/Assemblage," *Theory, Culture, and Society* 23, nos. 2–3 (2006): 108–9.

80. On assemblage theory and assemblage art, see Bill Brown, "Re-Assemblage (Theory, Practice, Mode)," *Critical Inquiry* 46, no. 2 (2020): 259–303. On assemblage theory and composition, see *Assembling Composition,* ed. Kathleen Blake Yancey and Stephen J. McElroy (Urbana, Ill.: Conference on College Composition & Communication, 2017).

81. Gilles Deleuze and Félix Guattari, *A Thousand Plateaus,* trans. Brian Massumi, vol. 2 of *Capitalism and Schizophrenia,* trans. Massumi et al. (Minneapolis: University of Minnesota Press, 1987).

82. DeLanda, *Assemblage Theory,* 68.

83. Jane Bennett, "The Agency of Assemblages and the North American Blackout," *Public Culture* 17, no. 3 (2005): 445–65.

84. N. Katherine Hayles, *Unthought: The Power of the Cognitive Nonconscious* (Chicago: University of Chicago Press, 2017), 118.

85. See Jasbir K. Puar, *Terrorist Assemblages: Homonationalism in Queer Times* (Durham, N.C.: Duke University Press, 2007), and *The Right to Maim: Debility, Capacity, Disability* (Durham, N.C.: Duke University Press, 2017). Notably, in discussing the turbaned body as an assemblage, Puar presents a comparative assembly that uses Edvard Munch's *The Scream* (*Terrorist Assemblages,* 190).

86. See Drew Daniel, *The Melancholy Assemblage: Affect and Epistemology in the English Renaissance* (New York: Fordham University Press, 2013); Nick J. Fox and Pam Alldred, "Re-assembling Climate Change Policy: Materialism, Posthumanism, and the Policy Assemblage," *The British Journal of Sociology* 71,

no. 2 (2020): 269–83; Amit S. Rai, *Untimely Bollywood: Globalization and India's New Media Assemblage* (Durham, N.C.: Duke University Press, 2009); Tony D. Sampson, *The Assemblage Brain: Sense Making in Neuroculture* (Minneapolis: University of Minnesota Press, 2016); Christopher Rosin, Angga Dwiartama, Darryl Grant, and Debbie Hopkins, "Using Provenance to Create Stability: State-led Territorialisation of Central Otago as Assemblage," *New Zealand Geographer* 69, no. 3 (2013): 235–48.

87. Hayles, *Unthought,* 117.

88. On technical modes of assembly, see Matthew Hockenberry, "Techniques of Assembly: Logistical Media and the (Supply) Chaîne Opératoire," *Amodern* 9 (April 2020), amodern.net/article/techniques-assembly.

89. See *Making Things Public: Atmospheres of Democracy,* ed. Bruno Latour and Peter Weibel (Cambridge, Mass.: MIT Press, 2005), 14. Also see Bruno Latour, *Reassembling the Social: An Introduction to Actor-Network-Theory* (Oxford: Oxford University Press, 2005), and Martin Müller and Carolin Schurr, "Assemblage Thinking and Actor-Network Theory: Conjunctions, Disjunctions, Cross-Fertilisations," *Transactions of the Institute of British Geographers* 41, no. 3 (2016): 217–29.

90. Elise Danielle Thorburn, "A Common Assembly: Multitude, Assemblies, and a New Politics of the Common," *Interface* 4, no. 2 (2012): 254–79, at 258; Michael Hardt and Antonio Negri, *Assembly* (Oxford: Oxford University Press, 2017).

91. Butler, *Notes,* 181.

92. Butler, 217.

93. Jonas Staal, "The Speculative Art of Assemblism," *PARSE* 7 (Autumn 2017), parsejournal.com/article/the-speculative-art-of-assemblism. See also Florian Malzacher, *Gesellschaftsspiele: Politisches Theater Heute* (Berlin: Alexander Verlag, 2020). For a counterargument to assemblism, see Jodi Dean, *Crowds and Party* (New York: Verso, 2016).

94. Jason Frank, *The Democratic Sublime: On Aesthetics and Popular Assembly* (Oxford: Oxford University Press, 2021), 92.

95. Frank, *Democratic Sublime,* 151.

96. Frank, 7.

97. Frank, 70 (italics original).

98. I mix metaphors in hopes of tempering the lens metaphor's ocularcentrism.

99. "Assemble" has long meant bringing people or things together. The sense of putting together the parts of a machine emerged in the nineteenth century. Other, obsolete (but also conceptually intriguing) uses include having sex and to liken or compare (*Oxford English Dictionary Online,* s.v. "assemble, v.1" and "assemble, v.2").

100. I learned about this practice through a Twitter thread by the historian of modern Japan Nick Kapur (@nick_kapur, mobile.twitter.com/nick_kapur /status/1436911092073058312).

101. See flickr.com/photos/arlis-reference/4996726871/in/album-721576243 87162740.

102. See Joe Hunt, *Mission without a Map: The Politics and Polices of Restoration*

Following the Exxon Valdez Oil Spill (Anchorage: *Exxon Valdez* Oil Spill Trustee Council, 2010), 89–90, and Riki Ott, *Not One Drop: Betrayal and Courage in the Wake of the Exxon Valdez Oil Spill* (White River Junction, Vt.: Chelsea Green, 2008).

103. Butler, *Notes,* 8.

104. Butler, 18.

105. See Ariella Azoulay, *The Civil Contract of Photography* (New York: Zone, 2008), and *Civil Imagination: A Political Ontology of Photography* (New York: Zone, 2015).

106. Nancy N. Chen, "'Speaking Nearby': A Conversation with Trinh T. Minh-ha," *Visual Anthropology Review* 8, no. 1 (1992): 82–91, at 87.

107. I hope other writers can address sonic, kinesthetic, ludic, and other modes of assembly in ways my training does not allow.

108. Catherine D'Ignazio and Lauren F. Klein, *Data Feminism* (Cambridge, Mass.: MIT Press, 2020), 5 (italics original).

109. Karen Barad, *Meeting the Universe Halfway: Quantum Physics and the Entanglement of Matter and Meaning* (Durham, N.C,: Duke University Press, 2007), 178.

1. What Is Assembly?

1. Rick Altman, *A Theory of Narrative* (New York: Columbia University Press, 2008), 10. All citations in this paragraph are from this page.

2. Ryan Milner uses the term "image meme" for a genre of meme that combines image and text (*The World Made Meme: Public Conversations and Participatory Media* [Cambridge, Mass.: MIT Press, 2016], 39).

3. Raúl Sánchez Cedillo, "The Rest Is Missing: On Constituencies as a Matricial Notion for New Institutions of the Commons," in *The Constituent Museum: Constellations of Knowledge, Politics and Mediation, A Generator of Social Change,* ed. John Byrne, Elinor Morgan, November Paynter, Aida Sánchez de Serdio, and Adela Železnik (Amsterdam: Valiz, 2018), 31.

4. "Works for the Now, by Queer Artists of Color," *New York Times Style Magazine,* June 29, 2020, nytimes.com/2020/06/29/t-magazine/queer-bipoc-artists.html.

5. Guanyu Xu, "Temporarily Censored Home," *Lens Culture,* 2019, lensculture.com/articles/guanyu-xu-temporarily-censored-home.

6. Guanyu Xu, "my neighborhood, the same block #blacklivesmatter," Instagram, instagram.com/p/CBUlhwOF3X8.

7. As noted in the Introduction, I draw this notion of "saying" from Judith Butler.

8. Altman, *Theory of Narrative,* 15.

9. Relevant here is Bruno Latour's concept of the "immutable mobile," which speaks to the ways inscriptions and media artifacts manage to persist in their combinations and expressions in spite of movement and displacement, and sometimes toward rhetorically and politically advantageous ends ("Visualization and Cognition: Thinking with Eyes and Hands," *Knowledge and Society* 6 [1986]: 1–40).

10. Rhizome, descriptions for Mariam Ghani and Chitra Ganesh, *How*

Do You See the Disappeared? A Warm Database, Net Art Anthology (Rhizome website), 2004, anthology.rhizome.org/how-do-you-see-the-disappeared-a-warm-database.

11. Altman, *Theory of Narrative,* 19.

12. N. Katherine Hayles, *How We Think: Digital Media and Contemporary Technogenesis* (Chicago: University of Chicago Press, 2012), 181. Like representation, assembly is (arguably) elemental, only perhaps in a manner harder to trace than storytelling, and perhaps often "fused" and "infused" with other forms.

13. Altman, *Theory of Narrative,* 20.

14. D. Brett King and Michael Wertheimer, *Max Wertheimer and Gestalt Theory* (New York: Routledge, 2005), 155, as quoted by Charissa N. Terranova, *Art as Organism: Biology and the Evolution of the Digital Image* (London: I. B. Tauris, 2015), 35.

15. N. Katherine Hayles, *Unthought: The Power of the Cognitive Nonconscious* (Chicago: University of Chicago Press, 2017), 119.

16. My thanks to an anonymous reader for encouraging these further reflections on drive via Hayles. That same reader notes the discussion of drive in Paul Ricouer's trilogy *Time and Narrative.* Although it is beyond the scope of this book, it strikes me that further inquiry around the drive to assemble (and the broader question of drives and cultural forms) could be valuable.

17. Okwui Enwezor, "Popular Theater, Photography and Difference," in *Samuel Fosso,* ed. Maria Francesca Bonetti and Guido Schlinkert (Milan: Five Continents Editions, 2004), 19.

18. Samuel Fosso, "Samuel Fosso in Conversation with Hans Ulrich Obrist," in *SIXSIXSIX* (Göttingen: Steidl, 2020), 8–9.

19. Fosso, "Samuel Fosso in Conversation," 9, 11.

20. Fosso, 10.

21. See Lev Kuleshov, "The Principles of Montage," in *Critical Visions in Film Theory: Classic and Contemporary Readings,* ed. Timothy Corrigan, Patricia White, and Meta Mazaj (Boston: Bedford / St. Martin's, 2010), 135–44.

22. Fosso makes this observation in an interview with Yves Chatap ("The Lives of Samuel Fosso," *Aperture,* June 1, 2017, aperture.org/editorial/lives-samuel-fosso).

23. Margaret E. Baron, "A Note on the Historical Development of Logic Diagrams: Leibniz, Euler and Venn," *The Mathematical Gazette* 53, no. 384 (1969): 113–25. Baron traces a long history of logic diagrams, referring to figures like Aristotle, Leibniz, and Ramon Lull. Also see A. W. F. Edwards, *Cogwheels of the Mind: The Story of Venn Diagrams* (Baltimore, Md.: Johns Hopkins University Press, 2004).

24. John Venn, *Symbolic Logic* (London: Macmillan, 1881), 510.

25. Peter Hamburger and Raymond E. Pippert, "Venn Said It Couldn't Be Done," *Mathematics Magazine* 73, no. 2 (2000): 105–10, at 105.

26. Baron, "Note on the Historical Development of Logic Diagrams," 113.

27. Altman, *Theory of Narrative,* 21.

28. Sarah Kember argues that analog and digital media "coexist in an ongoing, dynamic relationship of remediation that extends to the hybridization

of media with other media and cultural forces" ("Ubiquitous Photography," *Philosophy of Photography* 3, no. 2 [2012]: 331–48, at 335). For Joanna Zylinska, digital photography is "a continuation of users' practices enacted with the analog medium; only it is faster, even less permanent, and even more excessive" (*Nonhuman Photography* [Cambridge, Mass.: MIT Press, 2017], 179). For Meredith Hoy, an "aesthetic of digitality does not necessarily rely on electronic computational processing for its realization"; rather, it involves the presentation of "an array of discrete, discontinuous, and interchangeable units that make up the building blocks, and indeed the very materiality, of the world in question" (*From Point to Pixel: A Genealogy of Digital Aesthetics* [Hanover, N.H.: Dartmouth University Press], 210).

29. The information about the gold medal and the labels of collaborator and compiler come from Shawn Michelle Smith's text prepared for the exhibit *Photography on the Color Line* at the Center for the Humanities at Oregon State University in 1999, as excerpted in "African American Photographs Assembled for 1900 Paris Exposition," loc.gov/pictures/collection/anedub/dubois.html.

30. Whitney Battle-Baptiste and Britt Rusert, "Introduction," in *W. E. B. Du Bois's Data Portraits: Visualizing Black America,* ed. Whitney Battle-Baptiste and Britt Rusert (New York: Princeton Architectural Press, 2018), 7–22, at 19.

31. Battle-Baptiste and Rusert, 11.

32. Battle-Baptiste and Rusert, 11.

33. Aldon Morris, "American Negro at Paris, 1900," in Battle-Baptiste and Rusert, *W. E. B Du Bois's Data Portraits,* 23–36, at 35.

34. Battle-Baptiste and Rusert, 19.

35. Dignity + Debt, "The Student Debt Initiative," dignityanddebt.org/projects/student-debt-initiative.

36. April Glaser, "Where 8channers Went After 8chan," *Slate,* November 11, 2019, slate.com/technology/2019/11/8chan-8kun-white-supremacists-telegram-discord-facebook.html.

37. Battle-Baptiste and Rusert, "Introduction," 22 (italics original).

38. Hito Steyerl, "In Defense of the Poor Image," *e-flux,* no. 10 (November 2009), e-flux.com/journal/10/61362/in-defense-of-the-poor-image. I discuss trolling and recruitment in chapter 3.

39. For more on this and other works by Justesen, see Birgitte Anderberg, "Performing Feminism—Kirsten Justesen," in *A Cultural History of the Avant-Garde in the Nordic Countries, 1950–1975,* ed. Tania Ørum and Jesper Olsson (Leiden: Brill, 2016), 569–76, and Vibeke Vibolt Knudsen, "*Circumstances*—1973: An Unknown Work by Kirsten Justesen," *Statens Museum for Kunst Journal* 5 (2001): 178–201.

40. The Japan Disasters Digital Archive, jdarchive.org.

41. Arlette Farge, *The Allure of the Archives,* trans. Thomas-Scott Railton (New Haven, Conn.: Yale Univeristy Press, 2015), 96.

42. Farge, 94; 69; 113.

43. On scale shifts, see David Joselit, *After Art* (Princeton, N.J.: Princeton University Press, 2012). Joselit writes: "Images are a form of information that

may shift from two dimensions to three, from tiny to huge, or from one material substrate to another" (xv–xvi).

44. Ceci Moss, *Expanded Internet Art: Twenty-First Century Artistic Practice and the Informational Milieu* (New York: Bloomsbury, 2019), 21. My thanks to Aja Bond for pointing me to this book.

45. The phrase "eco-conscious lexicon" is from Rhizome's *Net Art Anthology,* anthology.rhizome.org/r-u-in-s-garden-club.

46. Kari Altmann, *Garden Club,* karialtmann.com/teams/garden-club.

47. Moss, *Expanded Internet Art,* 22.

48. Mark Leckey, "Art Stigmergy," *Kaleidoscope,* Summer 2011, as quoted by Moss in *Expanded Internet Art,* 9.

49. On these aphorisms as "interchangeable, authorless, repetitive and empty," see Cary Levine, "Unset in Stone: Jenny Holzer's Materialized Missives," in *Jenny Holzer: Retro,* ed. Brady Doty and Dina Shaulov-Wright (New York: Skarstedt Gallery, 2011), 6.

50. For Levine, Holzer's works "relate to (and complicate) both conventional agitprop and prior conceptualist efforts to dematerialize the work of art" ("Unset in Stone," 3).

51. Robert Storr, "Paper Trail," in *Jenny Holzer: Redaction Paintings* (New York: Cheim & Read, 2006), 9.

52. Jenny Holzer, interview with Diane Waldman, July 6 and 12, 1989, in *Jenny Holzer,* 2nd ed. (New York: Solomon R. Guggenheim Foundation, 1997), 33.

53. *Walter Benjamin: The Work of Art in the Age of Its Technological Reproducibility, and Other Writings on Media,* ed. Thomas Y. Levin, Brigid Doherty, and Michael W. Jennings (Cambridge, Mass.: Harvard University Press, 2008).

54. On this shift in dissemination, see Hannah Ewens, "Jenny Holzer's Art is Powerful On and Off Screen," *Vice,* October 9, 2017, vice.com/en/article/8x8bd5/jenny-holzers-art-is-powerful-on-and-off-screen. Also see Leisha Jones, "'Being Alone with Yourself is Increasingly Unpopular': The Electronic Poetry of Jenny Holzer," *Journal of Narrative Theory* 48, no. 3 (2018): 423–51.

55. Moss, *Expanded Internet Art,* 19.

56. *Border Spaces: Visualizing the U.S.–Mexico Frontera,* ed. Katherine G. Morrissey and John-Michael H. Warner (Tucson: University of Arizona Press, 2018).

57. Samuel Truett and Maribel Alvarez, "A Conversation on Border Landscapes through Time," in Morrissey and Warner, *Border Spaces,* 23–38, at 31–32.

58. Katherine G. Morrissey and John-Michael H. Warner, "Introduction," in Morrissey and Warner, *Border Spaces,* 3–19, at 7.

59. Morrissey and Warner, 13–14.

60. Truett and Alvarez, "Conversation," 35–36.

61. Truett and Alvarez, 33.

62. See Katherine G. Morrissey, "Monuments, Photographs, and Maps: Visualizing the U.S.-Mexico Border in the 1890s," in Morrissey and Warner, *Border Spaces,* 39–65.

63. Amelia Malagamba-Ansótegui and Sarah J. Moore, "A Conversation on Border Art and Spaces," in *Border Spaces,* 113–33, at 132.

64. Kirby Ferguson, *Everything Is a Remix,* 2021, everythingisaremix.info/watch-the-series.

65. See, for instance, "Appropriation," in *Keywords in Remix Studies,* ed. Eduardo Navas, Owen Gallagher, xtine burrough (New York: Routledge, 2017), 17: "Regardless of how much remix may or may not rely on appropriation to create new works, appropriation is play, and at the core of creating. Without it there is no making, no production, no art, no science."

66. Beretta E. Smith-Shomade, "Appropriation," in *Keywords for Media Studies* (New York: New York University Press, 2017), 14–15.

2. Art, Assembly, and the Museum

1. See "Charlie Brown," art21.org/read/richard-serra-charlie-brown, as referenced in Samantha Friedman, "To Collect," *Inside/Out: A MoMA/MoMA PS1 Blog,* October 20, 2011, moma.org/explore/inside_out/2011/10/20/to-collect.

2. When the group-show version went missing, Serra had to write a second version (Lynne Cooke, "Thinking on Your Feet: Richard Serra's Sculptures in Landscape," in *Richard Serra Sculpture: Forty Years,* ed. Kynaston McShine and Lynne Cooke [New York: Museum of Modern Art, 2007], 102n1).

3. Benjamin H. D. Buchloh, "Process Sculpture and Film in Richard Serra's Work," in *Richard Serra: Arbeiten 66–77, (Works 66–77); Kunsthalle Tübingen 8.3 – 2.4.* (Tübingen: Kunsthalle Tübingen, 1978), 233. The quote from Friedman is in "To Collect."

4. Rosalind E. Krauss, *Passages in Modern Sculpture* (Cambridge, Mass.: MIT Press, 1977), 276.

5. Cooke, "Thinking on Your Feet," 77.

6. The work has been used as a prompt. See, for instance, Don Ball, "Visualizing Verbs," *Art 21 Magazine,* March 30, 2016, magazine.art21.org/2016/03/30/visualizing-verbs, and Celia Lury, "Introduction: Activating the Present of Interdisciplinary Methods," in *Routledge Handbook of Interdisciplinary Research Methods,* ed. Celia Lury et al. (New York: Routledge, 2018), 1–26.

7. Maurice Denis, "Definition of Neo-Traditionalism," in *Art in Theory: 1815–1900,* ed. C. Harrison (London: Blackwell: 1998), 863.

8. As Étienne Gilson puts it, "a picture exists from the moment these simple conditions are fulfilled; . . . painting is by definition abstract and not representational" (*Forms and Substances in the Arts* [1966], trans. Salvator Atlanasio [Chicago: Dalkey Archives Press, 2001], 114).

9. Via Kant, Hegel, and others, it seems possible to trace a larger intellectual history of Western assumptions about representation that have made deriding "mere arrangement" such a seemingly obvious critical move as to not require justification. One starting point is Jacques Rancière's notion of the "mimetic order" or the "representational regime of the sensible" and its interpretation by Davide Panagia (*Rancière's Sentiments* [Durham, N.C.: Duke University Press, 2018], 40). Also relevant are theoretical movements that decenter representation, as in Nigel Thrift, *Non-Representational Theory: Space, Politics, Affect* (London: Routledge, 2007).

10. Susanne K. Langer, *Feeling and Form: A Theory of Art Developed from Philosophy in a New Key* (New York: Charles Scribner's Sons, 1953), 40.

11. Interestingly, Langer also expresses appreciation for the "tremendous readiness" of verbal symbols to "enter into *combinations*" (Susanne K. Langer, *Philosophy in a New Key: A Study in the Symbolism of Reason, Rite, and Art,* 3rd ed. [Cambridge, Mass.: Harvard University Press, 2009], 76, [italics original]). She also notes that visual forms are equally capable of "complex combination" (77).

12. Marta Gili, *Milagros de la Torre: Photographs 1991–2011* (Barcelona: RM, 2012), 172.

13. According to a 1961 MoMA press release, "assemblage" is "a more inclusive term than the familiar 'collage.'" ("The Art of Assemblage," October 4, 1961). Also see William C. Seitz, *The Art of Assemblage* (New York: Museum of Modern Art, 1961).

14. The quote is from Brandon Taylor, *Collage: The Making of Modern Art* (London: Thames & Hudson, 2006), 210–11. Also see Ari H. Merjian and Mike Rugnetta, "From Dada to Memes," *Art in America,* December 2, 2020, artnews.com/art-in-america/interviews/memes-dada-political-collage-1234577740.

15. Poggi observes that the "coexistence of images, words, and objects is now a familiar feature of twentieth-century art" (Christine Poggi, *In Defiance of Painting: Cubism, Futurism, and the Invention of Collage* [New Haven, Conn.: Yale University Press, 1992], 257).

16. Felix Thürlemann adds the intriguing term "hyperimage," linking artistic practices like those of Pierre Bonnard and Wolfgang Tillmans with methods of multipicture display and art historical arranging (*More Than One Picture: An Art History of the Hyperimage,* trans. Elizabeth Tucker [Los Angeles: Getty, 2019]).

17. Patrizia McBride, *The Chatter of the Visible: Montage and Narrative in Weimar Germany* (Ann Arbor: University of Michigan Press, 2016), 5. Of course, "montage" is not just one thing. It can be film sequences cutting between perspectives (à la D. W. Griffith), forms of editing that yield distinct perceptual effects (à la Sergei Eisenstein), and any image-making, poetic, or other practice that uses combination to effect disruption and disunification. On the varieties of montage, see Rane Willerslev and Christian Suhr, "Montage as an Amplifier of Invisibility," in *Transcultural Montage,* ed. Rane Willerslev and Christian Suhr (New York: Berghan, 2013), 1–16. Also see Craig Buckley, *Graphic Assembly: Montage, Media, and Experimental Architecture in the 1960s* (Minneapolis: University of Minnesota Press, 2018).

18. Christiane Paul, "The Database as System and Cultural Form: Anatomies of Cultural Narratives," in *Database Aesthetics: Art in the Age of Information Overflow,* ed.Victoria Vesna (Minneapolis: University of Minnesota Press, 2007), 95.

19. Sharon Daniel, "The Database: An Aesthetics of Dignity," in Vesna, *Database Aesthetics,* 150.

20. Griselda Pollock, *Encounters in the Virtual Feminist Museum: Time, Space and the Archive* (London: Routledge, 2007), 59.

21. Many fields debate the difference between typology and taxonomy. I

use "typology" because I emphasize many, coequal possibilities rather than sets and hierarchies. I call it "critical" because it's not presented as complete, and because it's partly oriented toward what *ought* to be done. Relevant here is Graham Beryl, "Taxonomies of New Media Art: Real World Naming," in *Museums and the Web 2005: Proceedings,* ed. J. Trant and D. Bearman (Toronto: Archives & Museum Informatics, 2005).

22. On the problems with naming as "art" that which was not understood as such in the time or culture of its creation, see Carolyn Dean, "The Trouble with (the Term) Art," *Art Journal* 65, no. 2 (2006): 24–32.

23. Ben Davis, "I Looked Through All 5,000 Images in Beeple's $69 Million Magnum Opus. What I Found Isn't So Pretty," *Artnet,* March 17, 2021, news.artnet.com/opinion/beeple-everydays-review-1951656.

24. Peter Carpreau, "The Paradox of the Value of Art: Constructing Meaning and the Boundaries of History," in *The Transhistorical Museum: Mapping the Field,* ed. Eva Wittocx, Ann Demeester, Peter Carpreau, Melanie Bühler, and Xander Karskens (Amsterdam: Valiz, 2018), 110.

25. Hans Belting, *Hieronymus Bosch: Garden of Earthly Delights,* trans. Ishbel Flett (London: Prestel, 2016), 21.

26. As quoted in Belting, 14 and 17.

27. Belting, 14, 122.

28. Belting, 62.

29. Belting, 17; 98; 62; 47.

30. Belting, 47.

31. Jil Evans and Charles Taliaferro, "Representations," in *The History of Evil in the Early Modern Age,* vol. 3, *1450–1700CE,* ed. Daniel N. Robinson, Chad Meister, and Charles Taliaferro (New York: Routledge, 2018), 282.

32. The phrase "formative power" is in Paul Crowther, *The Transhistorical Image: Philosophizing Art and History* (Cambridge: Cambridge University Press, 2002). The phrase "transhistorical surplus" is in Nicola Setari, "Notes on Transhistoricity: Between Art Theory and Curatorial Practice," in Wittocx, Demeester, Carpreau, Bühler, and Karskens, *Transhistorical Museum,* 32.

33. Lev Manovich, "What Is Digital Cinema?," in *Post-Cinema: Theorizing 21st-Century Film,* ed. Shane Denson and Julia Leyda (Sussex: REFRAME, 2016), 40. While the statement I have quoted does not refer to Lialina's project, Manovich does frame Lialina's project along similar lines in an interview with Rick Silva available at art.colorado.edu/archive/hiaff/interviewc154.html?id=133&cid=12.

34. Carpreau, "The Paradox of the Value of Art," 111.

35. Joseph Keckler, as quoted in Olivia Laing, *Funny Weather: Art in an Emergency* (New York: Norton, 2020), 332.

36. David Joselit, *After Art* (Princeton, N,J.: Princeton University Press, 2013), 14.

37. Belting, *Hieronymus Bosch,* 79–84.

38. *Jheronimus Bosch: Transmediaal drieluik,* jheronimus-bosch.nl.

39. Annalisa Merelli, "Photos: The 500-year-old Painter Who Can Still Blow Any 16-year-old's Mind," *Quartz,* May 14, 2016, qz.com/682847/photos-the-500-year-old-painter-who-can-still-blow-any-16-year-olds-mind.

40. Thomas McMullan, "This Bonkers Bot Is the Only Twitter Account Worth Following Right Now," *Wired,* October 17, 2018, wired.co.uk/article /bosch-twitter-bot-digital-art.

41. David Britton, "This Bosch Painting Twitter Bot Is Great Meme Material," Daily Dot, November 11, 2018, dailydot.com/unclick/bosch-bot-twitter -earthly-delights-painting-memes.

42. Melanie Bühler, "(Re)Discovering Art History's Philosophical Foundations—An Interview with Hanneke Grootenboer," in Wittocx, Demeester, Carpreau, Bühler, and Karskens, *Transhistorical Museum,* 42.

43. Both quotes derive from McMullan, "This Bonkers Bot," the first by Eley Williams, the second by Anna Riddler.

44. The name is an allusion to Christo and Jeanne-Claude's 1972–1976 work *Running Fence.* David Hopkins, *After Modern Art: 1945–2017* (Oxford: Oxford University Press, 2018), 271.

45. These other quotes come from the statement by the artists of Postcommodity on their website, postcommodity.com/Repellent_Fence_English.html. Additional details are drawn from the documentary *Through the Repellent Fence.*

46. I derive "in spite of all" from Georges Didi-Huberman, *Images in Spite of All: Four Photographs from Auschwitz,* trans. Shane B. Lillis (Chicago: University of Chicago Press, 2003).

47. Postcommodity, postcommodity.com/Repellent_Fence_English.html, (italics mine).

48. Kaja Silverman, *The Miracle of Analogy, or The History of Photography: Part 1* (Stanford, Calif.: Stanford University Press, 2015), 11.

49. Silverman, 11.

50. Silverman, 95.

51. Silverman, 61.

52. Silverman, 63–64.

53. Silverman, 64–65.

54. See Fontcuberta's artist statement for Zabriskie Gallery, web.archive .org/web/20190421010037/www.zabriskiegallery.com/-joan-fontcuberta --artist-statement.

55. "Claudia Schmuckli of the Fine Arts Museums of San Francisco: Battery Member and Museum Curator Interview," *The Battery Candy* 5 (2019): 53–54.

56. Huey Copeland, "Close-Up: Specters of History," *Artforum,* September 2014, artforum.com/print/201407/carrie-mae-weems-s-lincoln-lonnie -and-me-2012-47844.

57. de Young Museum, *Specters of Disruption,* e-flux Announcements, e-flux .com/announcements/216303/specters-of-disruption.

58. Strike MoMA, "Frameworks and Terms for Struggle," strikemoma.org.

59. Alexander Nagel, whose work includes discussion of assemblage and other supposedly modern modes in medieval art, calls for a "way of proceeding" that refuses the "organizing lines of history" and is instead "its own form of thought" (Melanie Bühler, "Undoing Time: Art's Anachronistic

Capacities—An Interview with Alexander Nagel," in Wittocx, Demeester, Carpreau, Bühler, and Karskens, *Transhistorical Museum,* 84–87).

60. María Íñigo Clavo and Olga Fernández López, "Transhistoric Display and Colonial (Dis)encounters," in Wittocx, Demeester, Carpreau, Bühler, and Karskens, *Transhistorical Museum,* 68.

61. Setari, "Notes on Transhistoricity," 27.

62. Pollock, *Encounters in the Virtual Feminist Museum,* 13.

63. Íñigo Clavo and Fernández López, "Transhistoric Display," 67.

64. Eva Wittocx, Ann Demeester, Peter Carpreau, Melanie Bühler, and Xander Karskens, "Introduction," in *Transhistorical Museum,* 13.

65. Michelle Raheja, "Imagining Indigenous Digital Futures: An Afterword," *Studies in American Indian Literatures* 29, no. 1 (2017): 172–75.

66. Nikos Papastergiadis and Charles Esche, "Assemblies in Art and Politics: An Interview with Jacques Rancière," *Theory, Culture & Society* 13, no. 7/8 (2014): 38.

67. Paul Arnett, "Self-Taut: On Dial's Style," in *Thornton Dial in the 21st Century,* ed. William Arnett, John Beardsley, Alvia J. Wardlaw, and Jane Livingston (Atlanta: Tinwood, 2005), 127.

68. Fred Moten, *Black and Blur* (Durham, N.C.: Duke University Press, 2017), 155–56.

69. Wittocx, Demeester, Carpreau, Bühler, and Karskens, "Introduction," 14.

70. Wendy Hui Kyong Chun, *Discriminating Data: Correlation, Neighborhoods, and the New Politics of Recognition* (Cambridge, Mass.: MIT Press, 2021), 52.

71. On these terms relative to museums, see, e.g., Fiona Cameron, "The Liquid Museum: New Institutional Ontologies for a Complex, Uncertain World," in *The International Handbooks of Museum Studies,* vol. 1, *Museum Theory,* ed. Kylie Message and Andrea Witcomb (Hoboken, N.J.: Wiley, 2015), 345–61, and Adam Muller, "Deterritorializing the Canadian Museum for Human Rights," *Museum and Society* 18, no. 1 (2020): 82–97.

72. Manuel DeLanda, *Assemblage Theory* (Edinburgh: Edinburgh University Press, 2016), 22.

73. Wittocx, Demeester, Carpreau, Bühler, and Karskens, "Introduction," 14.

74. Hito Steyerl, "A Tank on a Pedestal: Museums in an Age of Planetary Civil War," *e-flux journal,* no. 70 (February 2016), e-flux.com/journal/70/60543/a-tank-on-a-pedestal-museums-in-an-age-of-planetary-civil-war.

75. See Maanvi Singh, "Native American 'Land Taxes': A Step on the Roadmap for Reparations," *The Guardian,* December 31, 2019, theguardian.com/us-news/2019/dec/31/native-american-land-taxes-reparations.

76. Yaiza Hernández Vélazquez, "A Constituent Education," in *The Constituent Museum: Constellations of Knowledge, Politics and Mediation, A Generator of Social Change,* ed. John Byrne, Elinor Morgan, November Paynter, Aida Sánchez de Serdio, and Adela Železnik (Amsterdam: Valiz, 2018), 167.

77. Raúl Sánchez Cedillo, "The Rest Is Missing: On Constituencies as a Matricial Notion for New Institutions of the Commons," in Byrne, Morgan, Paynter, Sánchez de Serdio, and Železnik, *Constituent Museum,* 84.

78. Vélazquez, "Constituent Education," 168.

79. Cedillo, "The Rest Is Missing," 85.

80. Olivia Laing, *Funny Weather: Art in an Emergency* (New York: Norton, 2019), 2.

81. Arlette Farge, *The Allure of the Archives,* trans. Thomas-Scott Railton (New Haven, Conn.: Yale Univeristy Press, 2015), 65.

82. Cooke, "Thinking on Your Feet," 95–97.

83. Cooke, 96.

84. Cooke, 96.

85. Andrew Alden, "About Basalt," ThoughtCo., February 3, 2019, thoughtco.com/what-is-basalt-1440991.

86. Juerg M. Matter et al., "Permanent Carbon Dioxide Storage into Basalt: The CarbFix Pilot Project, Iceland," *Energy Procedia* 1, no. 1 (2009): 3641–46.

87. Tim Smedley, "The Technology That Turns CO2 into Rock," DataDrivenInvestor (published on Medium), January 8, 2019, medium.com/datadriveninvestor/the-technology-that-turns-co2-into-rock-8ee34d4aad3b.

88. Among the many texts tracing these debates is Rachel M. Cohen, "The Environmental Left Is Softening on Carbon-Capture Technology. Maybe That's Okay," *The Intercept,* September 20, 2019, https://theintercept.com/2019/09/20/carbon-capture-technology-unions-labor.

89. Robert MacFarlane, *Underland: A Deep Time Journey* (New York: Norton & Company, 2019), 418.

90. The quote is from Wu Hung, "Material Art from China: An Introduction," in Wu Hung and Orianna Cacchione, *The Allure of Matter: Material Art from China* (Chicago: University of Chicago Press, 2019), 15. On the work in question as well as others by Huang, see "Huang Yong Ping: 'Book Washing' Projects" (in the same volume), 130–35.

91. See Benjamin P. Horton et al., "Mapping Sea-Level Change in Time, Space, and Probability," *Annual Review of Environment and Resources* 43 (October 2018): 481–521, and Jòn Bjarki Magnússon, "Where the Land Rises Faster than the Sea," Correctiv, July 28, 2017, correctiv.org/en/latest-stories/sea-level-rising/2017/07/28/where-the-land-rises-faster-than-the-sea.

92. See Ben Tarnoff, "Covid-19 and the Cloud," Progressive International, May 21, 2020, progressive.international/blueprint/d0b51aca-6c19-4216-b836-1974b74ee21f-ben-tarnoff-covid-19-and-the-cloud/en.

93. Tarnoff, "Covid-19 and the Cloud."

3. Memes, Assembly, and the Internet

1. Here I build on Ryan M. Milner's observation: "It's an easy shortcut to call a solitary image we scroll past on Twitter or Tumblr a *meme,* as if the term is synonymous with 'a quirky little JPG from the internet.' However, it takes memetic processes to turn an individual text into a memetic one" (*The World Made Meme: Public Conversations and Participatory Media* [Cambridge, Mass.: MIT Press, 2016], 3 [italics original]).

2. Limor Shifman, *Memes in Digital Culture* (Cambridge, Mass.: MIT Press, 2013), 7–8.

3. Gretchen McCulloch, *Because Internet: Understanding the New Rules of Language* (New York: Random House, 2019), 255.

4. /r/Memes, "About Community," reddit, reddit.com/r/memes.

5. Miles Klee, "Nazi Edgelords Ruined Big Chungus," *Mel Magazine,* 2020, melmagazine.com/en-us/story/big-chungus-nazi-reddit-ban.

6. According to the "Kyle" meme, people with that name love Monster Energy drinks and have a penchant for punching holes in drywall.

7. For Brennan quote, see An Xiao Mina, "Memes and Visuals Come to the Fore," NiemanLab, niemanlab.org/2017/12/memes-and-visuals-come-to-the-fore. Milner, *World Made Meme,* 1.

8. See Lauren Michele Jackson, "A Unified Theory of Meme Death," *The Atlantic,* December 7, 2017, theatlantic.com/technology/archive/2017/12/a-unified-theory-of-meme-death/546866; Jackson, "The Blackness of Meme Movement," *Model View Culture,* no. 35 (March 28, 2016), modelviewculture.com/pieces/the-blackness-of-meme-movement; Jackson, *White Negroes: When Cornrows Were in Vogue . . . and Other Thoughts on Cultural Appropriation* (Boston: Beacon, 2019).

9. I'm partaking in a meme based on a line from Peter Jackson's 2001 film adaptation of J. R. R. Tolkien's *Lord of the Rings: The Fellowship of the Ring*: "One does not simply walk into Mordor." I am far from alone in using this meme in scholarship.

10. Jackson, "Unified Theory of Meme Death."

11. Ben T. Pettis critiques Know Your Meme, which he defines as "a curated collection of user-submitted meme instances and partially crowd-sourced definitions." See Ben T. Pettis, "*Know Your Meme* and the Homogenization of Web History," *Internet Histories,* August 19, 2021, 14.

12. See Know Your Meme, "Object Labeling," knowyourmeme.com/memes/object-labeling.

13. Heather Schwedel, "Memes Are Object-Labeled Now," *Slate,* March 22, 2018, slate.com/technology/2018/03/memes-are-object-labeled-now.html.

14. This description is from Christianna Silva, "Let Aiden Arata, the Meme Queen of Depression Instagram, Take You through Guided Meditation," *Mashable,* July 30, 2021, mashable.com/article/meet-aiden-rata-meme-queen-of-depression-instagram.

15. Lauren Michele Jackson, "We Need to Talk about Digital Blackface in Reaction GIFs," *Teen Vogue,* August 2, 2017, teenvogue.com/story/digital-blackface-reaction-gifs.

16. TikTok user hippityhoppity2929, tiktok.com/@hippityhoppity2929.

17. Philodox, "Fashion Though the Decades TikTok Compilation | Popular Tiktok Memes Compilation," March 3, 2020, YouTube video, 11:46, at 1:43 to 2:15, youtube.com/watch?v=x_XZM_nZfEM.

18. On "stance" in memes, see Shifman, *Memes,* 40.

19. Among the many writings on folksonomy, see: Thomas Vander Wal, "Folksonomy Coinage and Definition," December 11, 2005, reproduced on vanderwal.net, February 2, 2007, vanderwal.net/folksonomy.html; Isabella Peters, *Folksonomies. Indexing and Retrieval in Web 2.0* (Berlin: De Gruyter, 2009); and James MacDevitt, "The User-Archivist and Collective (In)Voluntary Memory: Read/Writing the Networked Digital Archive," in *Revisualizing Visual Culture,* ed. Chris Bailey and Hazel Gardiner (London: Routledge, 2016), 109–24.

20. See Mark Peters, "Womyn, Wimmin, and Other Folx," *Boston Globe,* May 9, 2017.

21. Equating "memetic sub-cultural spaces" with "The Internet," writes Milner, works to cover up the "multiplicity and diversity of mediated participation" (*World Made Meme,* 122).

22. Judith Butler, *Notes Toward a Performative Theory of Assembly* (Cambridge, Mass: Harvard University Press, 2015), 33.

23. Whitney Phillips and Milner write: "Irony can be especially difficult to parse from earnestness online, and problematic perspectives can be amplified just as easily as pro-social ones." See *The Ambivalent Internet: Mischief, Oddity, and Antagonism Online* (Cambridge, Mass.: Polity, 2017), 21.

24. Milner, *World Made Meme,* 118 and 146.

25. Jules Gleeson, "Judith Butler: 'We Need to Rethink the Category of Woman'" (interview), *The Guardian,* September 7, 2021, theguardian.com/lifeandstyle/2021/sep/07/judith-butler-interview-gender.

26. Gleeson, Butler interview.

27. Butler, *Notes,* 33.

28. Gleeson, Butler interview.

29. Butler, *Notes,* 63.

30. Butler, 33.

31. Butler, 57.

32. Butler, 33.

33. Milner, *World Made Meme,* 138.

34. Jonathan Crary, *24/7: Late Capitalism and the Ends of Sleep* (New York: Verso, 2013), 52.

35. Hito Steyerl, "In Defense of the Poor Image," *e-flux journal,* no. 10 (November 2009), e-flux.com/journal/10/61362/in-defense-of-the-poor-image.

36. Ronald E. Day, *Indexing It All: The Subject in the Age of Documentation, Information, and Data* (Cambridge, Mass.: MIT Press, 2014), 137.

37. Day, 133.

38. Shoshana Zuboff, *The Age of Surveillance Capitalism: The Fight for a Human Future at the New Frontier of Power* (New York: Public Affairs, 2019), 201.

39. Safiya Umoja Noble, *Algorithms of Oppression: How Search Engines Reinforce Racism* (New York: New York University Press, 2018), 82.

40. Noble, 124–25.

41. Noble, 163; Wendy Hui Kyong Chun, *Discriminating Data: Correlation, Neighborhoods, and the New Politics of Recognition* (Cambridge, Mass.: MIT Press, 2021), 96.

42. Noble, 179.

43. Day, *Indexing It All,* 152.

44. Aria Dean, "Poor Meme, Rich Meme," *Real Life,* July 25, 2016, reallifemag.com/poor-meme-rich-meme.

45. Eloghosa Osunde, "& Other Stories," *The Paris Review,* July 22, 2021, theparisreview.org/blog/2021/07/22/other-stories.

46. Wendy Hui Kyong Chun, *Updating to Remain the Same: Habitual New Media* (Cambridge, Mass.: MIT Press, 2016), 62.

47. For more on "lulz," see wired.com/2011/11/anonymous-101. For more on "I did it for the lulz," see knowyourmeme.com/memes/i-did-it-for-the-lulz.

48. Mike Godwin, "Meme, Counter-meme," *Wired,* October 1, 1994, wired.com/1994/10/godwin-if-2.

49. Timothy Morton, *Hyperobjects: Philosophy and Ecology after the End of the World* (Minneapolis: University of Minnesota Press, 2013).

50. Snigdha Bansal, "Gen Z is Roasting Millennials for Their Side Parts and Skinny Jeans," *Vice,* February 5, 2021, vice.com/en/article/5dp4w5/genz-millennials-skinny-jeans-generation-wars.

51. Najma Al Zidjaly, "Memes as Reasonably Hostile Laments: A Discourse Analysis of Political Dissent in Oman," *Discourse and Society* 28, no. 6 (2017): 573–94.

52. Milner, *World Made Meme,* 220.

53. This is Richard Dawkins's response to the question "how do you feel about your word meme being reappropriated by the internet?" (Olivia Solon, "Richard Dawkins on the Internet's Hijacking of the Word 'Meme,'" *Wired,* June 6, 2013, wired.co.uk/article/richard-dawkins-memes).

54. Shifman, *Memes in Digital Culture,* 15; Lynne McNeill, "The End of the Internet: A Folk Response to the Provision of Infinite Choice," in *Folklore and the Internet: Vernacular Expression in a Digital World,* ed. Trevor J. Blank (Logan: Utah University Press), 80–97.

55. See An Xiao Mina, *From Memes to Movements: How the World's Most Viral Media Is Changing Social Protest and Power* (Boston: Beacon Press, 2019), 12: "Memes are the street art of the social web, and, like street art, they are varied, expressive, and complex, and they must contend with the existing politics of our public spaces."

56. Milner, *World Made Meme,* 2.

57. Milner, *World Made Meme,* 220.

58. The phrase "memetic payloads" appears in Matt Goerzen, "Notes Toward the Memes of Production," *Texte Zur Kunst* 106 (June 2017), textezurkunst.de/106/uber-die-meme-der-produktion.

59. Toni Morrison, Nobel Lecture, Nobel Foundation, December 7, 1993, nobelprize.org/prizes/literature/1993/morrison/lecture.

60. Keith Collins and Kevin Roose, "Tracing a Meme from the Internet's Fringe to a Republican Slogan," *New York Times,* November 5, 2018, nytimes.com/interactive/2018/11/04/technology/jobs-not-mobs.html.

61. For a partial history of this meme, see knowyourmeme.com/memes/pepe-the-frog. This entry does not cover all aspects of the history and uses of the meme; see "*Know Your Meme* and the Homogenization of Web History," 12.

62. Erin Gallagher, "Trump Trains," *Medium,* September 15, 2019, medium.com/@erin_gallagher/trump-trains-84bea1c3170d.

63. For further perspective, see Goerzen, "Notes," and Maxime Dafaure, "The 'Great Meme War': The Alt-Right and Its Multifarious Enemies," *Angles* 10 (2020), journals.openedition.org/angles/369.

64. Stephanie Mencimer, "'The Left Can't Meme': How Right-Wing Groups Are Training the Next Generation of Social Media Warriors," *Mother Jones,*

April 2, 2019, motherjones.com/politics/2019/04/right-wing-groups-are-training-young-conservatives-to-win-the-next-meme-war.

65. Jessica Bateman, "The Far-Right Is Weaponizing Instagram to Recruit Gen Z," *OneZero,* September 27, 2019, https://onezero.medium.com/the-far-right-is-weaponizing-instagram-to-recruit-gen-z-43257ddb2c9f.

66. Jessica Bateman, "'#IAmHere': The People Trying to Make Facebook a Nicer Place," BBC News, June 10, 2019, bbc.com/news/blogs-trending-48462190.

67. Jacob Davey, "Gamers Who Hate: An Introduction to ISD's Gaming and Extremism Series" (London: Institute for Strategic Dialogue, 2021), 9.

68. On Pizzagate and the roles of trolls on 4Chan in Trump's election and the spread of extreme right-wing ideologies, see Dale Beran, *It Came from Something Awful: How a Toxic Troll Army Accidentally Memed Donald Trump into Office* (New York: All Points, 2019).

69. Goerzen, "Notes."

70. Christina Kulich and Elizabeth Iams Wellman, "The United States Has a Democracy Problem: What Democratic Erosion Scholarship Tells Us about January 6," *items: Insights from the Social Sciences* (Social Science Research Council), January 26, 2021, items.ssrc.org/democracy-papers/the-united-states-has-a-democracy-problem-what-democratic-erosion-scholarship-tells-us-about-january-6.

71. Godwin, "Meme, Counter-meme."

72. On the multiple valences of "internet," see Thomas Streeter, "Internet," in *Digital Keywords: A Vocabulary of Information Society and Culture,* ed. Benjamin Peters (Princeton, N.J.: Princeton University Press, 2016), 184–96.

73. Relevant here is Michael Caulfield, "Info-Environmentalism: An Introduction," *EDUCAUSE review,* November–December 2017, 92–93, er.educause.edu/articles/2017/10/info-environmentalism-an-introduction. Also relevant is Whitney Phillips and Ryan M. Milner, *You Are Here: A Field Guide for Navigating Polarized Speech, Conspiracy Theories, and Our Polluted Media Landscape* (Cambridge, Mass.: MIT Press, 2020).

74. Federico Fastelli, "'The Argus Complex': Interview with W. J. T. Mitchell," *Lea* 8 (2019): 304–6.

75. Fastelli, 306.

76. Janet Murray, *Hamlet on the Holodeck: The Future of Narrative in Cyberspace* (New York: Free Press, 1997), 271.

77. Murray, 359.

78. Lev Manovich, *The Language of New Media* (Cambridge, Mass.: MIT Press, 2001), 225.

79. N. Katherine Hayles, *How We Think: Digital Media and Contemporary Technogenesis* (Chicago: University of Chicago Press, 2012), 176.

80. Hayles, 181–83.

81. Tara McPherson, "Digital" in *Keywords for American Cultural Studies,* ed. Bruce Burgett and Glenne Hendler, 2nd ed. (New York: New York University Press, 2014), 80.

82. Shoshana Zuboff, *Age of Surveillance Capitalism,* 185.

83. Zuboff, 185.

84. See Tim Hwang, *Subprime Attention Crisis: Advertising and the Time Bomb at the Heart of the Internet* (New York: Farrar, Straus & Giroux × Logic: 2020).

85. Salomé Viljoen, "Data Relations," *Logic,* May 17, 2021, logicmag.io/distribution/data-relations.

4. Generative Assembly after Disaster

1. This chapter is a revised and expanded version of Kyle Parry, "Generative Assembly after Katrina," *Critical Inquiry* 44, no. (3) (2018): 554–81.

2. It is noteworthy that several scholarly texts on Katrina refer to this assembly.

3. Alexia, comment on Daily Kos, "Another Katrina Open Thread," August 30, 2005, *Daily Kos* (blog), dailykos.com/comments/142664/3505929#comment_3505235.

4. Appearing alongside comedian Mike Myers on NBC's "A Concert for Hurricane Relief" on September 2, 2005, West stared into the camera and flatly stated, "George Bush doesn't care about black people" (youtube.com/watch?v=UJUNTcOGeSw).

5. Tania Ralli, "Who's a Looter? In Storm's Aftermath, Pictures Kick Up a Different Kind of Tempest," *New York Times,* September 5, 2005, nytimes.com/2005/09/05/business/whos-a-looter-in-storms-aftermath-pictures-kick-up-a-different.html.

6. See Colleen Shalby, "What's the Difference Between 'Looting' and 'Finding'? 12 Years after Katrina, Harvey Sparks a New Debate," *Los Angeles Times,* August 29, 2017, latimes.com/nation/la-na-harvey-20170829-story.html.

7. Lisa-Marie Ricca, "Online Image Contribution, Hurricane Digital Memory Bank," Hurricane Digital Memory Bank, hurricanearchive.org/items/show/112.

8. Valorie Thomas, "'Dust to Cleanse Themselves,' A Survivor's Ethos: Diasporic Disidentifications in *Zeitoun,*" *Biography* 35, no. 2 (2012): 271–85, at 279.

9. On media frames, see Kathleen Tierney, Christine Bevc, and Erica Kuligowski, "Metaphors Matter: Disaster Myths, Media Frames, and Their Consequences in Hurricane Katrina," *The Annals of the American Academy of Political and Social Science* 604 (March 2006): 57–81.

10. See e.g.: Karen J. Leong et al., "Resilient History and the Rebuilding of a Community: The Vietnamese American Community in New Orleans East," *Journal of American History* 94 (December 2007): 770–79; Dave Eggers, *Zeitoun* (San Francisco: McSweeney's Books, 2009); DeAnne K. Hilfinger Messias, Clare Barrington, and Elaine Lacy, "Latino Social Network Dynamics and the Hurricane Katrina Disaster," *Disasters* 36, no. 1 (2012): 101–21.

11. Among the many books written on the disaster, see: Douglas Brinkley, *The Great Deluge: Hurricane Katrina, New Orleans, and the Mississippi Gulf Coast* (New York: Harper Collins, 2006); Michael Eric Dyson, *Come Hell or High Water: Hurricane Katrina and the Color of Disaster* (New York: Basic Civitas, 2005); *Hurricane Katrina: America's Unnatural Disaster,* ed. Jeremy I. Levitt and Matthew C. Whittaker (Omaha: University of Nebraska Press); and Andy Horowitz, *Katrina: A History, 1915–2015* (Cambridge, Mass.: Harvard University Press, 2020). On the mediation of Katrina, see *Old and New Media after*

Katrina, ed. Diane Negra (New York: Palgrave Macmillan, 2010), and Bernie Cook, *Flood of Images: Media, Memory, and Hurricane Katrina* (Austin: University of Texas Press, 2015).

12. Douglas Brinkley, "The Broken Promise of the Levees that Failed New Orleans," *Smithsonian Magazine,* September 2015, https://www.smithsonianmag.com/smithsonian-institution/broken-promise-levees-failed-new-orleans-180956326/.

13. Dyson, *Come Hell or High Water.*

14. Michael Mizell-Nelson, "Not Since the Great Depression: The Documentary Impulse Post-Katrina," in *Civic Engagement in the Wake of Katrina,* ed. Amy Koritz and George J. Sanchez (Ann Arbor: University of Michigan Press, 2009), 59–77.

15. Jamelle Bouie, "Where Black Lives Matter Began," *Slate,* August 23, 2015, slate.com/articles/news_and_politics/politics/2015/08/hurricane_katrina_10th_anniversary_how_the_black_lives_matter_movement_was.html.

16. Here I adapt the term "documentary landscape" as used by Michelle Caswell and Anne Gilliland in "False Promise and New Hope: Dead Perpetrators, Imagined Documents and Emergent Archival Evidence," *The International Journal of Human Rights* 19, no. 5 (2015): 615–27.

17. Josh Neufeld, *A.D.: New Orleans after the Deluge* (New York: Pantheon, 2009).

18. Richard Misrach, *Destroy This Memory* (New York: Aperture Foundation, 2010).

19. I engage with a critique presented by Kate Parker Horigan below. On outside volunteers and nongovernmental organizations (NGOs), see Jordan Flaherty, *Floodlines: Community and Resistance from Katrina to the Jena Six* (Chicago: Haymarket, 2010).

20. See, for instance, James Thompson, *Humanitarian Performance: From Disaster Tragedies to Spectacles of War* (London: Seagull Books, 2014).

21. Matthew Seeger and Timothy L. Sellnow, *Narratives of Crisis: Telling Stories of Ruin and Renewal* (Stanford, Calif.: Stanford University Press, 2016); Madeleine Wattenbarger, "Why Do We Turn to Stories in the Midst of a Disaster? On Narrative and Trauma in Mexico City," *Literary Hub,* March 21, 2018, lithub.com/why-do-we-turn-to-stories-in-the-midst-of-a-disaster; and *Sandy Storyline,* sandystoryline.com.

22. Seeger and Sellnow, *Narratives of Crisis,* 162.

23. John O'Neal, Carol Bebelle, Nicholas Slie, Catherine Michna, John Grimsley, and Raymond "Moose" Jackson, "Performance and Cross-Racial Storytelling in Post-Katrina New Orleans: Interviews with John O'Neal, Carol Bebelle, and Nicholas Slie," *TDR: The Drama Review* 57, no. 1 (2013): 48–69.

24. Kate Parker Horigan, *Consuming Katrina: Public Disaster and Personal Narrative* (Jackson: University of Mississippi Press, 2018), 8.

25. For further reflection on narratives around Katrina, see Arin Keeble, *Narratives of Hurricane Katrina in Context: Literature, Film, and Television* (London: Palgrave Pivot, 2019).

26. James Johnson, "Aggregates Unseen: Imagining Post-Katrina New Orleans," *Perspectives on Politics* 10 (September 2012): 659–68.

27. On curation, social media, and disaster, see Sophia Liu, "Socially Distributed Curation of the Bhopal Disaster: A Case of Grassroots Heritage in the Crisis Context," in *Heritage and Social Media: Understanding and Experiencing Heritage in a Participatory Culture,* ed. Elisa Giaccardi (New York: Routledge, 2012), 30–55.

28. In psychology, "generativity" names a theory of novel behavior, and in the work of Erik Erikson, "generativity" names the fact or quality of social contribution (Erik Erikson and Joan M. Erikson, *The Life Cycle Completed* [New York: Norton, 1998]). For Noam Chomsky, generative grammar indicates a theory of the infinitude of utterances from finite means (*Language and Responsibility: Based on Conversations with Mitson Ronat,* trans. John Viertel [New York: Pantheon, 1979]). For Jonathan Zittrain, the generativity of technology lies in its capacity to facilitate unanticipated creative uses (*The Future of the Internet—And How to Stop It* [New Haven, Conn.: Yale University Press, 2009]). In contexts of artistic production, the term generative indicates a work that involves the introduction of processes, like algorithms or chemical reactions, that partially or wholly determine the evolution of a piece. For Ron Eglash, "generative justice" is a social, ecological, and technological movement oriented around communities' production and retention of unalienated value ("Generative Justice: The Revolution Will Be Self-Organized," *Tikkun,* April 15, 2014, tikkun.org/nextgen/generative-justice-the-revolution-will-be-self-organized). Finally, on generative art, including the use of "GANs" (generative adversarial networks), see Joanna Zylinska, *AI Art: Machines Visions and Warped Dreams* (London: Open Humanities Press, 2020).

29. Fred Moten, *Black and Blur* (Durham, N.C.: Duke University Press, 2017), 224.

30. Judith Butler gestures to generativity in their book on political assembly. "So this movement or stillness, this parking of my body in the middle of another's action," Butler writes, "is neither my act nor yours, but something that happens by virtue of the relation between us, arising from that relation, equivocating between the I and the we, seeking at once to preserve and disseminate the generative value of that equivocation, an active and deliberately sustained relation, a collaboration distinct from hallucinatory merging or confusion" (*Notes Toward a Performative Theory of Assembly* [Cambridge, Mass.: Harvard University Press, 2015], 9).

31. In what follows, I forgo the extensive discussion required to account for acoustic and moving-image generative assembly after Katrina. This is not for lack of examples. I discussed one in the first chapter: the frame-infused closing of Spike Lee's *When the Levees Broke* (2006). Another is Larry Andrews's pioneering animated film *OwnerBuilt* (2013). Of especial note from this chapter's perspective are Andrews's generative fusions of split screen, aural performance, and sound collage.

32. Selections from this vast literature include Jan Assmann, *Moses the Egyptian: The Memory of Egypt in Western Monotheism* (Cambridge, Mass.: Har-

vard University Press, 1997), Maurice Halbwachs, *On Collective Memory,* trans. and ed. Lewis A. Coser (Chicago: University of Chicago Press, 1992), Alison Landsberg, *Prosthetic Memory: The Transformation of Public Memory in the Age of Mass Culture* (New York: Columbia University Press, 2004), Pierre Nora, "Between Memory and History: Les Lieux de Mémoire," trans. Marc Roudebush, *Representations* 26 (Spring 1989): 7–24, and Michel Rolph-Trouillout, *Silencing the Past: Power and the Production of History* (New York: Penguin, 1995).

33. Andrew Hoskins, "Memory of the Multitude: The End of Collective Memory," in *Digital Memory Studies: Media Pasts in Transition,* ed. Andrew Hoskins (New York: Routledge, 2018), 92.

34. Diane Negra, "Introduction: Old and New Media after Katrina," in *Old and New Media,* 5.

35. Cook, *Flood of Images,* 125.

36. Shannon Lee Dawdy, *Patina: A Profane Archaeology* (Chicago: University of Chicago Press, 2016), 8, 2.

37. In terms of the limits of historiography, see Hayden White, *Metahistory: The Historical Imagination in Nineteenth-Century Europe* (Baltimore, Md.: Johns Hopkins University Press, 1973). Keith Jenkins provides a useful overview in *Re-thinking History* (New York: Routledge, 2003). In terms of the question of the unrepresentable, the literature is vast, but one important contribution is Jean-Luc Nancy, "Forbidden Representation," in *The Ground of the Image,* trans. Jeff Fort (New York: Fordham University Press, 2005), 27–50. Also see: Hillary Chute, *Disaster Drawn: Visual Witness, Comics, and Documentary Form* (Cambridge, Mass.: Harvard University Press, 2016), 17; W. J. T. Mitchell, *Cloning Terror: The War of Images, 9/11 to the Present* (Chicago: University of Chicago Press, 2011), 60; Alexander Galloway, "Are Some Things Unrepresentable?," *Theory, Culture & Society* 28, no. 7–8 (2011): 85–102. The last responds to an essay by Jacques Rancière of the same name.

38. Hayden White, "The Modernist Event," in *The Persistence of History: Cinema, Television, and the Modern Event,* ed. Vivian Sobchack (New York: Routledge, 1996), 17–38.

39. Saidiya Hartman, *Scenes of Subjection: Terror, Slavery, and Self-Making in Nineteenth Century America* (New York: Oxford University Press), 14.

40. Johnson, "Aggregates Unseen," 665.

41. Aric Mayer, "Aesthetics of Catastrophe," *Public Culture* 20 (Spring 2008): 180.

42. I adapt this notion from Okwui Enwezor, "Archive Fever: Photography Between History and the Monument," in *Archive Fever: Uses of the Document in Contemporary Art,* ed. Okwui Enwezor (New York: International Center of Photography, 2008), 11.

43. The literature on trauma, visuality, and witness is vast, including the many important debates that have arisen in response to the Shoah and the history of slavery and anti-Black violence in the United States. Important texts include: Shoshona Felman and Dori Laub, *Testimony: Crises of Witnessing in Literature, Psychoanalysis, and History* (New York: Taylor & Francis, 1992); *Trauma and Visuality in Modernity,* ed. Lisa Saltzman and Eric Rosenberg

(Lebanon, N.H.: Dartmouth College Press, 2006); Bracha Ettinger, *The Matrixial Borderspace,* ed. Brian Massumi (Minneapolis: University of Minnesota Press, 2006); Griselda Pollock, *After-Affects, After-Images: Trauma and Aesthetic Transformation in the Virtual Feminist Museum* (Manchester: Manchester University Press, 2013); Huey Copeland, *Bound to Appear: Art, Slavery, and the Site of Blackness in Multicultural America* (Chicago: University of Chicago Press, 2013); Courtney R. Baker, *Humane Insight: Looking at Images of African American Suffering and Death* (Champaign: University of Illinois Press, 2015).

44. Martin Jay, *Adorno* (Cambridge, Mass.: Harvard University Press, 1984), 15.

45. Kara Walker, *After the Deluge* (New York: Rizzoli, 2007).

46. The assembly starts at hurricanearchive.org/items/show/33222. It concludes at hurricanearchive.org/items/show/33260. My understanding is that Kirsch did not upload these images himself; they were instead downloaded from Flickr by project staff.

47. I adapt a notion of photographic density from Allan Sekula, who suggests that photobooks can allow photographs to "offer their density of meaning" ("Photography between Labour and Capital," in Benjmain H. Buchloh and Sekula, *Mining Photographs and Other Pictures, 1948–1968: A Selection from the Negative Archives of Shedden Studio, Glace Bay, Cape Breton* [Halifax: Press of the Nova Scotia College of Art and Design, 1983], 150).

48. AlienGraffiti, comment on skeletonkrewe, "Flood Line—Zoom In," flickr.com/photos/skeletonkrewe/1252063529.

49. Dawdy, *Patina,* 2.

50. Walker, *After the Deluge,* 7–9.

51. On artists as curators, see Alison Green, *When Artists Curate: Contemporary Art and the Exhibition as Medium* (London: Reaktion, 2018), 22.

52. Walker, *After the Deluge,* 9.

53. Walker, 3.

54. Michael P. Bibler, "The Flood Last Time: 'Muck' and the Uses of History in Kara Walker's 'Rumination' on Katrina," *Journal of American Studies* 44 (August 2010): 508.

55. Bibler, 509.

56. Bibler, 517–18.

57. Hoskins, "Memory of the Multitude," 94.

58. Roger I. Simon, *The Touch of the Past: Remembrance, Learning, and Ethics* (New York: Palgrave Macmillan, 2005), 4.

59. Simon, 9.

60. Walker, *After the Deluge,* 9.

61. Will Eisner, *Comics & Sequential Art* (Tamarac, Fla.: Poorhouse Press, 1985), 5.

62. Chute, *Disaster Drawn,* 35.

63. Chute, 63, 35.

64. Chute, 17.

65. Anthony Dyer Hoefer, "A Re-Vision of the Record: The Demands of Reading Josh Neufeld's *A.D.*," in *Comics and the U.S. South,* ed. Brannon Costello

and Qiana J. Whitted (Jackson: University Press of Mississippi, 2012), 293–324, at 315.

66. Horigan, *Consuming Katrina,* 62.

67. Patrice Pascual, introduction to Joseph Rodriguez, *Still Here: Stories After Katrina* (Brooklyn, NY: powerHouse Books, 2008), 9.

68. See Gilles Deleuze and Félix Guattari, *A Thousand Plateaus,* vol. 2 of *Capitalism and Schizophrenia,* trans. Brian Massumi (London: Athlone, 1988), 500: "Of course, smooth spaces are not in themselves liberatory. But the struggle is changed or displaced in them, and life reconstitutes its stakes, confronts new obstacles, invents new paces, switches adversaries. Never believe that a smooth space will suffice to save us."

69. Brooke Marine, "Why You Should Think Twice Before Sharing Your 'Blackout Tuesday' Post on Instagram," *W Magazine,* June 6, 2020, wmagazine.com/story/blackout-tuesday-instagram-post-why-you-should-think-twice.

70. On the related but not coextensive notion of archival art, see Hal Foster, "An Archival Impulse," *October* 110 (Autumn 2004): 3–22.

71. This much is evident in *Help Us* (2008), in which Bradford placed the eponymous words, first expressed from a rooftop in flood-stricken New Orleans, on the top of the gallery, or in subsequent pieces of explicit and trenchant material critique, not directly related to Katrina, like *Paris is Burning* (2010) and *150 Portrait Tone* (2017). Bradford discusses the "confrontational" in relation to Katrina with Tyler Green during the unedited version of his interview with Steve Roden on the "Modern Art Notes Podcast" on March 15, 2012 (manpodcast.com/portfolio/no-19-mark-bradford-steve-roden).

72. I draw these words (and those on the slowness of recovery efforts) from the Albright-Knox Art Gallery's description of the work, available at https://www.albrightknox.org/artworks/200814-mississippi-gottdam.

73. It is notable that Bradford's *Mithra,* which was eventually removed, left several legacies: the photograph *Ark in Snow* (2008) by John Mullen III; the derivative installation *Details* (2009–2010), made for Bradford's 2010 retrospective; and an associated documentation of the building of the ark called *Across Canal* (2009–2010) on Super 8 film.

74. From https://www.albrightknox.org/artworks/200814-mississippi-gottdam.

75. Mark Bradford, interview with Hamza Walker, in *Mark Bradford,* ed. Christopher Bedford (New Haven, Conn.: Yale University Press, 2010), 100.

76. For a critique of the digital archive as a site of neoliberal "prosumption," see Timothy Recuber, "The Prosumption of Commemoration: Disasters, Digital Memory Banks, and Online Collective Memory," *American Behavioral Scientist* 56 (April 2012): 531–49. For a critique relative to politics of national belonging, see Courtney Rivard, "Archiving Disaster and National Identity in the Digital Realm: The September 11 Digital Archive and the Hurricane Digital Memory Bank," in *Identity Technologies: Constructing the Self Online,* ed. Anna Poletti and Julie Rak (Madison: University of Wisconsin Press., 2014), 132–43.

77. Mari E. Ramler, "Beyoncé's Performance of Identification as a Diamond: Reclaiming Bodies and Voices in 'Formation,'" *constellations: a cultural rhetorics*

publishing space, no. 1 (May 2018), constell8cr.com/issue-1/beyonces-performance-of-identification-as-a-diamond-reclaiming-bodies-and-voices-in-formation. Among the critiques of the "Formation" video, see Maris Jones, "Dear Beyoncé, Katrina is Not Your Story," *BGD* (blog), February 10, 2016, www.bgdblog.org/2016/02/dear-Beyonce-katrina-is-not-your-story, and Shantrelle Lewis, "'Formation' Exploits New Orleans' Trauma," *Slate,* February 10, 2016, slate.com/human-interest/2016/02/beyonces-formation-exploits-new-orleans-trauma.html.

78. Walter Benjamin, "Theses on the Philosophy of History," in *Illuminations,* trans. Harry Zohn (New York: Schocken, 1969), 249.

79. For further reflection on Benjamin's response to the work, see Stuart Jeffries, "The Storm Blowing from Paradise: Walter Benjamin and Klee's *Angelus Novus,*" Verso Books blog, August 2, 2016, versobooks.com/blogs/2791-the-storm-blowing-from-paradise-walter-benjamin-and-klee-s-angelus-novus. For Apetkar's account of Klee's work and his response to it, see Ken Apetkar, "Paul Klee's *Angelus Novus* Flies to Paris, Repainter Reminisces," *Repainter Diary* (Ken Apetkar blog), July 21, 2016, repainterdiary.com/2016/07/21/paul-klees-angelus-novus-flies-to-paris-repainter-reminisces.

80. Jesse McCarthy, *Who Will Pay Reparations on My Soul?: Essays* (New York: Liveright, 2021), 42.

81. McCarthy, 49.

82. Doreen St. Félix, "Kara Walker's Next Act," *New York Magazine,* April 17, 2017, feature article.

83. McCarthy, *Who Will Pay Reparations on My Soul?,* 50.

84. McCarthy, 50.

5. The Powers and Perils of Media Assembly

1. Andy Horowitz, *Katrina: A History, 1915–2015* (Cambridge, Mass.: Harvard University Press, 2020), 153.

2. Jenna Marie Christian and Lorraine Dowler, "Slow and Fast Violence: A Feminist Critique of Binaries," *ACME: An International Journal of Critical Geographies* 18, no. 5 (2019): 1070.

3. Rob Nixon, *Slow Violence and the Environmentalism of the Poor* (Cambridge, Mass.: Harvard University Press, 2011).

4. Christian and Dowler, "Slow and Fast Violence," 1072.

5. Nixon, *Slow Violence,* 2.

6. Nixon, 3.

7. For recent examples, see *The Routledge Companion to Contemporary Art, Visual Culture, and Climate Change,* ed. T. J. Demos, Emily Eliza Scott, and Subhankar Banjeree (New York: Routledge, 2021). On the problem of indifference, see Thom Davies, "Slow Violence and Toxic Geographies: 'Out of Sight' to Whom?," *Politics and Space* 40, no. 2 (2019): 409–27.

8. Lindsey Dillon, review of *Slow Violence and the Environmental of the Poor* by Rob Nixon, *Progress in Human Geography* 36, no. 6 (2012): 831.

9. Nixon, *Slow Violence,* 263.

10. Nixon, 265.

11. Nixon, 266.

12. Carrie Lambert-Beatty, "Make-Believe: Parafiction and Plausibility," *October* 129 (Summer 2009): 51–84, at 54.

13. Jason Burke, "Former Maldives President Mohamed Nasheed Jailed for 13 Years," *The Guardian,* March 14, 2015, theguardian.com/world/2015/mar/14/former-maldives-president-mohamed-nasheed-jailed-for-13-years; Reuters (staff), "Supporters of Maldives Ex-president Hold Underwater Protest," *Reuters,* April 11, 2015, reuters.com/article/uk-maldives-protests/supporters-of-maldives-ex-president-hold-underwater-protest-idUKKBN0N20FG20150411.

14. See, for instance, Hedley Twidle, "Rachel Carson and the Perils of Simplicity: Reading *Silent Spring* from the Global South," *ariel: A Review of International English Literature* 44, no. 4 (2014): 49–88. On the charge that Carson's activism against DDT insecticide led to deaths by malaria, see Leo Hickman, "What is the Legacy of Rachel Carson's *Silent Spring?*" *The Guardian,* September 27, 2012, theguardian.com/global/blog/2012/sep/27/rachel-carson-silent-spring-legacy.

15. Nixon, *Slow Violence,* 10.

16. Karin Reisinger, "Abandoned Architectures: Some Dirty Narratives," in *Architecture and Feminisms: Ecologies, Economies, Technologies,* ed. Hélène Frichot, Catharina Gabrielsson, and Helen Runting (New York: Routledge), 203.

17. Nixon, *Slow Violence,* 3.

18. Nancy Scheper-Hughes and Philippe Bourgois, "Introduction: Making Sense of Violence" in *Violence in War and Peace: An Anthology,* ed. Nancy Scheper-Hughes and Philippe Bourgois (Oxford: Blackwell, 2004), 1.

19. My understanding is that Liz Kelly first introduced the term "continuum of violence" in "The Continuum of Sexual Violence," in *Women, Violence and Social Control,* ed. Jalna Hanmer and Mary Maynard (Basingstoke, UK: Macmillan, 1987), 46–60. Some writers question whether the concept, which centers on sexual violence, could extend beyond straight relationships, while others argue that "it can be extended to encompass other forms of violence that have in common unequal power relations as a root cause" (Heather Fraser and Nik Taylor, *Neoliberalization, Universities and the Public Intellectual: Species, Gender and Class and the Production of Knowledge* [London: Palgrave Macmillan, 2016], 74).

20. Johan Galtung, "Violence, Peace, and Peace Research," *Journal of Peace Research* 6, no. 3 (1969): 171.

21. Paul E. Farmer, Bruce Nizeye, Sara Stulac, and Salmaan Keshavjee, "Structural Violence and Clinical Medicine," *PLoS Medicine* 3, no. 10 (2006): 1686 (italics original).

22. Michael Watts, *Silent Violence: Food, Famine, and Peasantry in Northern Nigeria* (Berkeley: University of California Press, 1983).

23. Nancy Scheper-Hughes, *Death without Weeping: The Violence of Everyday Life in Brazil* (Berkeley: University of California Press), 1992. The concept is used in Samantha Sabo et al., "Everyday Violence, Structural Racism and Mistreatment at the US–Mexico Border," *Social Science & Medicine* 109 (May 2014): 66–74.

24. "Letting die" is from James Tyner, *Genocide and the Geographical Imagination: Life and Death in Germany, China, and Cambodia* (Lanham, Md.: Rowman & Littlefield, 2012). "Creeping environmental change" is from Mickey H. Glantz, "Creeping Environmental Problems in the Aral Sea Basin," in *Central Eurasian Water Crisis: Caspian, Aral, and Dead Seas* (Tokyo: United Nations University Press, 1998), 25–52. I derive these references from Shannon O'Lear, "Climate Science and Slow Violence: A View from Political Geography and STS on Mobilizing Technoscientific Ontologies of Climate Change," *Political Geography* 52 (2016): 4–13.

25. Joan Cocks, *On Sovereignty and Other Political Delusions* (London: Bloomsbury Academic, 2014), 47.

26. Jacques Derrida, "Force of Law: The 'Mystical Foundation of Authority,'" in *Acts of Religion*, ed. Gil Anidjar (New York: Routledge, 2002), 234 (as cited by Cocks).

27. Joan Cocks, "The Violence of Structures and the Violence of Foundings," *New Political Science* 34, no. 2 (2012): 221–27, at 224. Also see Joan Cocks, "Foundational Violence and the Politics of Erasure," *Radical Philosophy Review* 15, no. 1 (2012): 103–26.

28. Mimi Ọnụọha, "Notes on Algorithmic Violence," GitHub, February 7, 2018, github.com/MimiOnuoha/On-Algorithmic-Violence.

29. Fernando de Maio and David Ansell note that "structural violence" is a "generative mechanism . . . an orienting concept, an analytical lens—and not a variable to be entered into a regression model" ("'As Natural as the Air Around Us': On the Origin and Development of the Concept of Structural Violence in Health Research," *International Journal of Health Services* 48, no. 4 [2018]: 752).

30. Kimberlé Crenshaw, "Demarginalizing the Intersection of Race and Sex: A Black Feminist Critique of Antidiscrimination Doctrine, Feminist Theory, and Antiracist Politics," *University of Chicago Legal Forum* 1989, no. 1, 139–67, at 142.

31. The notion of oppression as "interlocking" was articulated by The Combahee River Collective in 1977 (Combahee River Collective, "A Black Feminist Statement," in *The Black Feminist Reader*, ed. Joy James and T. Denean Sharpley-Whiting [Oxford: Blackwell, 2000], 261–70).

32. Bim Adewumni, "Kimberlé Crenshaw on Intersectionality: 'I Wanted to Come up with an Everyday Metaphor That Anyone Could Use,'" *New Statesmen*, April 2, 2014, newstatesman.com/lifestyle/2014/04/kimberl-crenshaw-intersectionality-i-wanted-come-everyday-metaphor-anyone-could.

33. Crenshaw, "Demarginalizing the Intersection of Race and Sex," 149.

34. Kimberlé Crenshaw, "Mapping the Margins: Intersectionality, Identity Politics, and Violence against Women of Color," *Stanford Law Review* 43, no. 6 (1991): 1241–99, at 1296 and 1265.

35. Adam Ramsay likewise links environmentalism and intersectionality. in "My Environmentalism Will Be Intersectional or It Will Be Bullshit," *Open Democracy* (blog), March 25, 2014, opendemocracy.net/en/opendemocracyuk/my-environmentalism-will-be-intersectional-or-it-will-be-bullshit.

36. Leah Thomas (@greengirlleah), "Social Justice Cannot Wait," Instagram, May 28, 2020, instagram.com/p/CAvaxdRJRxu.

37. Crenshaw, "Mapping the Margins," 1296.

38. Bullard, Miller-Travis, and Morton are quoted in Cameron Oglesby, "The Generational Rift over 'Intersectional Environmentalism': Environmental Justice Gets a Gen Z Makeover," *Grist* (blog), February 10, 2021, grist.org/justice/intersectional-environmentalism-justice-language. Oglesby also records Thomas's response to the critique of her commercial engagements: "If people are listening to me for whatever reason—and I think a lot of it has to do with privilege, with me having lighter skin—how [else] can I direct them to something that benefits others?"

39. I derive this formulation from Frederick Douglass, who observed in a lecture, "Poets, prophets and reformers are all picture-makers. They see what ought to be by the reflection of what is, and endeavor to remove the contradiction" ("Pictures and Progress," December 3, 1861).

40. Wendy Hui Kyong Chun, *Updating to Remain the Same: Habitual New Media* (Cambridge, Mass.: MIT Press, 2016), 44.

41. Rebecca Solnit, *Infinite City: A San Francisco Atlas* (Berkeley: University of California Press, 2010), 51–56.

42. Holmes's *Petropolis* appeared at http://environmentalobservatory.net/Petropolis/map.

43. Claire Reddleman, *Cartographic Abstraction in Contemporary Art: Seeing with Maps* (London: Taylor & Francis, 2017).

44. Anita Hill, "Anita Hill in conversation with Mark Bradford," in *Mark Bradford* (London: Phaidon, 2018): 28.

45. Hill, 25.

46. Jesse J. Holland, "Hundreds of Black Deaths in 1919 are Being Remembered," Associated Press News, July 23, 2019, apnews.com/article/arkansas-ar-state-wire-chicago-red-summer-us-news-d7830d62a99f4cdd8f0a0d08cefb92c5.

47. Hill, "Anita Hill in conversation with Mark Bradford," 27.

48. Scott Ellsworth, *The Ground Breaking: An American City and Its Search for Justice* (Boston: Dutton, 2021), 42–45.

49. See, for instance, Chris M. Messer, Thomas E. Shriver, and Alison E. Adams, "The Destruction of Black Wall Street: Tulsa's 1921 Riot and the Eradication of Accumulated Wealth," *The American Journal of Economics and Sociology* 77, no. 3–4 (2018): 789–819.

50. Dreisen Heath, "The Case for Reparations in Tulsa, Oklahoma: A Human Rights Argument," Human Rights Watch, May 29, 2020, hrw.org/news/2020/05/29/case-reparations-tulsa-oklahoma.

51. Heath, "Case for Reparations."

52. George Yancy, "Robin D.G. Kelley: The Tulsa Race Massacre Went Way Beyond 'Black Wall Street'" (interview), *Truthout,* June 1, 2021, truthout.org/articles/robin-kelley-business-interests-fomented-tulsa-massacre-as-pretext-to-take-land.

53. Eric Foner uses these terms in a review of the book by Ellsworth,

building on Gore Vidal's notion of the "United States of Amnesia"; see Foner, "United States of Amnesia," *London Review of Books* 43, no. 17, (2021), lrb.co.uk /the-paper/v43/n17/eric-foner/united-states-of-amnesia.

54. Whyte included the chart in the presentation "It's Too Late for Indigenous Justice: Problems with Climate Change Advocacy." The subsequent article is Kyle Powys Whyte, "Too Late for Indigenous Climate Justice: Ecological and Relational Tipping Points," *WIREs Climate Change* 11, no. 1 (2020): e603, doi.org/10.1002/wcc.603.

55. Emilee Gilpin, "Urgency in Climate Change Advocacy is Backfiring, Says Citizen Potawatomi Nation Scientist," *National Observer,* February 15, 2019, nationalobserver.com/2019/02/15/news/urgency-climate-change-advocacy -backfiring-says-citizen-potawatomi-nation-scientist.

56. Kyle Whyte, "Indigenous Climate Change Studies: Indigenizing Futures, Decolonizing the Anthropocene," *English Language Notes* 55, no. 1–2 (2017): 159.

57. I build on the observations of Karen Barad, who suggests that visual representations are "not (more or less faithful) pictures of what is," but instead "productive evocations, provocations, and generative material articulations or reconfigurings of what is and what is possible." Karen Barad, *Meeting the Universe Halfway: Quantum Physics and the Entanglement of Matter and Meaning* (Durham, N.C,: Duke University Press, 2007), 389.

58. *Environmental Justice Atlas,* https://ejatlas.org/about.

59. Jordan Engel, *Decolonial Atlas,* https://decolonialatlas.wordpress.com /2018/01/20/minneapolis-st-paul-in-dakota-and-ojibwe.

60. Engel, *Decolonial Atlas,* https://decolonialatlas.wordpress.com/2016/09 /07/dakota-access-pipeline-indigenous-protest-map.

61. Engel, *Decolonial Atlas,* https://decolonialatlas.wordpress.com/2017/03 /21/the-border-la-frontera.

62. Native Land project, native-land.ca.

63. Josh On, www.theyrule.net.

64. Josh On, "From They Rule to We Rule: Art and Activism," *Ars Electronica,* 2002, web.archive.org/web/20060207011251/http://www.aec.at/en/archives /festival_archive/festival_catalogs/festival_artikel.asp?iProjectID=11803 .

65. Mark B. N. Hansen, "New Media," in *Critical Terms for Media Studies,* ed. Mark B. N. Hansen and W. J. T. Mitchell (Chicago: University of Chicago Press, 2010), 174. Also see *New Media: 1740–1915,* ed. Lisa Gitelman and Geoffrey B. Pingree (Cambridge, Mass.: MIT Press, 2003).

66. Chloe Ahmann, "'It's Exhausting to Create an Event Out of Nothing': Slow Violence and the Manipulation of Time," *Cultural Anthropology* 33, no. 1 (2018): 142.

67. Ahmann, 164–65 (italics original).

68. Ahmann, 156.

69. Ahmann, 156, 155.

70. Ahmann, 154.

71. Ahmann, 155.

72. Roger Silverstone, *Why Study the Media* (Thousand Oaks, Calif.: SAGE, 1999), 143.

73. See *A Dictionary of Media and Communication,* ed. Daniel Chandler and Rob Munday, 3rd ed. (Oxford: Oxford University Press, 2020), 113–14.

74. See *The SAGE Handbook of Media Processes and Effects,* ed. Mary Beth Oliver and Robin L. Nabi (Thousand Oaks, Calif.: SAGE, 2009), 15.

75. David Roberts, *Global Warming, Politics, and the Media* (Washington, D.C.: Island, 2013).

76. See Lauren Pezzullo, "Eco-Warrior Profile: @climemechange Tackles Climate Change One Meme at a Time," *The Oxygen Project* (blog), July 11, 2020, theoxygenproject.com/post/eco-warrior-profile-climemechange-tackles-climate-change-one-meme-at-a-time, and Michael Elizabeth Sakas, "Memes About Climate Change Help Teens Laugh about Their Fears. Can They Also Get Them To Act?," CPR News, March 5, 2020, cpr.org/2020/03/05/memes-about-climate-change-help-teens-laugh-about-their-fears-can-they-also-get-them-to-act.

77. For a fact-check of this comparative assembly, see Angelo Fichera, "Manipulated Time Cover on Climate Recirculates," *FactCheck.org,* May 22, 2019, factcheck.org/2019/05/manipulated-time-cover-on-climate-recirculates.

78. That mockery took place in comments on Reddit and the Daily Caller, among other places. See twitter.com/aurabogado/status/784257358234996736, reddit.com/r/dankmemes/comments/57igbb/environmental_racism, and dailycaller.com/2016/10/07/sjw-blames-hurricane-matthew-deaths-on-environmental-racism.

79. Cameron Wilson, "Climate Deniers Are Making Memes About the Coronavirus to Argue Against Urgent Climate Action," *BuzzFeed,* April 1, 2020, buzzfeed.com/cameronwilson/right-wing-coronavirus-climate-change-memes-denier.

80. Tricia Hershey, *The Nap Ministry,* thenapministry.wordpress.com/about.

81. Patrise Cullors, "Q&A: Nap Ministry's Tricia Hersey talks rest and racial justice," *Prism,* September 3, 2020, prismreports.org/2020/09/03/qa-nap-ministrys-tricia-hersey-talks-rest-and-racial-justice.

82. Aliyyah Abdur-Rahman and Simone Browne, "Capture, Illegibility, Necessity: A Conversation on Black Privacy," *The Black Scholar* 51, no. 1 (2001): 71.

83. Zeynep Tufekci, *Twitter and Tear Gas: The Power and Fragility of Networked Protest* (New Haven, Conn.: Yale University Press), xiii.

84. Jonathan Crary, *24/7: Late Capitalism and the Ends of Sleep* (New York: Verso, 2013), 128.

85. @thenapministry, September 29, 2021, instagram.com/p/CUadcebFoR3.

86. Timothy Morton, twitter.com/the_eco_thought/status/1155643180135657473.

87. Naya Jones, "Dying to Eat? Black Food Geographies of Slow Violence and Resilience," *ACME: An International Journal of Critical Geographies* 18, no. 5 (2019): 1076–99, at 1082, 1084.

88. Jones, 1081. For further discussion of Blackness, surveillance, and sousveillance, see Simone Browne, *Dark Matters: On the Surveillance of Blackness* (Durham: Duke University Press, 2015).

89. Jones, "Dying to Eat?," 1077.

90. Christian and Dowler, "Slow and Fast Violence," 1072.
91. Jones, "Dying to Eat?," 1092.

Conclusion

1. Ryan M. Milner and Whitney Phillips refer to forms of collective and participatory communication via the internet as frequently ambivalent, not as in "I don't have an opinion either way," but the "tension, and often fraught tension, between opposites" (*The Ambivalent Internet: Mischief, Oddity, and Antagonism Online* [Malden, Mass.: Polity, 2017], 10).

2. Mimi Ọnụọha, *Us, Aggregated 3.0* (2019), mimionuoha.com/us-aggregated-3.

3. Lisa Nakamura, *Cybertypes: Race, Ethnicity, and Identity on the Internet* (New York: Routledge, 2002), 3.

4. Wendy Hui Kyong Chun demonstrates (and critiques) the way recommender systems collect "individuals and items" into these neighborhoods through a logic of homophily, doing so to "serve the interests of those who deploy them" (*Discriminating Data: Correlation, Neighborhoods, and the New Politics of Recognition* [Cambridge, Mass.: MIT Press, 2021], 158).

5. Mark Danner, "Be Ready to Fight," *The New York Review of Books,* February 11, 2021, nybooks.com/articles/2021/02/11/stupid-coup-be-ready-to-fight-capitol-riot.

6. Luke Mogelson, "Among the Insurrectionists," *The New Yorker,* January 25, 2021, newyorker.com/magazine/2021/01/25/among-the-insurrectionists.

7. Danner, "Be Ready to Fight" (italics original).

8. Danner.

9. Danner.

10. Lois Beckett and Vivian Ho, "'She Was Deep into It': Ashli Babbitt, Killed in Capitol Riot, was Devoted Conspiracy Theorist," *The Guardian,* January 9, 2021, theguardian.com/us-news/2021/jan/09/ashli-babbitt-capitol-mob-trump-qanon-conspiracy-theory.

11. Mogleson, "Among the Insurrectionists" (italics original).

12. Tim Elfrink, "He Wore a QAnon Shirt While Chasing Police on Jan. 6. Now He Says He Was Deceived by 'a Pack of Lies,'" *Washington Post,* June 8, 2021, washingtonpost.com/nation/2021/06/08/douglas-jensen-qanon-conspiracy.

13. Danner, "Be Ready to Fight."

14. Peter Galison, *Einstein's Clocks, Poincaré's Maps: Empires of Time* (New York: W. W. Norton & Company, 2003), 39–40.

15. Galison, 40.

16. Jason Frank, *The Democratic Sublime: On Aesthetics and Popular Assembly* (Oxford: Oxford University Press, 2021), 40.

17. I draw these figures and the quotations below from Mark Danner, "Reality Rebellion," *The New York Review of Books,* July 1, 2021, markdanner.com/2021/06/03/reality-rebellion.

18. Danner, "Reality Rebellion." "To millions of Americans the coup of January 6 represented direct and justified action," Danner explains. "Many of them believe that the Constitution, in its provision for citizens 'to keep

and bear arms,' provides for precisely this kind of violent rebellion against a tyrannical government."

19. Toni Morrison, "No Place for Self-Pity, No Room for Fear," *The Nation,* March 23, 2015, thenation.com/article/archive/no-place-self-pity-no-room-fear.

20. Toni Morrison, "Making America White Again," *New Yorker,* November 14, 2016, newyorker.com/magazine/2016/11/21/making-america-white-again.

21. Morrison, "No Place for Self-Pity, No Room for Fear."

22. Olivia Laing, *Funny Weather: Art in an Emergency* (New York: Norton, 2020), 3.

23. Laing, 115.

24. Eve Kosofsky Sedgwick, *Touching Feeling: Affect, Pedagogy, Performativity* (Durham, N.C.: Duke University Press, 2003), 139.

25. Laing, *Funny Weather,* 4.

26. Laing, 115.

27. Sedgwick, *Touching Feeling,* 146.

28. Laing, *Funny Weather,* 4.

29. Judith Butler, "What Value Do the Humanities Have?," McGill University Honorary Doctorate Address, Montreal, May 30, 2013, youtube.com/watch?v=lFlGS56iOAg.

Index

Page numbers in italics refer to illustrations.

Abdur-Rahman, Aliyyah, 249
#ablackhistoryofart, 67, *70,* 72
ableism, 43
#abortion, 158
abstraction, 1, 58, 94, 123, 206, 219, 257, 267, 290n8; in Bradford's work, 202, 229, 231–33; and critical opalescence, 266; and data visualization, 66; and feminist art, 12
#absurd, 158
Act for the Government and Protection of Indians (1850), 120
activism, 1–2, 11, 35, 40, 58, 100, 168, 170, 222, 225–26, 246; art-centered, 39; and comparative assembly, 5; environmental, 36, 77, 132, 213–17, 229, 241–43, 307n14; and hashtags, 14; Indigenous, 237; museum-directed, 115; and plural reading, 22; response to disasters, 17. *See also* climate justice; environmentalism; environmental justice; feminism
ACT UP, 217
"Adam and Eve" meme, 150
Adorno, Theodor, 192
advertising, 81, 106, 154, 165, 174, 177, 268
aesthetic assembly, 9, 11, 15, *70,* 73, 93, 96, 100, 106, 109, 127–28
affordances, 39, 47, 59, 61, 100, 104, 106, 189
Africa, 60, 66, 236, 277n4
Agbogbloshie, 249
agencement, 31, 124
Age of Sharing, The, 28
Agyemang, Brianna, 201
Ahmann, Chloe, 241–42, 248, 251
@aidenarata, 141
AIDS, 82, 221, 229–30
Akinkugbe, Alayo, 67, *70,* 72. *See also* #ablackhistoryofart
Alabama: Emelle, 120
Alaska, 35–36
Alaska Resources Library and Information Services (ARLIS), 36–37, *37, Plate 2*
algorithmic violence, 222
algorithms, 15, 35, 57, 60, *113,* 128, 142, 188, 261–62, 268, 302n28; algorithmic violence, 222; crime-prediction, 15; mutated search, 80; of oppression, 156; and social media, 52
allegory, 12, 60–61, 93–94, 122, 259, 279n11
@allisonholkerboss, *25*
Altman, Rick, 38, 45–46, 55, 59, 63
Altmann, Kari: *Garden Club,* 80–81, *81*
alt-right, 167, 169. *See also* America Firsters; QAnon; Trump, Donald
Amazon (region), 252
ambivalence, 22, 27, 41, 215, 226, 259, 312n1
America Firsters, 264. *See also* alt-right; extremism; misogyny; racism; white supremacy
American National Standards Institute, 101
Among Us, 136
Anable, Aubrey, 283n61

anachronism, 20, 117
analogy, 8, 32, 133, 218, 243, 257, 262, 265, 269; and assembly-based art, 39; and Bosch's work, 105–6; and disasters, 181, 188, 196; and Fontcuberta's work, 111–15; and Fosso's work, 61; and intersectionality, 223; and memes, 138, 141, 159, 169, 174, 177; and plural reading, 19–20, 31, 51; and Postcommodity's work, 108–10; and *Specters of Disruption*, 119. *See also* disanalogy
Andrews, Larry: *OwnerBuilt*, 302n31
angel of history, 40, 208–10
Anishinaabe, 244
Ansell, David, 308n29
Anthropocene, 234, 249
anthropology, 220
anti-Blackness, 266
Anti-Defamation League, 167
anti-imperialism, 27
ApachePunk, 237
apartheid, 43, 101. *See also* Jim Crow
appropriation, 39, 87–88, 148–49, 167–68, 172–73, 208, 290n65, 298n53
Aptekar, Ken: *Walter Benjamin is looking*, 209–10, *210*
Arata, Aiden. *See* @aidenarata
archival art, 99, 305n70
archives, 12, 98–99, 123, 148, 198, 270; archive noise, 112, 115; digital, 14, 17, 35–36, 52, 57, 146, 179, 181, 189–90, 194, 273; and disasters, 17, 20, 74–77, *78–79*, 179–81, 187–94, 202–7, 231; emergent archiving, 20, 202–7; participatory, 4, 74, 179–82, 189
Aristotle, 277n5, 283n55, 287n23
Arizona, 268; Douglas, 108; Nogales, *86*
Armstrong, Taylor, 5
Arnett, Paul, 122
arrangement, 38, *78–79*, 80, 221, 257, 261, 263, 267, 280n22, 284n79, 290n9; and algorithms, 52, 57; and art, 94–96, 98, 100–101, 291n16; and assembly, 3–4, 6, 9, 34–35, 64; and cognitive assemblages, 32; and disasters, 181, 187–89, 191, 195, 203, 209; and expression, 59; and intersectionality, 223, 239; in Justesen's work, 73–74; Langer on, 99; and the lens, 28–30; and memes, 144, 146, 148, 157, 160, 162, 165, 174, 176; in Postcommodity's work, 108–9; rearrangement, 28, 63, 74, 105, 157, 176, 209, 258–59; and *Specters of Disruption*, 115–16, 119, 125; and Strike MoMA, 123, 126; and violence, 218, 223, 225–26, 232, 238–39, 249; and *Well Now WTF?*, 116–17
Art + Feminism, 12
art galleries, 9, 56, 73, 93
art history, 2, 16–17, 20, 39, 67, 93, 214
artificial intelligence (AI), 15, 32, 56, 60, 63
Asawa, Ruth, 119
assemblage (concept), 45, 60, 75, 106, 190, 229, 265, 284n80, 291n13; and Deleuze/Guattari, 31–32, 36, 124, 218, 284n85; in premodern time tables, 12
assemblage (in art), 15, 28, 31–36, 98–99; in Dial's work, 120, 122; in Nagel's work, 293n59; in *Well Now WTF?*, 124; in Xu's work, 52
assembly, definition, 1, 3–4, 45–64
Atlanta University, 65
Atlantic (whaling vessel), *118*, 119
aura, 82
Australia, 245
avant-garde art, 117
Azoulay, Ariella Aïsha, 26, 29, 37, 125

Babbitt, Ashli, 264
Back the Blue, 52
Bailar, Schuyler (@pinkmantaray), 152, *153*
Bal, Mieke, 20
Barad, Karen, 44

Barthes, Roland, 281n42
Battle-Baptiste, Whitney, 66
Battle of Waterloo (1815), 4
Bauhaus, 66
Beeple (Michael Joseph Winkelmann): *Everydays: The First 5,000 Days,* 101
Being Libertarian, LLC, *246*
Belting, Hans, 102–3
Benjamin, Ruha, 15
Benjamin, Walter, 40, 82, 192, 208–11
Bennett, Jane, 32
Beyoncé, 208
Bibler, Michael P., 195
Biden, Joe, 264, 267
"Big Chungus" meme, 136
Big Data, 158
Bing (search engine), 17, 47, *48, 216*
#bitcoin, 158
Black Codes, 66, 71
black holes, 23, *24*
Black Lives Matter, 52, 183, 202, 217, 224
#BlackLivesMatter, 52–53, *53,* 201
Blackness, 67, 138, 157; distributed, 280n30; of meme movement, 137, 161. *See also* anti-Blackness
#BlackoutTuesday, 201
Black Wall Street, 232
Blitzer, Wolf, 180
#BLM, 159
blockchain, 101, 277n3
Boebert, Lauren, 263
Bogado, Aura, 245
Bogost, Ian, 19
Bonnard, Pierre, 291n16
border art, 84, 87
Border Spaces: Visualizing the U.S.–Mexico Frontera, 83–84
Borges, Jorge Luis, 282n45
Bosch, Hieronymus: *The Garden of Earthly Delights,* 9, 27, 101–7, *107, Plate 7*
@boschbot, 106, *107*
Bouie, Jamelle, 183
Bourgeois, Louise: *10 AM IS WHEN YOU COME TO ME,* 21–22, *Plate 1*
Bourgois, Philipe, 220
Bradford, Mark, 183; *Details,* 305n73; *Finding Barry,* 229–30, *230*; *Help Us,* 305n71; *Mississippi Gottdam,* 202–4, *204,* 305n73; *Mithra,* 203, *205*; *150 Portrait Tone,* 305n71; *Paris is Burning,* 305n71; *Scorched Earth,* 229–33, *Plate 11*
Braque, Georges, 96
Brave Fighter of Sun Fighbird, 138
Brenna, Amanda, 137
bricolage, 15, 98
Brinkley, Douglas, 182
Brock, André, Jr., 280n30
Browne, Simone, 249
#BTSFESTA2019, 159
@budomojo, *144*
Bullar, Robert, 225
Bundy, Kenya, 24
Burke, Tarana, 14. *See also* #MeToo
Bush, George W., 179, 182, 268, 300n4
Butler, Judith, 41; on gender, 149–51; on generativity, 302n30; on popular assembly, 33, 36; on sensate democracy, 270

cabinet of curiosities, 117
California, 34, 120, *230*; Bay Area, 116, 126, 226–28; San Francisco, 115, 119, 126, 226
Cameroon, 60
Campt, Tina, 20, 283n69
Canada, 108
capitalism, 140, 165, 171–72, 216, 226, 243, 246–47, 251; racial, 232; surveillance, 156
Capitol building, 38, 262–66, 268, 270. *See also* January 6 Capitol siege (2021)
Capitol Police, 264
capture, 158
Carbfix, 130, 132
carbonization, 39, 129–32
Carson, Anne: *Nox,* 111
Carson, Rachel, 221; *Silent Spring,* 217–18, 307n13

cartographic abstraction, 229
Chacon, Raven, 108. *See also* Postcommodity
chaotic enumeration, 12
Charters of Freedom, 270
Cheng, Ian: *BOB (Bag of Beliefs),* 128
China, 49, 51, 131
Chomsky, Noam, 302n28
Christian, Jenna Marie, 214, 254
Christie's, 101
Chun, Wendy Hui Kyong, 124, 157–58, 226, 312n4
Chute, Hillary, 197–98
#CiteBlackWomen, 14
citizen witnessing, 192
civil contract of photography, 37
Civil War (U.S.), 65
classification, 39, 63, 125, 147–49, 177
climate change, 17, 77, 131–32, 171, 213, 218, 234, 243, 252; and memetic drip, 30, 248–49; and social media, 77, 243, *245*
#climatechange, 158
climate justice, 77, 82, 132, 171
@climemechange, 243, *245,* 249
CNN, 180
Cockerell, Charles Robert, 20
Cocks, Joan, 221–22
Cocopah, 236
cognitive assemblage, 32, 56
Cohen, Kris, 283n61
Cole, Thomas, 122; *Prometheus Bound,* 120–21, *121*
collage, 15–16, 45, 98–99, 258, 291n13, 302n31
Collins, Keith, *Plate 10*
colonialism/imperialism, 26–27, 34, 88, 234, 249, 267; and data visualization, 65–66, 71; and mapping, 85, *86,* 226–28, 236–38; and Mexico–U.S. border, 84, 109–10; and *Specters of Disruption,* 120, 126. *See also* decolonization
Colorado, 263
comics, 85, 137, 146, 167, 181, 183–89, 197–204, 207
"coming ice age" meme, 244
comparison, 2, 34, 66, 71, 258, 281n42, 285n99, 311n77; comparative assembly, *7,* 8, 63, 85, 284n85; deceptive, 17, 262; and disasters, 179, 183, 190; and environmentalism, 228, 233–34, 243–44; and mapping, 85, *86*; and memes, 137, 159; and plural reading, 19–20; and violence, 221; viral, 5–6, 11, 31, 40
computer art, 98
concept mapping, 146
conceptual lenses, 28–31, 223, 259
conceptual reassembly, 40, 220–26, 233, 241, 253
configuration, 27, 61, 63–64, 222, 262, 265, 270, 279n12; and art, 9–10, 21, 39, 50, 73, 95–103, 108–9, 117–22, 126, *129*; and assembly, 3, 17, 28, 31, 38, 56, 87, 257–59; definition, 57–59; and disasters, 40, 181, *185,* 188, 192–93, 197–98, 207–8; and environmentalism, 77, 217, 228, 249–50; ephemeral, 36; and in-person gatherings, 35; and mapping, 228, 230–31, 233, 238–40; and memes, 140, 146, 161, 163, 170, 173–77; and social media, *25,* 249–50
constellation, 12, 64, 75, 101, 104, 112, 129, 148, 160–61, 258; definition, 192
Constituent Museum, The, 127
constituents, 17, 87–88, 231, 239, 257–58; and art, 10, 73, 80–82, 92–96, 101, 105–32, *118, 119, 129*; and assembly, 5–6, 38, 46–52, 55–64, 77; definition, 4; and disasters, 187, 205–6, 208; and distributed assembly, 14–15; and environmentalism, 35, 128, 131–32, 216–17, 228, 250; and January 6, 2021, siege, 266–68; and memes, 140–42, 146, 160, 162, 170, 174–77; and plural reading, 22

contemporary art, 92, 98, 100, 104
content creation/creators, 1, 245, 250
continuum of violence, 220, 225, 233, 240, 307n19
contradiction, 5, 33, 64, 73, 79, 114, 120, 125, 171, 176, 228, 309n39; and assembly, 85; and realism, 102
conversation, 4, 14, 17, 42, 71, 181, 221, 233, 237; and art, 93, 109–12, 116, 128; and assembly, 34, 37, 77; and disasters, 16, *78–79*, 198, 201; and environmentalism, 252; and memes, 39, 139, 162–65
Cook, Bernie, 187, 190
Cooke, Lynne, 91, 129
Copeland, Huey, 115–16
counter-memes, 159–61, 168, 170–71, 208
Covid-19 pandemic, 116–17, 124, 230, 257
Crary, Jonathan, 152, 251
Cree, 244
Crenshaw, Kimberlé, 223–24, 233, 239
crime production, 15
Crimp, Douglas, 278n8
critical opalescence, 41, 266
critical typology, 9, 39, 92–94, 98, 100, 106, 111, 191, 219, 241, 291n21
cryptocurrency, 135
Cubism, 99
cultural forms, 1–2, 117, 257–58, 262, 267, 278n8; and assembly, 15, 17, 35, 38, 44–46, 55, 59, 88, 161, 287n16; definition, 3–4, 279n11; and disasters, 181, 186–87; and memes, 172–73, 174, 176; mixtures of, 231; and plural reading, 22, 28, 259; and representation, 277n5; and slow violence, 215, 217. *See also* expressive strategies
cultural production, 2, 16, 19, 39, 57, 88, 257
curation, 58, 147, 258; and activism, 39, 195; and art, 82, 93, 98, 100, 115–17; and assembly, 14, 56, 60; curators, 9, 11, 56, 67, 82, 93, 98, 100, 115–19, 195; and disasters, 186, 195; horizontal, *78–79*; and mapping, 228, 235
Curtis, Layla, 229

Dadaism, 98
Daily Caller, 311n78
Daily Kos, 179
Dakota Wind, 236
Daniel, Sharon, 99
Danner, Mark, 267–68, 312n18
Danth's Law, 160
dark web, 17, 47–49, 51, 57
dark web memes, 49, 51, 57
databases, 45, 75, 80, 100–102, 173, 187, 204, 258–59; aesthetics of, 99; and data exhaust, 177; Manovich on, 2, 15, 172, 278n6; narratives of, 16, 98, 104; warm, 11, 58
data bodies, 58
data exhaust, 177
datasets, 15
Davey, Jacob, 168
Davis, Douglas: *The World's First Collaborative Sentence*, 128
Dawdy, Shannon Lee, 190, 194
Dawkins, Richard, 136, 159, 298n53
Day, Ronald E., 154, 157–58, 176
DDT, 218, 307n14
Dean, Aria, 157, 163
Dean, Carolyn, 2, 278n7
death by indirection, 221
decarbonization, 39, 132
@decolonialatlas, *86*
decolonization, 94, 214, 238, 244, 277n5; *The Decolonial Atlas*, 85, *86*, 236–38, 243
decontextualization, 26
deep web, 47, *48*
DeLanda, Manuel, 31, 34, 36, 124
de la Torre, Milagros: *Nocturnes II*, 9–11, *10–11*; *Untitled (Poland)*, 96, *97*
Deleuze, Gilles, 31, 34, 36, 124, 201, 305n68
Deloria, Philip J., 244

de Maio, Fernando, 308n29
Denis, Maurice, 93–94, 132
Denmark, 73
Derrida, Jacques, 221
deterritorialization, 34, 124–26, 226
de Young Museum: *Specters of Disruption,* 115–22, 125–26
Dial, Thornton: *New Light,* 120–22
digital art, 100
digital blackface, 142
digital media, 2, 154, 159
digital studies, 17
D'Ignazio, Catherine, 42–43
Dignity + Debt, 67, 72
Dillon, Lindsey, 215
disanalogy, 8, 19, 138
disasters, 30, 35, 45, 55, 60, 102–3, 105, 170, 270; and archives, 17, 20, 74–79, *78–79,* 179–81, 187–94, 202–7, 231; and distributed assembly, 40, 74, 77, 190, 198, *206,* 208; and generative assembly, *6,* 40, 179–211, 302n31; and memetic drip, 248; and methodology of book, 42–43; and slow violence, 213–14, 218–19, 252; and social media, *78–79,* 179, 187. *See also* Hurricane Digital Memory Bank (HDMB); Hurricane Katrina; Japan Disasters Digital Archive (JDA)
Discord (platform), 67, 168
disinformation, 3, 116, 217, 262
disruption, 16, 51, 99, 115–28, 170, 186, 188, 195, 236, 291n17
distant reading, 281n42
"distracted boyfriend" meme, 140, 147
distributed assembly, 82, 85, 128, 217, 222, 239; definition, 14–15; and disasters, 40, 74, 77, 190, 198, *206,* 208; hyper-, 39, 158, 160–61, 163–65, 167, 169, 171, 173, 208; and memes, 161, 164, 168
distributed disassembly, 168–71, 182–83, 262, 267
Domino Sugar Refining Plant, 210
Douglass, Frederick, 309n39
Dowler, Lorraine, 214, 254
drip (memetic), 30, 40, 240–52
drive, 12, 77, 87, 92, 112, 133, 154, 156, 161, 214, 239; artistic, 94, 109; to assemble, 33, 46, 59–65, 71, 109, 111, 174, 187, 189, 257, 259, 287n16; for data, 58, 235; and elemental witnessing, 194–95; for empire, 226; for justice, 34, 254; narrative, 38, 59, 63; for profit, 132, 177, 263; and violence, 240
drop-scenes, 20
Du Bois, W. E. B., 65–68, 71–72, 74, 207
#DuBoisChallenge, 72
dustin3000: "Racism," *6, 180*
Dutch still life painting, 21

Eco, Umberto, 12, 280n27
Ecology of Attention, The, 28
EcoTok (@eco_tok), 245, *247,* 250
Eglash, Ron, 302n28
8chan, 67
8kun, 67
Eisenstein, Sergei, 96, 291n17
El Anatsui: *Hovor II,* 117, 119
elemental witness, 191–97, 203, 207
El Escorial, 105
Ellsworth, Scott, 231
emergent archiving, 20, 202–7
emojis, 24, 26, 67, 151, 161, 167, 174–76
Engel, Jordan: *The Decolonial Atlas,* 85, *86,* 236–38, 243; "Tribes Spanning the U.S.–Mexico Border," 236
England, 63
environmentalism, 3, 29–30, 36, 42, 44, 132, 213, 307n14; and generativity, 77, 218; intersectional, 224–25, 243–44, *244,* 245, 308n35; and mapping, 226–35; and performativity, 77, 216–17, *216*; and slow violence, 214–21, 249–51; and social media, 17, 215, 240–55
environmental justice, 3, 30, 42, 44, 225, 235
Environmental Justice Atlas, 235

Environmental Protection Agency: Superfund sites, *227,* 228
environmental racism, 171, 225, 245, 248
Enwezor, Okwui, 60, 191
ephemerality, 10, 14, 36, 39, 50, 109, 254
Erikson, Erik, 302n28
ethnography, 27
Eurocentrism, 2
Europe, 2, 17, 27, 33, 45, 95, 149, 210, 213, 258
Evangelatou, Maria, 280n24
everyday violence, 221
expanded internet art, 80, 82–83
experimentation, 1, 12, 28, 76, 91, 110, 159, 216
Exposition Universelle (1900), 65–66, *68,* 71
expressive folksonomy, 31, 183, 205; and memes, 19–20, 39, 140–59, 167, 173, 208
expressive strategies, 1–2, 22, 28, 34, 40, 45, 61, 88, 91, 94, 100, 103, 215–16, 255, 258. *See also* cultural forms
extremism, 168. *See also* alt-right; America Firsters; January 6 Capitol siege (2021); QAnon; Trump, Donald; Unite the Right rally (2017); white supremacy
ExxonMobil, 239
Exxon Valdez oil spill, 35–36, *Plate 2*

Facebook/Meta, 67, 76, 140, *155,* 183, 239, *246,* 264
family resemblances, 17–22, 26, 99, 108, 117, 143, 162, 168, 259, 283n55
Farge, Arlette, 74–75, 128
Farmer, Paul, 221
"fashion through the decades" meme, 143, *145*
fast violence, 252–53
Fauvism, 93
Federal Emergency Management Agency (FEMA), 182, 200
feminism, 21, 167, 208, 214; attacks on, 150, 167; feminist art, 12–14, 20, 73; and intersectionality, 223–24
Fernández López, Olga, 119
filtering, 29, 75, 93, 99, 116, 235
firstness, 10, 280n20
F.I.S.H. (Frustrated Independent Fish Harvesters), 35–37, *37*
Flickr, *6,* 36–37, *37,* 179, 183, 192, 194, 304n46, *Plate 2*
Floyd, George, 42, 52, 201, 224
folklore, 39, 139, 161–64
folksonomy. *See* expressive folksonomy
Foner, Eric, 233, 309n53
Fontcuberta, Joan: Googlegrams, 111–14, *113, 114*
Fosso, Samuel: *SIXSIXSIX,* 60–61, *Plates 4–5*
foundational violence, 221
4chan, 67, 150, 167, 299n68
Fraenger, Wilhelm, 102
Frank, Jason, 33
Franklin, Benjamin, 140
Frascari, Marco, 278n8
Frege, Gottlob, *18*
Friedman, Samantha, 91
Fukushima Daiichi Nuclear Power Plant, 74
Furie, Matt, 137, 167. *See also* Pepe the frog memes

Galison, Peter, 265–66
Gallagher, Erin, 167
Gallenkuş, Uğur, 5, *7,* 22
Galloway, Alex: *Starrynight,* 101
Galtung, Johan, 221
games, 18–19, 81, 136, 167, 168
Ganesh, Chitra: *How Do You See the Disappeared? A Warm Database,* 58. *See also* Rhizome
Gates, Theaster, 71; *But to Be a Poor Race,* 66
General Motors, 223
generative assembly, 181, 215, 231–32, 254; and disasters, *6,* 40, 179–211, 302n31

generativity, 61, 64, 72, 88, 177, 181, 258, 302n30, 308n29; and archives, *79*, 105; and art, 11, 96, 103, 109–10, 113–14, 122, 124, 277n3; and critical opalescence, 270; definition, 302n28; and environmentalism, 77, 218; and intersectionality, 223–24; and memes, 160; and plural reading, 128; in psychology, 302n28
gender, 3, 15, 149–52, 157, 213, 233, 245; and methodology of book, 42–43
genocide, 119–20, 228
Gen Z, 161
GeoCities, 64
George Mason University: Roy Rosenzweig Center for History and New Media, *180*. *See also* Hurricane Digital Memory Bank (HDMB)
Georgia, 66, 68; Atlanta, 65, 252, 263
Germany: Berlin, 105
gestalt, 59
#GetThatBread, 159
Ghani, Mariam: *How Do You See the Disappeared? A Warm Database,* 58. *See also* Rhizome
GIFs, 23, 30, 77, 254–55, 257; and art, 23, 95, 104, 116–17, 122–24, 127; and memes, 141–42, 148, 151, 158, 167–68
Gilson, Étienne, 290n8
Github, 222
Godwin, Mike, 163, 168, 170; Godwin's Law, 159–60
Goerzen, Matt, 168–69
Gombrich, E. H., 9
Goodman, Eugene, 264
Google, 47, *48*, 205; Googlegrams (Fontcuberta), 111–14, *113*, *114*; images, 111, *114*, 156; reverse image search, 261
Gorovoy, Jerry, 21
Gqunta, Lungiswa: *Lawn 1*, 101, 105
Great Depression, 183
Green, Tyler, 305n71
Greenaway, Peter, 96
Greenberg, Clement, 281n41
Greenland, 252
Griffith, D. W., 291n17
Grootenboer, Hanneke, 9
Gropius Bau, 105
Guantánamo Bay Naval Base, 113–14, *114*
Guattari, Félix, 31, 34, 124, 201, 305n68
Gulf Coast, 180, 182–83, 185, 190. *See also* New Orleans

Haiti, 245
Halbwachs, Maurice, 190
Hamilton, Joe, 229; *Indirect Flights,* 98
Hammer Museum, 229
hands, 21–26, 283n69
Hansen, Mark B. N., 241
Hardt, Michael, 33
Hartman, Anne, 279n11
Hartman, Saidiya, 191
Harvard University: Reischauer Institute of Japan Studies, 74
hashtags, 14, 52, 57, 147, 158, 163, 165, 168, 201, 222, 240. *See also individual hashtags and platforms*
Havard, John O., 27
Hayles, N. Katherine, 4, 16, 32, 34, 56, 59–60, 173, 287n16
HBO, 194
Heath, Dreisen, 231
Hellisheiði Power Station, 130
Hernández Vélazquez, Yaiza, 127
Hershey, Tricia, 246–47. See also *Nap Ministry, The*
Hill, Anita, 229
"hippity hoppity get off my property" meme, 142–44, *144*, 147–48
@hippityhoppity2929, 143
historiographic experience, 191
Hitler, Adolf, 159
Höch, Hannah, 96
Holland, Faith: *Well Now WTF?,* 116–17, 123–24, 127, *Plate 9*
Hollenbach, Kate: *USER_IS_PRESENT,* 111

Hollywood, 143
Holmes, Brian: *Petropolis,* 228–29
Holzer, Jenny, 82–83, 161, 289n50; *Truisms,* 80–81
@holzertron, 82
Homer, Winslow: *The Gulf Stream,* 195
homonationalism, 32
Hong Kong, 137, 167
Horigan, Kate Parker, 186–87, 198, 301n19
Hoskins, Andrew, 190
Hoy, Meredith, 287n28
Huang Yong Ping: *The History of Chinese Art and A Concise History of Modern Painting Washed in a Washing Machine for Two Minutes,* 131
Hurricane Digital Memory Bank (HDMB), 179–80, *180,* 183, 190, 192, 205–7, *206,* 304n46
Hurricane Harvey, 179
Hurricane Katrina, 16, 52–53, 213, 218, 300n2, 305n71; and comparative assembly, 5–6, *6,* 179–80; and disaster media, 182–89; and distributed assembly, 40, 190, 198, 208; and elemental witness, 191–97, 203, 207; and emergent archiving, 202–7; and generative assembly, 179–82, 207–11, 302n31; and present blankness, 197–203, 207; and prevailing conditions, 40, 55, 182, 188–91, 197, 207. *See also* New Orleans
Hurricane Matthew, 245
hyperdistribution, 39, 158, 160–61, 163–65, 167, 169, 171, 173, 208
hyperobjects, 160
hyperpractice, 160

"I am not racist But" meme, *Plate 6*
iceberg-tier memes, 47–49
Iceland, 130; Reykjavík, 9, *129*; Viðey, 129
iconography, 17, 102, 108
Igbo, 60
Illinois: Chicago, 228
image macros, 67, 164, 257
image memes, 18, 47, 67, 69, 138, 142–43, 243, 250, 286n2
imagetext, 5, 171
immutable mobile, 286n9
incrementality, 242–43, 249–51. *See also* memetic drip
indexes, 93–94, 132, 154, 156–58, 176, 186, 219
Indian Removal Act (1830), 66
@indigenous_fememeisms, 244, 250–51
Indonesia, 252
infographics, 244
infotainment, 11
Íñigo Clavo, Maria, 119
injustice, 5, 27–28, 45, 156, 198, 213, 220, 224, 231, 235, 269
Instagram, *7, 244–45*; and art, 67, 82–83, *83,* 106; and memes, 141–42, *142, 153*; and police violence, 52–53, 224. *See also individual accounts and hashtags*
interpellation, 58
@intersectionalenvironmentalist, 243–*44*
intersectionality, 31, 51, 126, 138, 223, 226, 233, 239–41, 258; intersectional climate justice, 132, 171; intersectional environmentalism, 224–25, 243–44, *244,* 308n35
inventive vigilance, 41, 255
Iskin, Ruth, 12
"Is this a pigeon" meme, 138–40, 147
Italy: Milan, 91
@itsmayart, 143, *145*

Jackson, Lauren Michele, 137–38, 140, 142, 159, 161, 163
Jackson, Peter, 296n9
Jagoda, Patrick, 283n61
January 6 Capitol siege (2021), 38, 41, 169, 262–66, 268
Japan Disasters Digital Archive (JDA), 74, 76–79, *78–79*
Jay, Martin, 192
#JennyHolzer, 82, *83*

Jensen, Douglas, 264
Jet magazine, 66
Jim Crow, 66. *See also* apartheid
"jobs not mobs" meme, 163–65, 168, 262, *Plate 10*
Johnson, James, 187, 191
Johnson, Jasmine: *A Glossary of Gestures for Critical Discussion, 23*
Jones, Naya, 253–55
Joselit, David, 81, 105, 289n43
J. P. Morgan Chase & Co., 239
Justesen, Kirsten: *Circumstances,* 73–75, *74–75*

Kapur, Nick, 285n100
Katrina. *See* Hurricane Katrina
Katrina patina, 194
Keckler, Joseph, 105
Kelley, Robin D. G., 232–33
Kelly, Liz, 307n19
Kember, Sarah, 282n51, 287n28
Kenai River, 35–37, *37*
Kerry, John, 268
Kickapoo, 237
Kinder, Marsha, 279n10
Kirsch, Christopher: *Floodlines,* 190, 192–94, 304n46
Klee, Paul: *Angelus Novus,* 208–9
Klein, Lauren, 42–43
Know Your Meme, 140, 296n11
Krauss, Rosalind E., 91, 281n41
Kugle, Andrew (@AndrewJKugle), *166*
Kuleshov, Lev, 60–61
Kumeyaay, 236
Kunstkammer, 117

la frontera, 83–84, 236. *See also* Mexico–U.S. border
Laing, Olivia, 21, 128, 269–70
Lakota/Dakota, 236
Lambert-Beatty, Carrie, 216
land art, 109
Langer, Suzanne K., 95, 291n11
Latour, Bruno, 33, 286n9
Leckey, Mark, 80
Lee, Spike: *When the Levees Broke: A Requiem in Four Acts,* 52–54, *53, 54,* 302n31
Leonardo da Vinci: *The Last Supper,* 22
Lessing, Gotthold Ephraim, 281n41
Levine, Caroline, 279n12
Lialina, Olia: *My Boyfriend Came Back from the War,* 104–5, *105,* 292n33
liberalism, 167, 242, 262, 277n4
Lipan Apache, 237
Lippard, Lucy, 12
Lisjan Ohlone, 126
listening to images, 20
listicles, 11, 67
Little Bear, 141
Liu, Alan, 12
Los Angeles County Museum of Art: *The Allure of Matter: Material Art from China,* 131
lulz, 152, 158
Lüski, Aïm Düelle, 29

Mackern, Brian: *netart_latino database,* 101
macrocinema, 104
Malagamba-Ansótegui, Amelia, 87
Maldives, 215–16, *216*
Malraux, André, 20
Manovich, Lev, 2, 15, 98, 172–73, 292n33
mapping, 1, 38, 66, 75, 83–85, 87, 140, 149, 243, 258; and art, 10, 21, 80, 92, 98, 126; and colonialism/imperialism, 85, *86,* 226–28, 236–38; concept mapping, 146; and configuration, 228, 230–31, 233, 238–40; and disasters, 183, 205–7; and memes, 158, 248; thematic counter-mapping, 40, 226–41, 254
Marine, Brooke, 201
Marinetti, Filippo Tommaso, 96
Martin, Trayvon, 67, *69,* 71
Martinez, Cristóbal, 108. *See also* Postcommodity
Maryland: Baltimore, 241
material art, 131

material culture, 94, 119
Mayer, Aric, 191
McBride, Patrizia, 99
McCarthy, Jesse, 40, 209–11
McCulloch, Gretchen, 136
McGee, Barry, 229
McKittrick, Katherine, 253–54
McNeill, Lynne, 161
medium specificity, 17, 281n41
#meh, 158
Mehretu, Julie, 229
Mejia, John Paul, 225
meme coins, 172
meme generators, 8
memes, 2, 4, 14, 16, 27, 35, 45, 56, 63, 77, 179, 181–83, 257–58, 296n9, 298n53; "Adam and Eve," 150; and analogy, 138, 141, 159, 169, 174, 177; and arrangement, 117, 144, 146, 148, 157, 160, 162, 165, 174, 176; and art, 98, 104, 123, 133; and assembly, 171–77; "Big Chungus," 136; Blackness of meme movement, 137, 161; "coming ice age," 244; counter-memes, 159–61, 168, 170–71, 208; and cultural forms, 172–73, 174, 176; dark web, 49, 51, 57; definition, 135–38, 295n1, 298n55; "distracted boyfriend," 140, 147; and distributed assembly, 161, 164, 168; drip, 30, 248–49; and environmentalism, 30, 217, 243–52; and expressive folksonomy, 19–20, 39, 140–59, 167, 173, 208; "fashion through the decades," 143, *145*; "hippity hoppity get off my property," 142–44, *144*, 147–48; and hyperdistribution, 158–71; "I am not racist But," *Plate 6*; iceberg-tier, 47–49; image, 18, 47, 67, 69, 138, 142–43, 243, 250, 286n2; "Is this a pigeon," 138–40, 147; and January 6, 2021, siege, 17, 38, 262–63, 266; "jobs not mobs," 163–65, 168, 262, *Plate 10*; object labeling, *18*, 140–41, 146; "O.K.," 23–24, *24*; Pepe the frog, 137, 167–68; "put your hands in the air," *62*; and slow violence, 219, 252–53; Venn diagram, 61–62, *62*; "when," 143; "Woman Yelling at a Cat," 5, *8*
meme stocks, 172
memetic drip, 30, 40, 240–52
memetic payload, 164, 168–69, 250
memos, 151–52
Mencimer, Stephanie, 168
metadata, 140
metaverse, 172
methodology of book, 17–28, 42–44. *See also* critical typology; plural reading
#MeToo, 14
Metropolitan Museum of Art (Met), 190, 192–93, *193*, 195
Mexican muralism, 9
Mexico, 9, 114, 119–20; Agua Prieta, 108; Nogales, *86*
Mexico–U.S. border, 17, 30, 83–85, 108–9, 161, 236–37
Michigan: Detroit, 243, 263
Microsoft, 47, *216*. *See also* Bing
millennials, 161
Miller-Travis, Vernice, 225
Mills, Lorna: *Well Now WTF?*, 116–17, 123–24, 127, *Plate 9*
Milner, Ryan M., 150, 284n74; on the ambivalent internet, 22, 297n23, 312n1; on memes, 137–38, 161–63, 286n2, 295n1, 297n21
mimesis, 2, 102, 163, 220, 277n5, 290n9
Mina, An Xiao, 161, 298n55
misogyny, 150–51. *See also* America Firsters; QAnon; Trump, Donald; Unite the Right rally (2017)
Misrach, Richard, 191; *Destroy This Memory*, 184–88, 192–93
Mississippi River, 252
Mitchell, W. J. T., 5, 10, 171, 278n9, 280n20, 283n55
Mizell-Nelson, Michael, 183
modern art, 99–100
Modern Devotion movement, 102

modernism, 93, 98, 117
montage, 15–16, 45, 98–99, 104, 258, 291n17
MoreUtopia!: *A Glossary of Gestures for Critical Discussion, 23*
Morrison, Toni, 41, 164, 268–70
Morton, Taylor, 225
Morton, Timothy, 160, 252–54
Moss, Ceci, 80
Moten, Fred, 122, 188
Mount Vesuvius, 4
Mullen, John, III: *Ark in Snow,* 305n73
Murray, Janet, 172
Museo del Prado, 105
Museum of Modern Art (MoMA), 91, 116, 291n13; Strike MoMA, 116–17, 122–27, 157
museums, 16, 57, 93, 136, 229, 257; and activism, 115–28; and assembly, 4, 9; and deterritorialization, 34, 115–28; and environmentalism, 39, 131–32; virtual feminist, 2; without walls, 20. *See also individual museums*
Myers, Mike, 300n4
MySpace, 198

Nagel, Alexander, 293n59
Nakamura, Lisa, 262
Nap Ministry, The, 246, 251–52
narrative, 1, 257–59, 263, 277n4, 278n6, 278n8; Altman on, 38, 45–46, 55, 59, 63; and art, 102–3, 109, 119; and assembly, 2, 4, 45–46, 75; database narratives, 16, 98, 104; and disasters, 182–89, 192, 194, 197; drive for, 38, 59, 63; Hayles on, 59; and mapping, 226, 235; and memes, 152, 163, 165, 172–73; and race, 71, 180; and violence, 40, 214–20
Narratives of Crisis: Stories of Ruin and Renewal, 186
Nasheed, Mohamed, 215–17
National Archives, 270
Native Lands, 238
Nazis, 159
NCAA Division I, 152
Negra, Diane, 190
Negri, Antonio, 33
neoliberalism, 206, 216, 268
net art, 64, 94, 98, 100–101, 124
Neufeld, Josh: *A.D.: New Orleans after the Deluge,* 183–84, *184,* 187, 197–99, *199,* 204
new media, 15, 241
New Orleans, 182, 185–86, 191, 208, 211; as archaeological place, 190; Lower Ninth Ward, 196, 203–5; representations of, 5, 53, 180, 192–207. *See also* Gulf Coast; Hurricane Katrina
New York City, 82, 91, 190
New York Times, 164, 179
Ngai, Sianne, 279n12
Nicholson, Jack, 264
Niépce, Nicéphore: *View from a Window at Le Gras,* 111
Nigeria, 60, 221
9/11, 58
Nixon, Rob, 40, 214–17, 219, 221, 239, 242, 252–53, 255
Noble, Safiya Umoja, 56, 156–58, 177
nonfungible tokens (NFTs), 101, 172
nonhuman photography, 15
Nora, Pierre, 190
North America, 2, 27, 149, 258

object labeling memes, *18,* 140–41, 146
Oglesby, Cameron, 224, 309n38
Okanagan, 238
Oklahoma, 236; Tulsa, 231–33
Oman, 161
On, Josh: *They Rule,* 238–39, *239*
O'Neal, John, 186
Ọnụọha, Mimi, 56, 71, 222; *In Absentia,* 66; *Us, Aggregated,* 260–61, *260–61*
#oof, 159
Osunde, Eloghosa, 157, 176
Over the Edge, 16
Overton, Joseph P.: Overton window, 169

Paglen, Trevor, 15; *They Took the Faces from the Accused and the Dead... (SD18)*, 101
Palestine, 127
Palmer, Carole L., 282n48
Panagia, Davide, 280n22, 290n9
#panic, 158
paranoid reading, 269
Parler, 67
parody, 1, 22, 48, 63, 279n11
participatory archives, 4, 74, 74–79, *78–79*, 179–82, 189
@pattiegonia, 243
Paul, Christiane, 99
Payne, Daniel, 84
Peirce, Charles Sanders, 280n20
Pelosi, Nancy, 266
Pence, Mike, 263–64
Pennsylvania: Philadelphia, 231, 263
Pepe the frog memes, 137, 167–68
performance, 1, 4, 63, 216–19, 226, 248, 302n31; and art, 109; drive for, 61; and January 6, 2021, siege, 266–67; and memes, 148–49, 152–61, 250; and race, 69, 71
performativity, 33, 37, 71, 111, 122, 162; and environmentalism, 77, 216–17, *217*; and memes, 144, 149–51, 162
performed lists, 143
Peters, Benjamin, 26
Pettis, Ben T., 296n11
Phillips, John, 284n79
Phillips, Whitney, 22, 297n23, 312n1
photojournalism, 5, 191
photomosaics, 9, 111–14
Photoshop, 8
Picasso, Pablo, 96
Pinterest, 106
Pizzagate, 299n68
planking, 135–36
Plato, 277n5
Plummer, Ken, 277n4
plural reading, 17–28, 46, 65, 108, 112, 128, 138, 191, 259, 281n42
Poggi, Christina, 98–99, 291n15
Polaroid, 60
Poletti, Anna, 198
police violence, 42–43, 52, 82, 201, 224, 231
Polidori, Robert, 191
Political Electricity; or An Historical & Prophetical Print in the Year 1770, 27
Pollock, Griselda, 20, 99, 269
poor images, 152, 157
popular assembly, 31–38, 41, 123, 170, 217, 262–71
positions, 51–55
Postcommodity: *Repellent Fence/Valla Repelente*, 108–10, *Plate 8*
present blankness, 197–203, 207
prevailing conditions, 40, 177, 182, 188–90, 207
Prince William Sound, 36
privilege, 24–26, 88, 185, 196, 240, 268–69, 309n38; and methodology of book, 42–44
profane archaeology, 190
protest, 14, 33, 36, 37, 42, 55, 116, 123, 163, 167, 169, 202–3, 216, 224, 237
Puar, Jasbir, 32
Puerto Rico, 127
"put your hands in the air" meme, *62*

QAnon, 262–64, 266. *See also* alt-right; extremism; misogyny; racism; white supremacy
Quechan, 237
@queernature, 243
queerness, 21, 49, 147, 214, 243, 269
@queerquechua, 243

racism, 43, 68–69, *69*, 72, 201–2, 230–31, 251; anti-Blackness, 266; environmental, 171, 225, 245, 248; and Hurricane Katrina, 6, 179–83, 187–89, 193–96, 208; intersectional, 224; and January 6, 2021, siege, 262; and memes, 24, 137, 150, 164, 171; post-9/11, 58; of world's fairs, 65. *See also* alt-right; America Firsters; apartheid; Black Codes; Hurricane Katrina;

January 6 Capitol siege (2021); Jim Crow; Nazis; police violence; QAnon; Red Summer; slavery; Trump, Donald; Unite the Right rally (2017); white supremacy
Ramaytush Ohlone, 126, 226
Ramler, Mari E., 208
Ramsay, Adam, 308n35
Rancière, Jacques, 11, 121, 280n22
Rare and Endangered Memes for Edgy Environmentalists, 243
Raven, Arlene, 12
Real Housewives, The, 22; *of Beverly Hills,* 5
reassembly, 85, 218, 234, 238, 270; and art, 104, 106, 109, 125; conceptual, 40, 220–26, 233, 241, 253; and disasters, 189, 207; and listening to images, 20; and memes, 161, 163, 171; promise of, 11
Reconstruction, 66
Red Cross, 231
Reddit, 5, 67, 140, 150, 164, 311n78; /r/Memes, 136; /r/ShitRedditSays, 152; r/the_donald forum, *Plate 10*
Reddleman, Claire, 229
Red Summer, 230
Reisinger, Karin, 218
rematriation, 126
remembrance, 40, 190
remix, 39, 87–88, 104, 138, 161, 173, 176, 189, 290n65
Rentería-Valencia, Rodrigo, 277n2
repair, 3, 35, 38, 67, 93, 182, 188, 270; hyperdistributed, 171
reparative assembly, 41, 271
reparative reading, 21, 269–70
representation, 1, 16, 47, 231, 257–59, 277n5, 278n7, 290n9; and art, 9, 58, 94, 99, 103, 120, 290n8; and assembly, 2–4, 34, 45; and disasters, 75, 181–82, 187, 190–91, 198, 202, 207; and environmentalism, 77, 215–16; and gender, 76; and listicles, 12; and mapping, 234; and memes, 152, 154, 172, 174; and violence, 40, 214–16, 219
Republican Party (U.S.), 164–65, 263, 267–68
Resting Place, A, 252
reterritorialization, 124–27, 132
Rhizome: *How Do You See the Disappeared? A Warm Database,* 58; VocabWiki, 147
Ricca, Lisa-Marie, *180*
rickrolling, 135–36
Ricouer, Paul, 287n16
Roberts, David, 242, 248
Robinson, Katrina, 200
Rodchenko, Alexander, 96
Rodríguez, Joseph: *Still Here: Stories after Katrina,* 198–201, *201*
Rolph-Trouillot, Michel, 190
Roose, Kevin, *Plate 10*
Ruscha, Edward: *Raw, 118,* 118–20
Rusert, Britt, 65
Russell, Bertrand, *18*

Saar, Betye, 96
Sánchez Cedillo, Raúl, 47, 127
Sanders, Bernie, 85
satire, 23, 27, 28, 117, 245
#savePepe, 167
Scheper-Hughes, Nancy, 220–21
Schmuckli, Claudia: *Specters of Disruption,* 115–22, 125–26
Schwedel, Heather, 141
secondness, 10, 280n20
Sedgwick, Eve Kosofsky, 21, 41, 269–70, 283n61
Seeger, Matthew W., 186
Sekula, Allan, 304n47
Sellnow, Timothy L., 186
Senegal, 41
Serra, Richard, 290n2; *Áfangar,* 129–31; *Verb List,* 12, 39, 91–94, 100, 116, 128–29, 131
Servín, Luis, 84
sexism, 43, 150
sexual violence, 14, 43, 231, 307n19
shadow text, 177
Shiba Inu dog/Doge, 135
Shifman, Limor, 135–38, 161
Shirley, Matt, *62*

shitposters, 137, 167
Shoah, 303n43
Shore, Daniel, 281n42
Shuumi Land Tax, 126
Siberia, 252
Sigüenza, José de, 102
silent violence, 221
Silicon Valley, 116, *139*, 157, *227*, 228, 228
Silverberg, Mark, 283n55
Silverman, Kaja, 110–12
Simon, Roger, 196
Simon, Taryn: *Image Atlas*, 101
Simone, Nina, 202
Simpson, Lorna: *Easy to Remember*, 111
Skitt's Law, 160
slavery, 66, 195–96, 303n43
slow violence, 3, 35, 45, 214, 221, 226, 228, 248, 258; and environmental racism, 249–51; and fast violence, 40–41, 252–55; and methodology of book, 42–43; resistance to, 17, 215–20, 241–42, 251
Smedley, Tim, 130
Smith, Christen A., 14. *See also* #CiteBlackWomen
Smith, Shawn Michelle, 288n29
SMITH Magazine, 198
Smith-Shomade, Beretta E., 88
snowclones, 143, 150, 158
Snyder, Joan, 12, *13*, 280n28
social media, 2, 63–64, 77, 226, 269; and art, 82, 95, 106, 117; and assembly, 4, 9–10; and disasters, *78–79*, 179, 187; and environmentalism, 17, 215, 240–55; and January 6, 2021, siege, 38, 262–65; and memes, 38, 135, 154, 167–68, 174; and viral comparison, 5. *See also* hashtags; memetic drip; *individual platforms and accounts*
social media galleries, 52, 64, 77
Socrates, 277n5
Sogorea Te' Land Trust, 126
Solnit, Rebecca: *Infinite City: A San Francisco Atlas*, 226, *227*; *Poison/Palate: The Bay Area in Your Body*, 226, 228
Sontag, Susan, 265
South Africa, 43, 101, 283n69
South America, 108
speaking nearby, 41–42
Spongebob Squarepants, 243
Staal, Jonas, 33
Standing Rock, 236
Steam (platform), 168
Sterling, Linder, 96
Steyerl, Hito, 72, 125, 152
St. Félix, Doreen, 209
"Stop the Steal!," 170, 262
storycentrism, 277n4
storytelling, 2–3, 6, 77, 94, 104, 241, 278n8, 287n12; and database narratives, 16; and disasters, 186–87, 191, 197; humans as storytelling animals, 258, 277n4; and memes, 172, 174; and Rhizome's work, 58
Stradford, J. B., 232
street art, 39, 139, 161–64, 298n55
Strike MoMA, 116–17, 122–27, 157
structural violence, 3, 17, 31, 35, 40, 42–43, 45, 221, 232, 246, 258, 308n29; as analytic, 308n29
structured openness, 200
Superdome, 183, 195
surface reading, 281n42
surveillance, 58, 154, 156, 253
Swartz, Aaron: *Image Atlas*, 101
Sylvester, Terray, 277n2
Syms, Martine: *Reading Trayvon Martin*, 67, *69*, 71–72

Tamez, Margo (@indigifem), 237–38
Tarnoff, Ben, 132
technological redlining, 156
TED talks, 87
Telegram, 67
Tenor, 151
Texas: Denton, 199
#thanosdidnothingwrong, 159
thematic countermapping, 40, 226–41, 254
thematic list, 11–12, 15, 81, 92, 123, 143

"There's a War on For Your Memes," 142–43
#TheShowMustBePaused, 201
Thomas, Jamila, 201
Thomas, Leah, 224–25, 243, 309n38
Thomas, Nig, 106, *107*. *See also* @boschbot
Thomas, Valorie, 180
Thorburn, Elise Danielle, 33
Thunberg, Greta, 77
Thürlemann, Felix, 291n16
Tigua, 237
TikTok, 24–25, 76, 143, 145, 148, 156, 245, 250
Tillmans, Wolfgang, 291n16
time (concept), 233–34, 255. *See also* memetic drip
Time magazine, 244
TMZ, 264
Tohono O'odham, 237
Tolkien, J. R. R., 296n9
Transgender Pride Flag, *175*
transmedia, 4, 106, 239, 257, 279n10
Treme, 194
Tribe, Mark: *Starrynight,* 101
Trinh T. Minh-ha: *Reassemblage: From the Firelight to the Screen,* 41. *See also* speaking nearby
trolling, 152, 168, 288n38, 299n68
Trump, Donald, 164–65, 168–69, 244, 262–64, 267–68, 299n68; and "jobs not mobs" meme, *Plate 10*; Trump trains, 167. *See also* alt-right; extremism; January 6 Capitol siege (2021); misogyny; racism; white supremacy
Tufekci, Zeynep, 14
Tulsa Race Massacre (1921), 230–33, 236, *Plate 11*
Turner, Joseph: *Slave Ship (Slavers Throwing Overboard the Dead and Dying, Typhoon Coming On),* 195
Twist, Kade L., 108. *See also* Postcommodity
Twitter, *86*, 252, 285n100; and art, 82, 106, 122; Black Twitter, 122; and disasters, 74, *78*, 183; and environmentalism, 241; and January 6, 2021, siege, 263–64; and memes, 5, 17, 143, 164–67, 172, 295n1. *See also* hashtags; *individual accounts and hashtags*
2018 midterm elections (U.S.), 163
typology, 12, 28, 115, 131–32; critical, 9, 39, 92–94, 98, 100, 106, 111, 191, 219, 241, 291n21

United Farm Workers, 217
Unite the Right rally (2017), 169
U.S. Capitol. *See* January 6 Capitol siege (2021)
U.S. Congress. *See* January 6 Capitol siege (2021)
U.S. Immigration and Customs Enforcement (ICE), 66
U.S. Supreme Court, 264

Vander Wal, Thomas, 146
Venice Biennale, 81
Venn, John, 61
Venn diagrams, 61–63, 257
Vertov, Dziga, 72, 98
video art, 98
Viljoen, Salomé, 177
viral comparisons, 5–6, 11, 31, 40
viral dances, 26, 52, 77, 143
Virginia: Charlottesville, 169
virtual feminist museum, 20
visual bonds, 72, 154
visual culture, 2, 20, 35, 94, 98, 195, 274; invisible, 15
visual studies, 17
Vonnegut, Kurt, 4

Waku, *78*
Wales, 43
Walker, Kara, 40, 183; *After the Deluge,* 190, 192–96; *A Subtlety, or the Marvelous Sugar Baby,* 209–10
Wallerstein, Wade: *Well Now WTF?,* 116–17, 123–24, 127, *Plate 9*
Warburg, Aby, 99; *Mnemosyne Atlas,* 20
Wattenberg, Martin: *Starrynight,* 101

Watts, Michael, 221
WE ACT for Environmental Justice, 225
Weems, Carrie Mae: *Lincoln, Lonnie, and Me—A Story in 5 Parts,* 115–16
West, Kanye, 179, 300n4
Wheaton's Law, 160
"when" memes, 143
White, Hayden, 191
White House, 265
whiteness, 156, 211, 253
white privilege, 24, *25,* 196, 268
white supremacy, 23–24, 67, 167, 246, 262–63, 267. *See also* America Firsters; apartheid; Black Codes; January 6 Capitol siege (2021); Jim Crow; Nazis; QAnon; Red Summer; slavery; Trump, Donald; Unite the Right rally (2017)
Whitlock, Gillian, 198
Whyte, Kyle Powys: "Settler Time versus Indigenous Time," 233–34, *234*
Wikipedia, 13, 240
Williams, Alice May: *A Glossary of Gestures for Critical Discussion, 23*
Wilson, Fred, 195
Winkleman, Michael Joseph. *See* Beeple (Michael Joseph Winkelmann)
Wired, 159
Wisecup, Kelly: *Assembled for Use,* 27
Wittgenstein, Ludwig, 18–19, *18,* 280n20, 282n45, 282n49
Wölfflin, Heinrich, 20
"Woman Yelling at a Cat" meme, 5, *8,* 22
World Wide Web, 12, 159
#worsttimeline, 159
Wu Hung, 131
Wynter, Sylvia, 277nn4–5

Xu, Guanyu: *My Desktop, Plate 3*; "my neighborhood, the same block #blacklivesmatter," 52, *53*; *Parents' Bedroom,* 49–51; *Temporarily Censored Home,* 49

Yaqui, 237
#yeet, 159
YikYak, 67
Young, Liam Cole, 279n11
YouTube, 76, 143, 164, 183, 198, 262

Zimmerman, George, 67
Zittrain, Jonathan, 302n28
Zuboff, Shoshana, 156, 177
Zuckerberg, Mark, 157
Zylinska, Joanna, 15, 287n28

Kyle Parry is associate professor in the History of Art and Visual Culture department at the University of California, Santa Cruz. He is coeditor of *Ubiquity: Photography's Multitudes.*